WILDE'S
DEVOTED
FRIEND

To

J.-P. B. Ross

and the late

Professor Giles Robertson

WILDE'S DEVOTED FRIEND

a life of
Robert Ross
1869–1918

Maureen Borland

Lennard Publishing
1990

Lennard Publishing
a division of Lennard Books Ltd
Musterlin House
Jordan Hill Road
Oxford OX2 8DP

**British Library Cataloguing in Publication Data is available for
this title**

ISBN 1 85291 085 2

First published 1990
© Text Maureen Borland 1990
Robert Ross quotations © Executors of the late
Professor Giles Robertson 1990

Phototypeset in Plantin
by Nuprint Ltd.
Cover design by Pocknell & Co.
Reproduced, printed and bound in Great Britain by
Butler and Tanner Limited, Frome and London

Contents

Illustrations

(1) ROBERT ROSS, taken in 1916, two years before his death. *(Courtesy Exors. Professor G. Robertson)*

(2) OSCAR WILDE, at the pinnacle of his success, circa 1894. *(Courtesy Merlin Holland)*

(3) AUGUSTA ELIZABETH ROSS, Robbie's mother. Daughter of Robert Baldwin. *(Courtesy of J-P. B. Ross)*

(4) HON. JOHN ROSS, Robbie's father. Canadian politician and barrister. *(Courtesy J-P. B. Ross)*

(5) ROBBIE, aged about 13. *(Courtesy J-P.B. Ross)*

(6) JACK and ALEX, Robbie's brothers. *(Courtesy J-P. B. Ross)*

(7) ROBBIE with tutor and friends. *(Courtesy J-P. B. Ross)*

(8) JOHN (Jack) ROSS, Robbie's eldest brother. *(Courtesy J-P. B. Ross)*

(9) MARY ROSS, Robbie's eldest sister. Wife of Major Charles Jones. *(Courtesy Exors. Professor G. Robertson)*

(10) ROBERT ROSS, circa 1890, portrait by Frances Richards, Canadian artist, friend of Mary Jones. *(Courtesy Exors. Professor G. Robertson)*

(11) ALEX and ROBBIE, circa 1888. *(Courtesy Exors. Professor G. Robertson)*

(12) THE JONES FAMILY OF JESMOND HILL, circa 1898. Back row: Hilda, Ethel, Petica, Lillian, Edward. Front row: Emily, Margaret, William. *(Courtesy Exors. Professor G. Robertson)*

(13) JESMOND HILL, the home of Major and Mrs Charles Jones. *(Courtesy of J-P. B. Ross)*

(14) ETHEL JONES, Robbie's niece, second wife of Sir S. Squire Sprigge. A portrait by William Rothenstein. *(Courtesy Professor & Mrs T. S. Sprigge)*

(15) SIR SAMUEL SQUIRE SPRIGGE, Editor of *Lancet*, Secretary & Chairman of *The Society of Authors*. A Portrait by William Rothenstein. *(Courtesy Professor & Mrs T. S. Sprigge)*

(16) CECIL SQUIRE SPRIGGE, son of Squire Sprigge and Ada Moss, step great-nephew of Robbie's. *(Courtesy Professor & Mrs T. S. Sprigge)*

(17) SIEGFRIED SASSOON, devoted to Robbie and always true to his memory. *(Courtesy Sir Rupert Hart-Davis)*

(18) VYVYAN HOLLAND (Wilde's younger son) London 1914 after being commissioned. *(Courtesy Merlin Holland)*

(19) MORE ADEY, in the garden of his home at Wotton-under-Edge in 1920. *(Courtesy Merlin Holland)*

(20) THE FOUNTAIN at King's College, Cambridge, 1916. *(Courtesy King's College, Cambridge)*

(21) CHRISTOPHER SCLATER MILLARD, Graduate of Keble College, Oxford. Bibliographer and Wilde scholar. *(Courtesy Bodleian Library)*

(22) ALEXANDER GALT ROSS, Robbie's brother, stockbroker, businessman, a bachelor and man of impeccable tastes. *(Courtesy Exors. Professor G. Robertson)*

(23) SIR EDMUND GOSSE, lifelong friend and confidant of Robbie's. *(Courtesy Miss J. Gosse)*

(24) OSCAR WILDE'S tomb at Père Lachaise, Paris. Robbie's ashes also lay within the tomb. *(Courtesy Merlin Holland)*

Foreword

by Michael Halls

N *SWINBLAKE* (1906) Robert Ross imagined himself visiting Parnassus. On the giddy path that edges the cliff of immortality he meets Theodore Watts-Dunton:
  Beneath us lay the gulf of oblivion.
'Be careful, young man, not to tumble over; are you a poet or a biographer?'
I explained that I was merely a tourist.

Ross was never a mere tourist. Wilde's *St Robert of Phillimore* affected dilettantism partly as a defence, partly for the sheer pleasure of misleading; but his alert writer's intelligence, committedly modern, ardently progressivist, yet 'standing at a slight angle to the universe', combines richness and wit, both characteristically *fin de siècle*, with the fancy, the good humour—the sheer charm—of the new century: he lightened the Edwardian patchouli with pungent attar of ladslove.

Maureen Borland vividly shows us the *reality* of Ross. It is high time someone did. A lay-figure bearing Ross's name inhabits countless footnotes, labelled as Oscar Wilde's foul-weather friend or as Alfred Douglas's Aunt Sally, but even in biographies of Wilde he seems to be ancillary. This is obviously false: his highly individual personality is now visible in Maureen Borland's fascinating, minutely researched, affectionate portrait. Ross's friendship with Wilde—and, like his spiritual cousin John Wilkes a century earlier, Wilde was a connoisseur of friends—was important to Wilde himself after, as well as before, he met Lord Alfred Douglas and began that *gracilis descensus Averni*; and Bosie's feuding with Ross was more than the sleazy aftermath of Wilde's tragic end. It was a clash of human values: affection and integrity versus envy and self-contempt. That Douglas's mind was grindingly obsessed with libel actions speaks for itself. Both his upbringing and his conscience made him need authoritative reassurance that he was not worthless. That Ross should have evidently been the character against whom Douglas had to measure himself was a compliment, of a kind.

9

'The gods are strange. It is not of our vices only they make instruments to scourge us. They bring us to ruin through what in us is good, gentle, humane, loving.' Wilde's words in *De Profundis* might have been a warning to the friend to whom he entrusted his masterpiece; but in respect of Ross's life-story, at least, the 'gods' were no Olympians: they sat in Parliament and on the Bench, they owned or read newspapers... they made up those formidable masses of ignorance, fear and hypocrisy, the urban British middle classes. If, as we see below, Ross's life can now be written with humour and perception, it is partly because now at last, a century after the passing of the Labouchère Amendment, these gods are on the run. Even Bosie's love dare speak its name. Vice is returning to the carpenter's bench; Sin to the reptile-lair of theology; and Robbie and Oscar are Parnassians.

MICHAEL HALLS
King's College
Cambridge
July 1989

Acknowledgements

CONVENTION has grown up whereby biographers, at the end of their official acknowledgements, give a perfunctory mention to their respective spouses. I propose to break that convention, conscious of the fact, that without the generous support of my husband, Dr J. C. Borland, this book would not have been possible.

I owe a sincere debt of gratitude to Mr & Mrs J.-P. B. Ross, to the late Professor Giles Robertson and Mrs E. Robertson, who gave me the most gracious encouragement from the beginning.

Sir Rupert and Lady Hart-Davis responded instantly to my incessant requests for information which must have tried their patience yet they always treated me with the utmost courtesy—a memory I shall long treasure.

I thank Merlin Holland for permission to quote from the copyright works of Oscar Wilde and Vyvyan Holland, and for being ever available to answer my questions.

In thanking individual people, it is always hard to convey the real debt one owes to them. I can do no more than record my thanks to Sir John and Michael Rothenstein; Lord Bonham Carter; Michael Meredith; Michael Pennington; Owen Dudley Edwards; J. Robert Maguire; Robert M. Baldwin; Professor and Mrs T. Sprigge; Francis Guy F. Wyndham; and Miss Jennifer Gosse; Dr C. E. Blacker and her brother and sister; Mrs Sheila Colman on behalf of the Estate of Lord Alfred Douglas; A. P. Watt on behalf of the Executors of the Estate of Robert Graves; and Madame V. Eldin on behalf of the Estate of Arnold Bennett.

I received endless help from the staffs of Cambridge University Library; King's College, Cambridge; Slade School of Fine Art, University College, London; Brotherton Library, University of Leeds; University of Glasgow, Special Collections; Master and Fellows of Corpus Christi College; New College, University College; Bodleian Library, Oxford; University of Reading; John Rylands University Library of Manchester; William Andrews Clark Memorial Library, University of

California, Los Angeles; Houghton Library, Harvard University; Harry Ransom Humanities Research Center, University of Texas at Austin.

I am grateful, too, to the following organisations: Society of Authors on behalf of the Estate of Bernard Shaw; Imperial War Museum; Johannesburg Art Gallery; Tate Gallery; National Gallery; Whitechapel Art Gallery; National Gallery of Victoria, Melbourne; Public Record Office, Kew and Chancery Lane; Foreign & Commonwealth Office; Principal Probate Registry, Somerset House; Inland Revenue, Management Division; Provincial Government of Ontario, Registrar General's Office; Archbishop's House, Westminster Cathedral; Royal Automobile Club; Savile Club; Reform Club.

I must also thank the staff of the House of Lords Library; British Library, Great Russell Street and Colindale; National Library of Scotland; Brown, Picton and Hornby Library, City of Liverpool; Mitchell Library, Glasgow; Dick Institute, Kilmarnock; Oxford Public Library; Berg Collection, New York Public Library; Library of Congress; and Strathclyde University Library, who never queried why a metallurgist was suddenly so interested in English literature.

To the Proprietors of News International plc: *The Times* and *Times Literary Supplement; Daily Telegraph* and *Morning Post; Academy; Burlington Magazine*; Illustrated London News Group for the *Bystander*, I acknowledge with thanks permission to quote from their publications.

I must record a special mention to Dr Michael Halls of King's College Library, Cambridge, for all his assistance and for agreeing to write the Foreword; to Duncan McAra for editorial expertise; and to Roderick Brown of Lennard Publishing, for making the dream a reality.

If I have forgotten to include anyone, I apologise, as I do unreservedly to anyone whose copyright I have unintentionally infringed.

M.B.

I

MORAL DILEMMA

(1869-1900)

'Love is all very well in its way but friendship is much higher. Indeed, I know of nothing in the world that is either nobler or rarer than a devoted friendship.'

Oscar Wilde, 'The Devoted Friend'

One

Early Influences

ITH THE DEATH of Robert Ross in October 1918 a notable link was severed with the literary and artistic world of late-Victorian and Edwardian England. His particular claim to a place in the hall of fame is neither as a journalist and writer nor as a competent artistic administrator, but for his instinct for friendship. Having, as a young man, enjoyed friendships with his seniors, men as various and renowned as Edmund Gosse and Oscar Wilde, he, in turn, as an older man, offered hospitality, support and encouragement to the young poets, such as Siegfried Sassoon and Wilfred Owen, emerging from their ordeals on the Western Front.

Robert Baldwin Ross was born in Tours, France, on 25 May 1869, the youngest surviving child of the Honourable John Ross[1] and Augusta Elizabeth, the daughter of Robert Baldwin,[2] a prominent Canadian politician.

Of Scots-Irish descent, John Ross was taken to Canada by his parents Alexander and Jane Ross, née McMickin, shortly after his birth in Ireland in 1818. In 1839 he was called to the Bar of Upper Canada. Early in his legal career he developed a keen interest in politics, and was later elected to the Legislative Council. He was an able administrator, a special trait he passed on to his son, Robbie.

John and Eliza had seven children, the first five being born in Toronto: Maria-Louisa, in 1852, died in infancy; the first Robert Baldwin, 1854, died three days after his second birthday; Mary-Jane, 1855; John (Jack), 1859; Alexander Galt, 1860; Maria-Elizabeth (Lizzie) and Robert (Robbie) were born in Tours in 1867 and 1869.

From 1862 until his death, Ross concentrated on his legal practice, though he still remained a member of the Legislative Council; indeed in 1867, by Royal Proclamation, he was called to the Senate of Canada and, two years later, was appointed Speaker of the Senate.

By 1866 John Ross's health was failing and he took his wife and young family to France; he hoped the warm and gentle climate of the Loire valley would help him recover physically. In 1870 France was plunged into war with Prussia, and John, together with his enlarged family, returned to Canada. There he found that private fears about the competency of his business partner were well founded. He had been using the company accounts to finance his own private schemes. He had indeed embezzled thousands of dollars from clients' accounts, a debt of honour the ailing John Ross set about to repay in full; the effort, though, was too much for him and he died in January 1871.

Although not a wealthy woman, Eliza had inherited considerable property from her father's Estate, and this cushioned her from the worst effects of widowhood. She fully discharged her husband's debts, and in later life her Canadian property investments greatly increased in value and helped to provide her with quite a substantial income. Before he died John had expressed the wish, that if it were at all possible, he would like his children educated in Europe. He believed, that in Europe, they would learn to love and appreciate art and literature as he had done.

On 8 April 1872, Robbie, Jack, Alex, Mary, Lizzie and their mother left Quebec for England, arriving in London on 22 April. It was Robbie's second crossing of the Atlantic in less than three years. He never lost his Canadian heritage and he retained, for the rest of his life, his distinctive Canadian accent.

Eliza arranged for her two elder sons to become pupils at Cheltenham College; Mary was sent to a little finishing school in Bayswater; Robbie and Lizzie were not ideal nursery companions, their antagonism began the day Robbie was born and they never found pleasure in each other's company. It is possible that it was Lizzie's volatile feminine temper and the over-protectiveness of his mother that first sowed the seeds of Robbie's homosexual proclivities.[3]

On 8 April 1874 Mary married Major Charles Jones, a fellow Canadian, and their secure and loving home became a natural haven of peace for Robbie later when the rigours of his life became unbearable. As a child, Mary regarded him as completely spoiled and pampered, but, as an articulate and compassionate man, he became a very great favourite with her.

Robbie attended the Sandroyd House School in Cobham, Surrey, from 1875 until about 1882, when he won a classical scholarship to Clifton, though this was never taken up because of ill health. In later years Robbie was always vague about the precise details of his education; what is certain is the versatility of his knowledge. He liked to pretend to be an intellectual trifler, but he had a sound intellect and a natural ability to conquer any subject which interested him. Some of his education was entrusted to a tutor and together they made many artistic and cultural visits to the capital cities of Europe. His devotion to his mother and family were well defined and when Jack and Minnie (Mary McLeod) announced their engagement, the thirteen-year-old Robbie confided to his mother his hopes for the future of the name of Ross:

> I shall be very careful in my will that I leave my property to Jacks and Mary [sic] children...on condition that they won't go and lose the pedigree for our Jacks anyhow...it is a disgrace enough already to have it loosed. And I shall be very careful if our family extends to keep up a pedigree so far.[4]

During the period 1884-6 Robbie travelled with his mother to the continent of Europe; for a time they were joined by Jack and Minnie, Mary and her family and Alex. While Robbie enjoyed the art and architecture of Switzerland and Austria, it was a performance of the Passion Play at Innsbruck that appealed to his young senses and helped to heighten his interest in religion and religious ritual.

Eliza Ross and her young family rented furnished houses around Chelsea and Kensington before they finally settled in 85 Onslow Square in the early 1880s. In his mature years Robbie spoke and wrote very little about his early life; indeed he tended to shroud it in mystery and when he did mention it he distorted some of the facts. However he did recall, with some apprehension, an early acquaintance with the historian Thomas Carlyle; a meeting which, if it did happen, could only have been shortly before Carlyle's death on 4 February 1881:

> Mr Shorter regrets that he never knew Carlyle. Here I have the advantage of him. I used to see that bleak old sage when I lived in Chelsea. I regarded him with extraordinary aversion and fear. Though my parents did not move in literary circles or in the brilliant artistic life that was humming around us in Cheyne Walk, they revered Mr Carlyle as a Scotsman who shed lustre on the race inhabiting the northern part of this island. They clothed their minds in intellectual kilts; and I, their child, was also clothed for a brief period in that revolting costume which led to an early, premature sympathy for the perpetrators of the Glencoe massacre. The Ross tartan is particularly hideous, and wounded my nascent aesthetic sense. We were not even entitled to wear it, having no connection with the noble family which bears our name. That offended my sense of propriety, quite apart from the skirts, which I thought effeminate. However, they must have attracted the attention of the author of *Sartor Resartus*. He patted my head on several occasions, and addressed me in language generally incomprehensible to my little Cockney ears. One day he inquired my name. I replied that it

was *Bobby*. He animadverted thereon, in words I do not profess to remember, and urged that it should be *Robbie*—a reminiscence, no doubt, of Burns. This was faithfully reported by my nurse on returning home, and from that day I was called "Robbie". One day I was sent to post a letter. I suppose I was older; though unconscious, as always, of anything ahead, I cannoned into Carlyle. The impact laid me flat on the pavement, where I yelled for some minutes, though soothed eventually by England's great thinker. And then—this is the point of the story—Carlyle dived into his pockets, produced a halfpenny, and said kindly, "Here is a bawbee for Bobby." He had quite forgotten (and this hurt me) that my name had been changed out of deference to his opinion. I have the halfpenny to this day. When Mr Carlyle died I was put into deep mourning. He was the first, and perhaps the most interesting, of all my street acquaintances.[5]

On New Year's Day 1885 Oscar Wilde and his beautiful young wife Constance (née Lloyd) moved into 16 Tite Street, Chelsea; that fact is certainly known; what is less clear is when Robbie Ross first became acquainted with Wilde. Many writers have expressed views on when this took place, but regrettably this particular event was not documented. Frank Harris—after both Ross and Wilde were dead, and therefore unable to refute the allegations—said they had met in a public lavatory, and that their relationship began as an act of importuning. Frank Harris, Editor of *The Evening News*, however, was frequently guilty of distorting the facts in order to create a better story. There are at least three other ways how they could have met; and all more likely than the one Harris suggested. Wilde was in Toronto in 1882, and it is quite likely someone suggested to him, that when he returned to London, he should endeavour to make the acquaintance of Mrs Ross (a prominent Canadian exile) and her family. Secondly, the young painter Frances Richards, who met Wilde in Toronto in 1882, was a personal friend of Mary Jones and she could well have arranged for Robbie to meet Wilde. Thirdly, Alex could have made the introduction, being engaged in writing literary reviews and acquainted with many of the leading literary figures.

The relationship between Robbie, Oscar Wilde and Alfred (Bosie) Douglas[6] has produced more hyperbole than reasoned argument could expect to sustain. There is certainly no direct evidence that Ross was 'the first boy' to corrupt Wilde; the mere fact that a proposition is frequently repeated does not substantiate its credibility. The only indisputable fact is that all three of them did, at some time in their lives, indulge in homosexual practices.

In 1886 Robbie, aware that if his education was not more formalised he would be unable to gain admittance to a university, was persuaded to attend W. B. Scoones, the crammers' school in Covent Garden. Robbie spent the next two years gaining the necessary qualifications, but there were compensations to lighten the burden of his studies. When in 1887 his mother travelled abroad, she arranged for him to stay for three months as a paying guest at 16 Tite Street with Oscar and Constance Wilde and their young sons, Cyril and Vyvyan.

The friendship between Ross and Wilde progressed slowly, there were long periods when they did not meet or correspond; indeed it was not until ten years later that their lives became inextricably linked.[7] Wilde was at his wittiest in Ross's company and in many ways their divergent personalities complemented each other. Robbie, with his well-developed sense of humour and sharp intellectual perception, appreciated the special qualities of the other man. They differed in their approach to life, Wilde wishing to sample all the pleasures and despairs, regardless of the risk or the disgrace; Ross discreet and compassionate, concerned to protect the weak and the innocent, and aware from a very early age that what he took from life had to be paid for with tears and anguish.

Robbie, by the age of nineteen, was mentally and emotionally mature, although paradoxically, he was often racked by self-doubt and insecurity. He went up to King's College, Cambridge, in October 1888, and although he was not an old Etonian, this slight 'inconvenience' was not allowed to spoil his enjoyment. He immediately immersed himself in the life of the University, and was determined that both he and the College should benefit from his presence. On admission Robbie made two false declarations, the first that he was a Roman Catholic; and while he may have spiritually belonged to the Church of Rome, he was not admitted for another five years. His second lie was that he was a member of the Savile Club. Alex was a member and Robbie was frequently his guest, but he was not elected a member until 1893. Both lies, while not serious, were minor irritants to his fellow undergraduates, and his arrogant pose annoyed his friends and enemies.

If Robbie hoped to follow the success of his brothers at Cambridge, then he was going to have to work extremely hard and devote little time to pleasure. Jack had been up at Trinity from 1877 to 1883, when he obtained his BA; he had been ill during his undergraduate days, and had therefore stayed up longer than was normal. He was called to the Canadian Bar in 1887, and to the Inner Temple in London the following year. Alex also enjoyed his undergraduate days, entering Caius College in October 1879 and graduating with a BA in June 1884.

There was a nine- and ten-year difference in ages between Robbie and his brothers Alex and Jack, and as he grew towards maturity Robbie frequently sought their advice and support. Jack was the more dominant personality and he took his role as elder brother very seriously. Alex was less extrovert but was prepared to take on the world and win at everything he tackled. In 1888 he accompanied the writer, Rider Haggard to Iceland, but on the whole his tastes were rather more aesthetic, although he never lost a youthful passion for medieval weapons of combat, and he became an accomplished fencer despite having lost an eye at the age of five when trying to prime an archer's bow.

By the time Robbie entered King's College he had been friendly with Oscar Wilde for two years, and it was natural for Wilde, the elder and more mature, who had made a glittering academic and social success of his years at Oxford, to offer some general advice. A few days after the start of the Michaelmas Term, Wilde wrote to the new undergraduate:

> I congratulate you. University life will suit you admirably, though I
> shall miss you in town... Are you in College or lodgings? I hope in
> College; it is much nicer. Do you know Oscar Browning? You will
> find him everything that is kind and pleasant.[8]

Wilde also wrote to Oscar Browning, a History Fellow at King's, who, after meeting Robbie, was more than prepared to confirm Wilde's opinions of the Freshman. Browning's assessment was quickly confirmed by Fellows and tutors alike and even some undergraduates. Robbie's maturity, his sense of obligation and his willingness to be at the service of his fellow man made him a delightful companion.

As a Freshman Robbie was not in College, but in licensed lodgings at 13 Mill Lane. Much of his leisure time should have been devoted to study for his History Tripos, but there were more exciting things to do. He made friends almost at once with Walter Murray Guthrie of Trinity Hall, who was about to publish the first edition of the *Gadfly*. Robbie could not resist the smell of printer's ink, and the idea that he should help write and edit the new venture made the prospects of his first term doubly exciting. The magazine professed to be a 'mirror of morals, men and manners', and in the first leader the editors emphasised the aims of the journal.

The life of the *Gadfly* was short, a single issue only. This was due partly to the inclusion of an offensive and unflattering article on Oscar Browning, in which the author poured scorn on Browning's literary tastes, his social snobbishness and the validity of his 'vast intellect'. There is no direct evidence that Robbie wrote the article, but he was certainly involved with the magazine, and he shared the responsibility for its editorial policy. The *Gadfly* article was regarded by the College as a serious breach of discipline, and the Fellows were anxious to identify the King's Freshman who was thought to be responsible for the offending article. E.H. Douty, a young MA, decided to take on the role of amateur sleuth. He believed that, if his detective work was unsuccessful, he could shame the culprit into confessing. Douty was convinced that Ross was the guilty man, but his investigations were largely inconclusive, and all he managed to do was to make enemies of undergraduates, Fellows and even some tutors.

The vacation brought no rest for Robbie, he spent Christmas at Jesmond Dene, Newcastle, with his sister Mary and her husband Charles Jones and their seven children. Out riding one morning, Robbie had an 'ignominious fall' from a horse and slightly damaged his hand. He returned to London on 28 December and there were many pleasant distractions and a great deal of exciting news for the young Freshman to enjoy. One of Mary's daughters came back with him to Onslow Square; Jack and his wife were in London; and Alex was back from Iceland. Oscar and Constance Wilde were also in town, and Wilde was celebrating the publication of *The Happy Prince and other stories*, which Alex had favourably reviewed in the *Saturday Review*.

At the beginning of the Lent Term Robbie was again at the centre of events. His involvement in the Bump Races helped to counter-balance his long-haired, aesthetic reputation; he was not a particularly accomplished rower, but as King's were not regarded as a premier rowing College, he was able to row bow in King's second boat, which unexpectedly managed to make two bumps. However, more pressing problems awaited his attention. The *Gadfly* having folded soon had a successor; Oscar Browning, for some time, had been considering bringing out a rival magazine and had already chosen the title. Guthrie, however, pre-empted him, and his *Granta* (still published) appeared before the Browning version was ready. Robbie was naturally involved with Guthrie's new magazine, and already had a number of subjects for his capricious pen.

King's were also involved in the election of a successor for Vice-Provost Austen Leigh who had replaced Provost Okes, who had died the previous November. At a Union Debate on 19 February Robbie unequivocally declared where the Fellows' votes should be placed. He also used the occasion to express his deep regret for the part he had played in the production of the *Gadfly*, and for the regrettable slur on Oscar Browning. His contrition, however, did not last long. A few days after the Union Debate, writing in the *Granta*, he was again engaged in the political affairs of the College. In a wide-ranging article entitled 'The Coming Dean', he referred to the forthcoming elections and rashly

advised the Fellows how they should cast their votes. He was also far
from reticent in giving his enthusiastic support to the changes in
admissions procedures that had taken place at King's. As a non-Etonian
and educated mainly privately, he held no allegiance to a single public
school and felt eminently qualified to give his opinions without fear or
favour:

> Everyone will look with critical eyes on the responsible electors and
> their choice of a Vice-Provost, and those who are to fill the two
> vacant Fellowships. The development of the College has excited
> general interest in more ways than one during the last few years, for
> it has risen from comparative obscurity into one of the most pushing
> or even prominent colleges of the University. The partial severance
> of its connection with Eton is doubtless a cause of this. For,
> however much the lovers of Eton, and those whose conservative
> prejudices are something more than mere sentiment, may regret the
> admission of non-Etonians into the place, we believe it was the
> salvation of the college, for in these advanced days an exclusively
> Etonian college is impossible for Cambridge. The change naturally
> brought evil with good, and among those who battered at the doors
> for admission under the new regulations, there came some of the
> most undesirable Undergraduates that could well be imagined. Not
> only long-haired, but the short-haired and the no-haired came—the
> purely social and the socially pure.[9]

He ended his scathing article with an attack on Douty, who was
expecting to be elected to one of the vacant Fellowships, as well as being
appointed to the office of Dean:

> We protest most strongly against this proposal; it is one which will
> excite not only the indignation of King's, but of Cambridge
> generally. No one would ever have heard of Mr Douty, if he had not
> been unjustly shoved to the front by his own exertions and those of
> his supporters. Mr Douty, last term, endeavoured, without success
> to play the part of an undignified Lecoq. Owing to his detective
> energies, the Undergraduates failed to discover the King's
> correspondent of the *Gadfly*, and his semi-official interference
> disgusted even the Senior Proctor. So that even those who had been
> loudest in their threats of vengeance against the (then unknown)
> long-haired Freshman, were as eager to protect him against the
> pomposity and officiousness of an amateur policeman.[10]

Robbie's remarks were ill conceived and undiplomatic; it was impossible for the friends of Douty to ignore the actions of this precocious Freshman, and they decided he should be punished and made to atone for his lack of manners. It was, however, important to John Tilley, Francis Ford, Arthur Bather, Edward [Fred] Benson, later to write *Mapp and Lucia* and others, and William Hall, five of the self-appointed committee of retribution, that their actions in taming Ross should not result in their being sent down. The conspirators consulted Arthur Tilley, elder brother of John, and by involving a junior tutor, the whole affair took on a sinister aspect. A spontaneous undergraduate act of hooliganism would have been frowned on by the College authorities, but the culprits could have been dealt with by the Proctors and no real harm would have been done. A premeditated assault, with the connivance of a member of the academic staff, was obviously a different matter.

Robbie spent the first weekend in March at Oxford and arrived back in Cambridge at five o'clock on Monday 4th, unaware that a plot was being hatched against him. He resumed his studies and on the evening of the 8th he dined in Hall. As he emerged into the cold night he was accosted by six undergraduates and with no consideration for his delicate constitution he was manhandled and thrown into the Fountain in the Front Court. Such an act in high summer might have resulted in a hysterical outburst from the unfortunate victim, but in March, the foolish and silly act could well have resulted in the victim dying of pneumonia. Robbie might have been able to laugh off the indignity and shame of the attack, but, when his assailants went to dine with Arthur Tilley his humiliation was complete.

It was inevitable that the ducking would be viewed unfavourably by the College authorities: Bather and Ford asked for a meeting with Provost Austen Leigh to explain their actions. The meeting was arranged for Sunday 10th. Austen Leigh asked Browning if he wished to be present, because Bather had told him that, in making his explanation, he would mention Browning's connection with the incident. Austen Leigh was not alone in thinking Browning might be implicated, George Prothero, a Proctor, also thought he had advance knowledge. Browning emphatically denied the suggestion and demanded of Prothero: 'I should like to know on what you founded so rash and absurd an accusation.'[11] Prothero replied promptly saying that he had heard from many sources that ever since the *Gadfly* article and the identifying of Ross as the writer, Browning had wanted him punished. Prothero said he had also heard that Browning had been present when Bather and Ford had discussed the idea of ducking Ross. He told Browning, 'It is certainly the impression in certain quarters that you by no means disapproved the idea.'[12] Prothero was probably right in questioning Browning's involvement; it was in keeping with Browning's complex personality that such duplicity was thought to be in character. The fact that he regarded himself as a friend of Ross's would not prevent his encouraging and supporting Bather and Ford in their actions. It would, indeed, have been most unlikely that Browning was completely unaware of what Bather and Ford planned, but before the incident was discussed by the Council matters took a more serious turn. The original motion was for a vote of censure against Tilley for his part in the 'ducking incident'; but it was extended to include a statement charging Tilley with incompetence as a lecturer. It was an unfortunate widening of the issue and completely masked the serious breach of discipline, making it hard to resolve the matter to the satisfaction of the College, the assailants or even the assaulted. Indeed, the matter would drag on into the new term.

On Monday the 11th an extra-ordinary meeting of the Council was called, Austen Leigh, Vice-Provost Whitting, Browning, John Nixon, Gresham Professor of Rhetoric, Prothero, and Arthur Tilley, were among those present. In spite of the doubts about Browning's involvement he put forward a resolution accusing Ford and the others of committing a serious breach of College discipline and asked that they should be punished accordingly. After some discussion, while accepting that both the assailants and the assaulted had been guilty of breaking College rules, the Council decided to take no further action.

Robbie, however, was not inclined to let the matter drop so easily. He accepted that he had been lucky not to be sent down for writing as he had in the *Gadfly* and the *Granta* but he did not feel charitable towards his assailants. He had been insulted and abused and he wanted retribution and vengeance. Ever since childhood his physical health had caused concern, but he was also highly strung and excitable, and the 'ducking incident' played on his nerves. In a distressed emotional state he even contemplated suicide and his brother had to come down from London and take him back to the safety of his mother's home at Onslow Square.

The change of environment did not have a recuperative effect on Robbie; Lizzie was not an ideal companion for the invalid and there were the inevitable squabbles between them. Robbie's health deteriorated and on 25 March Mrs Ross telegraphed Oscar Browning telling him that her son was still having a recurrence of the 'attacks'.[13] She telegraphed Browning for the next four days, and finally she was able to say that Robbie was much better and Browning could visit anytime after the 29th.

As the Easter vacation continued Robbie recovered sufficiently to go with Alex to Naples; the trip was not a great success. Alex sustained a minor injury while on the outward journey by ship and Robbie's depression did not ease.

The summer term at King's started on 26 April. Robbie returned but the 'ducking incident' still clearly obsessed him. He thought he had been dealt with harshly, while Arthur Tilley and the conspirators had been let off lightly. He told Oscar Browning that his family had consulted solicitors and obtained counsel's opinion as to the advisability of bringing a criminal charge against Ford and the others. But if he blamed Ford and the others for the attack, he kept his most virulent comments for Arthur Tilley. He wanted Tilley punished and it distressed him that far from being censured it looked as if Tilley would be rewarded for his support of the attackers.

If Robbie was perplexed by the lack of official censure by the College authorities, John Nixon was equally annoyed and on 14 May he submitted a detailed report on the incident to the Congregation. In the report Nixon argued that 'lynch law cannot be tolerated in civilised society and any encouragement of it by a responsible officer seems to be inexcusable.'[14] He agreed that Ross's activities in journalism were to be deplored, but he added a note of caution to those who had objected: 'A natural disgust at the personalities of modern forms of society journalism ought not to blind him or us to the offensiveness and harm of retaliation by personal violence.'[15] Nixon expressed his own personal distress at the outcome of the whole incident in a particularly bitter letter to Browning. He complained that in trying to see that Tilley was censured for his part in the incident, he had put his own position in jeopardy: 'I belong to a College where the senior officer responsible for discipline (after the Provost and Vice-Provost) is likely to be harmed by proposing censure on a Tutor for complicity in a serious breach of discipline strongly condemned by the Council. Is not the suggestion a reproach to King's?'[16]

Robbie's obvious distress at the unsatisfactory outcome of the 'ducking incident' had indeed changed the opinion of many of those in College and a number of undergraduates including Frederic Wisden and E.F. Bulmer petitioned Browning and Nathaniel Wedd to take action on Robbie's behalf. Monty James contrived to arrange an interview between Robbie and Francis Ford but it achieved nothing. Robbie was not prepared to change his opinion of Ford and he still wanted satisfaction against Tilley, whose conduct in the whole affair he continued to deplore.

It is difficult to know how the matter could have been settled to the satisfaction of both parties, but in the end Arthur Tilley was obliged, one night in Hall, to make a public apology to Ross. It was a humiliation from which Tilley never recovered and it was said he never again dined in Hall.

Honour partially satisfied, Robbie could have expected to return to his studies; unfortunately illness intervened. He contracted measles, an unpleasant disease in children, but in a physically frail young man potentially lethal. Robbie returned, yet again, to Onslow Square, to be cared for by his mother. The illness precipitated a further crisis in his life; in spite of the efforts of Prothero and Browning, Robbie decided not to return to King's in October. He had not enjoyed his year as a Freshman and he saw no reason to repeat the misery. As he convalesced from his measles he again came into conflict with his mother and Lizzie. They were distressed by his homosexuality and tried to force him to change his mode of life. He would not conform to their demands and although he would be discreet in his affairs, the rift with Lizzie would deepen. The ensuing rows made life at Onslow Square unpleasant and as Alex told Browning, 'He [Robbie] must leave home...my present idea is to leave him to his own devices. I think it would be much better for him if he had to make his own plans and carry them out himself.'[17]

It was a harsh punishment from a loving family to expect a twenty-year-old to fight all his battles without their support. He needed their understanding and compassion but he was to learn a salutary lesson and one which would be invaluable: if he was to succeed in life, it would be by his own ability and personality. It is doubtful if Ford, Benson, John Tilley and the others realised that their act of hooliganism would end Robbie's university career, cause him to leave home, and prejudice any chance he had of fulfilling the great potential of his life.

Two

Friendship and Journalism

F ROBBIE THOUGHT he was going to live a life of unabashed pleasure now that his undergraduate days were over, he was quickly disillusioned. His mother and brother had decided he was to leave home but they were not prepared to allow him to enjoy his freedom. He was banished to Edinburgh on the grounds, perhaps his family hoped, that the Protestant atmosphere of the city would end Robbie's Roman Catholic leanings and by removing him from the secular pursuits of London they would end his homosexual practices. Robbie had little choice but to agree to go. He was financially dependent on his mother's generosity. In agreeing to go to Edinburgh to work for W.E. Henley, the editor of the *Scots Observer*, Robbie was taking the first step into a career in journalism where at first, he could earn only a pittance.

Robbie settled into rooms in Rutland Square, and if he was lonely and found his position on the *Scots Observer* less than fulfilling, he gained some pleasure by continuing to correspond with Oscar Browning. The 'ducking incident' was still important but as he admitted to Browning, 'there being no redress against Tilley I have abandoned all prospect of an action against Ford etc.'[1] A short time later, however, he had obviously changed his mind, and it is noteworthy that he considered at such a young age to use the laws of libel to solve his problems. He planned, if Tilley was appointed a lecturer in Classics, to publish the correspondence and full details of the 'ducking incident'. He told Browning, 'at all events I shall act in such a way as to make it incumbent on Tilley to bring an action against me. You can tell the Council that you know (privately) that if any attempt to bring Tilley back is successful that I shall make the whole thing public. It is perfectly disgraceful that he should be allowed to remain in Cambridge at all.'[2]

Isolated in Edinburgh Robbie let his anger against Tilley simmer, even Christmas brought him no release. His sister and brother-in-law Mary and Charles Jones and their growing family had left Jesmond Dene in Newcastle and, as they spent Christmas in Hanover, Robbie was unable to join them. Wilde was in London and had little time for the lonely exile, he was too busy writing and enjoying a series of new friendships. Robbie hated Edinburgh and his relationship with Henley

27

was fraught with difficulties; Henley was a cantankerous man, who had no place in his life for anyone save his little daughter. Depressed and bored Robbie hoped for a solution to his problems, and not for the first time, illness intervened and brought the change of environment he sought.

Early in February 1890 he developed peritonitis.[3] The illness ended his stay in Edinburgh and as soon as he was fit to travel his family arranged, by a series of ambulance wagons and trains, to get him back to London. At Onslow Square Eliza Ross nursed him back to health, but as soon as he was able he moved into an apartment of his own, and as Henley had transferred the *Scots Observer* to London Robbie was able to resume his duties.

It was not very long, however, before Henley began to disapprove of Robbie's behaviour, disliking, in particular, Robbie's growing intimacy with Oscar Wilde. The previous July, the *Scots Observer* had been very critical of Wilde's essay 'The Portrait of Mr W.H.', Henley declaring that the essay should not have been published in any magazine, let alone a journal as respectable as *Blackwood's Magazine*. Wilde had been justifiably annoyed by the slurs and had accused Henley of being a Philistine. Ross had been equally incensed; he had spent an enjoyable evening with Wilde discussing the story of Shakespeare's Mr W.H., in which Wilde suggested that W.H. was a boy actor whom Shakespeare loved. The mildly hinted-at love affair between the boy actor and the Bard was too much for Henley, and he never missed the opportunity to publish an unfavourable review of Wilde's work.

Ross's recovery was slow, but he was able to enjoy and share in Wilde's company and his growing literary reputation. In June *Lippincott's Monthly Magazine* published the first version of Oscar Wilde's 'The Picture of Dorian Gray'. In writing to congratulate Wilde, Robbie allowed his enthusiasm for the story to flow a little too freely:

> Even in the precincts of the Savile, nothing but praise for *Dorian Gray* , though of course it is said to be very dangerous. I heard a clergyman extolling it *he* only regretted some of the sentiments of Lord Henry as apt to lead people astray. Sprigge[4] tells me that *Lippincott's* has had a phenomenal sale. 80 copies were sold in one day at a Strand bookseller, the usual amount being about 3 a week in that part. I hope you will consent to speak tomorrow night at the Authors. My brother is particularly anxious that you should. Your article in the *19th Century* if possible eclipses the *Decay of Lieing* (sic) but it seems a pity it should have come out the same month as

> *Dorian Gray*. Perhaps it is as well that you should be in every
> magazine to correct the note of tediousness in all the other articles.
> Will you come to dinner some night this week.[5]

It was predictable that Henley and the *Scots Observer* would disapprove of 'The Picture of Dorian Gray', and the paper ran a long and, at
times, acrimonious correspondence between Wilde and Charles
Whibley, Henley's editorial assistant, and readers of the *Scots Observer*.
At dinner one evening with Wilde, Ross revealed that the correspondence had been solely between Wilde and Whibley. Annoyed yet amused
by the deception Wilde brought the correspondence to a close with a
characteristic flourish: 'A comedy ends when the secret is out'.[6] Henley
was sure that Ross had informed Wilde about the true nature of the
correspondence and Robbie's dealings with Henley became increasingly
difficult.

If his position with the *Scots Observer* gave Robbie little pleasure, this
was counterbalanced by his involvement with the affairs of the Society of
Authors. The Society brought him into contact with 'men of letters' and
this was very much more to his liking. The Management Committee
included such notable writers as Arthur Conan Doyle, Henry Harland,
Rudyard Kipling, Justin McCarthy and John Addington Symonds. Alex
had become Honorary Secretary of the Society in 1885, when he was
approached by Walter Besant, the driving force behind the Society since
its inception in February 1884. He held the position until January 1889,
when he resigned and joined the Management Committee; Alex worked
for an honorarium of £10 per annum, and incidentally had supplied,
from his own means, much of the furniture for his office. Alex's place as
Secretary was taken by a young doctor, Samuel Squire Sprigge. Besant
offered Robbie the post of assistant editor of the Society's magazine the
Author, a position Robbie held in very special regard. He listed it
amongst his prime achievements for the rest of his life, although with a
salary of only two shillings a quarter. Besant ended his letter of appointment with: 'You could draw it weekly [weakly] if you pleased.'[7]

A salary so minute was hardly sufficient for Robbie to enjoy himself as
'a young man about town', but his mother was able to supplement his
meagre earnings. Robbie was also able to increase his income with paid
journalism. On 16 February 1891 he published in the *Author* a short
story, 'How We Lost The Book of Jasher'; set in the FitzTaylor Museum
at Oxbridge. Robbie's insight into the future was perceptive, while his
ambiguous humour was finely drawn:

Now, whenever a grant was made to the left wing of the building, as
I call it, I always used to say that science was being sacrificed to
archaeology. I mocked at the illuminated MSS over which
Girdelstone grew enthusiastic, and the musty theological folios
which Monteagle purchased. They heaped abuse upon me, of
course, when my turn came, and cracked many a quip on my
splendid skeleton of the ichthyosaurus, the only known specimen
from Greenland. At one time the strife broke into print, and the
London press animadverted on our conduct. It became a positive
scandal. We were advised to wash our dirty linen at home, and
though I have often wondered why the press should act as a
voluntary laundress on such occasions, I suppose the remark is a
just one.[8]

The 'positive scandal' was already being born. In January 1891 the young
poet Lionel Johnson took Lord Alfred (Bosie) Douglas, the third son of
the Marquess of Queensberry, to tea with Wilde; and so began a
sequence of events that would lead to Wilde's disgrace and imprisonment. Wilde did not introduce Ross to Douglas until early 1893[9]; he
knew Robbie would never play a subordinate role to Douglas and he
delayed the meeting for as long as he could. Douglas was twenty-two
years old and possessed a quite exceptional physical beauty. It was with
astute foresight that Wilde referred to him as a Greek youth. He was the
reincarnation of Narcissus, the mythical Greek youth who spurned the
love of the nymph Echo and was condemned by the gods to lose his heart
to his own image reflected in a clear pool. Douglas spurned love, yet he
needed to be loved. He had impeccable manners and a noble Scottish
ancestry and could charm his way into the hearts of men; unfortunately
his character was also flawed. He was vain and arrogant, and had a
vicious and violent temper; he destroyed all he touched.

Douglas, like Ross, had an adoring mother, but he had a father he
hated and despised; Robbie, however, needed a 'father-figure' in his life.
Wilde scholars have suggested that Ross's relationship with Wilde partially filled that void, but Wilde was not suited for the role of substitute
father. He needed to be loved and adored, not respected and revered. It
was fortunate that at the Society of Authors Robbie met Edmund Gosse
who was eminently fitted to play the role of stern/authoritative father and
considerate/compassionate friend. There was never any ambiguity in
Robbie's feelings towards Edmund Gosse; he greatly respected his scholarship and self-discipline, and was more than willing to sit at the master's
feet and absorb all that Gosse could teach him. He was never hesitant to
admit the debt of gratitude he owed Gosse and when, at a dinner party

one night, a fellow guest asked: 'Can you *stand* Gosse?' R.R.[replied] 'Yes. I try to put up with him, for, *like you*, I am deeply indebted to him.'[10]

In March 1892 Robbie sent Gosse a copy of a book in which he had written anonymously, but in collaboration with More Adey,[11] a new biographical introduction:

> I ordered that a copy of *Melmoth the Wanderer* should be sent to you which I hope you have received. Being responsible for part of the introduction I ventured to send it to you. I fear you have not much sympathy for the *école prestige* but I believe you will find *Melmoth* amusing enough for holiday reading. Though many people imagine it a mere repetition of Mrs Radcliffe it has little in common with the work of that estimable lady. In saying this I merely wish to spare you from reading the preface.[12]

Robbie's association with the 'Wandering Jew' was more lasting than he realised when he and More Adey wrote the introduction. Charles Robert Maturin, the Irish writer of *Melmoth the Wanderer*, was a great-uncle of Oscar Wilde, and it was Robbie who suggested to Wilde, when he left prison in 1897, that he should take the *nom-de-guerre* of Melmoth. Wilde accepted this suggestion readily, and added Sebastian, after the martyred Christian saint.[13]

In collaborating with More Adey Robbie was forging another lifelong friendship. Ten years older than Robbie, More Adey was an unlikely choice for the young Canadian, but as with his other friends, Robbie shared with More Adey a deep understanding of and admiration for Wilde and his writings; although Wilde, on occasions, could be hostile to More Adey and his eccentric manner. More Adey was a small, slightly built man, with deep set eyes, shielded by thick bushy brows. He had a receding hair-line, which made him look older than he was, and a short beard and thick moustache. There was something Eastern European in his looks, and people meeting him for the first time took him to be a revolutionary leader. He was pleased to play the role, assuming a sinister pose, though he was a charming man with a kindly disposition and a sympathetic nature. The two friends shared a home for the next fifteen years, and they were a perfect foil to each other's bouts of depression. More Adey was a Roman Catholic, and it may have been his faith which finally persuaded Robbie to become a convert.

Early in 1893 Robbie met another young man whose influence would be of a lasting nature. Aubrey Beardsley was born in Brighton in 1872; in his short life he achieved a reputation as a distinctive and talented artist. His highly individualistic draughtsmanship brought him into close contact, if not always in harmony, with many of the leading artistic and literary personalities of the late Victorian age. Robbie described their first meeting in vivid detail:

> I shall never forget my first meeting with Aubrey Beardsley, on
> February 14th 1892, at the rooms of Mr Vallance, the well-known
> disciple and biographer of William Morris. Though prepared for an
> extraordinary personality, I never expected the youthful apparition
> which glided into the room. He was shy, nervous, and self-
> conscious, without any of the intellectual assurances and ease so
> characteristic of him eighteen months later when his success was
> unquestioned. He brought a portfolio of his marvellous drawings, in
> themselves an earnest of genius; but I hardly paid any attention to
> them at first, so overshadowed were they by the strange and
> fascinating originality of their author. In two hours it was not hard
> to discover that Beardsley's appearance did not belie him. He was an
> intellectual Marcellus suddenly matured. His rather long brown
> hair, instead of being *ébouriffé*, as the ordinary genius is expected to
> wear it, was brushed smoothly and flatly on his head and over part
> of his immensely high and narrow brow. His face even then was
> terribly drawn and emaciated. Except in his manner, I do not think
> his general appearance altered very much in spite of the ill-health
> and suffering, borne with such unparalleled resignation and
> fortitude: he always had a most delightful and engaging smile for
> both friends and strangers.[14]

Robbie quickly became a favourite with Beardsley's mother and sister Mabel and it was not long before Mrs Beardsley was appealing for Robbie's help in controlling her wayward and difficult son:

> Please don't betray me by letting him know I have written to you,
> but you have great influence with him and I should be so grateful to
> you if you would remonstrate with him on his behaviour. To me it
> seems monstrous that he should even contemplate behaving in such
> an unprincipled manner....I am quite certain that Mr Vallance will
> agree with me and I know *he* will do his best to bring Aubrey to his
> senses. I rely upon you, too, to shame him into proper behaviour.
> Please forgive me for troubling you, but you have always been such
> a true friend.[15]

Ellen Beardsley displayed extraordinary confidence in Robbie; he was, after all, only twenty-four and, like Beardsley, was a member of the 'Decadents'; he was also a close and intimate friend of Oscar Wilde, yet he had sufficient balance and common sense to make it possible for a distraught mother to appeal for his help, in taming her 'wayward and unprincipled son'. There was something very special about this slightly built Canadian, that he could, and indeed did, all his life, 'hunt with the hounds and run with the fox'. It was a gift he exploited with considerable skill; he proved a good and true friend to all those to whom he gave his patronage. It is also true he never betrayed a friendship—once given.

Robbie had a difficult task in balancing his friendships and in trying to stop the inevitable quarrels which threatened to break out between them. Wilde, in particular, disliked Beardsley, yet when his biblical play *Salome* was to be published, he allowed Robbie to persuade him to let Beardsley do the illustrations. The relationship between artist and author was extremely bitter, but Robbie was certain the *Salome* pictures were brilliant; he regarded them as amongst Beardsley's finest works:

> In the illustrations to *Salome*, he [Beardsley] reached the
> consummation of the new convention he created for himself; they
> are, collectively, his masterpieces. In the whole range of art there is
> nothing like them. You can trace the origin of their development,
> but you cannot find anything wherewith to compare them; they are
> absolutely unique.[16]

If the illustrations for *Salome* caused Wilde distress, then so did the problems concerned with the translation of the play. Wilde originally wrote the play in French, with two Paris friends, Stuart Merrill and Pierre Louÿs assisting with the language and French grammar. When the play was considered for production in England, Douglas, who was still an undergraduate at Oxford, but also a very powerful influence on Wilde, asked to be allowed to do the translation. Wilde acquiesced. And when Douglas made a number of alterations to the French text, to which Wilde took great exception, Ross suggested that Beardsley should make the corrections to the final draft. It was the first time, since Wilde had met Douglas, that Ross had ever heard a whisper of criticism by Wilde of his new golden boy. In his own inimitable way Robbie took full advantage of the minor rift. Despite later denials, it would seem as if Douglas always bore Robbie great animosity from the very moment of the *Salome* row. Robbie, however, knew perfectly well where the blame lay, he was sure that Douglas the translator was more at fault than Beardsley the artist.

On 24 March 1893 Robbie was finally elected to membership of the

Savile Club, having been proposed the previous November by the Reverend Charles Middleton-Wake; his sponsors included Edmund Gosse, St John Hawkin and Martin Conway. Ross was contributing to the *Saturday Review* and saw little of Wilde, who was increasingly obsessed with Bosie Douglas and John Gray, who later became a Roman Catholic priest. In April, when *A Woman of No Importance* was first performed, Robbie was in the audience with the rest of Wilde's acolytes.

In July 'Alfred' the sixteen-year-old son of a military gentleman,[17] spent the night at Onslow Square with Robbie and his mother. Robbie had met him at Easter at the home of Biscoe Wortham, Oscar Browning's brother-in-law. It is hard to believe Eliza Ross would have allowed such a visit if she had suspected Robbie and the boy were indulging in homosexual acts. The next day Robbie made a fatal mistake by introducing 'Alfred' to Bosie Douglas; Douglas was infatuated with the boy and arranged to meet him again later. When they met there is no doubt they became lovers, and as a consequence 'Alfred' returned late to his school in Bruges, run by Biscoe Wortham. It was an unfortunate coincidence that the boy was a pupil of Wortham's; it made the subsequent allegations and counter-allegations difficult for Robbie to handle without involving Oscar Browning and his nephews Philip and Toddy Wortham.

Douglas, always an indiscreet letter-writer, wrote to 'Alfred'; Wortham, already suspicious of the boy's behaviour, intercepted his letters, which confirmed his worst fears. Wortham confronted 'Alfred' who confessed, but in doing so aroused in Wortham's mind, the awesome possibility that his own sons had been seduced by Robbie. Wortham interrogated Philip, who admitted that Robbie had seduced him three times. Wortham wrote to Browning seeking help and advice, unaware that Browning would report direct to Robbie. In his letter Wortham said: 'Ross is simply one of a gang of the most absolutely brutal ruffians...two other persons beside himself are implicated in this business.'[18] There can be no question but that the other two were Wilde and Douglas, yet it was Ross who seemed to bear the brunt of the allegations. He travelled to Ostend to try and negotiate with Wortham. The subsequent meeting, however, proved less than successful, and he was forced to write to Browning and admit:

> He [Wortham] refuses to tell me what he proposes doing. He says he possesses documentary evidence but what he intends doing with this (if it exists) he will not say. He also speaks of "coming to terms" but does not state what those terms are beyond the fact that I have certain letters....He will not tell me which letters they are. I have

no letters from him that could not be read in public. . . . I was also
confronted with Philip who repeated his story. It is an absolute
fabrication. If it were true I certainly would not attempt to conceal it
from *you*.[19]

'Alfred's' father consulted his solicitors and considered issuing writs
against Robbie and Douglas. Sir George Lewis, Robbie's wily solicitor,[20]
interceded and pointed out that while Robbie and Douglas might be sent
to prison, 'Alfred' would also serve a prison sentence. More Adey took
over the negotiations for Robbie and his family, and eventually he was
able to report that all thought of legal redress had been dropped. It was
an unsatisfactory conclusion to a sordid affair and none of them came out
of it with any credit. The repercussions would dog Robbie for the rest of
his life, although his part in the 'seduction' was never established beyond
reasonable doubt. Nor was his involvement any greater than that of
Wilde and Douglas, yet he would carry the scars; and Douglas would
eventually use the alleged 'seduction' against him in a court of law.
Wortham was able to assure his wife that her son Toddy had not been a
victim of Robbie's vice, although he did not feel able to issue the same
reassurance about Philip. There was, however, a sequel which must have
raised a few doubts in Robbie's mind: Biscoe Wortham was arrested for
disgusting behaviour, but was released after it was revealed it had been a
question of mistaken identity.

In consequence of all the allegations and stress Robbie's health again
caused concern to his mother and Alex, and it was advised that he should
leave London. He agreed to go to Cambridge for a few weeks. The
stresses continued to take a toll of his fragile nerves and his health did not
improve. His family realised that he needed a firm hand to curb his
excessive behaviour and in November he was sent to Davos and placed in
the capable hands of his brother Jack.

In Davos Robbie had time to reflect on the harshness of his punishment
and he wrote and told Douglas the reasons behind his sudden departure
from London:

I am not allowed to live in London for two years. As the purse
strings are in their hands, and a stoppage is threatened, I have to
submit. [Adey] had concealed everything, but the worthy Rev Mr
Squeers[21] wrote a full and particular account of how things were to
my brother. It was news to him, as [Adey] had hitherto concealed
everything, but the trouble with the noisy military gentleman. My
elder brother here gets letters about the disgrace of the family, the

> social outcast, the son and brother unfit for society of any kind,
> from people at home. I am sure you will be amused to hear this.[22]

His friends in London were distressed by his absence and Max Beerbohm wrote that his 'return would be triumphal'.[23] Beerbohm was
perplexed by Robbie's sudden departure and wanted to know all the
reasons for his protracted stay in Davos:

> As a matter of fact I have never learnt even the cause of your
> departure: from what you hint I suppose it was a kind of flight:
> though Bosey told me—to my relief—that you were merely feeling
> ill and had quarrelled with your people.[24]

Robbie's 'flight' and quarrels with his family were the inevitable
outcome of a youthful prank; he frequently upset his mother and sisters
by his thoughtless actions and his involvement with socially unacceptable
companions, which caused him to become the subject of whispered
confidences. Rumours of disreputable and imprudent behaviour were
circulating in London concerning Wilde, Douglas, John Gray and Reggie Turner[25] and Robbie could not hope to escape censure. It was also in
1894 that Robbie was finally received into the Roman Catholic Church,[26]
and his conversion must have been a sad disappointment to his mother,
whose Protestant faith was firm. It would have been as hard for Eliza
Ross to overlook her son's behaviour as it was for the Marquess of
Queensberry to turn a blind eye to his son's posturings.

He may have found disfavour with his relatives in London, but in
Davos he stayed with Jack and his sister-in-law Minnie. On Saturday 18
November 1893 he was in residence at the Posthaus, and if, as Beerbohm
suggested, Robbie was trying to escape from some terrible disgrace, he
did not behave as a penitent sinner. His precarious health may have
prevented him from taking an active part in the strenuous activities of
the spa; he did not ski or take part in the toboggan races, but he quickly
became a member of the English Literary Society, and was no passive
member despite his youth. On 2 January 1894, a few months short of his
twenty-fifth birthday, he read a paper to the assembled members of the
Society entitled 'The Didactic in Art and Literature'. His inexperience as
a lecturer and the overglowing announcement of his forthcoming talk in
the *Davos Courier* of 31 December were not allowed to mar his moment of
enjoyment, nor did he spare his captive audience in pursuing his
undoubted pleasure. His conscience, though, did prick him and he
began his lecture with a rebuttal of the *Davos Courier* announcement:
'Mr Ross has been accustomed to write for some of the leading London
journals as a literary critic.' He confessed:

> I find nothing better than praise even when it is insincere but I feel
> that you may have been inveigled here under false pretences in the
> belief that you are going to hear a professional critic and journalist,
> whereas I am neither.

With the formalities over he began his lecture in the conventional manner by recalling an early membership of a school literary society where he admitted he had spent some of the dullest moments of his life. He said he could have endured the boredom, but what he could not forgive was that he had never been asked to read a paper:

> I bore in silence the slight from my companions, but I left School
> with a cynical and bitter view of literary societies throughout the
> world. I promised myself that one day I should have my revenge;
> and that I would bore my fellow-creatures, if only for half an hour,
> as a retribution for what I had suffered from them.

His revenge was definitely very sweet and he enjoyed the moment to the full, savouring his own power and perhaps aware, even then, that his greatest gift was to be able to communicate with his fellow men. In later years, his friends—and they were indeed many and eminent—were to attest to his ability as a raconteur. His wit was never forced, his humour never contrived. Even in January 1894 there was something more that was visible to his audience; he knew the precise nature and derivation of words, and, with the wizardry of a man who can use humour as a positive weapon, he held his audience spellbound:

> When therefore I was asked by your innocent committee to read a
> paper, I saw my chance had come. You will say with some justice
> that it was a little cowardly to take advantage of a community in the
> secluded confines of a Swiss valley, where people resort chiefly for
> their health; but I trust you will be tolerant of despair, and look on
> yourselves as suffering for others.

In retrospect those last three words were a particularly poignant phrase; it was to be his destiny to suffer for others, not in the physical form of martyrdom, but simply by his unselfish concern for others less fortunate than he. He always considered other people's welfare and emotions before his own. If he had been a little more selfish he would not have suffered as much as he was destined to do. It is difficult to see how he could have changed events as he admitted to his audience of the English Literary Society:

> The joy of martyrdom will compensate you in some respect for your
> prospective boredom, together with the knowledge that the more
> you suffer the greater pleasure you will afford the reader of this
> paper.

It is doubtful if his audience were bored; his lecture was well written,
even if it did contain certain ideas and philosophies that he shared with
Oscar Wilde. There is evidence to suggest that Wilde obtained some of
his best dialogue from his conversations with Robbie. Perhaps, the hand
which guided Robbie that January afternoon in Davos was that of Oscar
Wilde. In April 1891 in the preface to *The Picture of Dorian Gray* Wilde
had written: 'There is no such thing as a moral or an immoral book.
Books are well written or badly written. That is all.' These sentiments
were to haunt both Wilde and Ross, and they must have wished that the
offending words had never been written. In Davos on that winter afternoon, Robbie, oblivious of the dangers he was facing, allowed his pas-
sions to run riot as he lectured his distinguished audience on his
definition of moral values:

> I hope no one will regard it as a compliment, when I say that an
> inability to forget their morals is a peculiarly English vice. No
> achievement in Literature or Art can occur, without the English
> asking if it is quite moral. No picture can be painted, no novel
> written, without the enquiry whether it is fit and proper for their
> under-aged daughters, their underfed sons, and their over-aged
> fathers. They do not first ask if this picture is "well" painted, if this
> book is "well" written. Yet that is the only spirit in which such
> things should be considered at all. It is often not till years afterwards
> when author and artist are dead, and those who blushed are dead,
> that someone asked, "Was this book well written? Was this picture
> well painted?"...I claim for Art and Literature the same immunity,
> the same freedom; that they be judged only by artistic and literary
> standards. Why should we hear that this writer is immoral or that
> painter's pictures are immoral? I do not know what an immoral
> book is and I have read a good many. I know what a pornographic
> book is. I think many books badly written. If that is what is meant
> by immoral, Archdeacon Farrar's irreligious novel *The Life of Christ*
> is a very immoral book. It is I think the most deleterious reading,
> not excepting Miss Marie Corelli, that I am acquainted with.

His condemnation of the writings of Marie Corelli was especially
unfortunate. The lady he maligned with such youthful exuberance had a

long memory; over a quarter of a century later she was to exact a terrible revenge.

Not content with giving the first lecture of the year, Robbie was also involved, with others, in an exchange of letters to the editor of the *Davos Courier*. In the final paragraph of his letter, he put into clear perspective his view of life:

> I, Sir, have only two objects in life. The first is to amuse myself, the second is to amuse other people, and though pained in the harshness of your correspondence I am compensated by the fact that she[27] was "rather amused" at what I said. Had she happily been present no doubt she might have been "much amused" as more courteous critics confessed themselves to have been.

While Robbie was still at Davos Beardsley wrote and told him of the proposed publication of a new quarterly magazine to be called the *Yellow Book*. Beardsley, as its art editor, was enthusiastic about the provocative venture and it says much for the mood of these young men that their enthusiasms were matched only by their appetite to shatter the conventions of their elders, to blow aside Victorian hypocrisy, and to pursue—without restriction—their own lives. Beardsley was equally convinced that the magazine would provide Robbie with another outlet for his fluent pen:

> We all want to have something charming from you for the first number. Say an essay or a short story. Now do send us something soon in your most brilliant style; and make up your mind to be a regular contributor.[28]

Robbie responded to Beardsley's request, and although he asked how long the proposed article should be, he never wrote for the *Yellow Book*. In view of the fact that he enjoyed seeing his work in print, this is surprising, and it is impossible to know exactly what were his reasons for failing to respond to the new magazine. The first issue of the *Yellow Book* appeared on 15 April 1894, and it was notable that not only was Robbie's contribution absent but there was no reference to Oscar Wilde and his art. The omission was astonishing, for he was at the height of his fame, and was undoubtedly the leader of the Aesthetic movement. The absence of Wilde's name from the magazine was deliberate. Beardsley's dislike of Wilde had increased since their quarrel over the illustrations for *Salome*; he was deeply superstitious, and was convinced that everything with which Wilde was associated would bring them all bad luck. Even John

Lane, founder of The Bodley Head and the publisher of the *Yellow Book*, was doubtful about accepting Wilde's contributions, despite having previously published his books. But in 1894 these were only reaching a small, exclusive readership; Lane hoped that the readership of the *Yellow Book* would be much wider and more diverse. There were some who thought that Lane's reticence also extended to Robbie Ross. This, however, would appear not to have been so, for Lane remained a friend throughout all the subsequent traumas.

Robbie left Davos in late January to return to London, but he did not remain there for long. With Alex and Major Charles Jones, he went to Canada to join Mary and her daughters Ethel and Lillian. They all returned to London in June, by which time there were new challenges waiting to occupy his heart and mind.

Three

A Life Destroyed

N 3 JANUARY 1895 Wilde's entertaining comedy *An Ideal Husband* had its first public performance. Robbie, concerned at the growing influence Douglas had on Wilde, was nevertheless delighted by the success of the play. Fifteen days later in the *St James's Gazette* Robbie wrote a long article entitled 'Mr Oscar Wilde on Mr Oscar Wilde: An Interview'. Written as a conversation between the reporter and the subject there is in the last exchange between the two men no hint of the traumas that were about to explode in their lives:

> "Well," I said, rising to go, "I have enjoyed myself immensely."
> "I was sure you would," said Mr Wilde. "But tell me how you manage your interviews."
> "Oh, Pitman," I said carelessly.
> "Is that your name? It's not a very *nice* name."
> Then I left.[1]

So much has been written about the relationships of Robbie, Oscar Wilde and Bosie Douglas, that it is difficult to be totally objective in trying to analyse their respective roles in the tragedy which overtook them. Perhaps it was predestined that they should find consolation in each other's company. That their relationships were based initially on homosexual practices cannot be denied; that each was introduced to such practices before they first met is equally hard to argue against; in the end it was the predilection shared by Douglas and Wilde for young street louts that caused Oscar Wilde's downfall. If Wilde had confined his activities to the young men of his own class, such as Robbie Ross, Arthur Clifton[2] and Reggie Turner, then Victorian society would have turned a blind eye, and there might have been no trials. It is doubtful, however, if the tragedy could have been prevented, for such was the streak of madness running through the Queensberry male line, that if Wilde had not responded to the jeers and taunts of Douglas's father, then the fighting Marquess would have found another way to destroy his son and his friends. Into this maelstrom Robbie was drawn and it must be regretted that he did not listen to the dictates of his own heart and ignore the affairs of Wilde/Douglas and Queensberry. But he was as incapable of turning his back on Wilde as he was incapable of turning away from the teachings of his Church. His own homosexuality was the cross he had to bear; he neither attempted to shift the blame for it on to others, nor did he ask others to help moderate his inverted impulses. Perhaps a modern psychoanalyst could have found a cause or reason for his sexual tastes. But when Wilde's and Douglas's love-affair ended in the fires of hell it was inevitable that Ross would rise like a phoenix from the ashes. Although a mere spectator in the drama Robbie never fully recovered from the emotional wounds inflicted on him by Wilde's love for Douglas.

Robbie could not end his friendship with Wilde, nor could he ignore Constance Wilde's suffering caused by her husband's indifferent and reckless behaviour. As Wilde's friendship with Douglas began to cause public comment, Constance turned to Robbie for help and comfort. Her dependence on him grew slowly; in 1893 she was still addressing him as 'Mr Ross'. A year before the final collapse of her husband's life, she had become more familiar and had started to call him Robbie; as the disaster grew closer he became 'my dear Robbie'. At Christmas in 1894 it was Robbie who remembered Constance and her young sons Cyril and Vyvyan, and she sent him a charming note for his consideration:

> Thank you so much for the exquisite flowers, and for so kindly remembering the two boys: we are all very grateful to you and send you our best wishes for a happy Xmas and New Year.[3]

Robbie's pleasure was short-lived and he experienced a sense of isolation and despair when Wilde and Douglas went off to Algiers for a brief winter holiday before the opening of *The Importance of Being Earnest* on 14 February. Constance and her sons were at Babbacombe near Torquay with Lady Mount-Temple, the widow of William Cowper-Temple and a distant cousin to Constance. Constance was short of money and she appealed to Robbie to contact Oscar and arrange for him to ease her poverty. With typical generosity Robbie immediately telegraphed back offering Constance the money from his own limited resources. Constance deeply appreciated the offer but was able to refuse it:

> How very sweet and kind; you are a real friend, such as I knew you always to be! If I do want anything I will let you know, and you shall let me have the £5, but at this moment I have no expenses and can well wait until Oscar returns.
>
> And now, is there any chance of your being able to come here for a week? Lady Mount-Temple wants you so much to come next week

> when she will have a room for you. And I should be so glad to have
> you here altho' at present it is so cold that it is quite unbearable.[4]

When the Marquess of Queensberry left his card with its obscene message, 'To Oscar Wilde, posing somdomite',[5] at the Albemarle Club on 18
February 1895, it began one of the most notorious and sensational
periods in English legal history. Oscar Wilde did not see the offending
card for ten days, and when he saw the ill-spelt message, his first action
was to write to Robbie, asking for his help. It says much for their
relationship, that at the moment of his gravest crisis, Wilde turned for
help to Ross with his unique qualities of common sense, calmness, and
control in moments of stress:

> Since I saw you something has happened. Bosie's father has left a
> card at my club with hideous words on it. I don't see anything now
> but a criminal prosecution. My whole life seems ruined by this man.
> The tower of ivory is assailed by the foul thing. On the sand is my
> life spilt. I don't know what to do. If you could come here at 11.30.
> please do so tonight. I mar your life by trespassing ever on your love
> and kindness. I have asked Bosie to come tomorrow.[6]

Robbie received the note from Wilde at 6.40 p.m. at his rooms at 24
Horton Street, and at 11.30 he went to the Hotel Avondale in Piccadilly
where Wilde was staying. Douglas was already there and his presence did
nothing to lighten Robbie's sense of impending doom.

Douglas was never in any doubt that the only course of action open to
Wilde was to sue Queensberry for criminal libel. Robbie was equally sure
that Wilde should simply ignore the insult and let Douglas and his father
fight their own battles. He considered it was purely a family squabble
and that both antagonists were well matched, and that Wilde was being
used as an expendable pawn in a lethal game. If only Robbie had been
able to foresee the consequences of taking Wilde to consult his own
solicitors, C.O. Humphreys, Son & Kershaw, he would, instead, have
bundled his friend into a hansom cab and rushed him to the nearest
railway station to catch the first train for the continent. Ironically,
eighteen years later, when forced to defend himself against the very same
libellous allegations, Robbie took the same coldly logical, but ill-advised
steps that Wilde pursued so recklessly. Both Humphreys, the solicitor,
and Sir Edward Clarke, the barrister he hoped to retain, asked Wilde if
he was innocent of the charge alleged on the Marquess's card. Wilde
replied gravely and earnestly that the charge was absolutely false and
totally groundless. The outrageous lie stunned Robbie, but he under-

stood only too well Wilde's attitude to the whole sordid business. Wilde used the English language in a precise and concise manner; he was right, the words on the card were not correct; Wilde was not 'posing'—he *was* a sodomite! As truth and lies collided, Robbie was aware of the likely outcome of the action against Queensberry. In the witness-box, questioned by the Prosecution, cross-examined by the Defence, Wilde would answer in precisely the same vein, with intelligence, with candour, with wit and with subtlety. And his replies would be misunderstood and distorted by a jury of his intellectual inferiors.

The warrant for the arrest of the Marquess of Queensberry for libelling Wilde was issued on 1 March 1895 and he was arrested the next day. He came up before the Magistrate at Bow Street and was bailed to appear for trial at the Old Bailey on 3 April.

The weeks leading up to the trial should have been a time for reflection and planning, but Douglas had other ideas and he and Wilde went to Monte Carlo. Ross was devastated by Wilde's sojourn with Douglas at such a sensitive time; even so when the trial opened he was so unconcerned by his own reputation that he drove to the court with Wilde. He was subpoenaed by Queensberry's solicitors, but was never called upon to give evidence against Wilde. The trial of the Marquess of Queensberry lasted only three days, but the outcome was to have a lasting impact on all the central players. Wilde thought he could use his Irish wit and literary reputation to prove Queensberry's libel to be untrue. Douglas wanted to go into the witness-box and tell the Court of his father's brutal and cruel treatment of his wife and family, but was prevented from doing so by both Wilde and his Counsel. Douglas's evidence would have been regarded as irrelevant and would not have been accepted by the Bench. Sir Edward Carson, Queensberry's Counsel, when he cross-examined Wilde about his writings was the butt of much of Wilde's wit, but when Carson said he would call Alfred Taylor,[7] Edward Shelley, Charles Parker, and Alfred Wood so they could all recount their loathsome experiences with Wilde, Wilde's demeanour changed. Alfred Wood, one of the four, had tried to blackmail Wilde. Wilde had paid Wood to go the United States and assumed he was still there.

Sitting in the witnesses' room Robbie was unaware of the drama being enacted in the Court, but that night as he journeyed back with Wilde he felt the first serious misgivings; if any of the young men entered the witness-box Wilde would indeed be ruined. Robbie's pessimism was justified, and was confirmed by Sir Edward Clarke who realised only too well that his case was lost and, the next morning, begged leave of the Court to state that on behalf of his client he wished to withdraw from the prosecution.

The jury, on the direction of the Judge, found Queensberry Not Guilty.

Wilde left the Old Bailey at noon on 5 April, fully aware that in view of the grave charges of homosexuality and buggery that had been made against him he was quite likely to be arrested. He went immediately with Robbie and Alfred Douglas to the Holborn Viaduct Hotel; Wilde seemed unable to take any positive action, except to write to the editor of the *London Evening News* explaining why he had been unwilling to allow Douglas to enter the witness-box on his behalf. He ended his short letter with an unselfish and noble gesture to his young friend: 'I determined to retire from the case, and to bear on my own shoulders whatever ignominy and shame might result from my prosecuting Lord Queensberry.'[8] Wilde undoubtedly saw himself at that moment as a martyr, but he was also a proud and arrogant man, and it would have been out of character for him to flee and live the tortured life of a hunted man. Ross and Wilde had both inherited a fierce thread of Celtic honour, and were unable to bear the indignity of turning away from a conflict, even if it meant they would be mortally hurt in the ensuing battle.

After lunch they moved on to the Cadogan Hotel in Sloane Street where Douglas had been staying. It was then that Douglas suggested going to see George Lewis, an old and valued friend of Wilde's, who was also, ironically, Queensberry's solicitor. Lewis had, however, declined to act for him during the trial, but there was now little he could do to help Wilde. The matter had already been placed in the hands of the Director of Public Prosecutions, and by 3.30 p.m. on 5 April, Detective-Inspector Brockwell of Scotland Yard, accompanied by a Treasury Official, appeared before John Bridge, the Bow Street Magistrate, to apply for a warrant for Wilde's arrest.

Ross desperately tried to persuade Wilde to flee to France, from where there was no extradition treaty, but Wilde could not be persuaded. Robbie was unable to relieve his friend's distress, and when Wilde asked him to go to see Constance and tell her what had happened he went willingly but with a heavy heart. In spite of his own despair Robbie was sympathetic and compassionate. Constance, understandably, was inconsolable and her distress only added to the burdens Robbie had to face. She urged him to plead with her husband to leave the country before he was arrested. Robbie assured her that he had been trying to do just that, but Wilde was strangely reluctant to leave. Ross returned to the hotel determined to try once more to urge Wilde to flee. Reggie Turner had arrived during the afternoon, and together they implored Wilde to leave; their pleas were in vain. Meanwhile, Douglas, unable to bear the agony of waiting, went to the House of Commons to seek help from his cousin, George Wyndham.

Thomas Marlow, a newspaperman with the *Star*, arrived at the Cadogan Hotel shortly after five o'clock, but Wilde was unable to see him. The ever-attentive Robbie was sent to deal with Marlow who told him of the issue of the warrant for Wilde's arrest.

At 6.30 p.m. Inspector Richard, accompanied by another officer, arrived at the hotel to serve the warrant on Oscar Wilde. Robbie and Reggie Turner were not allowed to go with Wilde to Bow Street. Beardsley's early superstition about the *Yellow Book* proved well founded; when Wilde left the hotel he had a yellow book under his arm—a fact that was well reported in the press. The association with Wilde's arrest killed the *Yellow Book*, even though, in truth, the book he carried was *Aphrodite* by Pierre Louÿs, which just happened to be bound in yellow. That Edward Shelley, a young clerk at The Bodley Head, was one of Wilde's lovers—and blackmailers—caused further distress to the publishers of the *Yellow Book*. At the time of Wilde's arrest John Lane was on his way to the United States. When he docked he found waiting for him cables from a number of his established authors, threatening to withdraw their work from The Bodley Head unless the publishers ended their association with Wilde and his group of 'decadent' young men. Lane had no option but to instruct his staff to withdraw all copies of the fifth issue of the *Yellow Book*, and to dismiss Beardsley and delete all his drawings from the next issue. The *Yellow Book* never recovered from the sacking of its controversial art editor, and after just four more issues it ceased to appear.

Robbie returned again to Tite Street to pack an overnight bag for Wilde; he found Constance and her sons had already left the house to stay with relatives. He took the overnight bag to Bow Street Police Station, but was unable to leave it or to see Wilde. Douglas in the meantime was harrying his friends and relatives in an attempt to secure bail for Wilde, but all his efforts were unsuccessful and Wilde remained in custody for three weeks.

Later that evening Robbie made yet a third trip to Tite Street; fearful that Wilde's manuscripts and possessions would be seized, he broke into the study and took away as many of Wilde's manuscripts as he could find. In view of the sale of the contents of Tite Street following Wilde's bankruptcy, Robbie's actions were courageous and far-sighted, and he certainly saved many valuable manuscripts from being lost permanently.

Exhausted and utterly despondent, Robbie returned to his mother's home, and then against the dictates of his own heart, but on the advice of his family, he left London for Calais. He had been told there might be further arrests following on from Wilde's, and he knew his own freedom was at stake. He was torn between duty to his friend and loyalty to his family; he did not care about his own future, but it went against everything he believed in to desert a friend in need. Ross wanted to share Wilde's burden; Wilde's guilt was his guilt. And if Wilde had the courage to face his accusers so should he. The decision to go or stay was the most difficult decision Robbie had ever made, but in the end he went to France, convinced that if he was free he would be able to fight the bigotry and intolerance that was destroying Wilde's life and that would, if not checked, destroy them all.

Douglas, to his credit, stayed in London and visited Wilde daily during his remand, and only left London on 25 April, the night before the trial, and then only after he had been advised to leave by Wilde's solicitors, who thought his presence might be injurious to their client. Douglas's actions were courageous and unselfish and at the time he was entitled to all the praise that was heaped on him. Douglas went to Rouen and immediately telegraphed Ross to join him. There, the two friends stayed until the end of Wilde's first trial when Douglas travelled to Paris and Ross returned to Calais.

Wilde was tried by the British Press long before he appeared in the dock. The public hysteria reached contemptible heights, and the hurt it caused innocent people, such as Constance and her sons and Robbie's family, was immeasurable. This trial and Wilde's action against Queensbury have been covered in much greater detail elsewhere.[9] The day Wilde was sentenced to two years' hard labour was a day Robbie would never forget: 25 May, his twenty-sixth birthday. There was little time, however, for personal mourning; Robbie had also to cope with the death in Davos of Jack's wife Minnie. She was brought home to England for burial at Hope near Shrewsbury on 28 May, and Robbie returned from France to be with his family. But if his sympathy was with Jack in his bereavement, his heart was with Wilde as he began his imprisonment. He knew that his future would be linked with that of his disgraced and shamed friend.

In much of the writings about that period of Wilde's life, there has been a certain amount of ridicule poured on the actions of his friends in deserting him in his hour of need. However, with the possible exception of Douglas, who should have been in the dock with Wilde, there was little his friends could have done—even if they had stayed in London—to alter the verdict of the jury.

There is little point in speculating on what a jury's verdict would have been if Douglas had been charged alongside Wilde, or if Robbie had stood beside his friend in the dock. There was much evidence, outside the trial as well as within, which showed that Wilde was the figure-head of a group of young men involved in homosexual practices. In January 1886 the Labouchère Amendment[10] had made homosexual acts in private and public a criminal offence and Ross, Douglas and Wilde were guilty of breaking that law. But the witnesses against Wilde were, on their own admissions, guilty of perjury, of blackmail and a multitude of other crimes, and were not the innocent victims of Wilde's predilections, nor had they been lured into homosexual acts against their wishes; they were, as Wilde and Ross were, willing accomplices. Oscar Wilde and Robbie Ross were both generous in rewarding their young 'friends', but they paid dearly for their sexual propensities. Two of Wilde's accusers were later sent to prison: one served seven years' penal servitude for extorting money with threats, whilst the other served a custodial sentence for receiving stolen goods. Justice may have been served when Wilde was sent to prison, but he should not have been convicted on the perjured evidence of these young louts.

The stressful events of that spring caused Robbie emotional and physical anguish and he had to seek the strength he needed from his mentor Edmund Gosse, although even Gosse's support was often ambivalent, and never more so than over his attitude to the disgrace of Oscar Wilde. Gosse might have said 'There but for the grace of God go I', but he did not; he wrote to Robbie in the manner of a stern father ashamed of the actions of his wayward son:

> Now the great thing is to forget. Your action throughout, so far as I
> understand it, has been quixotic and silly but honourable. In this
> dark world no one can do more than walk by the light of his
> conscience. If it is any pleasure to you to know it, you preserve all
> our regard (my wife's and mine), and in the future, calmer times we
> shall both rejoice to see you and give you any support we can, if ever
> you want support. I miss your charming company, in which I have
> always delighted, and we all miss it, for you are a favourite with
> every member of this family. I would say to you be calm, be
> reasonable, turn for consolation to the infinite resources of
> literature, which, to your great good fortune, are open to you more
> than to most men. Write to me when you feel inclined, and however
> busy I am I will write in reply, and in a more happy season you
> must come back, to be truly welcomed in this house.[11]

It was less than two months later, on 4 August, that Robbie visited Gosse at home.[12] Robbie needed wise counselling, and this Gosse was able to give, with fatherly affection and compassion. All his life Robbie let his heart rule his head. Frequently he needed to be reminded of his own needs and desires, and never more so than in his determination to restore Wilde's literary and social reputation.

Four

Love for the Imprisoned

OT CONTENT with getting Oscar Wilde sentenced to two years' hard labour on 21 June, barely a month after the harsh sentence was passed, the Marquess of Queensberry presented a petition for bankruptcy against Wilde. A Receiving Order was then made on 25 July and the first private hearing was a month later. Two public hearings took place on 24 September and 12 November, and it was at one of these hearings that Robbie Ross attended to give moral support and to pay respect to his friend. Wilde described the event touchingly in *De Profundis:*[1]

> When I was brought down from my prison to the Court of
> Bankruptcy between two policemen, Robbie waited in the long
> dreary corridor, that before the whole crowd, whom an action so
> sweet and simple hushed into silence, he might gravely raise his hat
> to me, as handcuffed and with bowed head I passed by him. Men
> have gone to heaven for smaller things than that. It was in this
> spirit, and with this mode of love that the saints knelt down to wash
> the feet of the poor, or stooped to kiss the leper on the cheek. I have
> never said one single word to him about what he did. I do not know
> to the present moment whether he is aware that I was even
> conscious of his action. It is not a thing for which one can render
> formal thanks in formal words. I store it in the treasury-house of my
> heart. I keep it there as a secret debt that I am glad to think I can
> never possibly repay.[2]

In that quotation from that most bitter letter which he wrote during his last months in Reading Gaol, Wilde lays to rest the presumption that his relationship with Robbie was purely one of sexual pleasure. Who other than a devoted friend, with nothing to conceal, would have made such a public act of homage as Robbie did that day in the corridor of the Court of Bankruptcy? Robbie was not a showman, he did not perform acts of generosity for the benefit of a wide audience. By his gesture of sincerity he told a hostile world that there were still people who did not regard Wilde as a perverted monster.

Ross was perturbed that the disclosures made during the public examination of Wilde's bankruptcy would cause Wilde more humiliation than he had already endured at his trials. Wilde had been highly extravagant and his taste for high-living would do nothing but further harm his reputation with the general public. Aware that Wilde's debts were substantial Robbie set about trying to persuade Wilde's many friends to contribute sufficient monies to enable the bankruptcy proceedings to be stopped. Robbie harried and pleaded to get the money. The task was immense—he needed to raise £2000[3]—but he was determined to succeed. He told Oscar Browning that he wished to make sure, that, on leaving prison, Wilde would 'be a perfectly free man and enabled to deal himself with any plays or literary work, which as an undischarged bankrupt he could not do'.[4] Wilde's friends had indeed already been most generous, paying most of the costs for his defence out of their own pockets, but even their resources were not limitless as Ross admitted to Browning: 'It is only *now* when they [Wilde's friends] have come to the end of their resources that they seek assistance.'[5] He ended his appeal to Browning with a plea and a promise that:

> No names of subscribers will be *made public* so none of the
> charitably disposed need fear lest the appearance of their names
> might give the impression that they were in any way connected with
> Oscar Wilde or sympathised with him except as one who has
> suffered or will suffer for the next two years the most terrible and
> cruel torture known to English injustice and Angle-Saxon hypocrisy.
> Several of those who have contributed most generously were his
> severest critics and outspoken opponents prior to his trial.[6]

The collection of monies was successful, but shortly before the hearing on 12 November further creditors came forward and, as it was impossible for Robbie to raise the additional £400, Wilde's friends realised they had no alternative but to let the bankruptcy take place. The Marquess of Queensberry was listed as Wilde's major creditor and Robbie was always convinced that if the Queensberry family had chosen, they could have settled Wilde's debts and averted the bankruptcy.

The imprisonment of Oscar Wilde left Robbie with a sense of guilt and despair; he could not write, and indeed for the next five years he was disinclined to continue his career in journalism. Robbie was also deeply concerned about the terrible consequences Wilde's imprisonment would have on Constance and her sons. She was emotionally and physically ill-equipped to handle the disgrace, and there really was no one but him who could salvage anything from the ruins of her life. Twelve years were to pass before Robbie again met Cyril and Vyvyan, although he never stopped thinking of them or striving to give them back their birthright. Robbie believed that if there was to be a future for Wilde once he had served his harsh sentence, he would have to find a way of reuniting Wilde with his wife and sons as well as solving his financial problems.

In December Robbie joined Douglas in Capri, in early January they moved on to Naples; Robbie was unable to pacify Douglas, who was bitterly hurt to find that Wilde was turning against him. Robbie pointed out that Douglas had only himself to blame for Wilde's change of attitude; he had rushed into print to defend Wilde, when a more prudent friend would have remained silent. Douglas saw himself as a martyr and regarded his own exile as a more savage form of punishment than Wilde's imprisonment. His selfish attitude enraged Robbie; Douglas was incapable of rehabilitating Wilde, yet he bitterly resented Robbie's desire to help. Robbie left Naples in late January to attend the marriage on 5 February 1896 of his sister Lizzie—who now insisted on being called Elise—to Morgan Blake, a young doctor.

On 23 February, Robbie accompanied by Ernest Leverson visited Wilde in Reading Prison, and it was through such visits that Wilde began to learn the extent of his financial and matrimonial problems. Robbie reassured Wilde that a solution could be found if the details were left to him and More Adey; although he had no real idea how this would be achieved, except by the continued generosity of Wilde's friends, such as the Leversons, Adela Schuster, and Mrs Helen Carew. The affairs of his family again demanded Robbie's attention and he was forced to turn his attention away from Wilde and his problems. On 7 March his brother-in-law, Charles Jones, died at the age of fifty-five, leaving a young widow and eight children. The eldest girl was twenty-one, and the baby of the family was barely three. To Robbie it seemed as if history was repeating itself; his own mother had been left a young widow, and now his sister Mary would have to learn to endure the same sense of loneliness and isolation. He took his role as uncle to the children very seriously, and they returned his love and affection. There were, from time to time, strains in his relationship with Mary and her family over his homosexuality; in spite of his discretion and his desire to keep that side of his nature entirely private, they tried to impose on him a code of behaviour he could not follow.

In late May Robbie paid a further visit to Reading; this time he was accompanied by Robert Sherard, and it was after this visit that Robbie wrote to More Adey, expressing feelings of sadness and compassion:

You must allow perhaps for my exaggeration but I try not to do so
and I am writing from pencil notes taken down immediately after
leaving the prison. I did not break down at all, although it is the
worst interview I have had with Oscar, because Sherard was nearly
breaking down all the time and shewed himself fearfully nervous,
both before Oscar arrived and afterwards. I do not know why I am
so sure but he was much shocked by the change for the worse. I did
not know he gave way to exhibitions of feeling, though I know he
feels things of course, as much perhaps as I do...If asked whether
he [Wilde] was going to die. It seems quite possible within the next
few months, even if his constitution remained unimpaired, but for
the causes that wives and husbands die shortly after each other, for
no particular cause or men who have lost all their money or their
"10 o'clock business" and young girls whose engagements have gone
wrong. I should be less surprised to hear of dear Oscar's death than
of Aubrey Beardsley's and you know what he looks like. However
all this you will think my exaggeration but I have endeavoured to be
judicious and have no reason to exaggerate to you and Bosie.[7]

It was at this period, as Wilde served his sentence, that the deep and
lasting friendship between him and Robbie began to grow, and as their
dependence on each other increased their friends and enemies formed
two warring factions. By those opposed to Wilde, Ross was always
referred to as 'a funny little queen'; to those supporting Wilde, Ross was
the loyal, caring friend. Those aligned against Douglas regarded Robbie
as the wronged man, while those defending Douglas looked upon Ross as
Lucifer's servant. None of these descriptions accurately fits Robbie. He
was no saint, but neither was he a sinner. He once said of himself:
'although not a moral man, neither was he immoral'.[8]

By 1896 Douglas had shown an irresponsible attitude to the letters he
had received from Wilde. He had, after all, carelessly left in the pocket of
his suit the damaging letter[9] which had enabled Alfred Wood and his
fellow conspirators, Allan and Clibbon, to blackmail Wilde. It was the
same incriminating letter that the Prosecution used so effectively against
Wilde at his trials. In August 1895 Wilde had to ask his friends to restrain
Douglas from including his [Wilde's] letters in an article he was writing
for *Mercure de France*, now Robert Sherard told Wilde that Douglas was
about to dedicate a book of poems to him. The day after Robbie's visit
with Sherard, Wilde wrote to him anxious to have his assistance in
restraining Douglas from his ill-advised actions. He was concerned that
Douglas was disposing of gifts and letters and he ordered Robbie to
recover from Douglas all these presents, and to effect the return of all his

letters. As Wilde began to appreciate the fickle nature of his friendship with Douglas, he insisted that Robbie should look after his affairs. There is in Wilde's letters to Robbie perhaps the first real sign of awareness over the events which had governed his life. He does not seek to exaggerate or attempt to justify his actions; he does not hide behind the clothes of the jester. He is true to himself, and true to his young friend. The play-acting is over, they know the secrets of each other's soul, and that artificial spirit, which they exhibited in the presence of others, is now missing.

Robbie's preoccupation with Wilde's problems continued through the spring and early summer of 1896. With the assistance and encouragement of More Adey, Robbie hoped to ensure that when Wilde was finally released from prison he would have a small income until he could write again. Robbie was also acting as an intermediary between Constance and her husband, but the more he tried to protect Wilde the more he lost the trust of Constance, the one person beyond all others he did not want to hurt. As if Wilde's own problems were not complicated enough, Robbie was also increasingly worried by the deterioration in the health of Aubrey Beardsley. His tuberculosis was worsening, he suffered from horrifying bouts of haemorrhages, and in early May Ellen Beardsley asked Robbie to go to Brussels to accompany her son back to England. In June Robbie stayed with Beardsley at Crowborough, but his own health was causing him much distress. As a child he had been struck in the kidney by a cricket ball, the blow had badly damaged the kidney and by June 1896 it was decided that only the removal of the organ would give him any relief from the excruciating pain and intermittent fevers. There was a high degree of risk in such a major and intricate operation, but it was performed by a leading surgeon, Sir Frederick Treves.[10] Robbie was fully aware of the risks involved, but as he prepared himself for the ordeal which lay ahead, he put his affairs in order and wrote a few letters of 'farewell'. For a month his life hung in the balance, but in the middle of July, Treves was able to tell Alex that providing there were no further post-operative complications the worst of the danger was over. Robbie spent much of August convalescing at his mother's home in Upper Phillimore Gardens, but his recovery was extremely slow. Later in the month, he moved with his mother to Margate, in the expectation that sea air would hasten his recovery.

Wilde, now able to write freely, made increasing demands on the invalid, and as always Robbie was unable or unwilling to ignore the incessant pleas for attention from his imprisoned friend.

More Adey, concerned about the detrimental effect of Wilde's demands on the invalid, wrote to Wilde, pointing out in rather subtle

terms that Robbie was hardly in a position to help himself, much less sort
out Wilde's problems:

> Robbie is going on well, the doctor says, but he suffers a great deal
> from dyspepsia which affects his spirits very much. You know how
> much he thinks of and feels for you. He looks very ill still. He had
> his hair cut very short while he was at his worst and, owing to his
> continued weakness, it has not yet grown again and is very thin.
> This makes him look different. He has had a photograph taken
> which I hope to have an opportunity of showing you before long. He
> amuses himself by reading Dickens and has become quite
> enthusiastic over *Barnaby Rudge* and *Our Mutual Friend*, etc. They
> just serve to amuse him without tiring his head.[11]

The autumn and winter passed slowly, Robbie's recovery continued
but he was still unable to work, and it was April before he found the
enthusiasm to write again, when he published a short story in the
Canadian Magazine.

As the final weeks of Wilde's imprisonment approached, Robbie became
increasingly disturbed by Wilde's physical condition; he was sure that
Wilde would not be able to endure the last weeks of his imprisonment.
More Adey tried to organise a petition to the Home Secretary to secure
Wilde's early release, but, with the exception of Bernard Shaw and the
Reverend Stewart Headlam, he found it impossible to obtain the signa-
tures of men whose importance would carry weight with the Authorities.
Robbie approached Edward Clarke to see if there was any chance of
getting the last weeks of Wilde's sentence remitted. Clarke replied that
he thought such a remission would not be granted.

In April, prior to his release, Wilde authorised Robbie to act as his
literary executor and in consequence he ensured that Robbie would
never again be freed from the bonds which tied him mentally and
physically to Wilde for the rest of his life:

> I want you to be my literary executor in case of my death, and to
> have complete control over my plays, books and papers. As soon as I
> find I have a legal right to make a will I will do so. My wife does not
> understand my art, nor could be expected to have any interest in it,
> and Cyril is only a child. So I turn naturally to you, as indeed I do
> for everything, and would like you to have all my works. The deficit
> that their sale will produce may be lodged to the credit of Cyril and
> Vyvyan.[12]

The first task Wilde gave him was to have control over the typing, copying and dispatch of his letter to Douglas which he had called *Epistola: In Carcere et Vinculis*, but which later became known as *De Profundis*.[13] The Prison Commissioners, however, refused Wilde permission to send the letter and on his release he took it with him and handed it personally to Robbie. The contents of the letter eventually resulted in years of anguish for Robbie yet he acted strictly according to Wilde's wishes. It is surely the final irony that the letter giving Robbie his executive powers was dated 1 April: April fool's day.

Robbie fulfilled Wilde's very detailed instructions except in one vital detail: he did not send the original of the letter to Douglas, but sent the typed copy. It is not known why he did this; Wilde might have changed his mind after his release and countermanded his earlier instructions, or perhaps Robbie, realising the historical value of the document and knowing Douglas's tendency to destroy what he did not like, decided not to risk losing the original.

Wilde's extravagant behaviour before his trial was a cause of concern to his friends, particularly Robbie and More Adey. They were certain that Wilde, once released from prison, would return to his former, maladjusted ways, unless they prevented it. While Wilde was still in prison they set about his rehabilitation; ignoring their own sexual preferences they sought to impose a code of behaviour on Wilde, which would ensure that Douglas would never again be the most important influence in his life. They hoped that by separating Wilde from Douglas, Constance would financially support her husband until such time as Wilde could again earn his own living by writing. Robbie and More Adey were not the most suitable individuals to solve Wilde's social affairs and they were certainly ill equipped to handle his financial problems, but what they lacked in business acumen they made up for in sincerity. Wilde was also far from convinced that the two friends were the right people to handle his business affairs and he was highly critical of their efforts:

> Everything that you [More Adey] do is wrong and done in the
> wrong manner. Robbie is better as a guide, for if he is quite
> irrational he has the advantage of being always illogical, so he
> occasionally comes to a right conclusion. But you not merely are
> equally irrational, but are absolutely logical: you start always from
> the wrong premises, and arrive logically at the wrong conclusion.[14]

If Robbie's and More Adey's efforts did not please Wilde they also brought them into conflict with Constance. Robbie wrote to Constance saying that he had heard that the Marquess of Queensberry was attempting to buy the life interest in her marriage settlement, and that this should be prevented at all costs. Constance, however, did not share his assessment of the situation, as she demonstrated in a letter from Heidelberg, dated 21 June 1896:

> The business matters of which you speak are quite incomprehensible to me. I have never heard that there was any rumour of Lord Q buying the Life-Interest of my Settlement but I was told and my lawyer was also told that I would be prevented from buying it by Oscar's friends who were prepared to bid against me to the extent of several hundreds of pounds with the intention of getting it into their own possession and of settling a portion on the boys and the remainder on him.
>
> This is a most short-sighted policy as I should not accept such a gift for my boys and if the Life-Interest is bought in this way over my head I should feel bound to withdraw my offer of an allowance to Oscar during his lifetime.[15]

It must have seemed to Robbie that in trying to help he had simply made matters worse, but he had been right to try to protect Wilde from the excesses of his own extravagances. Wilde had shown on many occasions that he was incapable of running his own life. He was over-generous to those he considered less fortunate than himself, and he was never able to curb this part of his nature. Robbie was unable to defend himself against Wilde's unjust criticism, and it was left to the third member of the Wilde circle, Reggie Turner, to put the other side of the story:

> And now, dear Oscar, you must allow me to say something to you about More and Bobbie, as you have written to me about them. The most beautiful thing I have ever known is Bobbie's devotion to you. He has never had any other thought than of you; never once, for one minute, has he forgotten you; he has only looked forward to one thing, the time when he would be able to talk to you freely and affectionately again. It is very rare to find such complete devotion, and I fear, dear Oscar, that you have gone very near to breaking his heart.... There may have been some mistakes and you may have been over-burdened with unnecessary details, but they have done nothing but what is good for you, and with regard to your wife they have done nothing which cannot be undone in two days if you and she be willing. They have never used any money for any other purpose than what it was given them for, though I feel that it is

shameful for me to attempt to excuse the actions of such dear and
devoted friends as More and Bobbie are to you. There have been, I
know, bitter cruel disappointments for you, but neither Bobbie nor
More are in any way responsible for them.[16]

Oscar Wilde completed his two years' hard labour on 19 May 1897; he
spent his last night of confinement in Pentonville Prison, where his
sentence had begun those long and bitter months before. Shortly after
his release, at 6.15 a.m., he was met by More Adey and Stewart Headlam, and they breakfasted at Headlam's home at 31 Upper Bedford
Place, Bloomsbury. Later they were joined by Ernest and Ada Leverson.
Robbie and Reggie Turner were waiting in Dieppe, they having expected
Wilde on the morning boat; but he was delayed in London and he wired
to say that he would come over on the overnight boat.

Wilde's arrival in France and the story of his first day's freedom are
poignantly recorded by Robbie in an unfinished foreword to a book of
Wilde's letters that he was compiling at the time of his own death:[17]

> According to the arrangements he was to come over by the morning
> boat to Dieppe where Reggie Turner and myself had got rooms for
> him at the Hôtel Sandwich. Wilde talked so much and insisted on
> seeing so many people that he missed the train, so in the afternoon
> went down with Adey to Newhaven, waited till late afternoon and
> crossed by the night boat.
>
> We met them at half past four in the morning, a magnificent
> spring morning such as Wilde anticipated in the closing words of *De
> Profundis*. As the steamer glided into harbour Wilde's tall figure,
> dominating the other passengers, was easily recognised from the
> great crucifix on the jetty where we stood. That striking beacon was
> full of significance for us. Then we began running to the landing
> stage and Wilde recognised us and waved his hand and his lips
> curled into a smile. His face had lost all its coarseness and he looked
> as he must have looked at Oxford in the early days before I knew
> him and as he only looked again after death. A good many people,
> even friends, thought his appearance almost repulsive, but the upper
> part of his face was extraordinarily fine and intellectual.
>
> There was the usual irritating delay and then Wilde with that
> odd elephantine gait which I have never seen in anyone else stalked
> off the boat. He was holding in his hand a large sealed envelope.
> "This, my dear Bobbie, is the great manuscript about which you
> know."... The manuscript was of course *De Profundis*...
>
> In the afternoon we drove to Arques[-la-Bataille] and sat down

on the ramparts of the castle. He enjoyed the trees and the grass and
country scents and sounds in a way I had never known him do
before, just as a street-bred child might enjoy them on his first day
in the country: but of course there was an adjective for everything—
"monstrous", "purple", "grotesque", "gorgeous", "curious",
"wonderful". It was natural to Wilde to be artificial as I have often
said and that is why he was suspected of insincerity. I mean when he
wrote serious things, of art, ethics or religion, of pain or of pleasure.
Wilde in love of the beautiful was perfectly, perhaps too, sincere and
not the least of his errors was a suspicion of simple things. *Simplicity*
is one of the objections he urges against prisons.[18]

In those first few hours Robbie was content and happy just to see
Wilde free again, and he sat and listened as his friend talked of his years
of torment. Wilde, compiler of fairy stories, immediately on his release,
saw Reading Prison as an 'enchanted castle of which Major Nelson was
the presiding fairy'.[19] Wilde teased and delighted Robbie by recalling a
tale of a freemason he had encountered one day in the prison yard as he
exercised; Wilde, of course, knew that Ross had very decided views on
English freemasonry:[20]

> As I was walking round the yard one day I noticed that one of the
> men awaiting trial was signalling to me by masonic signs. I paid no
> attention until he made the sign of the widow's son which no mason
> can ignore. He managed to convey a note to me. I found he was in
> for fraud of some kind and was anxious that I should get my friends
> to petition for his release. He was quite mad, poor fellow. As he
> would always insist on signalling and I was afraid the warders would
> get to notice it, I persuaded Major Nelson to let me wear black
> goggles until he was convicted and sent to Portland.[21]

Wilde's enjoyment of his freedom lasted only as long as Robbie was
there to enjoy it with him. When in late May Robbie was forced to return
to London, the first bitter feelings of loneliness made Wilde appreciate
that he had merely exchanged a prison, with bars and warders, for an
even more restricted prison—a prison of absolute despair. He would
never regain his place in society or be the centre of an attentive audience;
he would never write another comedy to rival *The Importance of Being
Earnest*, or a tense drama such as *Dorian Gray*. He would write a ballad of
prison life, but the sparkling humour of his plays and the sensitive
insight of his fairy stories would never return. In the first few weeks at
Berneval-sur-Mer (near Dieppe), he wrote a letter to the editor of the

Daily Chronicle, and it must rank among the most percipient letters ever written on the subject of prison reform, and the appalling suffering of children in the penal system.[22] Robbie was doubtful of the wisdom of Wilde writing on such a subject, particularly as this was his first 'appearance' in print after his imprisonment. But the public's reaction to the letter was on the whole favourable, and Robbie was the first to admit his mistake. He apologised to Wilde for failing to appreciate that the truth in the letter was more important than the identity of the writer. Wilde was delighted with the apology:

> Your letter is quite admirable, but, dear boy, don't you see how
> right I was to write to the *Chronicle*? All good impulses are right.
> Had I listened to some of my friends I would never have written.[23]

Wilde's inability to cope with loneliness was a painful dilemma for Robbie to face; if alone, Wilde would return to his pre-prison bohemian ways, he would drink more than was good for him, and would quickly descend into a trough of despair and dejection. There was also, at the back of Robbie's mind, the fear that in his loneliness Wilde would return to Douglas; this, Robbie was determined to prevent at all costs. He believed, that if they were all patient, Constance would eventually return to her husband, and being again responsible for the welfare and future of his sons, Wilde would regain the joy of fatherhood that he had known for only a few short years. Robbie offered to forgo his own comfortable life in London, and to lose the respect of his family, and the affection of his friends, to go to France and live in exile with Wilde. In giving up all he valued most, Robbie was making the ultimate sacrifice to save his friend from the worst effects of his own loneliness.

In the early days of his exile Wilde at least understood his growing dependency on Robbie and what that dependence must be costing him. Douglas, angry that Wilde did not rush to join him, sent Wilde a particularly revolting letter and Wilde instinctively turned to Robbie, certain he would comprehend the depths of his agony:

> I have a real terror now of that unfortunate ungrateful young man
> [Douglas] with his unimaginative selfishness and his entire lack of
> sensitiveness to what in others is good or kind or trying to be so. I
> feel him as an evil influence, poor fellow. To be with him would be
> to return to the hell from which I do think I have been released. I
> hope never to see him again.
>
> For yourself, dear sweet Robbie, I am haunted by the idea that
> many of those who love you will and do think it selfish of me to

allow you and wish you to be with me from time to time. But still they might see the difference between your going about with me in my days of gilded infamy—my Neronian hours, rich, profligate, cynical, materialistic—and your coming to comfort me, a lonely dishonoured man, in disgrace and obscurity and poverty. How lacking in imagination they are! If I were rich again and sought to repeat my former life I don't think you would care very much to be with me. I think you would regret what I was doing, but now, dear boy, you come with the heart of Christ, and you help me intellectually as no one else can or ever could do.... No other friend have I now in this beautiful world. I want no other. Yet I am distressed to think that I will be looked on as careless of your own welfare, and indifferent of your good. You are made to help me. I weep with sorrow when I think how much I need help, but I weep with joy when I think I have you to give it to me.[24]

If Wilde had been able to sustain his contrition Robbie would have been a happy man, but he would also have been an unfulfilled man. It was part of his nature that he needed to help others less fortunate than himself, and he would have found that impossible had Wilde reformed and lived the life of a saint; he *needed* Wilde to be a sinner. Ada Leverson, of all Wilde's friends, understood better than most Robbie's special needs:

He [Wilde] had many devoted friends, who remained always loyal to him. Chief among these was Robert Ross. There indeed was no trouble he would not take to advance a friend's interest, and I think he rather resented any friend who was not in actual need of him.[25]

While Wilde was at Berneval it became obvious that the nature of his relationship with Robbie was undergoing a dramatic change. Ross was now the strong man, and Wilde turned into the demanding, fractious child who wanted that which he could not have. Robbie's joy was almost complete; he believed he had finally parted Wilde from the corrupting influence of Douglas, the strains in his own friendship with Douglas being almost at breaking point. In July Wilde wrote graphically on Douglas's short-comings:

As regards Bosie, I feel you have been, as usual, forbearing and sweet, and too good-tempered. What he must be made to feel is that his vulgar and ridiculous assumption of social superiority must be retracted and apologised for. I have written to tell him that *quand on est gentilhomme on est gentilhomme*, and that for him to try and pose as your social superior because he is the third son of a Scotch marquis and you the third son of a commoner is offensively stupid. There is no difference between gentlemen. Questions of titles are matters of heraldry no more. I wish you would be strong on this point; the thing should be thrashed out of him. As for his coarse ingratitude in abusing you, to whom, as I have told him, I owe any possibility I have of a new and artistic career, and indeed of life at all, I have no words in which to express my contempt for his lack of imaginative insight, and his dullness of sensitive nature. It makes me quite furious. So pray write, when next you do so, quite calmly, and say that you will not allow any nonsense of social superiority and that if he cannot understand that gentlemen are gentlemen and no more, you have no desire to hear again from him.[26]

Robbie returned to Berneval for three weeks on 1 August, and the two friends enjoyed a golden holiday. Wilde began to write his final work *The Ballad of Reading Gaol* and Robbie promised that he would act as agent between Wilde and Leonard Smithers, a publisher with a risqué reputation. Robbie, who had a poor opinion of all publishers, once said of Smithers: 'You always knew where you were with him, you knew he would cheat you and he always did'.[27]

Later in August Robbie, accompanied by Alex, joined Edmund Gosse and his family at the small fishing village of Bundoran in County Donegal. Robbie was a favourite with Gosse and his wife, and with their children, Tessa aged nineteen, Philip aged seventeen and fifteen-year-old Sylvia. There can be no doubt that in allowing Robbie to join his family on holiday, Gosse was quite convinced that his son was not in danger from Robbie's homosexual activities. It is notable that in his many friendships with families with teenage sons, there was never a conflict nor a suggestion that Robbie would be a corrupting influence. His homosexuality was wholly a private matter and he would never break his code of ethics and dishonour the son of a friend.

Robbie was involved with his own private affairs and he was guilty of neglecting Wilde. With the summer over and the autumn chills bringing an end to his visitors, Wilde became increasingly lonely and had to face the reality that the chance of being reunited with his wife and children was as far away as the day he left prison. It was inevitable that he should drift back into a relationship with Alfred Douglas. Ross was devastated by the news, and he wrote to Wilde pointing out the consequences of his actions. It was to Robbie a repudiation of everything Wilde had said during and after his imprisonment. In Naples with Douglas, Wilde tried to justify his actions to the grief-stricken Robbie:

> I cannot live without the atmosphere of Love: I must love and be loved, whatever price I pay for it. I could have lived all my life with you, but you have other claims on you—claims you are too sweet a fellow to disregard—and all you could give me was a week of companionship.[28]

Wilde was unable to appreciate that in going back to Douglas he was rejecting Robbie's love and devotion. Robbie had worked hard for two years to prevent Douglas again being the dominant influence in Wilde's life and now all his efforts had been wasted. He was not alone in his anger at the news that Wilde was again living with Douglas. Constance Wilde was appalled and promptly stopped her husband's meagre allowance. She told her brother Otho Lloyd that, 'in a short time war will be declared'.[29] Constance was right, war did break out! Robbie continued to write to Wilde expressing his hurt and anguish. As usual with Wilde, he wanted the best of both worlds; he wanted to live in Naples with Douglas, but he was also unable to do without the love, friendship and business help that Robbie so ably provided:

> I have not answered your letters, because they distressed me and angered me, and I did not wish to write to *you* of all people in the world in an angry mood. You have been such a good friend to me. Your love, your generosity, your care of me in prison and out of prison are the most lovely things in my life. Without you what would I have done? As you remade my life for me you have a perfect right to say what you choose to me, but I have no right to say anything to you except to tell you how grateful I am to you, and what a pleasure it is to feel gratitude and love at the same time for the same person.[30]

Robbie was not capable of accepting a subordinate role to Douglas, and, as the days passed, he returned to the security of his family and tried to shut Wilde out of his life. Despite the difficulties, he still negotiated with Leonard Smithers over the publication of *The Ballad of Reading Gaol*; however, in November 1897 even this help stopped, as he informed Smithers:

> I regret to inform you that I have ceased to be on intimate terms with Oscar Wilde or to enjoy his confidence in business or any other

matter...Alfred Lord Douglas has written to a common friend that
I have tried to prevent any considerable sum being obtained for the
poem.[31]

Wilde was concerned at the break in the friendship; it was the first
time he had seen Robbie in an unforgiving and petulant mood:

> I am greatly and rightly pained at your writing to him [Smithers]
> that our intimate friendship is over, and that you find you have no
> longer my confidence in business matters. The former is a question
> at any rate for yourself: the latter statement is unjust, unwarranted,
> and unkind.
>
> And on the whole I do think you make wonderfully little
> allowance for a man like myself, now ruined, broken-hearted, and
> thoroughly unhappy. You stab me with a thousand phrases: if one
> phrase of mine shrills through the air near you, you cry out that you
> are wounded to death.[32]

Wilde's 'second honeymoon' with Douglas lasted no more than four
months. They were both volatile and selfish; there was never really a
chance that they could live in peace and harmony. When the break came
it was to Ross that Wilde returned, even though he had not heard from
him for more than three months. It was also inevitable that Robbie
would be there waiting and prepared to forgive all the past hurts.

Five

Death of a Decadent

HERE IS in all human relationships much which is hard to define precisely; emotions become confused, logic and reason are replaced by irrational, hesitant actions. Robbie Ross, with his magnificent devotion to Oscar Wilde, displayed the whole spectrum of these emotions. He was often logical and reasonable, but he was also equally guilty of a wilful neglect of other people's feelings; above all he was totally unconcerned at the cost of his actions on his own high reputation. Wilde was equally careless with other people's feelings and needs; but, at least in one moment of honesty, he acknowledged the debt he owed to Robbie for all his selfless acts of charity:

> There was a certain Saint, who was called Saint Robert of Phillimore.[1] Every night, while the sky was yet black, he would rise from his bed and, falling on his knees, pray to God that He, of His great bounty, would cause the sun to rise and make bright the earth. And always, when the sun rose, Saint Robert knelt again and thanked God that this miracle had been vouchsafed. Now, one night, Saint Robert, wearied by the vast number of more than usually good deeds that he had done that day, slept so soundly that when he awoke the sun had already risen, and the earth was already bright. For a few moments Saint Robert looked grave and troubled, but presently he fell down on his knees and thanked God that, despite the neglectfulness of His servant, He had yet caused the sun to rise and make bright the earth.[2]

The friendship between the two men often seemed one-sided, with Wilde demanding and taking all, and Ross acquiescing and giving. Wilde could be cruel if he thought Robbie was being unnecessarily critical or unduly moral, and on one occasion he wrote: 'But Robbie is on horseback at present. He can ride everything, except Pegasus.'[3] Indeed, during Wilde's exile Robbie constantly lectured him about his excessive drinking and his loose moral behaviour. While deploring immorality and depraved behaviour in others Robbie was always able to square his own conscience and live with the sin of his own homosexuality. His dislike of

65

Wilde's mores, did not, however, prevent Robbie responding in his usual manner when Wilde was again short of money, but as with so much else he did, Robbie was loath to take personal credit for his generous actions:

> I had a fearful letter from poor Oscar who seems in a dreadful state of poverty even allowing for slight exaggeration. He says he had no dinner on Friday or Saturday. If you could sell the *Réjane* for me at once send Oscar £5 as soon as possible... Tell Oscar that a *friend* is sending him the money. There is no need to mention my name.[4]

Wilde's poverty was not as great as it appeared, he was still extravagant, but as Robbie had control over his allowance, Wilde had to appeal regularly to him to dispense more of the funds. Separated from Douglas and able only occasionally to enjoy Robbie's company Wilde spent many lonely days in Paris. As hard as he tried Robbie could not prevent Wilde's gradual decline. Wilde needed constant applause and failed to find it, except in the boulevard cafés where the dregs of society would buy him drinks and give him the only kind words he heard. He had fallen from his high position in society, and he could not find the way to climb back; his ability to write had gone, and he knew that with the approach of a new century there was no place left for him.

The weather of 1898 was exceptionally harsh. Robbie's own health was still causing concern, but he had little time for self-pity. On 16 March Aubrey Beardsley's slender hold on life finally snapped. Robbie was unable to attend the funeral in Menton, but he wrote an appreciative eulogy to the memory of one whose life had been so short yet so creative:

> There is no need to disturb ourselves with hopes and fears for the estimation with which posterity will cherish his memory; art history cannot afford to overlook him; it could hardly resist the pretext of moralising, expatiating and explaining away so considerable a factor in the book illustration of the nineties. As a mere comment on the admirations of the last twenty years of the nineteenth century, Beardsley is invaluable: he sums up all the delightful manias, all that is best in modern appreciation.... In his imagination, his choice of motive, his love for inanimate nature, his sentiment for accessory— rejected by many modern artists, still so necessary to the modern temper—his curious type, which quite overshadowed that of the pre-Raphaelites, the singular technical qualities at his command, Beardsley has no predecessors; no rivals. Who has ever managed to

> suggest such colour in masses of black deftly composed?...His style
> was mobile, dominating over, or subordinate to the subject, as his
> genius dictated. He twisted human forms, some will think, into
> fantastic peculiar shapes, becoming more than romantic—
> antinomian. He does not appeal to experience but to expression.
> The tranquil trivialities of what is usually understood by the
> illustration of books had no meaning to him; and before any attempt
> is made to discriminate and interpret the spirit, the poetical
> sequence, the literary inspiration which undoubtedly existed
> throughout his work, side by side with technical experiments, his
> exemption from the parallels of criticism must be remembered
> duly.[5]

Beardsley's death was not the only one which shattered Robbie's peace of mind that spring. Three weeks later, on 7 April, Constance Wilde died. Three years before she had fallen at her home, and she died during surgery to relieve the pain caused by the injury to her spine. Wilde immediately telegraphed to Robbie, who hurried to Paris, but as Robbie told Smithers, Wilde was not exactly the conventional grieving husband, although like all Wilde did, what he said was not exactly what he was really feeling. Robbie also had to apologise to Smithers for being somewhat late in letting him have opinions on two manuscripts he had been reading for the publisher. In his own defence he explained that while he was with Wilde it was impossible to get anything done. Robbie, although saddened by Constance's death, was far more worried about the effect her death would have on Wilde's financial stability:

> You will have heard of Mrs Wilde's death. Oscar of course did not
> feel it at all. It is rather appalling for him as his allowance ceases and
> I do not expect his wife's trustees will continue it. He is in very good
> spirits and does not consume too many. He is hurt because you
> never write. I explained you had been ill and rather worried with the
> domesticities of publishing.[6]

Constance was buried in the Staglieno Cemetery in Genoa, but neither Robbie, Wilde nor his sons were there to pay their last respects to the gracious lady, who was emotionally and spiritually unable to cope with the traumas in her life. Robbie held her in high esteem, and in trying to ensure that after Wilde's release he would never again live with Douglas, Robbie hoped that Constance would find a measure of happiness. Alas, his wish was not fulfilled. Constance did forgive Wilde, but not until it was too late for both of them. She was grateful to Robbie for what he was

doing to help Wilde, but she was never totally convinced that he was not
equally as guilty as Douglas in perverting Wilde. Two years before her
death Constance had written to Robbie, explaining her reluctance to
trust him:

> The question whether your desire to be my friend and your affection
> for me are genuine, I leave to your conscience and to God to decide.
> I have gone through too much and too much has crumbled beneath
> my feet for me to be at all now able to judge of the genuineness of
> anyone's professions on any subject. I have always had a great
> affection for you which I had once thought and hoped that you
> returned.[7]

Constance's funeral was private and the grief of her family was muted,
but for Aubrey Beardsley there was a public declaration of mourning.
Robbie was responsible for arranging on 12 May a Memorial Service at
the Jesuits' Farm Street Chapel. Ellen Beardsley was duly appreciative of
all Robbie's considerations, especially as he had arranged a carriage for
her use:

> How can I thank you for all your kindness yesterday: you managed
> everything so beautifully, it was very good of you. I am most
> grateful to you and I suppose I cannot tell you how deeply touched I
> am at this evidence of your affection for my precious boy...Dear
> Robbie, how you have worked to arrange the beautiful service we
> had yesterday...I cannot bear that you should be put to such
> expense as paying the half of the cost, so although I am only sending
> you a cheque for six pounds it is because I am afraid without your
> leave to send more.[8]

Robbie found it hard to pick up the threads of his life, he could find little
enthusiasm for writing, and he was disinclined to concentrate on anything else. He was preoccupied with family matters. On 15 September
Jack, a widower for three years, married Alice Strange, and Robbie still
hoped there would be a son to continue the name of Ross. On Sundays he
was often a guest at the Gosses' home, but even Edmund Gosse was
unable to lift Robbie from his depression. Wilde's decline bothered
Robbie a good deal; and in spite of the generosity of his friends Wilde
wandered aimlessly round Europe, and his restlessness increased Robbie's own irresolution. In November Douglas returned to England for
the first time since April 1895. Robbie offered the hand of friendship, but
they would never again achieve the closeness they had known before
Wilde's fall from grace.

The last year of the old century brought little respite for Robbie. Wilde stayed with Frank Harris at Cannes, but the visit was not a success. In March Wilde went to Gland in Switzerland with Harold Mellor, but again he was bored and miserable and moved on to Santa Margherita. In spite of illness, Robbie, after repeated appeals from Wilde, travelled to Switzerland; again he had to pay Wilde's debts before he took him back to Paris. If Wilde was causing him anguish then at least his other friends were able to give him odd moments of pleasure; in June Robbie was a guest at the wedding of William Rothenstein[9] to Alice Knewstub at Kensington Registry Office. As more of his friends were settling down to respectability and domesticity Robbie's sense of isolation increased, but at least in Rothenstein he had a friend with whom he could share an interest in art and art appreciation. In 1898 Edward Warren provided financial support for William Rothenstein, Arthur Clifton and John Fothergill[10] to open the Carfax Gallery in Ryder Street, St James's. The new gallery would show primarily the work of Charles Conder, as the Art Establishment and academic circles were disinclined to exhibit or recognise his work. Robbie took a connoisseur's interest in the development of the gallery, and gradually it became a dominant interest.

He was ill again during August and for a week he stayed with More Adey at Wotton-under-Edge, but by early September he was back with his mother at Upper Phillimore Gardens where he entertained Max Beerbohm and his fiancée, the actress, Grace (Kilseen) Conover to supper. John Fothergill was another friend who came to call. Robbie had first met the young architect in May 1897. When Wilde began his exile in Berneval, he had asked Robbie to arrange for John Fothergill to come to France and design him a villa. Wilde had hoped to recreate the 'House Beautiful' but the lack of money, or perhaps more significantly the lack of real resolve on his part, prevented the plans reaching a satisfactory conclusion. Fothergill was more than just a promising architect; he devoted much of his time to the study of art and archaeology and, as Robbie told Rothenstein, Fothergill was also developing a passion for philosophy:

> John Fothergill turned up the other day. He is very much changed
> in some ways I suppose for the better; but has lost that fine romantic
> look in his face, owing to his study of modern philosophy and
> archaeology at Leipzig and Rome. He has become quite an expert
> with antiques, at least some of his purchases have been highly
> extolled by American and German savants. Let me, however, relieve
> your mind by saying that he bought them for his own amusement
> and does not expect Carfax to deal with them. He is much delighted

> with Carfax and the appearance of the shop, but that does not
> compensate me for his loss of romanticism. There is, however, no
> nonsense about art in him. Everything has to be B.C.(C.C.X.) and
> good period and thoroughly battered with a certain amount of
> secrecy as to where it came from. John takes it all very seriously and
> says, of course, what is quite true that I know nothing of philosophy
> or art. He is a pupil of Professor Vundt, a pundit I never heard of.[11]

Later in September Robbie journeyed to Paris and spent a few days with
Wilde; he had arranged to spend the autumn and winter in Italy and the
south of France with his mother and niece Lillian.

His mother was in poor health and the family decided that a period
out of London would benefit her, and they thought that if Robbie
accompanied her, he might regain his own purpose for life. London
undoubtedly lacked the sparkle of the days before Wilde's imprisonment, but, as Robbie discovered, Rome did have its compensations,
although, as he told Rothenstein, he was not exactly leading a life of
excitement and extravagance:

> I need hardly tell you that in the ancient capital of the world, or the
> capital of the ancient world, nothing ever happens so I cannot write
> you a letter with any news. My niece Lily and myself go round every
> morning seeing ruins and churches and museums, and in the
> afternoon we drive out with my mater. That is really all that
> happens. Most of the pictures here are rather painful to me, so I
> have kept them for the last but there are many delightful frescoes
> discovered previous to Bernard Berenson[12]; which please me very
> much, but I fear that the absence of what for want of a better word
> we have agreed to call the artistic or aesthetic would get in to your
> nerves and you would only come for the Greek things in the
> museums though there are very few absolute Greek things even in
> the galleries.[13]

Robbie was not lonely in Rome; his friends Fothergill and Warren
were there to provide amusement:

> I have seen John Fothergill. He is looking so well and happy. He is
> here with Warren. He really has I believe a "Phlair" (American
> spelling) for antics at all events. He got a beautiful Greek head
> which is going to Boston. He works most fearfully hard every day in
> the new museum where recent finds are placed and is becoming
> quite learned about forgeries. Now that he has got over his

exaltation at being elected to the august brotherhood of
archaeologists and is no longer mysterious he is as charming as he
used to be. I fear I was rather harsh in my criticism of him in
London.[14]

In February 1900 Robbie was again ill for two weeks with influenza;
he told Alice Rothenstein that he felt like 'a washed-out cat',[15] although
he admitted that the Italian influenza was a less virulent kind than the
virus affecting those in England. Wilde had also been ill in Paris, and he
was annoyed with Robbie for daring to criticise him for not writing. In
March Wilde, having again made friends with Harold Mellor, allowed
him to pay his expenses for a visit to Italy. Wilde wrote telling Robbie of
his forthcoming trip and immoderately ordered him to, 'tell me a good
hotel. Also bed out some Narcissi. It is their season.' [He signed his
letter with a barbed insult] 'with best love, dear horrid irritating Robbie.'[16]

The paradox in the relationship between Ross and Wilde is difficult to
analyse. Each could not deny his homosexuality, yet Wilde never learned
to be discreet in actions or words. Robbie instinctively understood the
dangers in their love but Wilde could never see them or even admit they
existed. As Wilde wandered aimlessly round Europe indulging in
homosexual affairs the fear of another scandal was very real. Robbie
could not afford to become involved in another sordid scene, and often
despaired of Wilde's lack of caution. In April Wilde wrote, 'At Naples
we stopped three days. Most of my friends are, as you know, in prison,
but I met some of nice memory, and fell in love with a Sea-God, who for
some extraordinary reason is at the Regia Marina School, instead of
being with Triton.'[17] If Robbie had been able to persuade Wilde to be
faithful to a long-term relationship they could have both enjoyed a period
of contentment and happiness. Wilde, unfortunately, could not give
himself to monogamous love and Robbie could only pray that the inevitable scandal would be delayed for as long as possible.

Robbie's few days in Rome with Wilde were to be all too short. In
early April he moved with his mother and niece to Venice. Wilde stayed
in Rome for a little longer, before returning to Gland with Mellor, but by
the end of May or the beginning of June he was back in Paris. Robbie
and his family returned to London about the same time. He felt better
and began again to write seriously, and that summer he produced what is
perhaps one of his best short stories, 'A Case at the Museum', published
in the *Cornhill Magazine*[18] in October. He did not neglect Wilde, but
there is no doubt he did not correspond as regularly as Wilde wished.
When Wilde acknowledged his monthly allowance in September, he

complained that the letter accompanying the cheque contained no
information about Robbie's activities:

> Your letter is very maddening: nothing about yourself: no details,
> and yet you know I love middle-class tragedies, and the little
> squabbles that build up family life in England. I have had delightful
> letters from you quite in the style of Jane Austen. You, I know, are
> the Cinderella of your family, and you lead them all a dreadful life,
> like your *Märchen*-prototype. You turned your dear mother's
> carriage into a pumpkin, and won't let your sisters wear your
> slippers, and always have the comfortable ingle-nook by the fire,
> except in summer, when you make poor Aleck sit there.[19]

On 9 October Robbie informed Wilde that he would be in Paris on
Thursday the 18th and would be able to stay for a few days; it was now
his turn to complain that he had not received a letter from Wilde. Two
days later Robbie received a telegram saying that Wilde had been oper-
ated on that day, and that he was asking for him. Wilde had fallen and
hurt his ear while in prison, the injury had not healed and had continued
to cause him a great deal of pain. There is some debate about the exact
nature of the operation, but it is generally agreed that its purpose was to
relieve inflammation caused by a mastoid infection. Robbie wired back
immediately that he would do his best to advance his travel plans. The
next day he received a further telegram informing him that Wilde's
condition was extremely weak, and emphasising that Wilde was anxious
to see him. Robbie travelled overnight on 16 October, Wilde's forty-sixth
birthday. At 10.30 the next morning he went to see Wilde in his rooms at
the Hôtel d'Alsace, in the back streets near St-Germain-des-Prés. He was
rather surprised to find Wilde in a remarkably good mood, though the
invalid assured him that he was suffering excruciating pains. His wound
needed dressing daily, and although he was very poorly he showed
admirable courage and was often in excellent spirits. His incomparable
sense of humour and ready wit rarely deserted him when Robbie was
there to applaud him.

Robbie was joined at the Hôtel d'Alsace by Reggie Turner, who had
also been summoned to the bedside of the sick man. They listened
sympathetically to Wilde's grievances against Frank Harris, and earnestly assured him that all his debts would be paid. They both knew,
however, that Wilde had never been able to come to terms with his
poverty and still longed for the riches he had enjoyed as the foremost
dramatist of the day. He was unable to endure the life of a social leper,
and although he was more than grateful to the hotel proprietor, Edouard

Dupoirier, for all his many little kindnesses, he could not bear the dull and dreary atmosphere of his rooms. If Wilde received any genuine pleasure in those last bitter days, then it was probably from the company of Maurice Gilbert, a young Anglo-French dilettante.

On 25 October Robbie was joined in Paris by his brother Alex: Wilde was in particularly good form, and when his sister-in-law[20] and her new husband stopped in Paris during their honeymoon, his enjoyment of their company seemed in no way forced. On the 29th, for the first time since his operation, Wilde decided to rise from his sick-bed, and after dinner insisted on going out. Robbie thought the action rather foolhardy, but Wilde was determined and they went out into the Latin Quarter. Wilde found it hard to adjust to being away from the sanctuary of the hotel; they walked very slowly to a small café, and, much against Ross's wishes, Wilde insisted on drinking absinthe. Although while lying in bed he had appeared quite well, up and dressed and out in the cool evening air Wilde seemed extremely ill; he had aged considerably, and his hair, which had retained its soft brown tint all the time he was in prison, had now become tinged with grey.

The day after the outing Wilde was much worse; he had a cold and the pain in his ear was unbearable, but by the following afternoon he had recovered sufficiently to accompany Robbie on a drive to the Bois de Boulogne. On All Saints' Day Robbie went to a service at Père Lachaise. Wilde expressed a wish to be buried at Père Lachaise, and asked Robbie if he had yet chosen a site for his [Wilde's] tomb. They discussed the subject of epitaphs in a light-hearted manner, but it was doubtful if either of them realised just how little time there was left. A couple of days later Robbie had a meeting with Dr Tucker, Wilde's doctor, and he learned the full extent of Wilde's illness and its likely prognosis.

Robbie wrote immediately to Douglas, breaking the news of the gravity of Wilde's illness, explaining that Wilde's concern over his mounting debts was retarding his recovery. He told Douglas he would shortly have to leave Paris and urged him to come over and spend some time with Wilde before it was too late. In view of all that had gone before, Robbie's gesture was exceedingly gracious; Wilde, despite all his protestations to the contrary, was still very fond of his former golden boy. Douglas, to his shame, did not hurry to Paris; he did, however, send Wilde a small cheque. Robbie was very downhearted. Douglas had inherited a considerable sum of money from his father, who had died in January: Robbie suggested that Douglas should pay Wilde's debts and arrange to pay him a small annuity. Robbie confidently expected that out of Douglas's inheritance of some £25,000, he could, without effort, pay off Wilde's debts, annul the bankruptcy and so acquire the copyright to

Wilde's works. Knowing that Bosie Douglas disliked all matters connected with business, Robbie offered to act as manager, but Douglas, unable to believe that Wilde's Estate would ever again be solvent, refused the offer. It was a decision he later regretted, and to his dying day he maintained that Robbie had unfairly benefited from the Wilde Estate. He was unable to appreciate that it was his own selfishness which had prevented him from enjoying the full fruits of Wilde's brilliant writings. Douglas did, from time to time, send Wilde small cheques, but they were wholly insufficient to meet his needs. Robbie never forgave Douglas that gross act of meanness and it was this action, more than any other, that soured their relationship in the years following Wilde's death.

Robbie left Paris on the evening of 13 November to join his mother, who planned to stay in the south of France over the winter. On the 27th he wrote to Wilde, telling him of his plans for the next few weeks:

> I enclose December cheque for £10. I will write to Harris on the
> basis I suggested directly I get to Nice. For ten days we shall be at
> the Hôtel Suisse. I will let you know when we move. I expect it will
> be to Cannes. I hope that with the new century Frank Harris is
> going to turn over at least a new cheque in your favour, and I
> somehow feel that if you had ever known my undistinguished uncle,
> "an angel in the Irvingate Church",[21] you would, in spite of this
> disadvantage, have felt very much as you do now. Seriously you
> must not get too depressed. Things are sure to come right, and
> remember violent letters though justifiable in every way are of no
> use in the present case.[22]

As a heading to the letter Robbie had written: 'Reg will send me bulletins about you I hope.' Wilde probably never read this letter. The day after it was written Robbie received an urgent telegram from Turner, saying that Wilde's condition was: 'Almost helpless'. Robbie caught the night express to Paris, and the next morning Dr Kleiss,[23] the specialist, called in by Turner, confirmed that Wilde had little more than two days left to live. Devastated, Robbie went in to see Wilde, who was barely conscious. Robbie prayed silently that Wilde was aware of his presence. He suppressed his own grief and set about contacting those persons who would be most concerned about Wilde's impending death. He cabled Mr Holman, Adrian Hope's[24] solicitor, who would have the painful duty of breaking the news of Wilde's condition to his two sons. He sent telegrams to Frank Harris and to Douglas, who was in Scotland shooting. He then remembered his own promise to Wilde, that, if he were able, he would bring a priest to him before he died. Father Cuthbert Dunne, an

Irish priest from the Passionist Church of St Joseph, agreed to attend, and Wilde was very close to death when he was received into the Holy Roman Catholic Church. Robbie objected to what he considered 'easy conversions', but he felt he had done as much as he could for the immortal soul of his devoted friend.

Oscar Wilde died at 1.50 p.m. on Friday 30 November 1900 and was buried on Monday 3 December. Robbie was unable to contact Cyril and Vyvyan Holland[25] direct but he wrote to them via their mother's family solicitors. He received an emotional reply from the fifteen-year-old Cyril:

> Thank you so much for the kind letter you sent me. It was very kind of you to give the flowers for us. I am glad you say that he loved us. I hope that at his death he was truly penitent; I think he must have been if he joined the Catholic Church and my reverence for the Roman Church is heightened more than ever.[26]

After the funeral service Robbie returned to Menton and began to readjust his life. He received many letters of condolences and in replying to these he touched on the depths of his sorrow and the feeling of emptiness he felt following Oscar Wilde's death. To William Rothenstein, he acknowledged the true nature of his sadness:

> I have been so touched by your letter, the only one of several kind ones I have received that has given me any pleasure. I feel poor Oscar's death a great deal more than I should and far more than I expected. I had grown to feel, rather foolishly, a sort of responsibility for Oscar, for everything connected with him except his genius and he had become for me a sort of adopted prodigal baby. I began to love the very faults which I would never have forgiven in anyone else.[27]

If to Rothenstein he briefly touched on his own feelings, then in writing to Adela Schuster Robbie underlined the terrible conflict he had with himself where Wilde was concerned. In his own tormented heart he longed for the Wilde of former years, the man who had dominated London theatre-land, the man who had, before his imprisonment, been destined to become one of the greatest dramatists of the century. Robbie mourned the waste of that genius, but, in writing to Miss Schuster, he admitted honestly that Wilde was to blame for his own disgrace. He also laid some of the blame on the shoulders of a hypercritical world who could not find in their hearts enough compassion to forgive a fallen giant his moral sins. In writing of his distress Robbie revealed more about himself and showed the conflict with which he was forced to come to terms. He was not blind, though, and admitted that Wilde had many faults, but that these were overshadowed by the special gifts Wilde had for the world of literature. It is perhaps a pity that Robbie did not write the biography of Oscar Wilde for he would have written it with compassion and understanding and he would have told the truth:

> Two things were absolutely necessary for him, contact with comely things, as Pater says, and social position. Comely things meant for him a certain standard of living, and this, since his release, he *was able to have* except for a few weeks at a time or perhaps months. Social position he realised after five months he could not have. Many people were kind to him, but he was too proud, or too vain, to be forgiven by those whom he regarded as social and intellectual inferiors. It galled him to have to appear grateful to those whom he did not, or would not have regarded, before the downfall....He chose therefore a Bohemian existence, entirely out of note with his genius and temperament. There was no use arguing or exhorting him. The temporary deprivation of his annuity produced no result. You cannot ask a man who started on the top rung of the ladder to suddenly start again from the lowest rung of all. Among his many fine qualities he showed in his later years was that he never blamed anyone but himself for his own disasters. He never bore any ill will to anybody, and in a characteristic way was really surprised that anyone should bear any resentment against him...Some time I should be very grateful if you allowed me to have your views as to the advisability of a memoir, and its scope or plan, and if done with discretion whether it would please and interest his friends. I would not care for it to appeal to morbid curiosity, and I remember Mr Wilde's remark, "that it is always Judas who writes the biography".[28]

It was not long before publishers and writers were seeking Robbie's views on what he would regard as a suitable written memorial to the late Oscar Wilde. The first serious offer came from the publisher and bookseller, Arthur Humphreys, but Robbie declined the invitation to write the first memoir, giving the reasons for his decision as:

> 1st I think the interest in his work and his personality at the present moment to be confined to a very few people comparatively and 2nd I think such interest as there is, too confined to the unpleasant and later end of his life.[29]

Humphreys suggested that Ross might like to write a *Memoir* of Wilde jointly with Douglas and Frank Harris, but Robbie rejected the idea as unworkable. He went on to say that although he was very friendly with Douglas and was acquainted with Harris, he would find it impossible to collaborate with them as his views and theirs would be diametrically opposed. Robbie intimated that Arthur Humphreys[30] should write the memoir himself, and he would be pleased to give whatever assistance was required. Silence should have been Wilde's memorial, but silence was to be denied him. As Oscar Wilde's literary executor Robbie set about his duties diligently, his actions were always compassionate, and he was always mindful of the damage that would be further inflicted on Wilde's sons, if the tragedy of their father's life was constantly revived.

II

TRANQUIL YEARS

(1900-13)

'Nay, I'll do him justice. I'm his friend, I won't wrong him—And if he had any judgement in the world,—he would not be altogether contemptible. Come, come, don't detract from the merits of my friend.'

William Congreve, *The Way of the World*

Six

The Carfax

HE CARFAX GALLERY was well named; it was a constant reminder to Robbie of the Oxford he loved, and it became the crossroads of his life. The death of Oscar Wilde left him a sad and lonely man, and when he returned to London in the spring of 1901 the Gallery helped to fill the void. Robbie had inherited his father's love of art and with most of his education being gained in Europe, he had by the start of the new century acquired a sound knowledge of classical and contemporary art.

William Rothenstein and John Fothergill were finding the management of the Gallery irksome, and their frustrations were eased when Robbie offered to buy out their holdings. The little picture shop needed a strong and firm management and Robbie was convinced he was capable of the task; it was also inevitable that More Adey would join him in the new venture. Arthur Clifton remained to help the two friends, and the inexorable and efficient general factotum, Jack Stepney, was there to protect Robbie from the harassment of patrons and painters. By August Robbie was able finally to sort out the affairs of the Gallery, although, as he told Rothenstein, there were many questions which demanded urgent answers:

> There are a large number of items in the stock book which cannot
> be accounted for, viz a number of drawings which are not marked
> off as sold or returned to their original owners. A great many of
> them belong to you and so it is presumed that you either took them
> away or that they were sent back to you. Williams could not offer
> any explanation, except that it all happened in [Robert] Sickert's
> time. Adey and myself hoped that in going over things again after
> Williams went away some of these things would turn up and such as
> has been the case in many instances, but there are some drawings by
> Rodin belonging to him which we have no record of unless they
> were returned in a lot of 29 drawings which Arthur remembers
> being returned to him. There are some of Strang's (belonging to
> him) missing and as I said some of your own property (not actual
> drawings by you). There are of course a good many belonging to

> Carfax but I am chiefly anxious about those which we are
> responsible for. The stock book has been kept disgracefully both by
> Sickert and Williams.[1]

He told Rothenstein that he was most concerned that Rodin had written 'a cold...unenthusiastic letter' and he was worried that the Gallery owed Rodin money. He asked Rothenstein to give him full details of the Rodin sculpture so he could answer the complaint:

> 1st What Head?
> 2nd Who bought the Head?
> 3rd Has the purchaser ever paid?[2]

Robbie apologised for having to bother Rothenstein with such trivia while he was in Norfolk working. He explained he could not afford to offend artists or patrons of the Gallery, and as Arthur Clifton was away he had no one else to turn to for advice. He was particularly critical of the way the former employees of the Gallery had handled matters:

> When we are straight you shall not be bothered about such piddling
> matters, but I know you agree with me that artists and especially
> Rodin should not be kept waiting (anymore than is necessary).
> Williams among other idiocies never revealed that various dues had
> been sent in and the other day we received a threatening letter from
> a collector over the [late] bill. Williams explained that he had
> forgotten to mention the matter to Clifton. At the present moment
> the artistic side of Carfax is rather lying fallow, but I hope to get
> fairly straight before the end of September.[3]

The autumn was a time for stocktaking and planning for the future, but by November Robbie was ready to hold the first exhibition of the work of Max Beerbohm. Beerbohm had been developing his own special skills as a caricaturist for some years, and his growing reputation made him an obvious choice for an exhibition of one hundred caricatures. The subjects of his penetrating wit and fluent pen were famous politicians, including such notables as H.H. Asquith, the Earl of Rosebery and the Duke of Marlborough; neither rank nor social position excluded the subject from becoming a target for Beerbohm's genius. He was often accused of accentuating the physical disabilities of his subjects, yet such was the cleverness of his pen that most people who saw his caricatures, far from being embarrassed or angered, regarded them as a compliment. Mimicry is, after all, often regarded as a form of flattery, and rarely is it taken as insult.

Beerbohm was concerned with all aspects of the exhibition; for example, he thought the previous design of the invitation cards was not effective. In his opinion, the artist's name and the character of the exhibition were of supreme importance—not the name of the gallery. As the day of the opening drew nearer Beerbohm began to panic and it needed all Robbie's diplomacy to quieten and steady the nervous young designer.

The exhibition of Beerbohm's caricatures opened late in November. Robbie, aware that publicity was essential to any business venture, did not hesitate to contact those who were in the best position to give help to his little picture gallery. Edmund Gosse was a regular contributor to *The Times*[4] and the ideal man to approach and, as Gosse's reply proved, he did not resent the request for favourable publicity:

> We were much gratified by your kind and thoughtful note, but we blushed to think that you and your colleagues should exaggerate the value of our little friendly lead. I am sure you need no such friendly lead. (Perhaps the best I could do for you appears in the tempered slating of *The Times* this morning, which would have been much more savage if I had not been lucky enough to buttonhole the critic.)...
>
> If you can only get people to visit your gallery, and I am telling everybody to go, I think you will have a large sale. I shall be most glad, for your sakes and for Max's, too. Do let me hear how you get on.[5]

Edmund Gosse may have taken some of the sting out of the criticism in *The Times*, but Robbie must have been less than delighted with the review, and Beerbohm must have been furious, for in spite of the barbed praise there was nothing in the critical report to inflate his ego. The criticism in *The Times*, however, did not prevent Beerbohm's exhibition from being a great success, and the Carfax continued over the next few years to show Max Beerbohm's work. Beerbohm was much more than just a gifted caricaturist, he was also an accomplished writer, publishing many witty and amusing articles on art and drama. His gratitude to Robbie was genuine, and although they clashed occasionally over the adverse publicity Robbie attracted from those opposed to his work on behalf of the Wilde Estate, Beerbohm's letter at the time of his first exhibition does give a vivid account of the true nature of his feelings:

> How like you! Of course I shall be most extremely pleased to be written about by Vallance in the *Studio*. Why all these apologies and

> arguments? I am sure that if you were charged to tell someone that a
> large sum of money had just been bequeathed to him, you would
> begin by telling the man to prepare for some unpleasant news, to
> take a glass of brandy and pull himself together, and to believe you
> that it gives you as much pain to have to deliver the blow as it will
> give him to receive it.[6]

Robbie's involvement with Beerbohm was not confined to art and art
exhibitions, but also involved Beerbohm's affairs of the heart. Beerbohm's engagement to Kilseen Conover proved to have more than its
share of 'lovers' tiffs'. He was unable to take the whole business of
marriage seriously, being more in love with the ideal than with the
reality. Robbie, who had few illusions about the state of marriage,
nevertheless came to Kilseen's defence. He was concerned that she
would get hurt by her protracted engagement with Beerbohm, and he
tried to warn her of the consequences of the liaison, but she wasn't to be
so easily persuaded:

> Don't think I didn't enjoy my lunch. It was awfully nice of you to
> ask me and I am not stupid enough not to understand your reasons
> for speaking on such a difficult subject and I do appreciate the
> kindness in it. I won't say any more about it. I feel mean discussing
> it even. Mean to Max, for either I should not discuss it, or I should
> break it off. But all the arguments on the earth cannot undo the last
> six years. All I ask Max's friends is not to judge him too
> unkindly,... Don't misjudge him though. You *might* be wrong and I
> don't want the added unhappiness of thinking that Max has lost any
> of his friends through me.[7]

His friendship with Kilseen endured even after her engagement to
Beerbohm ended, and, as she grew older and poorer, Robbie frequently
gave her financial assistance. Robbie observed in Beerbohm's relationship with women the same degree of irresponsibility and selfishness that
typified Wilde's and Douglas's attitude to women. They were all
dreamers who tried to live out their fantasies in a world that had no
understanding of them. The worry over Kilseen and Beerbohm's engagement was not the only 'affair of the heart' that concerned Robbie at the
beginning of 1902. When Olive Custance[8] considered eloping with Bosie
Douglas, Robbie, in spite of his reservations about the match, allowed
them to use the privacy of the Gallery to arrange the details of their
flight. There was family hostility from the bride's parents to the marriage
of their only daughter to the third son of the late Marquess of Queens-

berry. His involvement with Oscar Wilde and his own very dubious reputation did not make Douglas an obvious choice as a son-in-law; even his own family were far from convinced that the marriage should take place. In the end, Olive and Douglas were married, but it was not a grand social occasion, as befitted the son of a Marquess or a rich man's only daughter. Robbie attended, but he sat alone in the almost deserted church. Apart from Douglas's sister, the only other witness to the ceremony was Cecil Hayes, a young barrister, who, a little over eleven years later, was to play a leading role in the litigation battles between Robbie and Douglas.

Douglas's selfishness and extravagance were hardly good qualities for an 'ideal husband', and he had very little to offer a young wife except a name tarnished by conflict and scandal. The marriage did not last; Douglas could not reconcile his conflicts, and it was not long before he saw his father-in-law as a common trader, and not fit company to associate with, in view of his own aristocratic lineage going back to the Royal House of Scotland. His disdain for trade extended in time to Robbie as well, and Douglas never lost an opportunity of making disparaging comments about 'Robbie's unsuccessful little picture shop'.

The management of the Carfax and the affairs of his friends left Robbie with little opportunity for leisure, and as the first anniversary of Oscar Wilde's death passed he began to realise the immensity of the task that lay before him. Wilde's debts were still unpaid and what royalties were forthcoming were immediately paid to the Court of Bankruptcy. Robbie, for some months, had been in negotiation with the Official Receiver in the hope of being able to secure for himself the copyright of Wilde's works; Adrian Hope, as trustee of Wilde's Estate, offered no objections to his acquiring the copyright. Robbie wanted to make a written declaration that once Wilde's debts had been paid and his bankruptcy cleared Cyril and Vyvyan should be the beneficiaries of the royalties, but Hope was adamant that the boys should not have 'any official benefit from their father's works'.[9] He was fearful that, as their names had been changed to avoid their being tainted by their father's guilt, any official recognition of them would undo all the good the years of anonymity had achieved. Sir George Alexander, the actor-manager, had purchased from the Official Receiver for £100 the literary and dramatic copyright of *The Importance of Being Earnest* and *Lady Windermere's Fan*; Robbie had vigorously objected to the sale but the Official Receiver had assured him that Wilde's works were worthless. In the second week of January 1902, Alexander proposed to stage *The Importance of Being Earnest* at the St James's Theatre, and Robbie hoped that Alexander would keep his promise and send him a contribution towards paying off Wilde's debts. Robbie was not all that optimistic, others including Frank Harris and Douglas had promised help, but the money had not been forthcoming.

A couple of publishers had assured Robbie that if he could secure all the copyrights they would be prepared to advance him the money for the purchase. Arthur Humphreys was keen to bring out an expensive library edition, but Grant Richards was more interested in a popular edition. Robbie, however, was more interested in stopping the pirating of Wilde's works, as the loss of royalties was a serious blow to his chances of paying off all Wilde's creditors. He was particularly concerned that Dupoirier in Paris had not been paid; although he did not think Adela Schuster should again come to his assistance, he could only accept her offer with gratitude:

> I do not know that I quite approve of your being bled when it is really incumbent on several others to subscribe, but I don't want to interfere with the excellent Dupoirier getting anything he can and I know he will be cheered by the smallest contribution, so if you are really able to do so will you send anything direct to him and let me know the amount so that I can keep count.[10]

Robbie's executorship of Wilde's works was to bring him despair and joy, but it also brought him many new friends. One of the most lasting of the friendships began in June 1902, when Walter Ledger[11] wrote soliciting his help and advice in compiling a bibliography of the works of Oscar Wilde. Ledger had first approached Douglas, who suggested he should contact Robbie, who knew more about Wilde's literary works than he did.

Walter Ledger was in many ways an archetypal bibliographer, an eccentric bachelor with a passion for sailing. He preferred to dress as an old-fashioned sailor in an open-necked shirt with a blue-and-white collar, and bell-bottomed trousers. He suffered periodically from manic depression, and on occasions his illness became so severe that it would result in bouts of homicidal mania. He would withdraw from the world and become a virtual hermit until the mood had passed. Robbie, ever willing to befriend yet another of life's casualties, shared with Ledger a mutual love of first editions and beautiful bindings.

After the receipt of Ledger's first letter, Robbie replied immediately, suggesting that they should meet at the Carfax and discuss at greater length Ledger's projected bibliography. On 22 July Robbie replied to another letter from Ledger, but this time apologised for the delay in his answer, explaining that he had been away on business. He added that, unfortunately, through pressure of work at the Gallery he would have to refuse the invitation to dine at Ledger's home in Wimbledon. He did, however, suggest that Ledger should dine instead at 24 Hornton Street,[12] where he would introduce him to Lord Alfred Douglas, if the latter was in London at the time. The proposed meeting with Douglas did not take place until later in the year. On 29 December in a postcard confirming the date and time of the dinner, there is just a hint that Robbie wished that protocol should be upheld. He was worried that Ledger's eccentric mode of dress would shame him in the eyes of Douglas; he underlined the words 'morning dress', as if to emphasise that he expected Ledger to make a special effort when he came to dine with the son of a Marquess.

The Carfax was, indeed, occupying much of his time. The exhibitions held during the summer and autumn of the works of Conder and Muirhead Bone had not been a success and Robbie had been forced to borrow money to pay the debts of the Gallery. He hoped at the start of the New Year the Carfax would be able to show the works of William Orpen, Roger Fry and Dugald Sutherland MacColl and that the resulting sales would improve the financial health of the Gallery. The exhibition of William Rothenstein's work, which had been scheduled for May, was finally held in December 1902, but the adverse comments in the Press did little to increase sales or help lessen Rothenstein's depression.

The relationship between Rothenstein and Ross was not always smooth, but perhaps the conflict of interests was due as much to their individual dominant personalities, rather than to a genuine disagreement about actual matters of fact. Their clashes were more often a case of mistaken intentions and poorly expressed wishes. There is an edge of bitterness in a letter from Rothenstein to Ross in December and he does little to hide his annoyance at what he has taken to be Robbie's condescension:

> It is very kind of you to suggest that you will give me a panel of 6
> pastels. I will accept your offer willingly; it was churlish of me to
> ask for all the things back.[13]

Rothenstein admitted he was grateful for Robbie's encouragement and assistance over the past few years but there is still an edge of bitterness to his words. He cannot avoid, however, asking Robbie to do a number of chores for him, although again there is an undercurrent of stress in his request:

> Will you be good enough to send my brother's 2 pastels the first
> thing tomorrow morning to Morley's Hotel, Trafalgar Square. He
> will be passing through there and will most likely take them with
> him. I am writing to ask Gray to photograph one or two of the
> pastels for myself tomorrow, before they go off. The rest will be sent
> to me through Dickson, at your early convenience, won't they?[14]

It was too much to expect Robbie not to see the underlying implications in Rothenstein's letter, and he replied in a less than sympathetic frame of mind. Disposing first of the matter of the photography, which Gray had been unable to do at the Carfax and had to remove two of the sold paintings from the Gallery for a few days, Robbie then tried to answer some of Rothenstein's criticisms. He stressed his actions had been misconstrued by Rothenstein, and that illness and tiredness had made him less attentive than he was normally. In trying to defend his actions Robbie revealed much of his complex and Delphic character:

> You always see me when I am dead beat and that is why I seem
> unsympathetic. Do you remember Oscar once said that a dealer was
> a person who knew the price of everything and the value of nothing.
> If that is true a dealer must be lacking in sympathy. Let me assure
> you that I never thought you churlish the other day at all. I merely
> made the suggestion that you should leave a few things out of
> commercial policy, but I quite enter [sic] with your feelings on the
> question. As you know I always believe in pacifying the mammon of
> unrighteousness *at once*, and not resisting, as in the end one has to
> submit. I always think you make a virtue of resistance and a virtue
> of capitulation as well. It is only a question of ethics on which we
> differ. You very often say things from which I dissent violently, but
> do not say so except by silence as I do not want to offend you. By an
> odd coincidence, since your marriage, your wife understands me a
> great deal better than you do. You have elaborate *impromptu* theories
> about people and things and are over-superstitious about them.
> When you have doubts about me and my lack of sympathy if you
> will consult Alice without reference to me I can leave my views and
> my character with her in trust. Being much simpler from an ethical
> standpoint, she is able to understand complex people including Will
> Rothenstein.[15]

The strains in their relationship, however, did not prevent Rothenstein asking Robbie and John Fothergill to be godfathers to his infant son John.

As the second anniversary of Oscar Wilde's untimely death passed, Robbie found his confidence returning. He would not claim to be happy, but he had found a purpose in life. He would always mourn the loss of Wilde, but with his work at the Carfax, his executorship of Wilde's Estate and with his growing circle of friends he was not unduly miserable. Early in 1903, however, he met a young man who gave him a degree of contentment he thought he would never find again. Frederick Stanley Smith was a handsome eighteen-year-old clerk; and although he lacked many of the social graces, Robbie found his personality and presence pleasing, and he was willing to teach the young man all that he could absorb. Smith could never replace Wilde in Robbie's affections, but his devotion and love would endure, when many other friendships would end in bitterness and recriminations.

In April 1903 the Carfax held an exhibition of the work of Roger Fry, and for once the Press, the public, the artist and the management of the Gallery all agreed the exhibition was a success. Robbie had first met Fry at Cambridge in 1888, but their friendship developed only when they became involved in the world of art. Fry never became the Establishment figure he thought his talents merited. He wanted the Slade Professorship at Cambridge or Oxford but it was not until 1933 that he was appointed to Cambridge, just one year before his death. He was offered the Directorship of the Tate Gallery but refused it, a decision he bitterly regretted in later years. He did, though, become a prolific writer and lecturer, and will perhaps best be remembered for his involvement with the Post-Impressionist Movement. Robbie was unimpressed by the new school of painting, but he was prepared to accept that his friends had divergent tastes, and he was always, regardless of the consequences, willing to show the work of up-and-coming artists at the Carfax. He was delighted to tell Fry how successful they had been in selling his work:

> We have sold *24 pictures* of yours.... The whole exhibition has really been a *terrific* success from our point of view and I hope from yours. It has far exceeded our expectations, especially in view of the fact that so few people have responded to the invitations. I suppose a good many have been away, but those who came have bought and that is more important. Of course those who turn up now complain that all the best things have gone and this is inevitable. We rehung the gallery a few days ago bringing unsold watercolours into the light and this was a success in that four sold from the newly hung wall. I have rearranged it again today.... I think I told you that *numerically* we have never done so well at any exhibition except Max. If we could only be sure of a success of our autumn shows

> Carfax could really just pay its expenses. Under the former
> management nothing modern except Conder ever paid expenses.
> Steer, Max and yourself have been our *three* triumphs in new fields.
> Sargent is only an advertisement as nothing is to be for sale.[16]

There were only two more exhibitions at the Carfax during 1903, and
in spite of Robbie's pessimism the reputation of the Gallery continued to
grow and it began to attract shrewd collectors and connoisseurs of art.
On 3 July, almost eight years to the day since Oscar Wilde had been
declared bankrupt, his trustees paid a dividend of 13s 4d to his creditors.
The major portion of the money had come from the production of
Wilde's plays in Germany; a debt to the discerning German public that
Robbie never forgot or ever felt he could sufficiently repay. It niggled
Robbie that Bosie Douglas, as a beneficiary under his father's Estate,
would receive a quarter share of the dividend; it had, after all, been
Douglas's father who had first made Wilde bankrupt, and it had been
Douglas who had urged Wilde to take the rash and imprudent litigation
which ended in his imprisonment. Robbie was not vindictive by nature,
but there were old scores to be settled with Douglas, and the day of
reckoning would eventually come.

The first exhibition at the Carfax, in January 1904, was of the work of
William Blake; in April they showed the work of Edward Calvert, and in
May Max Beerbohm was given a further show. But if artists were
important to the Carfax, then so were buyers. One of the most prolific
was Edward Marsh, a career Civil Servant; it is not known where and
when Robbie met Marsh, but it is quite possible that it was at the home
of Herbert and Margot Asquith. Marsh was initially guided in his art
purchases by the young painter Neville Lytton but by 1904 he felt able to
make independent decisions. In late March Robbie was asked to arrange
the disposal of a private collection of English paintings, and he
approached Edward Marsh as a possible buyer:

> A personal friend of mine and a client of Carfax wishes to dispose of
> an extremely fine Collection of English drawings. They number 200
> and he asks £2400 (*i.e*) at the rate of £12 a drawing, but of course he
> will not separate any of them, as he wants the money for a particular
> purpose.
>   The price is really absurdly cheap and I can praise the drawings
> without suspicion of partisanship because none of them as far as I
> can remember came from Carfax. If I had some capital I would buy
> them myself and I could rely on getting at least 15% profit in a
> couple of years. Many of the drawings could be sold quite quickly

for *at least* £40 and I could sell any of them separately for any
purchaser who might not care to have so many examples of one
particular master.[17]

He listed the paintings that were in the Collection, assuring Marsh
they were among the finest in private hands. He declined to name the
owner of the Collection, but told Marsh that if he decided to view, he
would, then, of course, name the Collector, and Marsh could deal with
him direct. In reply Marsh said that he would inspect the Collection if he
could bring Neville Lytton with him. Robbie agreed, explaining why he
had offered Marsh the first refusal: 'My reason for approaching you was a
chance remark of yours that you were rather looking out for something
important and did not want to waste money over an unimportant picture
however charming. I did not imagine you were a Pierpont Morgan.'[18]
Marsh eventually saw the Collection on 10 May and agreed to purchase
it. Robbie was able to tell Marsh the Collection belonged to Herbert
Horne, who was selling his paintings in order to live in Florence, where
he wished to continue his study into the history of early Italian Art.
Herbert Horne and Robbie were very close friends, and one of the most
amusing stories in *Masques and Phases*, 'The Hootawa Vandyck', is
dedicated to Horne. They both shared the same hard-headed business
sense and they both had a eye for a bargain. Horne had been delighted to
tell Robbie that he had just 'sold to an American for £200 etc a picture
which I bought for 100 francs. But you need not pass that on.'[19]

In May Martin Conway founded the Arundel Club to reproduce by
photography works of art which the general public would not otherwise
have had a chance of seeing. Robbie, who constantly complained of
being over-tired and ill, and whose spare time was extremely limited,
was, nevertheless, co-opted onto the committee and quickly appointed
Honorary Secretary. It was fortunate that he had Freddie Smith to act as
his secretary and his help became invaluable.

At the same time as Robbie was arranging the sale of the Horne
Collection, he was also negotiating with Marsh over the holding of an
exhibition of the work of Neville Lytton:

Friday July 1st is the first possible day for a press show. Saturday
2nd for private view. The English picture season lasts until July
20th, barring natural disasters, national rejoicings or "mourning
ladies" all of which detract public attention. The first fortnight of
July is or *ought to be* one of the best times for modern work. The
Americans come first week in August (for Old Masters only) that is
the position and on hearing from you we will write a formal letter

> from the firm to Mr Neville Lytton stating our terms which are 25%
> on the sales; the artist delivers the pictures framed and mounted. If
> however the *mounts* are made 19 inches x 24 inches we can *lend* our
> stock frames and that saves expense to the artist. Anyone wishing to
> buy the frame of a particular drawing can have one at 7/6.[20]

He went on to tell Marsh that both More Adey and Arthur Clifton
were of the opinion that Lytton's exhibition should be delayed until at
least the autumn and preferably until the following year. He pointed out
that the previous July they had held an exhibition of J.T. Wellington's
work which had been a total failure. He tried not to influence Marsh's
decision unduly by admitting that: 'With one or two exceptions as you
may know we never expect to do more by our *modern* exhibitions than
pay expenses, so we are not looking at the question from the financial
side, but from a *success of esteem* and the artist's point of view. Our
reward comes from making new clients and advertisements. I am sure
the exhibition will be a great success from our point of view whenever it
happens.'[21]

Neville Lytton's exhibition was held in June and July, and, unlike
some earlier shows held at the Carfax, the Press viewed the work on
display with favour:

> At the Carfax in Ryder Street a new artist appears with an
> interesting little exhibition. This is the Hon Neville Lytton, in
> whom an hereditary interest in poetry has taken the form of love for
> art, which has been cultivated by some years of careful training. Mr
> Lytton is as yet only in the first stages of his career but his work
> both in portraiture and in landscape is full of promise. The heads in
> chalk are excellent: still more so are two small full-length portraits in
> oil, which show a sound instinct for colour and a decided gift for
> "placing" a subject.[22]

In November the Carfax, much to Robbie's great joy, held a
posthumous exhibition of the work of Aubrey Beardsley. The show was
the largest gathering of Beardsley's work that had ever been assembled,
and included Robbie's own personal collection. The reaction to
Beardsley's work was no less divided than it had been when he was alive.
Some thought him a genius while others considered him obscene and
depraved; Robbie's belief in Beardsley's genius never wavered, and the
exhibition was a success. It was also a high note on which to end a year
which had enhanced Robbie's reputation as an art expert and art dealer.

Seven

Poisoned Chalice

F, WHEN Oscar Wilde had begun his exile in France, he had realised that in handing the manuscript of *Epistola: In Carcere et Vinculis* to Robbie, he was giving him a poisoned chalice, he would have sent his final work of prose straight to Lord Alfred Douglas— and that would have been the last the world would have heard of that most damning letter.

It is to be regretted that he gave the letter to Robbie with such precise instructions as to its future; Robbie carried out those orders diligently and compassionately. It can only be a matter of supposition as to when Robbie first read that bitter and censorious letter, but undoubtedly he must have been aware of its poignancy as he arranged for a typewritten copy to be taken, as Wilde had ordered.[1] As he dictated to a lady typist at 24 Hornton Street, Wilde's words had a terrible and lasting impact on him.

The original letter remained in Robbie's care, although in August 1897 he did send a typed copy to Alfred Douglas. Wilde wanted the letter published, but both he and Robbie knew there was no chance of publishing the letter in its unabridged form in the lifetime of Douglas or his family. The existence of the letter became known to Dr Max Meyerfeld; Wilde had never made any secret of the fact that, while in prison, he had written a prose work of great importance. Meyerfeld began to pester to be allowed to publish part of the letter; at first Robbie resisted all his advances, but finally Meyerfeld's persistence wore him down:

> But for you I do not think the book would have ever been
> published. When first you asked me about the manuscript which
> you heard Wilde wrote in prison, I explained to you vaguely that
> some day I hoped to issue portions of it, in accordance with the
> writer's wishes; though I thought it would be premature to do so at
> that moment. You begged however that Germany (which already
> held Wilde's plays in the highest esteem) should have the
> opportunity of seeing a new work by one of her favourite authors. I
> rather reluctantly consented to your proposal; and promised, at a
> leisured opportunity, to extract such portions of the work as might

be considered of general public interest. I fear that I postponed what
was to me a rather painful task; it was only your visits and more
importunate correspondence (of which I frankly began to hate the
sight) that brought about the fulfilment of your object.[2]

It was only after Robbie had sent the extracts to Meyerfeld for
publication in *Die Neue Rundschau* that he saw the possibility of a
simultaneous publication in England. His decision was 'not reached
without some misgiving...[as] Wilde's name unfortunately did not
bring very agreeable memories to English ears.'[3] Robbie still doubted the
wisdom of his decision when he sent the manuscript to Methuen. He did
not believe any London publisher would touch the work, and he was
suitably astonished when Methuen agreed to accept the commission. The
decision to publish was made on the advice of Methuen's reader, E.V.
Lucas. Lucas suggested certain modifications to the manuscript, to
which Robbie readily agreed. The title of the book caused some difficulty, but in the end Robbie had the final say: 'the title *De Profundis*,
against which some have cavilled, is...my own; for this I do not make
any apology.'[4]

As the day of publication approached, Robbie's pessimism and
apprehension increased. He could not believe that in the four years since
Wilde's death, public opinion had changed sufficiently for them to
accept that the tragedy of Wilde's life should be laid at the door of
entrenched bourgeois attitudes, and that he had never been a depraved
and corrupt monster.

In the weeks leading up to publication Robbie was again involved with
solicitors, when the Board of Trade issued a prosecution against him for
allowing a translation of *The Duchess of Padua* into German. Robbie was
learning that as Wilde's literary executor he would have to come to terms
with the vagaries and intricacies of the law as it applied to copyright
infringements. Coming as it did at the same time as the publication of *De
Profundis*, it was a particularly difficult period as he explained in a letter
to Walter Ledger:

> I dare not issue the English version of *The Duchess* yet. The pros and
> cons are too intricate to describe but apparently I have quite a fair
> case. My copy of *The Duchess* is now reposing with Counsel
> somewhere in Lincoln's Inn.
>   I have bought the copyright from Hambleton of *Pomegranates
> Sainte Cour[tisane]* and *Intentions*, and am trying to prosecute (*this is
> private*) the pirates. Could you send me notes of any piracies about

> these three and where they were supposed to be published?
> Methuen is ready to bring out a complete edition of Wilde directly
> all these law suits are settled.[5]

Negotiations with his solicitors and the Board of Trade continued and finally *De Profundis* appeared on 23 February 1905. In publishing the abridged edition Robbie took an enormous gamble; if the gamble failed he would not be given another opportunity to restore Wilde's literary reputation for many years to come.

Robbie contributed a brief introduction to the Preface but allowed Wilde's own moving, eloquent words to speak for themselves:

> For a long time considerable curiosity has been expressed about the manuscript of *De Profundis*, which was known to be in my possession, the author having mentioned its existence to many other friends. The book requires little introduction and scarcely any explanation. I have only to record that it was written by my friend during the last months of his imprisonment, that it was the only work he wrote while in prison, and the last work in prose he ever wrote. *The Ballad of Reading Gaol* was not composed nor even planned until he had regained his liberty.
>
> In sending me instructions with regard to the publication of *De Profundis*, Oscar Wilde wrote:
>
> "I don't defend my conduct. I explain it. Also there are in my letter certain passages which deal with my mental development in prison, and the inevitable evolution of my character and intellectual attitude towards life that has taken place; and I want you and others who still stand by me and have affection for me to know exactly in what mood and manner I hope to face the world. Of course, from one point of view, I know that on the day of my release I shall be merely passing from one prison into another, and there are times when the whole world seems to me no larger than my cell, and as full of terror for me."[6]

Robbie concluded his introduction with a plea for readers to be compassionate and objective in assessing the merits of the book: 'I venture to hope that *De Profundis*, which renders so vividly, and so painfully, the effect of a social *débâcle* and imprisonment on a highly intellectual and artificial nature, will give many readers a different impression of the witty and delightful writer.'[7]

If Robbie made one mistake in his handling of the manuscript, it was that he failed to make it clear the letter was not addressed to him, but to another. It was a lapse which lay him open to the accusation of committing a massive literary fraud. The authenticity of the letter was questioned as Robbie feared it might be: 'Certain people (among others a well-known French writer) have paid me the compliment of suggesting that the text was an entire forgery by myself or a *cento* of Wilde's letters to myself. Were I capable either of the requisite art, or the requisite fraud, I should have made a name in literature ere now.'[8] In his attempt to shield Douglas and his long-suffering family, Robbie failed to appreciate the effects the baseless accusation would have on his own good name. In thinking of others, Robbie left himself open to attack from the enemies of Wilde, of whom in 1905 there were still far too many. If the letter had been written to Robbie and not, as it was, to Douglas, then his reaction to it could not have been more genuine. It was as if Robbie could understand and appreciate Wilde's terrible suffering, which others could not begin to comprehend. Writing later, in the Foreword to another book by Wilde's great friend, Ada Leverson, Robbie said of Wilde's prison letter:

> The publication of *De Profundis* revived the interest in a personality which, apart from sad associations, was unique in English literature. To many people that personality was a repellent one—to others, such as the writer of this book, it was peculiarly fascinating. It will always be difficult for us to convey to those who never knew him or who, knowing him, disliked him, the extraordinary magnetism which he exercised at least on the needles, if not the silver churns, of life. As in the fable of the gold and silver shield every one received entirely different impressions according to the method of their approach and the accident of acquaintance.[9]

Public reaction to the book was even better than Robbie could have believed in his wildest dreams, but the joy he felt was offset by a personal tragedy; on 14 March, his mother Augusta Elizabeth died. It was a bitter blow. Robbie's relationship with her had often been stormy, and she had been shocked by his involvement in the sordid scandals which involved Wilde and his circle. She knew he was different from her other sons, Jack and Alex, but she was never able to fully understand that difference, or appreciate that his homosexuality was his private burden, which he was prepared to carry without her assistance. Her unreality and desire to 'live in the land of make-believe',[10] had made it hard for him to show the degree of affection he actually felt. She had, though, nursed him with love and tenderness as he fought his many battles against ill-health; she had been generous to his friends, she had helped Wilde's mother financially when he had been sentenced to imprisonment. She had sent Wilde messages of love and respect when he was at his lowest ebb. She had been emotionally and physically ill-prepared to cope with her thirty-four years of widowhood, yet she had asked for nothing more from life than to be surrounded by her family. Her home had been a haven of peace for Robbie when the strains of his life had become too hard to bear alone, and for a few short hours in the company of his mother he had been able to regain his sense of perspective.

His mother was cremated at Golders Green on 16 March, and although there were many tributes to her memory, none was more touching in its simplicity than that written by Max Beerbohm:

> I only heard this afternoon that the funeral was held this morning. I had thought it would not be before the end of the week. I had wanted to send some flowers—just a token of the sort of thing that I (not an Englishman, but brought up in England) could not say to you yesterday—yet felt all the same.[11]

Two weeks later, tragedy struck again. On 31 March Jack, Robbie's eldest and deeply respected brother, died at the age of forty-six. The Ross/Baldwin lineage had been cursed by the early death of its menfolk; his brother-in-law Charles Jones had also died in his mid-fifties. These early deaths left a void in Robbie's life, but the death of Jack robbed him of the gentle but firm hand that he needed so desperately in the years which followed. His wildly erratic character needed a restraint placed on it. The full tragedy of 1905 was that in its moments of extreme personal sorrow he achieved the most rewarding joy for his service to the memory of Oscar Wilde. The gods had decreed that he should divide his life between his personal and private sorrows and the needs and demands of Oscar Wilde and his sons.

There was little time for private mourning; Robbie was still deeply involved with the publication of *De Profundis*, and by March it was already into its third reprinting. Perhaps more encouragingly, it had been reviewed by thirty national newspapers and journals, and on the whole the criticisms had been favourable. Robbie said of the critics that they 'have shown themselves ready to estimate the writer, whether favourably or unfavourably, without emphasising their natural prejudices against his later career, even in reference to this book where the two things occasion synchronous comment.'[12]

Of all the reviews, however, there was one that Robbie read with more than usual relish. He must indeed have wondered why Douglas had not recognised the edited version of the letter that he had received at Nogent-sur-Marne in the summer of 1897. There is sufficient evidence now, however, to suggest that Douglas had, after receipt of the letter, read only the first few paragraphs before discarding it; he refused to accept, then or later, the criticism from Oscar Wilde whilst in prison. In the course of a long article,[13] Douglas wrote in a cynical and ill-tempered manner; he was never able to accept he bore some of the blame for Wilde's disgrace both before he went to prison and later when he wandered aimlessly round Europe in lonely exile. In Douglas's article there is a definite hint that he had begun to distance himself from Wilde and everything for which he stood.

The review of *De Profundis* in the *Times Literary Supplement* by E.V. Lucas was perhaps the least surprising, in view of Lucas's earlier commitment to the letter:

> This is an unfailing and now and then poignantly interesting work;
> it contains some beautiful prose, some confessions that cannot leave
> the reader unmoved and may even touch him a little with shame at
> his own fortunate rectitude; and in a passage of theological
> conjecture that is most engaging in its ingenuity and of a very
> delicate texture. The book contains all this and more, and yet while
> realizing the terrible conditions under which it was written, and
> possessed by every wish to understand the author and feel with him
> in the utter wreck of his career, it is impossible, except very
> occasionally, to look upon his testament as more than a literary feat.
> Not so, we find ourselves saying, are souls laid bare. This is not
> sorrow, but its dexterously constructed counterfeit.[14]

Lucas went on to quote from Wilde's text, and concluded a long discourse on Wilde's works, his life, his philosophy and his religion, and he ended his piece with what is perhaps one of the best eulogies on the life of the stricken man to whom Robbie devoted so much of his own short life:

> We do not say that this is a great criticism; but it is the true and the
> best Wilde. It is the kind of happy, swift, inverted commentary of
> which he had the secret and which we hold is his chief gift. And,
> right or wrong, it is very gay and charming, and it makes the reader
> think. Indeed, everything which Wilde says of Christ in this little
> book is worth reading and considering reading again. What, then, is
> the value of *De Profundis?* Its value is this—that it is an example of
> the triumph of the literary temperament over the most

disadvantageous conditions; it is further documentary evidence as to
one of the most artificial natures produced by the nineteenth century
in England; and here it makes a sweet and reasonable contribution
to the gospel of humanity.[15]

Robbie, with his customary generosity, sent copies of the book to
many people, friends, admirers and those who had befriended Wilde in
his hour of need. Major Nelson, that most humane of all prison gover-
nors, wrote a touching letter of thanks, adding: 'I think it one of the
grandest and saddest efforts of a truly penitent man. One has to read but
little to recognize what literature has lost in the death of a man like poor
Oscar Wilde.'[16]

If Wilde's prison captor had been delighted with the published letter,
his old friends were not united in their praise of the book. Indeed, in the
years that followed its publication, more words would be expounded
analysing Wilde's spiritual and emotional state than Wilde wrote in the
original work. Bernard Shaw, with his customary caustic wit, summed
up the whole *De Profundis* affair better than most:

> It is really an extraordinary book, quite exhilarating and amusing as
> to Wilde himself, and quite disgraceful and shameful to his stupid
> tormentors. There is pain in it, inconvenience, annoyance, but no
> unhappiness, no real tragedy, all comedy. The unquenchable spirit
> of the man is magnificent: he maintains his position and puts society
> squalidly in the wrong—rubs into them every insult and humiliation
> he endured—comes out the same man he went in—with
> stupendous success.... It annoys me to have people degrading the
> whole affair to the level of sentimental tragedy.[17]

In trying to apportion blame it is always difficult to be certain that it is
placed at the feet of the right person; during the Wilde trials reference
was made to a story called 'The Priest and the Acolyte'. At first it was
thought Wilde had written the piece, but later the writer was exposed as
J.F.Bloxam. If Wilde was cast in the role of the priest, then as the priest
he was condemned and destroyed, but in making Robbie his acolyte he
was guilty of a far more serious crime—Robbie drank from the chalice
and the poison ruined his life. Bosie Douglas was Wilde's true acolyte,
and Wilde should have sent him the original manuscript of *De Profundis*;
then, unable to accept its condemnations, Douglas would have destroyed
it. The tragedy of *De Profundis* was not that Robbie published it when he
did, but that Douglas could not then or at any time in his long life accept
the letter for what it was: the emotional outpourings of an imprisoned

genius, who knew no other way to purge his guilt than to lay the blame on the shoulders of another man. In later years Douglas disclaimed ever having seen the full text of the letter, but the more he denied its existence the more ridiculous he sounded. If Douglas had been given the original letter and had destroyed it; and if Robbie had not pre-empted his actions, the world of literature would have lost a great work. Such a loss would indeed have been a tragedy, and the sad truth of Wilde's torment would never have been made known. If the publication in 1905 had been the end of the *De Profundis* story, it would have been a fitting tribute to both the author and his literary executor; unfortunately its history was destined to be very acrimonious, and it was not long before Robbie learnt how fatal the poison in the chalice was and how little he could do to mitigate its effects. It is debatable, however, whether Robbie would have acted differently than he did; his motives at all times were altruistic. In the years that followed the publication of *De Profundis*, the gap between Robbie and Bosie Douglas widened to the point where the break in their friendship was final and irrevocable. Douglas never sought to gain control of the manuscript until he realised just what a valuable document it was, by which time it was too late. Robbie had placed the manuscript out of harm's way.

De Profundis was not only an outstanding literary accomplishment, it was also a financial success. Unfortunately with Wilde's Estate still bankrupt, the Official Receiver took the first £1000 of the royalties. Robbie proposed that if the bankruptcy was discharged, and if he was appointed official legal administrator of Wilde's Estate, he would hold all royalties in trust until Wilde's sons reached the age of maturity. Robbie was determined that the future proceeds of the Estate would be as great as he could make them, and with the death in 1904 of Adrian Hope, there was no longer a family objection to his working for the benefit of both Cyril and Vyvyan Holland. Discussions with the Board of Trade and the Official Receiver of Oscar Wilde's bankrupt Estate continued throughout 1905, and whenever possible Robbie purchased the copyright of Wilde's work. He objected most strongly to the pirating of Wilde's plays and books, but with appreciation of the needs of the bibliographer he gave his blessing to Walter Ledger to avail himself of any unauthorised editions he was able to secure:

> By all means, as far as I am concerned smuggle any books you like but I only possess the copyright of *Saville Crime, Pomegranates* and *Intentions*. As a matter of fact, I think Jones and Evans can get you all the American editions.
>
> No one will object because no one will know.[18]

The interest shown by the public in Oscar Wilde began to revive with the publication of *De Profundis* and a number of books about him began to appear, including among others a work by Stuart Mason, the pseudonym of Christopher Sclater Millard.[19] When Millard announced his intention to publish his own bibliography of the works of Oscar Wilde, it was inevitable that Robbie would introduce him to Walter Ledger, and would offer Millard professional help as well as the hand of friendship. The friendship caused Robbie much misery in the years ahead, yet surprisingly it outlasted many of those which had been built on more substantial ties. Millard never denied he was homosexual, and remained always, a totally unrepentant man, who refused to conform to the rigid moral codes of a civilised society. Robbie certainly found him an uncomfortable friend, but he needed to pick up and befriend the casualties of life—as he had done with Oscar Wilde.

On 24 June the marriage of Robbie's niece, Ethel Jones, to the widower Squire Sprigge took place; Robbie's friendship with Sprigge had developed over the years, and although they differed in their outlook on life, Robbie was delighted to welcome Sprigge as a full member of his close-knit family. Robbie's life, though, was becoming more complicated and he began to feel that he was dividing himself into separate compartments. The Carfax demanded much of his attention; the Gallery had held a number of exhibitions during 1905, but he and his partners More Adey and Arthur Clifton were aware they needed more space. Towards the end of the year they moved from their cramped Ryder Street quarters into more spacious and convivial premises round the corner at 24 Bury Street. The reputation of the Gallery continued to grow, and it was not frightened to experiment. On the whole the Gallery's bold policy was welcomed by painters and patrons, but, naturally, there were dissenting voices among the art critics as to the merits of the exhibitions held there. Bernard Sickert, art critic of the *Academy*, was highly critical of the exhibitions, and wrote that the Carfax was developing an archaistic school of the watercolours painted by maiden aunts, which made 'an idol of insipidity and a *culte* of incompetence'.[20]

Sickert's criticism was too savage and personal for Robbie to ignore. He did not object to constructive criticism, but his chivalrous nature demanded he come to the defence of the artist, especially when biased criticism came from a fellow artist:

> Though it is contrary to all precedent for dealers to discuss their own wares in the public press or to challenge the criticism they invited by exposing them to public view, you will perhaps allow us the privilege of breaking an honourable convention.

>While your critic B.S. has paid us a high compliment in speaking
>of the *Carfax School*, we fear the distinguished artists of whom he
>disapproves will hardly care for the kettle which he had tied to their
>tails, to indulge in retort. But we do not profess to act as their
>spokesmen. None of them requires any defence; if that was
>necessary they would find more eloquent and learned champions
>than we can pretend to be. We merely wish to remonstrate with
>your critic on a question of fact...Certain pictures do not belong to
>any time or movement, and illustrate no particular theory; they are
>never old-[f]ashioned because they have never been fashionable.
>That certain critics do not like them or become ribald about them is
>an interesting circumstance in the life of the *critic* but has nothing to
>do with art. Venus is painted looking into a mirror by Velasquez, or
>sleeping in a green meadow by Giorgione or at her toilet by Charles
>Shannon, but these pictures of her are never archaistic—they are
>archetypes.[21]

The response from Sickert was immediate. He attempted to shift the
blame directly on to the Carfax's policy of showing inferior art and
experimenting with modernism: 'What the artists I have mentioned
show in common is a distrust and dislike of their own talent, their own
eyesight, their own period and environment.'[22]

It was impossible for Robbie to leave the matter unresolved, and here
it was necessary for him to have the last word; in a long letter to the
editor of the *Academy* he stated his case in no uncertain terms. The first
paragraph of his letter, however, is the most revealing, for it took all the
pomposity out of his rebuke:

>I do not know that a difference of opinion between myself
>and...B.S. can be of much interest...but in an age when every
>one, even the artist, is allowed to write about art, I claim the same
>privilege for a dealer. In a wide experience I have never met a real
>artist who disliked or distrusted his own talent or eyesight, but
>many who disliked and distrusted their own period and
>environment. Nor have I ever met a critic suffering from this
>superfluous modesty. The capacity for ignoring one's period and
>environment forms part of the equipment of the artist.[23]

The year of 1905 had been a year of deep personal tragedy and much
public acclaim, and it ended on another jarring note. On 19 December
Robbie was in Dresden for the first performance, by the Royal Opera
House, of Richard Strauss's opera, *Salome*, based on the German transla-

tion of Oscar Wilde's play. Robbie did not enjoy the glittering occasion; his appreciation of the music was clouded by the knowledge that Wilde had always regarded *Salome* as his finest dramatic work, but as an opera it lost much of its mystique. If Wilde had been haunted by the spectre of *Salome* as she craved the head of John the Baptist, then Robbie was haunted by the ghost of *De Profundis* and its future would be as traumatic as *Salome*.

Eight

Bibliography Men

HE EARLY part of 1906 was a time for celebration: on 2 February, almost eleven years after Wilde had begun his imprisonment, his bankruptcy was finally annulled. The Trustees of his Estate made a final payment of one shilling in the pound, as well as 4 per cent interest. With all Wilde's creditors satisfied and with the copyright of many of Wilde's works in his possession, Robbie could consider bringing out a uniform edition of Wilde's works. Methuen had further agreed to publish with the *Collected Works*, the bibliography that Walter Ledger and Christopher Millard were compiling, and Robbie was naturally taking an active part in all the arrangements with the publisher and the two bibliographers:

> I have seen Methuen and have persuaded him to consider the
> Bibliography by yourself [Millard] and Ledger in a separate volume
> uniform with the de-luxe edition. What would you be inclined to
> quote as a figure for buying it outright? Methuen is very stingy and I
> promised to contribute half of what they asked. I don't say this in
> order to cheapen your figure at all. Please don't think that. The
> reason Methuen insists on the Bibliography being bought outright is
> that he will only deal with it as a portion of the whole edition, for
> which he has made arrangements with the Estate of Wilde. The sum
> he will advance will eventually come out of the Estate and be
> deducted from the accounts, and my half will be out of my pocket.[1]

Millard did not think Methuen's suggestion was particularly generous, and felt sure that Ross was being asked to shoulder an unfair share of the financial burden. Ledger agreed with Millard, and Ross was asked to try and make better arrangements with the publisher. On 12 April Ross informed Millard of the latest proposals, which he in turn passed on to Ledger:

> I [Ross] have persuaded Methuen to consent to publication on a
> royalty basis and you [Millard] or Ledger, assuming Ledger
> consents, will have to go and see Methuen and make your own

arrangements. I do not think the Bibliography by itself will have a
very large sale, but I think it would always have a very steady sale
and I suggest that it should be published uniform with the de-luxe
edition, but should always be sold separately for the benefit of those
who do not wish to indulge in the uniform edition.[2]

Robbie's efforts were, however, largely wasted. Before the month was
out, the whole bibliography venture was put in jeopardy by the indiscreet actions of Millard. On 3 April from Oxford where he was staying,
Millard sent Robbie a fragrant reminder of the University city he loved:
'How can I thank you for the whiff of Oxford Meadows which you sent
me. The flowers remind me of Pater and Amohol, and indeed everything
connected with the divine city.'[3] Millard undoubtedly sought pleasures
with 'gay abandon' and on 24 April he was arrested at Iffley and charged
with committing, the previous July, an act of gross indecency with
nineteen-year-old Harry Tinson. Millard wired immediately to Robbie,
pleading for his help—a request that Robbie could not ignore, even if he
must have known the dangers he faced in again being involved in a case
of gross indecency. Writing to Walter Ledger on the Sunday evening
after Millard's arrest, Robbie confessed to feeling despair at the detention of the unfortunate man:

> I wrote to you hoping you would have particulars. On receiving your
> answer I wired to the Inspector of Police Station, sending a message
> to Millard and asking *what* the charge was. This morning I got a
> wire to say, "Gross Indecency".
>
> If I can I will go to Oxford *tomorrow*. It is very terrible but of
> course there is nothing to be done.
>
> I know nothing of Millard or his people or what his means are. I
> only know him as a student of Wilde's works.[4]

Robbie travelled to Oxford to be with Millard when he appeared
before the County Magistrate at the Bullingdon Petty Sessions on 5 May,
and as he admitted the next day to Ledger, his visit to the Court was
painful and extremely unpleasant:

> I really don't think it is necessary to go into details about poor
> Millard. His case has been remanded for seven days, but a new and
> more serious charge had been proposed against him, and if he is
> sentenced he is liable to get 10 years' penal servitude. I saw him in
> Prison before the case came on. He was extremely amusing and self-
> confident. I did not mention your name as he did not do so. I am

glad to say that his mother and his cousin Lord Basing have
instructed Counsel to represent him. I was only in Court for about
an hour as I could not endure the evidence.[5]

Millard was remanded for a further week and bail was refused. The
Counsel instructed by his family was Charles Mathews; a rather unfortunate choice, since he had been junior Counsel at the trials of Wilde. At
his next appearance before the Bullingdon Magistrates, Millard was
found guilty of the lesser charge of gross indecency and was sent to the
Assizes for sentencing, where he received a term of three months'
imprisonment. Millard was probably very lucky not to be treated as
harshly as Oscar Wilde.

The imprisonment of Millard should have been a salutary lesson to
Robbie, but whatever he might have said in public about Millard's
crimes, it certainly did not prevent him from making a major change to
his own style of living. On 27 May 1906 Freddie Smith, who had been
working as Robbie's secretary for nearly three years, celebrated his
twentieth birthday. Shortly before the anniversary, Robbie took him to
live at 15 Vicarage Gardens. Smith had developed into a gifted and
talented actor and was in constant demand by amateur dramatic clubs
including the St James's Dramatic Society, where he was often called
upon to play the leading romantic role. He possessed a fine voice and
when reciting poetry could hold an audience spellbound, an unusual
achievement in such a young actor.

Robbie's sisters and his nieces and nephews were horrified by his
blatant disregard of social conventions. A family conference was called
and it was decided that Mary's eldest son Edward[6] should immediately
go to see his uncle and remonstrate with him. The family all agreed that
Robbie should be ordered to end forthwith the living arrangements with
Smith. Robbie did not enjoy being lectured to by his elders and he
definitely was not going to have his private life dictated by the whims of a
twenty-eight-year-old nephew, even if he was only acting as spokesman
for the rest of the family. The ensuing row with Edward left an indelible
mark on Robbie's tolerant nature. Robbie never forgave Edward or his
two sons, who continued to be deprived of his generous and sympathetic
company.

It is difficult to know if Alex was a party to the family deputation; he
was always willing to forgive his brother's indiscretions and to make
allowances for him. His support of Robbie rarely if ever faltered,
although he was often at the end of his tether by the actions of his
impulsive and eccentric brother. Edward's mother must also have had

divided loyalties in the row between her son and her brother. She had a
deep affection for Robbie and this would never diminish, but his relationship with Smith was an intolerable burden for her to bear.

In spite of the hostilities of the family, Robbie continued to share his
home with Freddie Smith, on a more or less permanent basis, for the
next ten years. It was an odd flaunting of convention, and although he
had, since leaving home in 1890, shared his home with More Adey, in
taking Smith to live with him he was publicly admitting his homosexuality. He was also breaking both the criminal law and ecclesiastical law;
the former could have resulted in his arrest, conviction and imprisonment, the latter in his excommunication from the Church of Rome. In
later years Robbie admitted, somewhat ruefully, that after Oscar Wilde
and Bosie Douglas, Freddie Smith came closest in his affections. With a
strange lack of comprehension of the dangers, Robbie even encouraged a
friendship between Freddie Smith and Christopher Millard. This con-
voluted behaviour is hard to understand, but Robbie was all his life able
to keep entirely separate his personal relationships from his public
persona.

Freddie Smith brought into Robbie's life a measure of contentment and
he went some way to easing the loneliness Robbie had endured since the
death of Oscar Wilde. In 1906 Robbie took up his neglected career in
journalism, and began to contribute almost weekly to the *Academy*. Of
the many journals, magazines and newspapers to which Robbie contributed, the *Academy* always held a very special place in his heart. It was a
weekly magazine devoted to literature, drama, art and music, and it
fulfilled many of the cultural requirements of Robbie's life. First published in 1870 the *Academy*, had, under the editorship of Harold Hann-
yngton Child, become a journal of literary and artistic excellence, though
perversely it was never a financial success. Its reputation remained high
for as long as Child remained its editor. He was the first to recognise all
the differing aspects of Robbie's writing talents, and he was not reticent
in saying exactly what he felt:

> Next, for doing what you have done singled out my little paper for
> honour. I consider it no less. Such brilliant work as yours could find
> a home in any paper in London. You chose me, and are content
> with our wretchedly inadequate pay, when you could get double the
> amount and (alas!) many more readers, anywhere else. It is unselfish
> of me to point this out to you: for Heaven's sake, and mine, don't go
> and act on it. If the *Academy* "dies in my arms", I shall still regard
> my connection with it with pride, as having enabled me to print
> your articles.[7]

In his early articles in the *Academy* Robbie was often modest and failed to sign his name to the work, but his delicate and suggestive wit rarely masked completely that the words had indeed come from his persuasive pen. In an appreciation of the work of Aubrey Beardsley his anonymity fooled no one:

> I am led to these reflections by the memory of Aubrey Beardsley and the reception which his work received, not from the British Public, but from the inner circle of advanced intellectuals. Too much occupied with the obstetrics of art, his superfluity of naughtiness has tarnished his niche in the Temple of Fame. "A wish to *épater les bourgeois*", says Mr Arthur Symons, "is a natural one." I do not think so; at least in an artist. Now much of Beardsley's work shows the *éblouissement* of the burgess on arriving at Montmartre for the first time—a weakness he shared with some of his contemporaries.[8]

Later in the article, Robbie recalled with pleasure the publisher Leonard Smithers and his association with Beardsley:

> When no one would publish Beardsley's work Mr Smithers stepped into the breach. I do not know that the *Savoy* exactly healed the breach between Beardsley and the public, but it gave the artist another opportunity; and Mr Arthur Symons an occasion for song and prose. Mr Leonard Smithers, too, was the most delightful and irresponsible publisher I ever knew. Who remembers without a kindly feeling that little shop in the Royal Arcade (et in Arcadia ego) with its tempting shelves; its limited editions of 5000 copies; the shy, infrequent purchaser; the upstairs room where the roar of respectable Bond Street came faintly through the tightly closed windows; the genial proprietor?[9]

Smithers, in replying to the article, was justly critical of Robbie's 'one besetting sin—over-great modesty'; and he rightly corrected Robbie's fallible memory, by pointing out that he never published more than five hundred copies of any of Beardsley's books, and even then he would be left with unsold copies. He admitted, however, that since Beardsley's death his work was now selling at a handsome premium over the original cover price.

The appreciation of art and artists remained Robbie's first love and when, in May, the Carfax purchased part of the Butts Collection of William Blake's drawings,[10] he used the opportunity to stage an exhibition at the Gallery of Blake's works. As well as the Butts Collection, he arranged the loan of Blake's largest and most spectacular picture *The Canterbury Pilgrims* from Sir William Stirling Maxwell. Sir Charles Dilke and Graham Robertson were among many other generous contributors. Unable to conceal his pride in the exhibition, and contemptuous of the dictate that a dealer should not praise his own wares, Robbie wrote appreciations for both the *Burlington Magazine* and the *Academy*:

> It is unlikely that an exhibition can ever be got together which would show Blake to greater advantage than this at Carfax: by its limitations it probably produces a greater cumulative effect than even the famous and comprehensive collection shown at the Burlington Fine Arts Club thirty years ago, for there are comparatively few of the worse class of his drawings on the walls, though those few might well have been eliminated. It is an exhibition of the utmost importance to all who are interested in imaginative art, and it will, no doubt, set seal on the appreciation which has grown of late to such a remarkable extent. But Blake is badly served by those who overpraise him. As a speculative mystic he would stand first in a far more distinguished company than that of his compatriots: as a poet and as a painter he might perhaps be accorded a place relatively similar—he is honourable among the thirty, howbeit he attains not to the first three. But by so much as the hierarchy of the poets of England exceeds in honour that of the painters does the glory of Blake the painter pale before the glory of Blake the poet.[11]

Robbie was not only art critic, under Child's generous editorship, but could indulge his love of drama, and, as expected, he brought his own inimitable style to the drama columns of the *Academy*; his wayward sense of humour was never far from the surface of his writings:

> Are dramatic critics any use? That question must often occur to actor-managers when distributing stalls for first nights of their plays. Is Sir Fretful really worth ten-and-sixpence? It was asked and answered two years ago; I ask it again. Useful and in many cases delightful contributors to their respective papers, do they affect the success of a piece? I know they nearly always say the same thing, and you can guess pretty well what that is going to be at the first *entr'acte* when they meet at the bar. But most of them are mere stylists who use the drama as a pianola for giving expression to their views on life and occasionally on actors. I foresee a time coming, a

time of revolution when, instead of actors craving notices from
eminent critics, as they are supposed to do, you will get the critic
pressing champagne and chicken on dramatic authors (N.B. Mr
Shaw is vegetarian and total abstainer) in order to get a "notice"
from over the footlights.[12]

Although he had perverse opinions on the value of drama critics,
especially those who wrote for a weekly magazine, Robbie, nevertheless,
continued to delight the readers of the *Academy* with his decisive criticisms. He rarely tried to emulate the drama critics of the daily press, and
he certainly saw no reason in the *Academy* merely to repeat what critics of
the calibre of Bernard Shaw and William Archer had already said so
eloquently and perceptively. He restricted himself to enjoying the toler-
ance of an editor who did not attempt to shackle him. In a comment on
an evening's entertainment at the Court Theatre, given by the English
Drama Society, he pricked the consciences of the archaic Royal Aca-
demicians, who were frequently the butt of his witticisms:

> How strange that social phrases retain their form and change their
> meaning or, perhaps, it is not strange at all. A lady the other day at
> dinner, where conversation flagged, asked me if I believed in *Ghosts*.
> I thought she referred to spiritual phenomena: but it was Ibsen's
> play. I have observed a similar mistake about the ACADEMY.
> "Have you seen the ACADEMY?" used to be a safe question from
> May till August bank holiday, and from January till March, when it
> referred to the summer and winter shows of pictures respectively;
> now it is a safe question all the year round and it never refers to that
> exploded institution at Burlington House.[13]

It was wholly consistent with Robbie's total lack of pretension and
sycophancy to social consciences, that when the Bijou Theatre put on an
amateur production of Arthur Symons's morality play, *The Fool of the
World*, with Freddie Smith in the role of Old Age, Robbie used the
freedom of the *Academy* to praise his young friend's acting abilities:

> (I find fault with Mr Symons in his symbolism), the part was
> rendered with marvellous skill by Mr F. Stanley Smith, who by a
> paradox very common on the stage was the youngest of the
> performers. I have heard him compared, not ineptly, with the child
> actor, Salathiel Pavy, immortalised by Ben Jonson. Elizabethan
> experts will remember the pretty conceit by which Ben Jonson has
> explained his early loss. I hope that Mr Stanley Smith may be seen

and heard, not only in Elizabethan drama, in which he has already
distinguished himself, but again in modern plays such as *The Fool of
the World*, where the adequate rendering of small parts counts for so
much.[14]

Always willing to poke fun at himself, Robbie, however, could never
resist the temptation of exposing the unjust censorship laws and the
arbitrary way in which plays were granted a performing licence. He
concluded his article with a frivolous invention:

> I have just written a morality play myself, prohibited by the County
> Council and the Censor, whom it satirises severely. It combines the
> poetry of Mr Arthur Symons with the actuality of Brieux's *Maternité*
> and will satisfy, I hope, the aims and ambition of all these
> associations. The play will be performed at the Bijou Theatre,
> William Archer Street, Bayswater. Admission Free. No tickets are
> necessary, but every one must bring a copy of the ACADEMY of
> next Saturday, and this will form the voucher, with date of
> performance. The play is entitled *Every Householder: A Mystery*, by
> Robert Ross.[15]

Robbie's articles were often written in the first person, yet they should
not be regarded as autobiographical; he chose which parts of his life to
include, which to leave out, which parts to exaggerate, and which parts
to belittle. He had a well-developed sense of humour, which at times
bordered on the bizarre, although beneath the mask of the jester, there
was a sensitive, lonely, insecure man, at odds with himself. He made
friends easily, but in giving his love to Oscar Wilde, he trapped himself
in a vortex from which there was no lasting escape. Given other circumstances, he might have developed into a serious playwright or a dramatic
author, but it was his destiny to play the trifler. He was, though,
concerned about the diversity and frequency of his signed articles, and
he chose to use a pseudonym which he had first used when writing for
the *Saturday Review* in the 1890s. It obviously appealed to his wry sense
of humour that at the time of his conversion to the Roman Catholic faith,
he should adopt the name of Christian Freeborn as a mask of anonymity.
He fooled no one. The delicate touch of his writings was too apparent to
all those who knew the sharpness and perception of his pen. In an article
which took a particularly devastating swipe at his fellow drama critics, he
was probably correct in trying to hide behind the religious garb of a
freeborn Christian:

> Could he [Mr Beerbohm Tree] be induced to start a school for
> dramatic critics? That there is a crying need for some such
> institution, the dramatic notices in the daily press afford a
> melancholy proof. My complaint against a particular class of
> journalist is not that his point of view is stupid or old-fashioned. It is
> only fair that stupidity should have its recognised mouthpiece on the
> staff of every paper, especially on a question of such commercial
> importance as the drama. The majority of plays are written down to
> the intelligence of the dramatic critics. A play, even when it is a
> failure, is seen and discussed by persons who never think of reading
> the other lies in a newspaper. Old-fashioned people, numerically less
> than the stupid, are also of considerable importance. Age does not
> wither for them the Robertsonian drama, nor does custom stale the
> infinite Variety stage. Age has nothing to do with prejudices and
> predilections.[16]

In June, the Literary Theatre Society staged for a private audience Oscar
Wilde's *Salome*, and as it was only a short play they asked Robbie if he
would allow them to stage another of Wilde's works on the same pro-
gramme. Robbie offered them the uncompleted *A Florentine Tragedy*.
Wilde had always meant to add the opening scene to the play, but as
Robbie commented: 'It was characteristic of the author to finish what he
never began.'[17] Thomas Sturge Moore, who was on the committee of the
Literary Theatre Society, asked to be allowed to add the opening scene,
to which Robbie readily gave his consent. When it was completed
Robbie was the first to agree that even Wilde would not have been
unhappy with the scene:

> It is not for me to criticise his work, but there is justification for
> saying that Wilde himself would have envied, with artist's envy,
> such lines as
>> We will sup with the moon,
>> Like Persian princes that in Babylon
>> Sup in the hanging gardens of the king.
> In a stylistic sense Mr Sturge Moore has accomplished a feat in
> reconstruction, whatever opinions may be held of *A Florentine
> Tragedy* by Wilde's admirers or detractors. The achievement is
> particularly remarkable because Mr Sturge Moore has nothing in
> common with Wilde other than what is shared by all real poets and
> dramatists. He is a landed proprietor on Parnassus, not a trespasser.
> In England we are more familiar with the poachers. Time and Death
> are of course necessary before there can come any adequate
> recognition of one of our most original and gifted singers.[18]

The stage scenery and dresses were designed by Charles Ricketts, which pleased Robbie a good deal; his admiration of Ricketts and Shannon had never diminished since they had first illustrated and published a number of Wilde's early works. At the performance on 18 June, the audience responded to the performance with enthusiasm; there were three curtain calls for *A Florentine Tragedy* and four for *Salome*. The press, however, were unanimous in their failure to give the production any critical coverage. The drama critic of *The Times* went so far as to return his tickets. Robbie, who was well used to such diverse attitudes, between the public and the press, said of the critics: 'And much pleasure has been derived from reading those criticisms, all carefully preserved along with the list of receipts which were simultaneously pouring in from the German performances.'[19] He could afford to ignore what the dramatic critics were saying about Wilde's plays, as theatrical producers and composers were showing an interest in Wilde's unfinished play; Puccini had indeed expressed a desire to turn *A Florentine Tragedy* into an opera, but unfortunately nothing came of the venture.

There were, though, other matters connected with Wilde's Estate that had a more successful outcome. On 14 August the Probate Court granted to Robbie Letters of Administration, and he was at last officially recognised as Wilde's literary executor. The Receiver of Bankruptcy valued Wilde's Estate at £100 and paid over to Robbie the sum of £79 16s, the balance left after all Wilde's creditors had been paid.

Christopher Millard served his sentence and on his release he appealed to Robbie to find him paid employment. Robbie obliged and Millard started work at the *Burlington Magazine* and was also able to assist Robbie with the editing of Wilde's *Collected Works*. At the end of September shortly before he left London on holiday, Robbie acquainted Millard with the problems he was encountering with the forthcoming publication, complaining bitterly that the cost and intricacies of publishing were causing him great distress:

> Every kind of effort has been made to obtain *Dorian Gray* but
> Carrington's final demand was for £425. Of course neither Methuen
> nor the Wilde Estate nor myself have got that amount of money and
> even if we had I do not really think it is worth that. Methuen would
> be fairly willing to pay a reasonable sum for a licence to include
> *Dorian Gray* in the uniform edition... Carrington only owns the
> English rights and all we really want of him is the right to sell five
> hundred copies and fifty Japanese [vellum]. We would if he
> preferred it give him a royalty of fifteen per cent which is the exact

amount that Methuen is giving for the other old books.... Except
for the sentiment of having all the books of Wilde's complete in at
least *one* edition *I am* really indifferent and I don't mind in the least
who publishes it. The only people who will be irritated are the
public. Methuen highly disapproves of *Dorian Gray* and is delighted
that there are so many difficulties. Carrington has not got such a
really great asset as he thinks. It is certainly not worth what he
thinks.[20]

In late October Edmund Gosse became literary editor of the newly
created *Books*, the *Daily Mail Literary Supplement*; but in spite of his
early enthusiasm Gosse did not particularly enjoy the experience. He
found the task of editor irksome, and the magazine unjustly earned the
reputation of being dull and boring although it had an impressive list of
contributors, including G.K. Chesterton, Thomas Hardy, Andrew
Lang, Arthur Symonds, and Robbie, who, of course, relished the prospect of writing for yet another magazine. He had completely regained his
appetite for the written word, and rarely a week passed when he was not
busily engaged in constructive criticism of a friend's artistic achievement, literary creation or dramatic rendition. He wrote a parody of *Faust*
entitled *A Little Doctored Faust*, a poem which he adapted from *The
Russian of Erick Schweiger: The Land-Grave*; and an essay called 'The
Eleventh Muse' which he called a 'Rehabilitation' which deflated any
pomposity he might have felt at the sheer volume of his literary achievements that year:

> In the closing years of the last century I held the position of a
> publisher's hack. Having failed in everything except sculpture, I
> became publisher's reader and adviser. It was the age of the *dicky
> dongs* [decadence] and, of course, I only advised the publication of
> deciduous literature and books which dealt with the history of
> decay. The business unfortunately closed before my plans were
> materialised, but we had a really brilliant series of works prepared
> for an ungrateful public. A cheap and abridged edition of Gibbon
> was to have heralded the *Ruined Home* Library, as we only dealt
> with the decline and fall of things, and eschewed motley in both
> senses of the word. *Bad Taste in All Ages* (twelve volumes, edited by
> myself) would have rivalled some of Mr Sidney Lee's monumental
> undertakings. It was a memory of these unfulfilled designs which
> turned my thoughts to an old note-book the skeleton of what was
> destined never to be a book in being.[21]

It had been another year of personal and private triumphs: Robbie was, perhaps, happier than he had been since Wilde's imprisonment. His reputation as an art critic and dealer was high; his work on behalf of Wilde's Estate was being recognised by both publishers and private citizens. His writing was liberally interspersed with humour and wit, and he had no difficulty in getting his work printed. His circle of friends had never been larger and Freddie Smith's friendship was an additional pleasure. The exhibitions at the Carfax had been widely acclaimed and he was also involved with the Whitechapel Art Gallery, which gave him a chance to further praise the work of his friends. In his art criticisms he often laid bare his own soul; he abhorred all forms of bigotry, he had compassion for all minorities, and this he well illustrated when writing of the exhibition of Jewish Art at the Whitechapel Art Gallery:

> One of the greatest bores on earth is the Anti-Semite, and for him, at least, the show should be a liberal education. He will be disappointed to find no examples of those peculiar knives used in the ritual murders of young boys...I will confess to a little disappointment myself at the exhibition, but for entirely different reasons. The art is inadequate. History, controversy, and archaeology predominate. No one expects the Jews to forget their wrongs, even in England; but Mr Zangwill is always here to jog their memories; and hideous news arrives from Russia at regular intervals to remind us that the Jewish question is still a political and economic problem of which we may be sure that social quacks of the Nordau type have not found the solution. For next to the Anti-Semite among bores the Zionist bears the palms...Mr Rothenstein is one of the dominating factors in the new English Art Club, and it is obvious to every one how much he has influenced the younger men Mr Orpen, Mr John, Mr McEvoy all of whom are now weaned and asserting their own vivid individualities; but how much they owe to Mr Rothenstein only future Berensons will appreciate. Though Mr Rothenstein is more of a painter than ever poor Solomon was, he stands in the same relation to his young Christian contemporaries as Solomon did to Rossetti and his circle. I wish it had been possible to have all his pictures brought together in the small single room, where, however, you observe a beautiful binding by Miss Josephine Birkenruth and admirable work by her brother Adolph.[22]

In praising the work of the young South African painter Adolphus Birkenruth, Robbie was forging another link in the chain between him and Reggie Turner, who was the young artist's generous patron. It was, though, to be a friendship that would bring him distress and despair and further increase the stresses in his relationship with Turner.

Nine

Art of Friendship

F THERE was a father-figure in Robbie's life, then it was Edmund Gosse. Robbie turned to Gosse whenever he needed moral or emotional comfort; he was a frequent visitor at Gosse's Sunday afternoon gatherings at Hanover Terrace; he also remained a family favourite with Ellen (Nellie) Gosse and her children. Gosse was very much an Establishment man, and he devoted much of his time to sitting on Committees: the London Library, Royal Literary Fund, the Royal Society of Literature and the Society of Authors. There was rarely a request made to Gosse that did not immediately receive a favourable response, so much so, that Robbie, on one occasion, remarked with typical witty insight, 'that, we were obliged some years ago to found a little secret society, of which he [Gosse] is not even an honorary member, for the protection of Edmund Gosse, for those seeking eleemosynary assistance, by a special arrangement with his family begging letters are carefully intercepted, and presentation copies of poems are consigned to the flames.'[1]

His friendship with Edmund Gosse brought Robbie into contact with many of the leading literary figures of the day; it was at one of Gosse's Sunday afternoon receptions that Robbie first met Henry James, Thomas Hardy, George Moore and Arthur Symonds. But it was not only the famous who attended Gosse's literary salons, many young and unknown writers were to be found at these gatherings. Gosse was an ideal companion for Robbie; they shared that unique ability which turned conversation into an art form. They were never boring or bigoted, although both were, perversely, egotistic and snobbish.

The disgrace and trauma of the Wilde trial had worried Gosse, mainly—it must be admitted—on Robbie's behalf; he had little sympathy for Wilde the man or Wilde the writer. Indeed he once wrote 'What I principally hated about him [Wilde], poor creature, was not at all his vices, but his unreality.'[2] Gosse never had the same problem with Robbie, who, in his own way, was as prone to romanticise as Wilde. In April 1907, after six uninspiring months, Gosse relinquished his position with the *Daily Mail Literary Supplement*; Robbie was left to express his regret at the loss of such a generous and thoughtful editor:

More than any other of your other contributors I am indebted to you
because you were the first editor (of a serious publication) who
appreciated my work and you are the first distinguished man of
letters to have expressed any appreciation of it by word or deed. It is
in no spirit of egoism that I claim to reciprocate in a special way that
emotion to which you refer but I cannot alas evince it in your
inimitable manner, while to express what must be the general feeling
of your contributors requires the art of the poets who were among
us—an art not mine. The knowledge that you were a fastidious
editor was to me stimulating and the labour in giving the best that
was in me became a pleasure, a delightful anxiety which I shall miss
more than I can tell you.[3]

Gosse could, though, still delight in the success Robbie was receiving
for his articles and particularly those which appeared in the *Academy* but,
like all Gosse's praise, there was an element of censure in his words:

The articles have given me a great deal of pleasure. They show that
you only need free space—I mean the good will of an admiring and
tolerant editor—to make you an excellent writer.... In the matter of
style, the only thing that jars upon me is the *vivisection* passage.[4]
This marks the difference between what is effective in speech and
writing. If people had been sitting round a table, this *boutade* would
have been highly successful—we should all have laughed. But for
written irony, it is too heavy. The mind is not stimulated, but
troubled by it, and is thrown off the track of ideas. Irony is a most
delicate artifice and it should always be used so as to aid and
illuminate, not to obscure, the line of thought. Your paragraph is
too startling and attracts attention to *itself*, and not to the general
trend of argument. Will you forgive me?...But I am delighted that
you are writing so much, and doing it so well. You ought to aim at
the highest distinction, and I don't see why you should not get it.
You have qualities of satiric humour and whimsical independence
which are altogether your own. Your courage is extraordinary—in
fact it is a snare to you. But these are lines on which you should go
far.[5]

It is surprising that in all of the many essays that appeared in the
Academy during 1906 and 1907, Robbie never once wrote about Oscar
Wilde the man. Indeed, throughout his life, he confined himself to
writing only Forewords to his dead friend's literary works. Seemingly,
he had decided very early on, that he would leave it to others to write the

fiction of Wilde's life, while he contrived to allow Wilde's own words to speak their beautiful messages.

In March he had the pleasure of seeing *The Duchess of Padua* performed for the first time at the St James's Theatre, loaned for the occasion by George Alexander. Even though the actors were only members of the dramatic society of the St James's Church, it was another memorable milestone in Robbie's campaign to salvage Wilde's literary reputation.

Later that spring Robbie developed, in an essay entitled 'Blunderbore', a theme which had long lain dormant in his mind: his heart never wholly belonged to England, his adopted home, but remained somewhere in France, the land of his birth, if not of his blood. He never lost his spiritual, physical or cultural ties with the people of France:

> Ideas, especially ideas connected with the Fine Arts, are quite often born in England; but a fresh idea about anything is always branded as illegitimate with us and dies from strangulation or neglect, unless sent over to be weaned in France, that dear country and benign foster-mother of intellect. The young bastard grows up strong and well and then is smuggled over one day when no one is looking, just as if he was one of the Tauchnitz edition. Like the Irishman, he gazes on his native shore for the first time, but he does not recognise it; the cut is reciprocated; English criticism brings out a sort of unrepealed Aliens Act from the recesses of its hollow mind; it invokes the public to resist the insidious *French* idea, which, it foresees, will undermine all that is *best and brightest* in English literature.... One of our chief debts to France is that she nourishes our ideas, transforms them, makes them her own, just as she transplanted and transmuted the flower of the Renaissance in an earlier day. With all our national vanity we never dispute the parentage. It is only territory and diplomatic prestige and commerce about which we quarrel with our *sweet enemy*. Paris is the cradle, or rather the intellectual crèche, of Europe. We can leave our ideas there with perfect safety, and they will come back to us in all the radiance of youth—royalists, socialists, chauvinists, clericals, freethinkers—but citizens of the Third Republic. How grievous, therefore, to find Paris turned into a dispensary for quack nostrums which we rightly discarded long ago. We are inventing others. America is our only lawful competitor.[6]

Early in the year Alfred Douglas wrote to Robbie confessing that he was bored with life, even though he had ample opportunities to hunt, shoot and fish, but his constant lack of money was causing him concern. In suggesting that Bosie Douglas should take paid employment as assistant editor of the *Academy*, Robbie was guilty of an extreme lack of perception. Douglas was a gifted poet and *littérateur*, but Robbie failed to take into account Douglas's unstable and inconsistent character. Douglas did, initially, have the help and guidance of Harold Child, who was able to exercise editorial control over Douglas's wilder eccentricities.

Robbie had little time to worry about Douglas's editorial expertise, although like other readers of the *Academy* he was pleased when poems by both Olive and Bosie Douglas began to appear, including Bosie's eulogy of Oscar Wilde, 'The Dead Poet', which was printed on 21 September 1907. Robbie was busy at the Carfax but Freddie Smith was still acting as his secretary and was able to ease his burdens. Millard was finding it hard to adjust to life after his imprisonment, but when he met a young Scottish Wykehamist, Charles Scott-Moncrieff, it gave both him and Robbie a great deal of pleasure. Scott-Moncrieff was at Edinburgh University when he first met Robbie and, in spite of Millard's questionable background, Robbie had no scruples about encouraging the friendship with the shy, charming but surly young Scot, who delighted them both by writing letters full of racy literary criticisms.

Millard was concerned, however, that his homosexual activities were attracting adverse attention from the Authorities, and after a period of unease he decided to go abroad. He hoped that in France, where there was a more tolerant attitude to homosexuality, he would be able to live without fear of arrest. Millard's decision did not please his brother. Robbie, though, was not dismayed; he expected his friends to behave illogically and irrationally, and they usually did not disappoint him:

> Moncrieff is due to come here Monday or Tuesday. He has told me
> the hour of his arrival and the method of his arrival; indeed
> everything except the *date*. He is obviously a real poet. I have had a
> long letter from your brother which I have not answered yet; it
> contained nothing important except that he thinks your residence
> abroad dooms you to destruction. I am going to write to him to say
> that I entirely differ from his point of view, and I will have an
> interview with him a little later on. You know I am awfully rushed
> during the day-time. When you write to Graham tell him I will
> answer his letter quite shortly.[7]

Millard did not remain in France for long; before the end of the summer he was back in London. Robbie was not displeased, for he had a great deal of work for Millard to do with the forthcoming publication of

Wilde's *Collected Works*. There had been, though, problems concerning
the bibliography, the collaboration with Ledger had come to an end, and
Robbie admitted he was unsure as to why this had happened:

> I cannot quite remember whether Methuen decided to give up the
> bibliography because Ledger would not deal or because of your
> disaster at Oxford. I have had so many rows with Methuen that I
> cannot now remember at the present moment.[8]

If Robbie had no problem in sharing a friendship with Millard,
Freddie Smith and Charles Scott-Moncrieff, Ledger was not so inclined.
Ledger seemed unable to be honest and truthful in acknowledging his
associations with the discredited man. There was a subtle difference in
the help Ledger gave; it was private and discreet, and he would not
consent to have his name publicly associated with the Wilde bibliography
after Millard had been convicted of gross indecency. In many ways they
were an odd circle of friends; they had many characteristics in common
and shared many interests. Yet each reacted quite differently to the
traumas which surrounded them. Robbie never once sought to renounce
his friendship with Oscar Wilde; indeed he frequently boasted of it, and
in the end he gave his life in defending it. He never came to terms with
the fact that in living his life as he did, he ignored the law just as
decisively as Oscar Wilde had broken it. Walter Ledger, by contrast, was
passionate in his love of Wilde's writings, but could not face a hostile
society and admit that he shared Wilde's sexual tastes. A gentle, solitary
man, he had a dreadful fear of being thought ridiculous. Millard, on the
other hand, did not care what society thought of him. He did not care
whether he was fairly judged for his sexual predilections. He was only
too aware that there were others who were more wicked and more
depraved than himself. He knew Oscar Wilde had been harshly judged
and he knew that Robbie Ross was being unfairly treated by a section of
British society who were no better than he.

In early June Robbie was confined to bed, his physical strength was
never a match for the enormous pressure he exerted on it. He was often
exhausted at the end of a working day, and the requests for assistance
were never-ending. At the Carfax Gallery he was arranging an exhibition
of the works of his old friends Charles Ricketts and Charles Shannon.
The exhibition opened in July and Robbie, under the initials of C.F.,
wrote an appreciation, which appeared in the *Academy*:

> Mr Ricketts perhaps alone of modern painters may be compared
> with artists of the Renaissance in the variety and skill with which he

practises in different mediums, and the modes of expressing one of
the most striking and intense individualities of the present
day.... The object of art criticism should, I believe, be directed
more towards urging people to go and see pictures for themselves
than to give readers an idea of what the critics think about them.
Modern painters have at all events a great advantage over old
masters. Their authenticity is unquestioned. You must judge for
yourself about modern pictures.... Those who cannot see the divine
beauty of Mr Shannon's *Hermes and the Infant Bacchus*, or that other
marvellous *tondo* the *Sleeping Nymph* and his half-dozen other
pictures had better not look at any modern work at all.[9]

Work continued to progress satisfactorily on the publication, by Methuen, of Wilde's *Collected Works*, but the first edition would not be ready until early in 1908. In the meantime, Robbie obtained a copy of a widely circulated prospectus, which announced the forthcoming publication in the United States of the *Collected Works of Oscar Wilde*. He was naturally furious that the American edition would be available before the authorised Methuen edition, and that it contained two disreputable works, 'The Priest and the Acolyte' and a translation from the French of Barbey d'Aurevilly's 'What Never Dies'. He had thought there was no longer any dispute in the literary world that Wilde had not written the former which Robbie regarded as 'a pornographic story which no one with any knowledge of the author's style—of any style—would dream of attributing to him: it is destitute of any literary *form*';[10] and Wilde had most certainly not translated the latter. Robbie might have overlooked these very obvious mistakes, but what he could not ignore was that the American publishers had not sought his approval for the publication; nor, as far as he could see, were they prepared to pay royalties to Wilde's Estate. However, what angered him most, was that the Introduction to the edition was written by Richard Le Gallienne, who claimed a friendship with Wilde, which Robbie regarded to be false. Robbie gave vent to his rage in a letter that was published in the *Times Literary Supplement* at the end of June:

Mr Le Gallienne, the American prospectus informs us, "aside from
being a writer of national reputation, was a lifelong friend of Oscar
Wilde and his college chum at Oxford". This will certainly be news
to many people in England; it points to grave omissions in the pages
of *Who's Who*; *Liverpool* and *Fleet-street*, to the compilers of that
ingenious Temple of Fame, are dearer names than Athens or
Thebes! Mr Le Gallienne, however, must have lost some of his

Oxford manner during his residence in America, for he can hardly claim ignorance on the vexed subject of "American rights"; it is amazing that he should lend his name and "his national reputation" to what he must know is a literary and financial offence, against the English publishers and the legal representatives of "his college chum at Oxford".[11]

With the difficulties of transatlantic communications, it was October before Le Gallienne's reply was published. In early August, shortly before he was due to go away on holiday, Robbie was granted one of his dearest wishes. He had never given up the hope that, one day, he would be able to renew his friendship with Cyril and Vyvyan Holland, Oscar Wilde's sons. Every action he had taken since the death of Wilde had been dictated by his feelings of remorse for the suffering inflicted on the two little boys he had last seen in April 1895. There was, perhaps, the hand of destiny guiding Vyvyan Holland when he attended the crammers' school of Scoones in July 1907; he quickly made friends with Sir Coleridge Kennard, thus opening the way for a meeting with Robbie. Sir Coleridge Kennard was the son of Mrs Helen Carew, a friend of Oscar Wilde, who, after his disgrace and subsequent death, remained true to his memory. At dinner in Hans Place, Mrs Carew's home, Vyvyan Holland heard, for the first time in twelve years, someone speak of his late father with respect and admiration. Later in the evening, Mrs Carew tentatively asked Vyvyan if he would object to meeting Robbie Ross. She was mortified when Vyvyan admitted he had no recollection of Robbie and could not recall ever having met him, nor did he know what Robbie had done for his late father. He listened attentively as Helen Carew outlined all that Robbie had done to rescue Wilde's literary reputation from oblivion. It was a shock for Vyvyan to learn that there were, in London, people who envied him for being Oscar Wilde's son and did not, as he had always been told by his mother's relatives, regard him as an object of pity.

On 7 August, a week after the dinner at Hans Place, Vyvyan returned again to Mrs Carew's home and there he met Max Beerbohm, Reggie Turner and Robbie. If he felt apprehensive, Robbie did not show it, and it was obvious from the first that he and Wilde's younger son shared a common sense of destiny. Vyvyan later wrote of that first meeting: 'I knew that I had found a true friend of my own, one who would be loyal and true and never betray me.'[12] Vyvyan was certainly attracted to the older man, and Robbie, on returning to his own chambers, committed his thoughts to paper, saying in a letter to Vyvyan, what he could never have said at the dinner table:

I regret very much that I was not allowed to see both you and Cyril
in the years that have intervened since the tragedy which has
darkened your life and about which I know you yourself must feel so
bitterly. I believe that I could have made your childhood happier,
and it would have made me happier too to know that you realised
how fond and devoted I was to you both, because you were the sons
of my greatest friend and the most distinguished man of letters in
the last years of the last century.[13]

Robbie recognised in Wilde's son all the charm and sensitivity of
Constance and the gaiety and enthusiasm for life of his father. Robbie
acted as mentor and guide to Vyvyan Holland, introducing the young
man to all his father's old and valued friends, including Adela Schuster,
the lady from Wimbledon, who had given Oscar Wilde £1000 towards
the legal expenses for his defence at the Old Bailey. He met Ernest and
Ada Leverson, who had sheltered Wilde when all other doors in London
were closed to him. Robbie delighted in the company of the young man,
but there was still a doubt about how Cyril would react to him. As the
elder of the two boys, Cyril had been more aware of the tragedy which
had shattered his life and ruined the happiness of his mother. He still
carried the unhealed wounds of that terrible episode in his young life.

Robbie was nervous and uneasy as the first meeting with Cyril
approached. Vyvyan had given him dire warnings to be careful in his
choice of topics of conversation. They dined in the convivial and liberal
atmosphere of the Reform Club. Most of Robbie's fears were unfounded,
although he and Cyril differed on the relative merits of literature and art;
Robbie's charm and generous spirit soon won the admiration of the elder
brother, and he very quickly regarded him as a 'lifelong friend'.

There is an illusion of unreality surrounding the friendship between
the three men; if, as many of Wilde's friends and enemies believed,
Robbie was the boy who had led Wilde into his homosexual ways both
before and after his imprisonment, then the friendship between him and
Wilde's sons is almost beyond belief. But if the stories were based on
animosity and myth, then the truth of their friendship was more prosaic
and it became a truly great memorial to them all. Robbie gave much of
his life to defending his friendship with Oscar Wilde, and in giving the
hand of friendship to Cyril and Vyvyan Holland he returned to them
their natural birthright. The callousness and bigotry of the general
public was such that Wilde's sons could never again carry his name with
pride, yet, in restoring his literary reputation Robbie gave them more
than just a proud name—he gave them a place in the history of the
twentieth century.

Richard Le Gallienne did not take kindly to Robbie's rebuke, and in a bitter letter of complaint, published in the *Times Literary Supplement* on 3 October, he took Robbie to task and tried to correct the errors in Ross's letter published back in June. He stressed he was not the editor of the American edition of Wilde's *Collected Works*, but had merely written the Introduction, indeed, he said he had not even read the complete works. He was particularly incensed at what he regarded as Robbie's cheap satire about his alleged friendship with Wilde; then he widened the argument into a personal attack on Robbie, declaring: 'when a man is fighting, it is as well that he should know what he is fighting about. Mr Ross does not seem to know.'[14]

Robbie's sponsorship of the Wilde Estate brought out in many people a spark of envy and jealousy. Le Gallienne was not alone in believing that Robbie had personally benefited from his association with Oscar Wilde; yet it was an allegation without foundation. In the final paragraph of his letter, Le Gallienne did not attempt to hide his own sense of envy as he added sourly: 'They [Keller & Co.][15] would be glad to know to whom they can pay a royalty on their edition. Perhaps Mr Ross would be kind enough to inform them in the interest of Mrs Wilde's children, or, shall I say his "executor".'[16]

The attack was too bitter and too personal for Robbie to ignore, and a week later his reply appeared, sparing neither Le Gallienne's sensitivities nor the American publisher's feelings. He attacked with all the vigour of a victim who has been savaged by an enemy without prior provocation:

> Mr Le Gallienne says truly that, "when a man is fighting, it is as
> well that he should know what he is fighting about". I am fighting,
> Sir, if that is the right expression, for the feeling of indignant protest
> against what is a violation of the rights of Wilde's family, a violation
> of the rights of Messrs Methuen, the accredited literary agents for
> the Wilde Estate. Still more, I am fighting for Wilde's literary
> reputation, which is being again jeopardised by the attribution to
> him of spurious works, one of which I can hardly imagine being
> published in the virtuous State of New York.[17]

There is about the correspondence with Le Gallienne the passionate intensity which Ross, as Wilde's literary executor, felt for his task, there was nothing careless or casual in the way he administered Wilde's Estate. He was courageous in his defence of Wilde, but his passion was never stronger than when he was defending the honour of Constance and her sons. The *Academy* gave its unconditional support to Robbie, and while there is no certainty that Douglas was responsible for it (and even if he

had he would have later repudiated the sentiments in the editorial)
nevertheless at the time the *Academy* was highly critical, saying that 'Le
Gallienne's defence is a quibble'.[18]

The *Academy*'s editorial support for Wilde and his official literary execu-
tor was almost its last act of charity. As the autumn days shortened into
winter the mood at the *Academy* underwent a significant moral change.
Robbie's days of freedom from editorial restraints came to an end when
Harold Child resigned to join the staff of *The Times*. Child suggested to
Robbie that if he could find someone to buy the magazine, the proprietors would be willing to sell, and the new owner could then appoint
Robbie editor. It is a pity Robbie did not act on Child's excellent advice.
Eventually, Lord Glenconner was persuaded to buy the *Academy*, and he
appointed Douglas as editor. It was a fateful decision and was to have far-
reaching consequences; the whole character of the *Academy* changed
rapidly. If Robbie made an error of judgement in recommending Lord
Glenconner to buy the *Academy*, Douglas exacerbated that error when he
appointed Thomas William Hodgson Crosland[19] assistant editor. The
magazine quickly became less a journal of cultural excellence and more
an organ of political and religious bigotry. Crosland loved success and
wealth, but when denied these twin pleasures he was a bitter man. He
had, originally, attacked and abused Douglas's writings in the many
small literary papers he started and closed after a few unprofitable
months but, by the time he became Douglas's assistant editor, the two of
them had formed an implausible working relationship. Crosland was a
loyal monarchist and a fundamental Tory; yet he detested the unequal
distribution of wealth, which gave to a few and left the majority with
nothing but despair. He had very few scruples. He would write, con-
structively, for one literary magazine, and then in another he would
denounce the former paper, its proprietor and its editorial policy. He
wrote scathing pieces about his friends and his enemies alike, who were
not amused by his satire. He had not been assistant editor of the *Academy*
for many weeks when he turned his jaundiced eye towards Robbie:
Robbie had submitted an objective criticism of a book, but, by his sub-
editing, Crosland turned the literary assessment into a vulgar and violent
abuse of one of Robbie's personal friends. Fortunately, Robbie's name
did not appear beneath the offending article; nevertheless, he was very
annoyed and demanded an explanation from Douglas. In replying,
Douglas simply admitted he had been obliged to take liberties with
Robbie's article. On Quarter Day, when Douglas sent payment for the
offending piece, Robbie returned the cheque, saying that he could not

possibly accept payment for something he no longer regarded as his work.

It is difficult to be precise about the exact timing of the quarrel between Ross and Douglas. Robbie placed the start of their differences as early as 1895 when he tried to stop Oscar Wilde taking legal steps to end the libels perpetrated by the Marquess of Queensberry. The rift widened when Wilde left prison and Robbie used financial blackmail to prevent him returning to Douglas. Robbie could still have forgiven Douglas his sins of omission, if he had been more generous to Wilde during his last bleak days in Paris. He never forgave Douglas that gross act of selfishness. He considered Douglas's marriage to Olive Custance a further act of betrayal; it was as if he was trying to hide his homosexuality behind the veneer of a respectable and loving husband. The rows simmered for years, each new hurt was recorded and stored in the memory, until their quarrel developed into an aggressive public confrontation. Their individual moral objectives were diametrically opposed; Robbie was motivated by the needs of others, Douglas's interests were wholly selfish. There is little doubt that Douglas viewed Robbie's success as Wilde's executor with increasing jealousy, and Robbie's friendship with Vyvyan and Cyril Holland was more than Douglas could bear.

On 3 November Vyvyan came of age, though his guardians, his mother's people, saw no reason to celebrate such an event. It was, for them, merely an unpleasant reminder of a part of the young man's life they would prefer to forget. Robbie, however, gave Vyvyan a birthday party at Vicarage Gardens; some of the guests were old friends of Wilde, the painters Charles Ricketts, Charles Shannon, Sir William Richmond and William Rothenstein; the writers, Henry James and Reggie Turner, and, of course, More Adey. Vyvyan's friends Ronald Firbank and Sir Coleridge Kennard completed the party. Douglas, who considered himself first among Wilde's friends, and certainly more intimate with Wilde than Sir William Richmond and Henry James, was not invited.

The insult did not go unnoticed, and although the seeds of the ensuing row were sown by Douglas, it was Crosland who cultivated them. The insidious forest of lies, deception and hatred, grew to the point where Robbie had no alternative but to wield the forester's axe. Their jealous squabbles over the ownership of Oscar Wilde's soul would be as passionate as their love had been.

Ten

Fulfilment of a Promise

N 6 JANUARY 1908 Freddie Smith gave a party. Unfortunately Robbie had already agreed to attend a Twelfth Night party given by Edmund Gosse, but he urged Christopher Millard not to let Freddie Smith down. There was, though, little time for party-going. Methuen were pressing for the manuscript of volume twelve of Wilde's *Collected Works* and Robbie, in turn, pressed Millard to complete the editing. Robbie's attitude to Millard continued to be ambivalent; he would frequently appear generous and caring, but in writing to Walter Ledger, he was disparaging about Millard's literary achievements:

> I quite agree with you about his somewhat trivial little works, but I
> am glad to give him some work to do as he is dreadfully hard up,
> and I would have to pay someone to do it, if he was not on the spot.[1]

Robbie was finally able to tell Ledger that Carrington's were, after all, bringing out a uniform edition of *The Picture of Dorian Gray*. He had added an Editorial Note, in which he wrote:

> The practice of adding introductions to thoroughly well-known
> works for the benefit of an already well-informed public has become
> almost ridiculous. Only in rare instances have the works been
> illuminated, even in cases where the text required elucidation, or
> when the editor was himself an author of distinction. I do not,
> therefore, propose to fail in fields where celebrated writers have
> scarcely succeeded. I can, however, take this opportunity of saying
> that the characters of this novel were entirely imaginary, in spite of
> assertions to the contrary by claimants to the doubtful honour of
> being the original of *Dorian Gray*: though it is obvious that,
> consciously or unconsciously, Wilde has put a great deal of himself
> into the character of *Lord Henry Wotton*.[2]

Robbie's time was, as usual, fully occupied. He told Millard, who was handling the day-to-day editing of the *Collected Works*, that 'unless something very important turns up I am invisible until after 12 February.

I have some very important work to finish.'[3] He was working on a lecture for the newly formed Independent Lecture Society which he gave at the Old Bluecoats School in Liverpool on the 12th. He was a gifted public speaker and during his long lecture he demonstrated his skill as a communicator. His audience laughed at his puns, acknowledged the strength of his arguments and applauded his masterful oratory. The next day his speech was widely reviewed in the *Liverpool Courier*, under the subtitle of 'A Brilliant Exposition', the review concluding with the words of Professor Ramsay Muir, one of the distinguished audience, who had enjoyed 'the charm, wit and eloquence of Mr Ross's address'. Taking as his theme 'Decadence in Art and Literature' Robbie argued that there was no such thing as decay in art, literature or society:

> Every few years distinguished men lift their voices, and tell us that all is over, *decay has begun*. The obscure and the anonymous echo the sentiment in the London Press. With the fall of any Government its supporters prophesy the rapid decomposition of the Empire; in the pulpit eloquent preachers of every sect and communion, thundering against the vices of Society, declare that Society is breaking up. Of course, not being in Society, I am hardly in a position to judge; and the vices I only know at second-hand from the preachers. Yet I see no outward signs of decay in Society; it dresses quite as well, in some ways better than, it did. Society eats as much, judging from the size and number of new restaurants; it patronises as usual the silliest plays in London, and buys in larger quantities than ever the idiotic novels provided for it. Have you ever been to a bazaar in aid of Our Dumb Friends' League? Well, you see Society *there*, I can tell you; it is not dumb. And the conversation sounds no less vapid and no less brilliant than we are told it was in the eighteenth century; the dresses and faces are quite as pretty. But much as I should like to discuss the decay of English Society and the English nation, I feel that such lofty themes are beyond my reach. I am concerned only with the so-called decay of humbler things, the abstract manifestations of the human intellect, the Arts and Sciences. And lest, weary at the end of my discourse, you forget the argument or miss it, let me state at once what I wish to suggest, nay, what I wish to assert, *there is no such thing as decay*.[4]

On his return to London Robbie had a number of pressing problems which resulted from a death that had occurred a couple of months earlier. Leonard Smithers, that incorrigible publisher, had died on 19 December 1907. In the last years of his life, Smithers sank further into deprivation and despair, and he died a broken and discredited man. In trying to salvage something from the ruins of her husband's business, Mrs Smithers tried to gain ownership of one thousand copies of *The Ballad of Reading Gaol*. Robbie could not allow sympathy to override his business acumen, and he had no alternative but to order the seizure of the copies of Wilde's prison poem. Mrs Smithers, a destitute widow, naturally contested the seizure of her only profitable asset. On 1 April, eleven years to the day since he had been appointed Wilde's literary executor, Robbie approached Ledger for help in preparing his legal case:

> Can you possibly do me the favour of lending me the 2nd, 3rd, 4th,
> 5th, 6th, and 7th Editions of *The Ballad of Reading Gaol* for the
> purpose of showing them to my solicitors and the authorities at
> Stationers' Hall; great care will be taken of them and I will see that
> they are kept clean. The widow of the late Leonard Smithers has
> commenced an action against me and it is very important to explain
> the details of the different editions to the Court.[5]

Two days later, Robbie was again seeking the loan of another book from Ledger's extensive library of Wilde's books. He told Ledger he now needed a first edition of Wilde's *Poems*, in order that it could be registered as his property at Stationers' Hall. He went on to explain that although there was no immediate action pending as to the ownership of the *Poems*, this would happen once he had established copyright of the book. On 29 May Robbie was able to tell Ledger of the successful outcome of the legal action:

> I have never thanked you sufficiently for your invaluable help in
> lending the books. I do hope they were not damaged. I fear they had
> to be shown to a great many people. The case actually came before
> the Judge, but Counsel for the defence got up and said he was ready
> to accept the injunction. I will send you for your "curios" a printed
> copy of the injunction which will be sent to all booksellers in
> England.[6]

The printed injunction, together with a list, compiled by Stuart Mason [Christopher Millard], of those editions of the works which could be legally offered for sale in the United Kingdom, was sent to all booksellers. It was the first time since Wilde's death that the pirating of his works would be controlled by legal enforcement. In the years which followed Robbie vigorously proceeded against any bookseller, publisher or printer who tried to break the injunction. Such was his enthusiasm for taking legal action against the pirates that in *Who's Who* he gave litigation as one of his hobbies. It was, unfortunately, a jest which he bitterly regretted.

In June 1908 Robbie had the pleasure of seeing the completion of the task that had been occupying him since Wilde's death. Methuen finally published a twelve-volume edition of the *Collected Works of Oscar Wilde*. Wilde's sins had not been forgotten by Society, but the literary world was, at last, prepared to judge his works on their obvious merit. Harold Child, the literary editor of *The Times*, was among those who favourably reviewed the *Collected Works*:

> bound in a white cover which is clearly the design of a good artist, printed in bold and handsome type on hand-made paper with deckled edges.... The real works of Oscar Wilde lie partly in the delight in art and letters, the joy in things of beauty of all kinds, experienced to-day by people who perhaps never suspect that to him they owe the impulse to seek their pleasure in such things; partly in the echoes of old laughter, the recollection of sallies that used to set the table in a roar, or of brilliant flashes of capricious wisdom struck out.... Through his personality, again, and his reckless Irish wit, he became the delight of dinner-tables, where he prodigally scattered the best of his genius. The spoken, not the written, word was his proper vehicle; and no one ever so lacked a Boswell.... It should be added that the set of volumes is not yet quite complete, though the coming volume or volumes are comparatively unimportant; and that it has been edited with self-effacement, with ability, and with scrupulous and loyal care by Mr Robert Ross.[7]

Included in the *Collected Works* was a fuller version of *De Profundis* which contained Wilde's letters to the *Daily Chronicle* on prison reform. As he had when he published the first edition of *De Profundis*, Robbie again received many letters of congratulations. Wilde's friends and per-haps, more importantly, his detractors, began to appreciate the extent of Wilde's suffering, only Bosie Douglas and Crosland failing to see the truth in Wilde's bitter confession. Edmund Gosse, however, in acknow-ledging the gift of the new edition, nevertheless admitted he still found it impossible to come to terms with Wilde's strange character.

The financial and critical success of the *Collected Works* was the high point of that summer, but Robbie's enjoyment of it was marred by the changes that were occurring in his private life. The lease on 15 Vicarage Gardens ran out and he did not renew it. For a couple of years he was practically roofless, taking service apartments or renting hotel rooms. It was an unsatisfactory period and Robbie did not solve his accommodation problem until the late spring of 1911. He spent the August Bank holiday weekend of 1908 at Brighton; the short break, though, was only a pleasant interlude in a troubled month. He quarrelled again with Bosie Douglas and this time Robbie did not seek to heal the rift. The argument simmered and festered all through the remainder of that year and Robbie was soon made aware of the fact that while Douglas had always been a difficult friend, he would be a dangerous and potentially lethal enemy.

The Carfax Gallery was still providing Robbie with enjoyment, but he felt restless now that he was no longer a regular contributor to the *Academy* and when Fabian Ware offered him the position of art editor on the prestigious *Morning Post* he happily accepted. His first article appeared on 4 August entitled 'Education in Art'. In his years at the Carfax he had gained a reputation for astute but fair dealing, and on the *Morning Post* he was soon regarded as an honest yet courteous critic. Controversy, however, was part of Robbie's character; he enjoyed a political, literary or dramatic fight and he deplored all forms of literary and artistic censorship. He was most scathing in his denunciation of petty officials, who, in his opinion, took decisions which, although strictly executed according to the law, were, nevertheless, arbitrary. He did not profess to be an expert on all subjects, but he rarely let an opportunity slip to correct a literary, dramatic or artistic wrong. When the Lord Chamberlain's office banned a play by the literary critic of the *Daily Telegraph*, W.L. Courtney, Robbie came to his defence and savagely ridiculed the unfortunate official responsible for the ban:

> All dramatic writers have or should have grievances against Mr Redford. Except that his name is George Alexander Redford, he has no qualification for the post. In his refusal to license *Waste* and *Mrs Warren's Profession*, he proved himself not a guardian of public morals, but an enemy of dramatic art in England. By his refusal to license Mr Courtney's adaptation of *Sophocles*, he has proved himself the personal enemy of all poets and dramatists. In the prohibition of *Waste* he was discourteous to the author, and dilatory in the exercise of his duty.
>
> On the other hand, it is idle to attack Mr Redford because he correctly interprets the law by prohibiting modern plays with scriptural characters, such as *Salome*, and permitting the performance of *Everyman* in which the Supreme Being appears. That is the fault of the stupid English law, not stupid Mr Redford.[8]

During September Robbie was busy writing his weekly column 'Art and Artists' for the *Morning Post*; early in October he went to Paris to write a piece on the Autumn Salon. In November Methuen published the last two volumes of Wilde's *Works*: *Reviews* and *Miscellanies*. In dedicating *Reviews* to Mrs Carew, Robbie repaid a debt to the gracious lady whose affection and admiration for Wilde had never wavered:

> The apparently endless difficulties against which I have contended, and am contending, in the management of Oscar Wilde's literary and dramatic property have brought me many valued friends; but only one friendship which seemed as endless; one friend's kindness which seemed to annul the disappointments of eight years. That is why I venture to place your name on this volume with the assurance of the author himself who bequeathed to me his works and something of his indiscretion.[9]

In a long Introduction to the volume Robbie explained his reasons for adding the work to the main set:

> The editor of writings by any author not long deceased is censured sooner or later for his errors of omission or commission. I have decided to err on the side of commission and to include in the uniform edition of Wilde's work everything that could be identified as genuine. Wilde's literary reputation has survived so much that I think it proof against any exhumation of articles which he or his admirers would have preferred to forget. As a matter of fact, I believe this volume will prove of unusual interest; some of the reviews are curiously prophetic; some are, of course, biased by prejudice hostile or friendly; others are conceived in the author's wittiest and happiest vein; only a few are colourless....It should be remembered, however, that at the time when most of these reviews were written Wilde had published scarcely any of the works by which his name has become famous in Europe, though the protagonist of the aesthetic movement was a well-known figure in Paris and London. Later he was recognised—it would be truer to say he was ignored—as a young man who had never fulfilled the high promise of a distinguished university career although his volume of *Poems* had reached its fifth edition, an unusual event in those days. He had alienated a great many of his Oxford contemporaries by his extravagant manner of dress and his methods of courting publicity.[10]

The final volume of the set, *Miscellanies*, Robbie dedicated to his

friend and Wilde's bibliographer, Walter Ledger. Harold Child again
reviewed both *Reviews* and *Miscellanies*. He paid a fitting tribute to
Wilde's ability as a critic-journalist and editor for Cassell of the magazine
Woman's World, and he also had a word of praise for Wilde's literary
executor and editor:

> The contents have been brought together from many quarters, and
> they include *everything that could be identified as genuine*, the editor
> having wisely *decided to err on the side of commission* rather than of
> omission... Mr Ross has permitted himself an introduction to each
> volume, of which we will only say that neither is among the least
> witty and delightful things between the covers.[11]

Miscellanies included Millard's bibliography of everything Wilde had
written and which had been published. Robbie hoped there would never
again be a doubt about the authorship of any of Wilde's works, and that
in the future Wilde's literary and artistic reputation would be safe from
forgers and copyright thieves.

A week after the publication of the final two volumes, there appeared in
the Court News of *The Times*, an intimation of a small public dinner for
Robert Ross in recognition of his services to the late Oscar Wilde's
Estate. The dinner was held on 1 December at the Ritz Hotel, eight years
after the death of Oscar Wilde. Far from being a small dinner, 160 people
were present to pay their tributes to Wilde's literary executor. Among
the distinguished company of Robbie's friends were Cyril and Vyvyan
Holland as well as Oscar Browning and George Prothero, his old King's
College tutors. There were also many members of his close family: Alex
to whom he deferred in all matters of principle; Jack's widow, Alice, who
had extended the generous hand of friendship; Mary and her daughter,
Lillian, whose love and devotion had often been stretched to breaking
point, but who had never failed him when he needed their love and their
understanding. Squire Sprigge and his wife Ethel were there. Christopher Millard, More Adey, and Freddie Smith were also among the
guests, a reminder that in Robbie's life there were still dark and tormented shadows.

Sir Martin Conway was in the Chair. Lord Alfred Douglas unfortunately did not attend, having told Reggie Turner, who was on the
organising committee for the dinner, that he did not wish to attend the
function. In a letter to Robbie, written four months after the dinner,
Douglas explained his reasons for not attending:

As to your absurd dinner to meet the Duchess of Sutherland and other people who have nothing whatever to do with Oscar or literature, I certainly did not feel inclined to go to a function to meet Frank Harris, Robert Sherard and about 20 other people with whom Oscar was not on speaking terms when he died. I said nothing about it except in a letter to Reggie in response to one asking me to attend the dinner. My letter was neither more or less *private* than the one you wrote me about the review copies of the complete edition, but I think it was indiscreet of Reggie to show it to you or repeat its contents.[12]

It must be said that Douglas's attitude was not shared by most of Robbie's friends, and it proved yet again that Douglas was never able to take a subordinate role. Only when he was at centre stage was he content.

After proposing 'The King' Sir Martin Conway announced, much to the amusement of the diners, that there were present, 36 journalists and critics, 20 authors, 12 poets, 11 art connoisseurs, 7 artists, 5 actors, 5 Government officials, 4 editors, 4 dramatists, 4 publishers, 4 men of science and medicine, 4 lawyers, 2 clergymen, and many whom he could not put into a *definite category*. Not least of the after-dinner speakers was Frank Harris, who used to the full his ability as a mimic to give an impression of the sheer brilliance of Oscar Wilde's conversation. He illustrated his talk with many personal reminiscences of the man whose ghost sat at dinner that night. He went into considerable detail about Robbie's various struggles with the Official Receiver over the proceeds from the Wilde Estate. He praised Robbie's tireless efforts to protect Wilde's Estate from pirates and forgers and mentioned, in particular, the American edition and Le Gallienne's involvement. Harris poured scorn on reports which had appeared in American papers that Wilde was still alive. He reminded the audience that Wilde had died exactly eight years before, and that Robbie, Reggie Turner and Dupoirier, the hotel proprietor, had been there to witness the sad event. In concluding his highly entertaining speech Harris could not refrain from a contemptuous comment on the actions of those who had not attended the dinner to honour Wilde's literary executor.

In reply to the tributes of his friends, Robbie spoke movingly and sincerely of his friendship with Oscar Wilde. In some detail he explained all the irritations and problems he had endured since he became the guardian of Wilde's literary reputation. In trying to justify his actions he quoted from an eighteenth-century poem he remembered from his boyhood, 'I hate the man who builds his name/On the ruins of another's fame.'[13] He admitted that that was exactly what he had done. If he had not become Wilde's executor, no one, other than his immediate family, would have heard of him. His modesty was, though, misplaced. It is quite possible that if he had not met Wilde he would have achieved more in his life. He might have become director of the National Gallery, or curator of the Wallace Collection, or Surveyor of the Royal Pictures.[14] He had the ability and the personality to succeed at everything he did, but his love for Oscar Wilde ruined his life; yet he never sought to repudiate that love.

In his speech Robbie paid tribute to all those who had helped Wilde in his last bitter years and he was quick to deny that he was the only friend that Wilde had at the end. There were, Robbie said, others who had done more for Wilde:

> It is only accident which made me the symbol of their friendship, and without their assistance Wilde could not have passed the many happy hours which he enjoyed so much even during the last actual year of his life. Without the assistance and friendship of these and others I could never have achieved what I have done.[15]

Robbie ended his speech by thanking the donor, who, a few days before, had given him a gift of £2000 to enable him to move Wilde's remains from Bagneux to Père Lachaise in Paris and to erect a suitable monument. Helen Carew, although he did not identify her at the dinner, was, with others, responsible for the gift. The decision as to which of the leading sculptors should be given the commission for Wilde's tomb had occupied Robbie for some time; it was, after all, a commission most sculptors would have been delighted to receive. But, in announcing at the Ritz dinner that Jacob Epstein would be given the work, Robbie prevented controversy and yet encouraged dissent. Epstein was a relatively unknown sculptor, although he had achieved a certain notoriety a few months earlier with his statues for the British Medical Association's new building in the Strand. In the years that followed, even Robbie, who loved to provoke an argument, must have wondered if he had blundered when he gave the commission to Epstein. The Epstein tomb would, from the moment it was conceived, be the subject of derision and hostility.

The dinner to honour Robbie was a public declaration that should have quietened his detractors for all time; unfortunately, public acclaim and rehabilitation of Oscar Wilde served only as a spur to those paragons of virtue who saw in Wilde's writings the hand of Satan; they were determined to destroy all the good that Robbie had achieved. The campaign, led inevitably by Bosie Douglas and encouraged by Crosland, lasted for forty years, until the death of Douglas. The poison he sprinkled so liberally contaminated the views of his many biographers and friends; their venom continued to blacken Robbie Ross's name and character.

No man is wholly a saint nor is he wholly a sinner. Oscar Wilde was not, as Douglas described him in 1918 from the witness-box at the Old Bailey, 'the greatest force for evil in Europe for the last 350 years';[16] nor was Robbie Ross, as Wilde's disciple, the purveyor of all that was depraved and debauched. 'There is good and bad in all of us',[17] Alfred Wood said, but in some men there is more good than bad. This was true of Robbie Ross. But for the insane jealousy of Douglas, he would have been able to enjoy the fruits of his many labours. As it was, he was subjected to a vicious and petty campaign of hate and abuse.

Eleven

Confederates in a Vendetta

Y THE SPRING of 1909 Robbie was in his fortieth year and had accomplished much. He was highly regarded as the art editor of the *Morning Post*; his criticisms were vibrant and fresh and he had many devoted readers. His 'word pictures' on painters and pictures did much to increase the enjoyment of those who later attended the exhibitions he reviewed. His articles were always liberally interjected with humour; his prestige and standing in the world of art was at its zenith. He was fêted by Society hostesses and was often to be seen at literary and artistic salons; he was especially popular with women, and they responded to his charming and generous spirit. He cultivated, and indeed enjoyed, the company and friendship of young artists, writers and poets. He was also a frequent and welcome guest at the country homes of some of the most influential people of the day, including the Prime Minister and Mrs Asquith. As the son and grandson of politicians he was able to move easily in political circles. He admitted to being an old-fashioned radical; the main political issues of the day interested him and his views on the Suffragette Movement, Home Rule and Free Trade made for lively and knowledgeable discussions.

At the beginning of the year John Lane of The Bodley Head published Robbie's illustrated life of Aubrey Beardsley; Aymer Vallance compiled a list of Beardsley's drawings. Robbie had written often about the life and art of Beardsley, but in bringing all the threads of his tragically short life together in one book, he failed to do justice to a rare talent. Perhaps he had been too close to his subject to be wholly objective; it would have been extremely painful for him to revive the last bitter years of Beardsley's life:

> No one could have wished him to live on in pain and suffering. I think the only great trials of life were the periods in which he was unfitted for work. His remarkable career was not darkened by any struggle for recognition. Few artists have been so fortunate as Aubrey Beardsley. His short life was remarkably happy at all events during the six years he was before the public. Everything he did met with success—a success thoroughly enjoyed by him. He seemed

indifferent to the idle criticism and violent denunciation with which
much of his art was hailed. I never heard of anyone of importance
who disliked him personally; on the other hand, many who were
hostile and prejudiced about his art ceased to attack him after
meeting him. This must have been due to the magnetism and charm
of his individuality, exercised quite unconsciously for he never tried
to conciliate people, or "to work the oracle", but rather gloried in
shocking "the enemy" a boyish failing for which he may be
forgiven.[1]

If all Robbie had done with his life was to secure the future of Oscar
Wilde's works, he would have earned a place in history. But he was not
content only to play the role of Wilde's literary executor; he had talents
which he could use to benefit other young writers. He introduced
unknown writers to editors and publishers; he encouraged the doyens of
literary critics to write constructive reviews. As a frequent guest at
society *soirées* he made sure their books were discussed. He used his
talents generously, and asked for nothing in return for these services
except that the recipient should not bring his friendship into disrepute.

When Arnold Bennett expressed a desire to become a member of the
Reform Club Robbie was happy to help, and, with the support of H.G.
Wells, Bennett was elected. On his first visit to the Reform Bennett was a
little apprehensive; Ross and Wells promised to be there to give him
moral support. Their carefully laid plans were thwarted when Wells
telephoned to say that unfortunately he was not able to keep the
luncheon appointment. Robbie himself was late in reaching the Reform
and when he eventually arrived he enquired of the head-porter if Mr
Bennett had arrived. He was told that Mr Bennett was indeed waiting for
him in the atrium. The obvious note of disapproval in the head-porter's
voice warned Robbie that all was not well. He hurried to the atrium and
his worst fears were confirmed: Bennett, oblivious to the rule that
smoking in the atrium was strictly forbidden, was enjoying a large cigar.
The members viewed Bennett with obvious distaste but when Robbie
greeted the miscreant they were reassured and thought to themselves:
'Ah, a friend of Robert Ross. That explains it.'[2]

There is a delightful sense of the ridiculous about the incident, and
the final comment is typical of the regard in which Robbie was held. His
friends were expected to be eccentric and ever so slightly outrageous, but
such was the affection felt by the liberal gentlemen of the Reform Club
for Robbie, they could only nod their heads and accept that his friends
would have to be taught to reform.

In Arnold Bennett, Robbie had a friend who brought much of the

Midlander's common sense to living and he was a good foil to Robbie's more whimsical and impractical view of life. Robbie strove after the impossible, regardless of his own material or physical needs, whereas Bennett urged on his impulsive friend a degree of caution. Bennett was able to prick the bubble of Establishment pomposity, which, for all his impudence, Robbie was never able to do. His head told him to conform to the rigid constraints of a puritan society, while his heart told him to adopt the Bohemian way of life which Wilde had advocated so frequently. It was a dilemma he never successfully solved.

H.G. Wells was not the least among the writers who shared Robbie's precious time. Three years older than Robbie, Wells was an original thinker, seeing clearly the divisions in society better than most of his contemporaries, and yet, in spite of, or perhaps because of, his essentially working-class background, he saw in Robbie, not only a literary friend, but a man who cared for his fellow man, whatever their social status. Nevertheless, the social gap between the two men was not unbridgeable; Robbie could ensure with his usual tact and diplomacy that H.G. Wells and Arnold Bennett did not commit too many *faux pas*.

As well as acting as the catalyst for writers, Robbie continued to champion the cause of painters and artists in the columns of the *Morning Post*. He was never frightened of taking the pomposity or snobbery out of art, and if he found something that offended his aesthetic taste he would allow his pen to roam freely; there was, however, a consistent theme running throughout his articles. He often ridiculed the pretensions of others, but without malice or cant; his generous nature continued to be the dominant code. He frequently let nepotism creep into his writings; he would flatter egos, while at the same time taking a backward swipe at officious and official administrators.

However, for all the pleasure Robbie gave to others there was an undercurrent of discord and despair in his own life. A deliberate campaign designed and fomented by Bosie Douglas—aided and abetted by Crosland—threatened to ruin his peace of mind. And in trying to understand the reasons behind this overwhelming hatred, it is necessary to understand something of the background to the feud. It had festered for many years, but it began to assume a ferocious bitterness after the publication in 1908 of the cheap edition of Wilde's *Collected Works* which produced a considerable increase in royalties for his Estate. The ghost of Oscar Wilde began to dominate all their subsequent actions. Robbie once wrote: 'Oscar is of course public property; only his grave, his body and his letters belong to me...'[3] Always jealous of the *riches* that Wilde accumulated, Douglas and Crosland used the popular appeal of the

Collected Works to intensify their campaign of hatred against the memory of Oscar Wilde and his literary executor Robbie Ross.

The two main antagonists were a very unlikely duo to be friends yet they made extremely dangerous enemies; they had few common bonds to link them, not rank, not education, not religion and not even social standing. The only common factor in their tortuous relationship was their intolerance and total disregard for the harm they did to Robbie and those close to him. It was their hatred for him and his circle of influential and prominent friends that fuelled their venom; as early as the spring of 1897 Wilde had been aware of Douglas's capacity for hate; in *De Profundis* he had written:

> Hate blinds people. You were not aware of that. Love can read the
> writing on the remotest star, but Hate so blinded you that you could
> see no further than the narrow, walled-in, and already lust-withered
> garden of your common desires. Your terrible lack of imagination,
> the one really fatal defect of your character, was entirely the result of
> the Hate that lived in you. Subtly, silently, and in secret, Hate
> gnawed at your nature, as the lichen bites at the root of some sallow
> plant, till you grew to see nothing but the most meagre interests and
> the most petty aims. That faculty in you which Love would have
> fostered, Hate poisoned and paralysed.[4]

After the death of his father, Douglas needed another figure on whom to vent his natural feelings of hatred. Robbie was an obvious victim, he had something Douglas could never imitate, a nature which did not know the meaning of hate. Robbie lived with love: love for his fellow man, regardless of, or in spite of, their faults; he saw in all men something worth preserving.

Encouraged by Crosland, Douglas began to insult Robbie whenever they met at the homes of mutual friends. He wrote Robbie offensive and abusive letters, accusing him of sodomy, anarchy and socialism. Douglas ordered his wife to end her friendship with Robbie; he instructed his servants that if Robbie called he was to be refused admission, imitating an action Wilde had taken, when he had instructed his servant that Queensberry was to be forbidden to again enter his home. Robbie's first instinct was to retaliate, but the nature of the retaliation remained a problem; it was difficult to stop Douglas without creating a social and personal scandal which would surpass Wilde's *cause célèbre*. It cannot, however, be ignored that Robbie did not behave with his usual good sense when the attacks became intolerable; he should have refused to be drawn into a fight he could not win. In stating publicly, as he did, that he was, like Caesar's wife, innocent of all crimes, and then proceeding to build his own pedestal, he could not really complain when his enemies knocked him from his perch of self-glorification. A more humble man would have handled his tormentors in a different manner, and would have come out of the battle less scathed. There is, after all, an argument which says that an innocent man does not need to defend himself, for the world knows his name is an honoured one. That should have been enough for Robbie. Many others had been aggrieved by Douglas's caustic tongue and had also suffered the sharpness of Crosland's poisoned pen: it was a mistake for Robbie to assume the mantle of standard-bearer.

Olive Douglas invited Robbie to lunch; in refusing her invitation he was polite but unnaturally stiff and formal. Olive wrote again admitting that his quarrel with her husband was causing her sadness and distress and she hoped it could be resolved. Deeply conscious that any quarrel with Bosie Douglas would increase Olive's distress, on 28 February Robbie wrote and tried to explain the reasons for his behaviour. He wrote that he had seen Douglas only twice since the previous summer, when Douglas had insulted him at the home of Frank Lawson. He said he had purposely been avoiding Douglas rather than risk another meeting, as there would obviously be another confrontation. He explained that they now disagreed on so many topics, and as Douglas had never learned to disagree in a pleasant way any meeting would invariably lead to another argument. He ended his letter by saying:

> I have no hostile feelings whatever because I know Bosie too well
> and have known him too long. But I decided some time ago to deny
> myself the privileges coincidental to friendship with him. I do not
> wish to reopen unnecessarily matters quite unimportant now to any
> one but myself; I merely wish to explain an attitude which otherwise
> may have seemed churlish to yourself for whom my regard may
> more adequately be described as homage.[5]

Douglas was certainly behaving in an irrational and perverse manner, and at the same time, in the *Academy*,[6] Crosland was expressing some highly objectionable and dangerous opinions on the law of libel, which only exacerbated an already difficult situation. Crosland thought it was his moral right to libel all who did not conform to his narrow and bigoted views; no one was safe from his pernicious pen. He was frequently issued with writs for libel, and on more than one occasion the libel was linked to blackmail.

The spring passed slowly. Robbie continued to write his weekly columns for the *Morning Post* and to live his life as he wished.

In June he went abroad, and as Freddie Smith told Walter Ledger, this was partly on business and partly for a rest from overwork in London. He took a short lease on 86 Church Street, Kensington, but was still unable to find suitable permanent accommodation. In July he finally severed all his connections with the Carfax Gallery, although it would still occupy a place in his heart.

With the gift by Mrs Carew of £2000, Robbie now felt able to consider a permanent resting place for Oscar Wilde's remains, which for nearly nine years had lain in a temporary concession in the Bagneux cemetery. On 20 July 1909[7] accompanied by Vyvyan Holland and Sir Coleridge Kennard, Robbie supervised the removal of Wilde's body to the National Cemetery at Père Lachaise in the east of Paris. Many stories were to be told of the removal, but the most grotesque was that told by Reggie Turner.[8] At the time of Wilde's death, the doctors had advised Robbie to place the body in quicklime, explaining that the lime would dissolve the flesh and leave the bones intact, thereby making later removal to a new coffin easier. However, when the coffin was opened at Bagneux, instead of a skeleton, Wilde's preserved body stared up at them. Turner declared Wilde's hair and beard had grown quite long. He then said that Robbie descended into the grave and carried Wilde's body into the new coffin.

The story is worthy of Turner's fictional adroitness. He did not, for instance, explain how Robbie descended into the grave, or how he climbed out again carrying Wilde's body. The truth was prosaic. There were endless bureaucratic complications, forms had to be signed and countersigned, revenue stamps had to be purchased, but Robbie, never a lover of petty restrictions, coped in his usual unflappable way. He had learnt, all those years before, when Wilde had died an alien in Paris, that French officialdom could not be circumvented but only tolerated and endured. He was, however, not amused when the Bagneux cemetery authorities would not allow him to transport Wilde's remains to Père Lachaise in the magnificent coffin he had ordered; they insisted on the removal being made in a plain oak coffin, made in the Bagneux cemetery workshop. Even this indignity he could have borne with equanimity, but the error in the engraving on the silver plate 'Oscard Wilde 1854-1900' was the final insult. The offending 'd' was removed by the undertaker, but he lacked any ability as a silversmith or engraver, and the result was a further affront to Robbie's artistic sensibilities. The simple ceremony at Père Lachaise was accomplished without further incident, but when the undertaker suggested that until a permanent memorial was erected, perhaps he should put up a small inscription, 'Robbie recoiled from him and raising his hands in horrified protest, cried in his rather drawling Canadian French: *"Oh, ma foi, non! Assez d'inscriptions!"* '[9]

Satisfied that Wilde was at last at peace, Robbie suggested to Vyvyan they should go to lunch. It seemed natural to Robbie to take him to the Café Weber in the rue Royale where Wilde had dined frequently, and where the Head Waiter still remembered him. Not for the first time, Vyvyan heard of the affection and regard ordinary people of Paris had for his father. Robbie, who always felt relaxed and content in Paris, could not resist the opportunity of showing his young companion the sights of Paris. Vyvyan, in his childhood, had travelled extensively in Italy and Switzerland, but, perhaps because of his father's association with Paris, had only passed through the city. As it was a glorious summer afternoon, they went up in the lifts of the Eiffel Tower, Robbie pointing out all the famous landmarks. If the events of the morning had distressed Robbie, they were more than compensated for by his delight in showing one of Wilde's sons the beauty of Paris. His friendship with Vyvyan healed many old wounds and swept the last vestige of sadness from him. He had achieved most of what he had set out to achieve, since that fateful day when Wilde had died. He had restored Wilde's literary reputation, paid all his debts and annulled his bankruptcy; but as important as all that was, it would not have been enough, had he not also been able to gain the respect, affection and friendship of Wilde's sons.

In arranging with Arthur Humphreys to publish a collection of his own articles in book form in September 1909, Robbie was indulging in a little light relief. *Masques and Phases*, described by E.V. Lucas as 'mischief between two covers',[10] was a typically irreverent and delightful example of Robbie's perverse wit and erudition. He played with words: the *Masques* revealed the drama of his life; the *Mask* would have disguised it. The *Phases* were only his stage character and not the *Faces* of his real nature. He was a Puck who needed the applause of an audience and in his delightful collection of essays, he received the acclaim he desired. In dedicating the book to Harold Child, Robbie repaid a debt to Child, who was the first editor to give him the freedom to write what he wished. Although as he admitted, in his dedication, he had often feared Child's editorial power:

> But I, who am not frightened of many things, have always been
> frightened of editors. I am filled with awe when I think of the
> ultramarine pencil that is to delete my ultramontane views. You
> were, as I have hinted, the first to abrogate its use in my favour.

> When you, if not Consul, were at least Plancus, I think the only
> thing you ever rejected of mine was an essay entitled, "Editors, their
> Cause and Cure".... There are essays in my book cast in the form of
> fiction; criticisms cast in the form of parody; and a vein of high
> seriousness sufficiently obvious, I hope, behind the masques and
> phases of my jesting. The psychological effects produced by works
> of art and archaeology, by drama and books, on men and situations
> such are the themes of these passing observations.
>
> And though you find them like an old patchwork quilt I hope
> you will laugh, in token of your acceptance, if not of the book at
> least of my lasting regard and friendship for yourself.[11]

The book was well reviewed, and not least by the *Times Literary
Supplement*. Harold Child, as literary editor, would undoubtedly have
overseen the wording and agreed with the sentiments it expressed, and
Robbie must have been flattered when he read:

> Will it seem inconsistent with what we have said of Mr Ross's
> modernity if we now insist that his style, an important part of him,
> belongs to yesterday rather than to the present? The *Yellow Book*,
> Aubrey Beardsley, Oscar Wilde, with their distinction and their
> limitations, are of yesterday, and it is with them that Mr Ross seems
> to dwell...The obvious thing and the important thing to say about
> his book is that it makes very pleasant reading.[12]

With his usual generosity and unrestrained modesty, Robbie sent
copies of the book to his friends. Roger Fry, always among the first to say
that which others wished they had had the wit to say, said of *Masques and
Phases*: 'Of course it wants annotating. A hundred years hence some fool
will do for you what I've done for Reynolds. It will cost him infinite
labour and everyone will be immensely proud of understanding your
jokes.'[13]

One of the essays 'Ego Et Max Meus' which Robbie called 'A Conversation', was dedicated to Mrs Beerbohm and in sending Max Beerbohm a
copy, Robbie wrote in a typically immodest fashion. It is certain his
affection for Beerbohm had not dimmed with the intervening years, in
spite of their all too frequent petty squabbles:

> A friend of mine, and a friend of yours (as Ernest Leverson used to
> call him) once told me that the most painful experience of his life
> (this was before he went to Reading) was to receive a presentation
> copy of a book by someone whose friendship he valued: especially

when the friend was a neophyte in literature, such gifts, he
considered, put a premium on insincerity. It is because I believe you
value my friendship, and not from mock modesty, that I offer you
my book, in the form of a symbol; if you cannot learn its contents,
at least you can mark and inwardly digest them, and your letter of
thanks which I shall look forward to will at least ring true, like one
of your dramatic criticisms. Though no bibliographer you will be
gratified, I think, to have an edition of which there are no large or
small paper examples, even for America, and to me it will be
gratifying (as Reggie would remark) to think that at least one friend
has enjoyed my book without being able to read it.[14]

It is difficult to understand why Crosland, on becoming assistant
editor of the *Academy*, should have found Robbie's essays so offensive,
and why he urged Douglas to sever all literary and social contact with
Robbie. Crosland insisted that Robbie's articles contained frequent references to homosexual practices, and that he advocated perverted
behaviour to the detriment of the moral welfare of the ordinary man. As
a bigot, Crosland could find a reason in the most innocent assembly of
words or phrases, and it is true, as Roger Fry admitted so eloquently,
that Robbie's humour was not always easy for a mere mortal man to
follow. To understand his humour it was necessary to have a greater level
of perception than Crosland possessed. It is easy enough to find perver-
sion if the reader is determined to find it, and there are similarities in
some of Robbie's essays to the writings of Wilde. In trying to define the
subtleties in Robbie's approach to humour, it is perhaps worth stating,
that like many of his homosexual circle, he used the language of humour
in such a way that a purely innocent joke could also have a sexual
connotation. Humour is lost on narrow, unimaginative souls, and here,
surely, is the difference between Robbie and his tormentors; they did not
understand the delicate touch of the jester.

In some people humour can be found by grossly distorting human
characteristics. Such humour is cruel, crude and obscene, and the use of
blasphemous words, usually with an explicit sexual innuendo, is degrad-
ing and unacceptable. On the other hand, humour which is wholly
reliant on perception and intelligent observation of the contemporary
scene and its players is not hurtful or corrupting to either the teller or the
audience. Robbie's delicate touch reflected the contemporary scene and
he rarely strayed over the boundary of social acceptability.

Crosland accused Robbie of corrupting the moral values of the man in
the street, yet it was his own crude and hurtful satire that was the more

corrupting influence. In this, Douglas was as much a victim as Robbie; Douglas was a highly talented poet who squandered his genius.

In October 1909 Robbie decided it would be in the interests of future historians if the manuscript of *De Profundis* was offered to the British Museum for safe-keeping. He knew that neither in his own lifetime, nor in the lifetime of Douglas, would he be able to publish the entire letter; the campaign of hatred, orchestrated by Douglas and Crosland, would prevent it being made public. In offering the manuscript to Sir Frederick Kenyon, Robbie acknowledged that the British Museum was the only place to be trusted with the future of the manuscript:

> I may say that I should like to be guided entirely by you as to the conditions about *De Profundis* and meanwhile will ask you to regard the MS as entirely under your control, to be shown to, or read by, anyone you think desirable or fitted. You will entirely understand that I merely do not wish to hurt the susceptibilities of living people.[15]

The gift of the manuscript was discussed by the Trustees on Saturday 13 November; two days later Sir Frederick Kenyon wrote and accepted the gift. In his letter he expressed the Trustees' special thanks, and said that they were aware that in offering the manuscript to the British Museum Robbie was making a considerable financial sacrifice. In demanding that the manuscript should be kept sealed for fifty years Robbie was ensuring that neither Douglas nor his family would be hurt by the contents of Wilde's prison letter. But, in safeguarding the future of the document, he was giving historians a document of immeasurable importance. He did, though, keep in his own possession a typed copy of the manuscript; this was rather fortunate because, as the hostilities between Douglas, Crosland and himself became more violent, he needed to use it as a powerful weapon with which to beat them. Unfortunately, in making a gift of the manuscript to the British Museum, Robbie only added to Douglas's grievances, which he exploited to the full. Douglas did not want to accept Wilde's outpourings and he certainly did not want them made public; in the end, it was his own actions and his own greed that made the world aware of the whole contents of that damning letter. In trying to destroy Robbie's good name, Douglas failed to realise that eventually Robbie would have to retaliate, and would have to use the only effective weapon that Wilde had given him. It is also worth bearing in mind that when the letter was composed, Wilde was at his lowest ebb, emotionally and physically. Notwithstanding, the letter was still a terrible indictment of Douglas.

The autumn gave way to the rigours of winter. Robbie wrote his weekly
column for the *Morning Post* but it did not prevent him from becoming
involved in artistic controversies when a topic appealed to him. He had
become one of the foremost experts on the art of Aubrey Beardsley; his
relationship with Ellen Beardsley had undergone a change since her son's
death. She was distressed by Robbie's prominent support of Wilde and
his works; the social stigma which Wilde had attracted at the time of his
disgrace had hurt her a great deal, and she could not forgive Robbie for
his involvement. Robbie, on the other hand, could forgive most things,
except those unscrupulous members of the art world who perpetrated
Beardsley forgeries on an innocent public. He was often called in to
judge the authenticity of a picture; to William Lang of Manchester, he
was prepared also to give a lesson on the art of Beardsley and how to
decide whether a particular picture was genuine:

> The first and best test of a Beardsley drawing is its history; if there
> is any mystery as to who it belonged to and where it came from, you
> can be fairly certain that something is wrong. Selling a Beardsley is
> not like selling a family-portrait or a well-known Old Master;
> although they have changed hands a good many times since the
> artist's death, the vendor ought to be able to give an account of the
> last couple of private owners at least. The second test is that every
> drawing when unframed, with the exception of some immature
> sketches, ought to show in each corner the holes made by the
> drawing pins, for Beardsley always attached his paper to a drawing
> board; the third test is the correspondence of the alleged drawing to
> the published reproduction in various books published during
> Beardsley's lifetime. Leaving aside indecent drawings, I doubt if
> there are more than about twenty that have not been
> reproduced...Armed with these facts and your own judgement you
> can now be an expert on Beardsley as well as on anything else.[16]

The final sentence of his letter has about it all Robbie's self-conceit; he
did not suffer fools gladly and he saw no reason to believe ignorance was
an excuse for foolish opinions or muddled thinking. The year ended with
two very pleasant social interludes. On 30 November he attended the
second revival of *The Importance of Being Earnest* at the St James's
Theatre, and to celebrate the performance of Oscar Wilde's most successful play, he dined at the Reform Club with Harold Nicolson, Max
Beerbohm, Reggie Turner, H.G. Wells, Arthur Clutton-Brock and the
young writer Hugh Walpole.

Twelve

Prelude to Discord

OBBIE WAS never frightened to give his views and opinions but he reserved some of his sharpest criticism for the Lord Chamberlain's Office, and the often arbitrary way in which plays were refused a performing licence. In January 1910 the controversy over their decision to refuse to license Wilde's *Salome*, while allowing the performance of other plays that featured the 'Supreme Being', occupied the letter columns of *The Times*. Robbie was angry that the Lord Chamberlain's Office would permit the paying public to see *Everyman*, a sixteenth-century morality play, yet still denied a public performance to *Salome*. He was also incensed that a burlesque dance of the seven veils by Maud Allan was allowed. He could not understand why Wilde's beautiful and reverential play should be forbidden a public performance while a music-hall dancer could titillate an audience with her strange gyrations to erotic music.

Robbie rarely saw Douglas, but from various friends he heard that Douglas was still actively involved in his campaign of hate. In February Crosland was sued by the Honourable Frederick Manners-Sutton,[1] for libel over an article in the *Academy*. As a witness for Crosland, Douglas was at his vitriolic best and he used the privilege of the witness-box to great effect. The lies told by Crosland and Douglas so enraged Robbie that he wrote to Edward Marshall Hall, Counsel for Manners-Sutton, offering to give evidence against Crosland. Unfortunately his offer came too late, but to Douglas, even the offer of help was an insult and he intensified his efforts to ruin Robbie's good name. Although Robbie bore all the abuse in silence he knew that one day he would be forced to take action against Douglas as he told André Gide in a letter written in March 1910:

> I am delighted that you have reprinted your brilliant *Souvenirs of Oscar Wilde*.... I have told many friends, since your study appeared first in *L'Ermitage*, that it was not only the best account of Oscar Wilde at the different stages of his career, but the only true and accurate impression of him that I have ever read; so I can only repeat to you what I have said so often to others.

149

Some day, perhaps, I shall publish letters of Oscar Wilde to
myself which will confirm everything you have said if there can be
any doubt as to the truth of what you so vividly describe.

This may one day become necessary in order to refute the lies of
Alfred Douglas. You no doubt heard reported in a recent libel action
that he swore in the witness-box that he was unaware of Oscar
Wilde's guilt, and that he was the "only decent friend who remained
with Oscar Wilde". You know perfectly well that Alfred Douglas
was the cause of Oscar Wilde's ruin both before and after the
imprisonment. I would like to have pretended this was not the case,
out of old friendship and regard for Douglas: and the fact that I had
quarrelled with him personally would not have affected my
determination to let the world think he was really the noble friend
he always posed as being. But since he has taken on himself, in his
new character of social and moral reformer, to talk about Oscar
Wilde's *sins* (in most of which he participated) and has betrayed all
his old friends, there is no longer any reason for me to be silent.[2]

The *Academy*, under the editorship of Douglas and with the assistance
of Crosland, was losing a great deal of money. Lord Glenconner was
unwilling to continue his sponsorship, and sold the ownership to Douglas for a nominal sum. Douglas did not have adequate resources and, as
advertising revenues were not sufficient to meet the weekly overhead
costs, Douglas was forced in July 1910 to sell. Robbie mourned the
passing of the *Academy*, he had enjoyed contributing to it, but he was
still very busy with his weekly articles in the *Morning Post* and he was
also contributing to other journals, including the radical *New Age*. The
General Election in January had not resolved the political turmoil. The
Liberals had retained power, but they needed the support of 40 Labour
and 82 Irish Nationalist members to have a workable majority. There
had been much discussion during the election campaigns that if the
Liberals were returned to power they would create sufficient Liberal
peers to stop the perpetual Conservative House of Lords from vetoing all
the legislation they wished to block. There were those in the country who
thought the only solution to the crisis was the abolition of the hereditary
House of Lords and its replacement by an elected second chamber. The
King had reluctantly agreed to the Liberal decision providing the results
of two general elections proved that it was what the electorate wished.
Robbie, a frustrated politician and a self-confessed snob, was happy to
give his reasons why the House of Lords should be retained in its present
form:

It was always a joke against the members of my dwindling party that
we had a tenderness for titles. I own to the soft impeachment.
Brought up in the middle classes, I have never succeeded in shaking
off the awe with which my kind regard the nobility. Staunch old
Radical as I am, believing in the payment of members, endorsing
nearly everything in Mr Lloyd George's Budget, I am ready to
postpone all these things rather than lose my House of Lords. And
there are many thousands of Radicals who *think* with me, if they
have not the courage to say so. They may declare that I am not
sincere or that I am not writing seriously.... Alas, it will not be so![3]

The benefits to be obtained from an elected assembly, whether it be
a first or second chamber, are, I think, apt to be exaggerated. The
result of the present elections prove that both political parties will
have to shelve their convictions. They will have to pretend to think
dishonestly, even if they do not do so, because the next election
must be near and hanging over their heads. The Lords, on the other
hand, are morally in a superb position. They have nothing to
pretend. Abolish them; reform them into an elective assembly; and
one of the first things that will be damaged is our Foreign Office.[4]

Early in March Robbie was back in Paris, having admitted to Walter
Ledger that 'I am rather stale. Journalism has rather occupied me.'[5]
Robbie did not leave an itinerary of his holiday, though, undoubtedly, he
went to Père Lachaise to see Wilde's grave and pay his respects to his
friend. The memorial on which Jacob Epstein was working would not be
ready for another two years, and Wilde's grave remained unadorned.
There were also some important changes in his personal life. Freddie
Smith, who had been his secretary and companion for seven years,
became financially independent when he inherited from the estate of a
distant relative. Freed from financial dependence Smith, nevertheless,
continued to live with Robbie, but his secretarial duties were taken over
by Christopher Millard. In July the Contemporary Art Society was
formed by Lord Howard de Walden, Lord Henry Cavendish Bentinck,
his sister Lady Ottoline Morrell and Roger Fry. Robbie immediately
became a subscriber fully supporting the aims of the new society.

On 10 October, Robbie gave his second lecture to the Sandon Society
at Liverpool. His theme was 'The Present and Future for English Art'
and he was particularly bitter about the adoration the Post-Impressionists were receiving from his fellow art critics:

You will have heard of the Post-Impressionists, of whom the late
Cézanne is regarded as the founder, and of whom Matisse is the
present protagonist. Many of my personal friends, the critics, have
joined the chorus of praise which greets the new revelation from
France....But they have also, in their dread of prettiness, of the
obvious, said good-bye to form, anatomy, to harmony, and to
artistic probity. Beauty they had none to part with. Of design they
know nothing. Of nature that much-abused factor they cared
nothing...I am the first to hail any new manifestation in art or
literature; to see excellence where it may be hidden from my fellows
in the auditorium. For I am a listener, not an actor on the
intellectual stage. From what I have seen of the neo-Impressionists
there is nothing of permanent value in their work. If there is, let the
public learn it; and if it buys, let it sell out quickly. Do not be
deceived by the pseudo-scientific art jargon of the apologists, who
are mere sheep in wolves' clothing. There is nothing for our young
artists to learn from them. None of them can draw as well as
Augustus John, none of them can paint as well as Charles Shannon
or Nicholson, none of them could teach as Professor Tonks teaches,
because they are not nearly so proficient in the grammar of art.[6]

A month later Robbie returned to the subject of the Post-Impressionists; Roger Fry had organised at the Grafton Gallery an exhibition,
which included the first London showing of work by Cézanne:

> A date more favourable than the Fifth of November for revealing
> the existence of a wide-spread plot to destroy the whole fabric of
> European painting could hardly have been chosen....To my
> uninitiated eyes they appear sketches or underpainting of pictures
> by someone who, if he cannot draw very well, sees though he does
> not seize the true aspects of Nature at rather commonplace
> moments. We are told, "that he aimed at design which should
> produce the coherent architectural effect of the masterpiece of
> primitive art". All I can say is that he failed; whether from
> insufficient knowledge of the manipulation of paint or an entire
> misunderstanding of the aims or methods of the primitives I do not
> profess to judge.[7]

His harsh denunciation of the exhibition and its painters provoked a
lively correspondence in the *Morning Post* between those who supported
him and those who passionately disagreed with his accusations, but
Robbie did not alter his opinion. History proved him wrong; seventy

years later Cézanne and the work of the Post-Impressionists attract collectors and connoisseurs from all parts of the world, and they pay enormous sums of money for their work; while the English painters Robbie so admired, would, with only a few exceptions, slip into obscurity.

As the controversy inspired by the Post-Impressionist exhibition continued Robbie entertained himself by writing a literary-log for the *Bystander*, a forerunner to the glossy society magazines:

> Some ten years ago I chanced to be present at the death of Oscar Wilde in Paris. It was in a little hotel in the Latin quarter. Last July I learned that the room had been turned into a show place, and that a franc was charged by the proprietor for seeing it. Out of curiosity I went, and found three Americans and a German at the hotel entrance, sightseers with the same objective. The former *patron* had left. With much ceremony we were invited to sign our names, and pay our entrance money. We were then harangued by the new *patron*, who gave an entirely fantastic and sensational account of the death at which myself, the former proprietor, and a friend were the only persons present. I have nothing to complain of in the narrative. He provided me with a halo, under the weight of which I still totter. I was given the undreamed honour of a title. I had become the *Vicomte de Rosse*, a scion of one of the oldest families in Middlesex; but I will skip that. We were then ushered into the WRONG room, and shown the wrong bed, on which *le pauvre poète* breathed his last. It was the best franc's worth I ever had. The German burst into tears, and the Americans told me it was the *bulliest* thing they had seen in Paris. They invested in some false relics, which I shall see, I hope, one day in some American museum of *Old Paris*.[8]

These gossipy reviews in the *Bystander* were among some of the most amusing and delightfully unpretentious that he ever wrote. This was also true of his *Morning Post* articles; whether on the vexed subject of the Post-Impressionists or when praising the poetry and art of William Morris, his fluent and elegant pen never let him down. It is hard to see what Crosland found so corrupting in such articles, and it is true that when asked to produce evidence of Robbie's writing which advocated and glorified 'unnatural vices' he was unable to do so. Douglas, too, when called upon to justify his allegations that Robbie's writing supported and promoted homosexual practices, could produce only personal letters which Robbie had written as a very young man.

On 8 December, to mark the production at Covent Garden of Richard

Strauss's opera, based on Wilde's *Salome*, Robbie wrote an informative
article in the *Morning Post*. He gave a full history of the play, and said he
wished 'to remove certain erroneous impressions which have gained the
general acceptance of writers too idle to "verify their misquotations".'[9] It
is still hard to understand why a production of Strauss's opera was
allowed but a dramatic performance of Wilde's play was still banned.

Twice in December, on the 1st and 13th, he dined at Hanover Terrace
with Edmund Gosse and his family; and on the 21st he attended a dinner
at the Café Royal in honour of the painter Philip Wilson Steer; John
Singer Sargent gave an accomplished after-dinner speech. The guests
included William Rothenstein, D.S.MacColl, Roger Fry, Max Beerbohm, Walter Sickert, and Charles Holmes.

Early in 1911 Robbie paid a visit to Berlin in his capacity as Wilde's
literary executor, but he did not remain long. In March he competed for
the Directorship of the Tate Gallery, but he was unsuccessful, and
Charles Aitken was appointed to the post. He would continue to compete
for a position at one of the major galleries, for, as he told Millard only a
couple of years before his death, he would have dearly loved to have been
curator of the Tate or Wallace Collection. His disappointment, though,
was not allowed to interfere with the help he gave to the galleries and the
art world in general.

As a Committee member of the Poets' Club, Robbie had always hoped
that they could honour Edmund Gosse, and on 17 May, a dinner was
held at the Hotel Richelieu in Oxford Street. The guests included
'literary London';[10] the Grand President, Maurice Hewlett, was also
present; Henry Simpson was in the chair and in recalling the dinner
many years later he gave an interesting insight into Robbie's complex
relationship with Gosse: 'Ross had the profoundest admiration, not
unmixed with fear, of Gosse.'[11]

Gosse gave an address entitled, 'The Example of Keats' and his
delivery 'positively sang'. Robbie responded by paying a well-deserved
tribute to Gosse's ability as a poet and writer, and in praising Gosse's
autobiography *Father and Son* he was perhaps reflecting on his own
problems: 'Anyone who has been unappreciated, misunderstood, especially by those nearest and dearest to them; anyone who has suffered, as
someone timely said, in the silence that is heard only of God.'[12] It was,
though, to Gosse's attributes for friendship that Ross paid his most
eloquent tribute and once again his words were synonymous with his
own interpretation of the duties of a friend:

> I could not tell you without a gross breach of confidence the endless
> kindness, the material assistance which Mr Gosse has given, not
> only to less fortunate contemporaries, but to younger writers....It is
> very much easier to assist damaged reputations which are destined to
> dazzle posterity, than to give a helping hand to those who are
> destined in the natural course to pass into oblivion.[13]

In conclusion he asked the assembled company to greet 'one who has been the friend of poets and the friend of literature and drinking a draught of blushful *Hippocrene* to Edmund Gosse the friend of friends.'[14]

The storm clouds were, however, gathering, and he began to appreciate how serious his quarrel with Douglas would become. Robbie heard in May 1911 that Douglas had become a member of the Roman Catholic Church, this in spite of his protestations of only a year earlier, when the Reverend Doctor R.F. Horton, a Nonconformist Minister, had accused Douglas of using the *Academy* to promulgate the teachings of the Church of Rome. Douglas sued for libel, and at the trial, presided over by Mr Justice Darling, Douglas declared that he could be a loyal member of the Church of England without hating or detesting the Church of Rome. After an initial disagreement the jury returned a verdict in favour of the defendant. It was a sorry little squabble which affected Robbie profoundly. The conversion of Douglas ended all hope of a reconciliation. The final indignity was compounded even further when Robbie heard a rumour that Crosland was also toying with the idea of renouncing his Methodist beliefs and joining the Church of Rome. He could not understand how the Church he loved and respected could allow men like Douglas and Crosland into its Faith. Robbie believed in forgiveness, but it was asking too much of him simply to accept that Douglas and Crosland had undergone a change of heart and would now become good Catholics and good Christians. Indeed, Robbie must have doubted their sanity.

Robbie was sure Douglas would degrade the teachings of the Church of Rome, and he regarded Crosland's proposed conversion as an act of treachery. Douglas's cousin, Wilfred Scawen Blunt, in his diary for 16 November 1905, had recounted a story Robbie had told him about his attitude to converts to the Roman Catholic Faith:

> When Oscar came out of prison he had the idea of becoming a
> Catholic, and he consulted me about it, for you know I am a
> Catholic. I did not believe in his sincerity and told him if he really
> meant it, to go to a priest, and I discouraged him from anything

hasty in the matter. As a fact, he had forgotten all about it in a
week, only from time to time he used to chaff me as one standing in
the way of his salvation. I would willingly have helped him if I
thought him in earnest, but I did not fancy religion being made
ridiculous by him. I used to say that if it came to his dying I would
bring a priest to him, not before. I am not at all a moral man, but I
had my feeling on this point and so the matter remained between us.[15]

Robbie had, since his conversion in the 1890's, sustained his Roman
Catholic Faith, and had held firm to the teachings of his chosen Church.
An integral part of his beliefs was the observance of that Faith, and he
never lost his youthful passion for religious ritual. Yet he could not
maintain his Faith when Douglas became a Catholic. He mistrusted easy
conversion and he feared Douglas would bring ridicule to the Holy
Roman Church. In spite of what Aitken later admitted: 'Now you are an
atheist all is well',[16] Robbie continued to mourn the loss of his Faith.
Douglas's conversion also broke the last remaining link with Wilde; he
would spend the next couple of decades denying he was ever 'Oscar's
golden boy'.

At the end of June Robbie took a lease on an apartment at 13 Lower
Grosvenor Gardens; it was his first settled home since leaving Vicarage
Gardens in 1908. Reggie Turner also occupied an apartment in the same
building, although he spent the greater part of his time abroad. The
decision to move into number thirteen was one that Robbie came to
regret. His friendship with Turner had endured all the strains of Wilde's
disgrace and death, but, as his quarrel with Douglas developed, Turner
was more inclined to take Douglas's side than his. Robbie tried to put his
side of the argument, but living in such close contact with Turner only
emphasised their different attitudes to life: Ross always striving to be
discreet and circumspect, Turner fearful of scandal but, nevertheless,
incautious in his relationships. Living in the same building they would
find it impossible to have casual homosexual liaisons, and there would
always be the suspicion that each was spying on the other's activities.
Jealousies and recriminations would intensify and reconciliations and
forgiveness would be difficult.

In the autumn of 1910 Martin Secker, the publisher, had suggested to
Arthur Ransome that he should write another book of criticism, now that
his book on Edgar Allan Poe had received such favourable reviews.
Ransome wanted to work on a book on Hazlitt, as he had already made
some preliminary notes on the subject, but Secker was more interested in
a book of criticisms of Robert Louis Stevenson. In the end they judged

that a compromise would be for Ransome to write a critical study of Oscar Wilde. As it turned out, this was a momentous decision, and one that would have bitter consequences for all concerned, particularly when Ransome's cousin, Laurence Binyon, Keeper of Oriental prints and paintings at the British Museum, agreed to introduce him to Robert Ross.

Robbie was willing to meet Arthur Ransome, as he was all writers who might benefit from some help and encouragement, and especially if they were interested in Wilde's literary genius rather than his sexual predilections. During the preparatory stages of the book Ransome experienced moments of uncertainty and inevitably turned to Robbie for support and encouragement, which Robbie gave as generously as he gave his time and professional expertise:

> I am very anxious, when your book comes out, to nurse the press
> properly and to persuade various editors that it belongs to an
> entirely different category to the Sherard, Comtesse de Bremont sort
> of thing. It will be the first serious study of Wilde that has ever
> appeared, and I want it to be recognised as such. Why don't you
> begin to make arrangements about having it translated into German?
> You ought to make something by the rights. I recommend
> Meyerfeld because he will be careful to boom it all over Germany.
> He ought to have the proofs, of course, before the book is
> published.[17]

By the summer of 1911 the project was well under way; Robbie was answering various points that Ransome raised in his correspondence, but he was careful not to influence Ransome's own interpretation of Oscar Wilde's life and work. Although Robbie, as Wilde's literary executor, gave his support to the book, Ransome still needed Methuen's consent before using quotations from Wilde's writings. But as Ransome pointed out in a letter to Robbie, he had heard via Secker that Methuen were giving him only very lukewarm support, and wished to see a complete set of proofs before giving their consent. Nevertheless, when Ransome sent him the introduction to the book, Robbie responded with generous praise:

> If the rest of your book has the eloquence and excellence of the
> introduction I shall have no cause to be disappointed. It is really
> admirable. You have adopted a brilliant method of *ringing up your
> curtain*.
>
>   There are two points (nothing to do with Wilde) on which

pedants might trip. By 1854 Rossetti had been discussed in *The Times* and *Athenaeum* and was better known then, than a few years later when he ceased to exhibit. If you omit *unknown* you will be all right. *Rising* and *Promising* are rather dreadful substitutes?...

Let me hear what Methuen says. I am sure the book would have a success with them, only I doubt if Secker will part. I would not mind advancing a certain amount to buy Secker out if necessary but don't tell Methuen that. He is stingy and if he thinks anyone else will risk, he will do nothing himself.[18]

Methuen had indicated they would have preferred to publish his book, an offer Ransome would have liked to accept, as his own relationship with Secker had reached an impasse. He continued to worry over the matter of the quotations; and Methuen's delay in giving their permission affected Ransome's ability to work. Robbie again took on the role of diplomat, smoothing down Ransome's ruffled feathers, stressing that his only concern should be to see that the work on the book went ahead unhindered by petty worries and distractions caused by the machinations of his publishers:

You can tell Methuen you have sent me the list. But don't write more letters to Secker than you can help. I fear it was your interview with Secker that was melodramatic. However your *attitude* must now be one of *helplessness* leaving it to Methuen and Secker to fight out. Methuen would in *any case* have cut up rough about the quotations, so that has nothing to do with the previous wish that they should eventually publish.

You have only to go on with the work as if nothing happened. When Secker writes reply that "you are really in his hands and cannot say or do anything more, but that the quotations are *essential* to your book". Even if the book is held up a little it does not affect either its value or your position.[19]

Ransome continued to be unhappy with the way Secker was treating him and it only tended to make the events which followed even more difficult to resolve peacefully. But Robbie had other reasons for worry. He was fearful that, however true and honest Ransome's assessment of Wilde was, Douglas would find a way of commenting adversely on the book. Douglas and Crosland might vent their spleen in the letter columns of the national press, but Robbie was far more concerned that they would use the grossly unfair libel laws to harm Ransome and his book. As publication day approached Robbie still had to placate Ransome's resentment towards the two publishers:

> I really think Secker's contention is fairly reasonable and I don't
> think you must attempt to jockey him out of the book but I think
> you might reasonably show the letter to Methuen and ask them to
> advance what money you require as Secker has proposed to withhold
> payment of your dues on account of Methuen's demands. I would
> send a copy of Secker's letter to Methuen leaving out the words
> *unjustifiable extortion* as that will only make mischief and trouble if
> they read that. I presume of course that Methuen has some contract
> with you by which sums will be due to you for your other books.[20]

In spite of all the difficulties, Ransome was grateful for all Robbie's
generous help:

> He [Robbie] was extremely amusing, alert, witty and selflessly
> devoted not only to Wilde but to any artist whose work he liked. He
> was at that time much interested in Eric Gill. He showed me one
> day a beautiful little gilt figurine of a Madonna and Child that he
> was buying for some gallery or other. He saw that I admired it.
> "Take her home", he said, "I don't need her for a week. You take
> her home and look at her whenever you can. Let me have her back
> by next Saturday". I did not take the risk of having the little statue
> in my care, but Ross's offer was just like him.[21]

There is no doubt that Robbie showed Ransome a copy of *De Profundis*; he certainly had in his possession a typed draft of the letter, but it
was not a complete or accurate transcript of Wilde's prison letter,
although Ransome always believed he had seen the only typed copy.
What is not in dispute, however, is that Ransome's book and his assertion that he had seen the whole of *De Profundis* were to have calamitous
repercussions. Robbie never made any secret of the fact that the suppressed parts of the letter were critical of Douglas and his father; but he
had certainly never actively sought to make Wilde's criticisms public. It
is possible that Douglas's actions of the past three years had made
Robbie certain that only a public humiliation of Douglas would end their
quarrel. The time had long passed when he could view Douglas's denun-
ciations as merely irritating, they were becoming dangerous and
increasingly difficult to ignore.

If only Robbie and Bosie Douglas had been able to settle their differences and to admit that they had more in common than they both
realised. They could have grown old and content together—boring or
enthralling, according to the tastes of their audience—as they remin-
isced about their days as Wilde's acolytes.

In his single-minded devotion to Wilde's memory, Robbie left himself exposed to attack from his enemies, which they exploited without mercy. It must be a matter for regret that Douglas ever met Crosland; that meeting and their subsequent association ruined Robbie, mirroring the ruin that Lionel Johnson caused when he took Bosie Douglas to tea with Oscar Wilde.

In December D. S. MacColl, Keeper of the Wallace Collection, wrote an article on the problems of resources and administration of the National Gallery. It was inevitable he should ask Robbie for help in publicising the problems of the Gallery:

> It would be a great help if the *Morning Post* were to take it up, and give an article or leader, I don't mind how critical.
>
> By the way, I hope you are going to join the National Art-Collections Fund.[22] It is the Fund that has made changes possible, and that has got a whip-hand of the situation. I desire, if I could work it, to see you on the executive where your knowledge of works of art and of the market and judgement generally would make a great addition to our forces.[23]

Robbie responded in his usual generous manner, and as art editor he was able to do much. He was particularly scathing that neither the Government nor the general public seemed concerned that the nation's art treasures were being sold to wealthy collectors in the United States and Germany. In a long article in the *Morning Post* which included interviews with Charles Ricketts and D. Croal Thomson of the French Galleries in Pall Mall, who both supported him, Robbie urged the Government to take action:

> It is well, therefore, that we should be moved to some definite measure of preservation. If the present agitation reaches the ears of the Government it may induce its members to consider how far they can help to retain the works of art that have been for centuries a symbol of our national culture, and in bringing about a more reasonable state of affairs in the administration of our National Galleries.[24]

If Robbie, at the start of his service as Wilde's literary executor, had been granted one wish, it is quite probable he would have asked for a Copyright Bill to be given the Royal Assent. The Berne Convention of 1886 and the Berlin Conference of 1908 had laid the groundwork for the

ROBERT ROSS, taken in 1916, two years before his death. *(Courtesy Exors. Professor G. Robertson.)*

OSCAR WILDE, at the pinnacle of his success, circa 1894. *(Courtesy Merlin Holland)*

AUGUSTA ELIZABETH ROSS, Robbie's mother. Daughter of Robert Baldwin. *(Courtesy of J-P. B. Ross)*

HON. JOHN ROSS, Robbie's father. Canadian politician and barrister. *(Courtesy J-P. B. Ross)*

ROBBIE, aged about 13. *(Courtesy J-P.B. Ross)*

ROBBIE (right) with tutor and friends. *(Courtesy J-P. B. Ross)*

JACK (seated) and ALEX, Robbie's brothers. *(Courtesy J-P. B. Ross)*

JOHN (Jack) ROSS,
Robbie's eldest brother.
(*Courtesy J-P. B. Ross*)

MARY ROSS, Robbie's
eldest sister. Wife of Major
Charles Jones. (*Courtesy
Exors. Professor G.
Robertson*)

ROBERT ROSS, circa 1890, portrait by Frances Richards, Canadian artist, friend of Mary Jones. *(Courtesy Exors. Professor G. Robertson)*

ALEX (left) and ROBBIE, circa 1888. *(Courtesy Exors. Professor G. Robertson)*

THE JONES FAMILY OF JESMOND HILL, circa 1898. (Left to right) Back row:
Hilda, Ethel, Petica, Lillian, Edward. Front row: Emily, Margaret, William.
(Courtesy Exors. Professor G. Robertson)

JESMOND HILL, the home of Major and Mrs Charles Jones. *(Courtesy of J-P. B.
Ross.)*

ETHEL JONES, Robbie's niece, second wife of Sir S. Squire Sprigge. A portrait by William Rothenstein. *(Courtesy Professor & Mrs T. S. Sprigge)*

SIR SAMUEL SQUIRE SPRIGGE, Editor of *Lancet*, Secretary & Chairman of *The Society of Authors*. A Portrait by William Rothenstein. *(Courtesy Professor & Mrs T. S. Sprigge)*

CECIL SQUIRE SPRIGGE, son of Squire Sprigge and Ada Moss, step great-nephew of Robbie's. *(Courtesy Professor & Mrs T. S. Sprigge)*

SIEGFRIED SASSOON, devoted to Robbie and always true to his memory.
(Courtesy Sir Rupert Hart-Davis)

VYVYAN HOLLAND (Wilde's younger son) London 1914 after being
commissioned. *(Courtesy Merlin Holland)*

MORE ADEY, in the garden of his home at Wotton-under-Edge in 1920. *(Courtesy Merlin Holland)*

THE FOUNTAIN at King's College, Cambridge, 1916. *(Courtesy King's College, Cambridge.)*

CHRISTOPHER SCLATER MILLARD, Graduate of Keble College, Oxford.
Bibliographer and Wilde scholar. *(Courtesy Bodleian Library)*

ALEXANDER GALT ROSS, Robbie's brother, stockbroker, businessman, a
bachelor and man of impeccable tastes. *(Courtesy Exors. Professor G. Robertson)*

SIR EDMUND GOSSE, lifelong friend and confidant of Robbie's. (*Courtesy Miss J. Gosse*)

OSCAR WILDE'S tomb at Pére Lachaise, Paris. Robbie's ashes also lay within the tomb. *(Courtesy Merlin Holland)*

British Government to introduce the necessary legislation, but the two general elections of 1910 delayed the passage of the Bill and it was not until 16 December 1911 that the Bill finally reached the statute book. After twenty-seven years of campaigning, it was a reason indeed for the Society of Authors to celebrate, and this they did, at the annual dinner on 8 December. The guests included Robbie and his nephew-in-law, Squire Sprigge, Chairman of the Management Committee, who had succeeded Alex as Secretary to the Society in the 1890s.

In the first few weeks of 1912 the columns of the *Morning Post* carried many long articles and letters from the leading art experts of the day, more than fulfilling MacColl's wish for publicity for his cause. But alongside the debate on the finances of the National Gallery, Robbie was involved in a potentially more damaging dispute concerning the display of paintings at the Royal Academy by the recently deceased Edwin Austin Abbey. In a wide-ranging review of the winter exhibition at Burlington House,[25] Robbie was particularly critical of Abbey's work, but his remarks were made with his usual good humour and lack of pomposity, something which could not be said of some of the other participants in the debate. His comments brought forth a storm of protest, not least from the artist J. Walter West, who, not content with disagreeing with Robbie's views on Abbey's art, added his own opinion of art critics.

Robbie could not fail to respond to such a challenge. He had to defend his reputation as a critic, which he did with a rare and delightful show of pretentiousness:

> My criticism is based on long and earnest study, not only of ancient and modern drawings, but of those who prize and collect them. The critic is concerned only with the point of view of the collector and the public. No artist ought really to be concerned as to what any critic says of his own or anyone else's work. The function of the critic is to stimulate people to take an intelligent interest in pictures, and where possible to make them form opinions of their own, independently of artist or critic.... The critic (who is sometimes an artist) is often wrong, or at least posterity does not always endorse his criticism.[26]

The years of peace and tranquillity were coming to an end. Robbie's easy-going relationship was disturbed; Fabian Ware, his editor on the *Morning Post*, had retired and was replaced by H.A. Gwynne who did not always appreciate Robbie's free spirit. Their simmering disagreements reached a climax in February 1912. Robbie wrote an appreciation of the 'Futurists' Exhibition' which was diametrically opposed to the views held by Gwynne, although, as Robbie told Edmund Gosse, there were other reasons for his subsequent resignation:

> What I have been expecting for some weeks and always thought might happen occurred the day before yesterday. I have been compelled to resign my position on the *Post*. Nothing was done rashly on my part, a pistol was held at my head. I have nothing to complain of whatever, everything is decency and order. Of course I was *intrigued* out of the office just as Ware and Belloc and others have been. Briefly I was invited either to take a smaller salary or to undertake definite office work from 7-11 p.m. and 3-7 p.m. on alternative evenings. The Editor with charming candour said he never expected I would accept either suggestion. About a month ago there was a complaint that I was "too slow in getting art notices" and "that my colleague had too much to do". This was quite a reasonable and true charge. But I was able to point out that in a letter I wrote to [the] former Editor I warned him that I was always a slow worker and would always be one and that he must accept that among my other disabilities. That my colleague (whose duties are different to mine) had too much on his hands I always conceded and pointed out myself to the new Editor when he took the chair. Of course I am very sorry and it is a little awkward for the moment from a financial point of view.
>
> As I have no technical grievance against the Editor and manager I don't want my friends to say I have. I would rather they said the *Post* was foolish to let me go. Of course no one is indispensable but I can claim to have raised the prestige of the paper as an authority on artistic questions. My official duties cease on March 31st.[27]

Philip Wilson Steer voiced the disappointment of many of the leading artists at Robbie's departure from the *Morning Post*: 'I am naturally disappointed that you, who have always in the past stood by me through thick and thin and whose writings I so much admire, should be muzzled.'[28]

Thirteen

Ups and Downs

ITH THE imminent loss of his position on the *Morning Post* it was inevitable that Robbie's friends should come to his aid with ideas for alternative paid employment. Charles Holmes said, 'I venture asking only because I have the hearty support of Roger F[ry]—is it too late to stand for the Slade? You would be a godsend there besides I should dearly like to be able to answer you someday with "tu quoque".'[1] Robbie did not go to the Slade, although his administrative expertise would have been a considerable asset to the School. He was, however, offered another equally prestigious, if not as financially rewarding, position.

If things had worked out differently, Robbie's involvement with the Johannesburg Art Gallery would have been among his finest memorials. As it was, the fates conspired against him, and although he held his directorship for only a short time, he remained committed to the fine ideals of the Gallery until his death.

The two people most responsible for the creation of the Johannesburg Art Gallery were Sir Lionel Phillips, a politician and diamond merchant, and his wife Lady Florence. The building was designed in 1909-11 by Sir Edwin Lutyens, with the assistance of two South Africans, Herbert Baker and J.M. Solomon. Sir Hugh Lane was the first London-based director of the Gallery, but, regrettably, by December 1910 he felt it was time for him to withdraw; his health was failing and he wanted to retire to the peace of the country. Lane recommended to Lady Phillips that the work of honorary director and chief purchaser could be done by either Henry Tonks or Robert Ross. In the event it was some time before the Johannesburg Municipal Council recommended a replacement for Sir Hugh, by which time Henry Tonks was committed to teaching at the Slade School and could not spare the time to become officially involved. He did, however, retain a keen interest in the affairs of the Gallery, and bought a number of pictures on their behalf. Lady Phillips, unhappy at the delay in appointing a successor, and frustrated by the procrastinations of the Municipal Council in building the Gallery, decided to act on her own initiative and in February 1912 she appointed Robbie as the new London director. She agreed to pay him a sum of £150 per annum from

her own resources, but she did not immediately inform the Municipal
Council of the appointment.

Arthur Ransome's book *Oscar Wilde: A Critical Study* appeared in March
1912. Without asking permission Ransome dedicated the book to Robbie, which embarrassed and annoyed him. Before publication Ransome
wanted Robbie to read the final proofs but he refused; although he came
to regret his decision. His reasons had seemed right at the time. He told
Carlos Blacker that his decision was 'because I felt that there would be
much in it of which I disapproved, and I thought the value of Ransome's
opinion (the fresh opinion of a younger generation) would be vitiated if I
began to doctor it.'[2] Ransome had been scrupulous in his treatment of
Douglas, to the extent that Douglas's name did not even appear in the
text. Robbie was concerned that there were obvious libels which anyone
intimate with the details of Wilde's friendship with Douglas could not
fail to see. Nevertheless the book looked as if it would have a well-
deserved success. *The Times* Book Club agreed to put it on its list and it
was reviewed favourably by many of the leading literary critics.

It was therefore not surprising that it came to the notice of Bosie
Douglas, who thought he saw the sure hand of Robbie behind Ransome's
oblique references and masked insults and he was determined to seek
retribution from his enemy. He turned to Crosland for advice and,
predictably, Crosland advised Douglas to issue writs against the author,
the publisher, the printers and *The Times* Book Club. Crosland's advice
should have been ignored for it was based solely on his own petty
grievances against Wilde, on his own personal prejudices and on his own
enjoyment of litigation. Unfortunately, Douglas's behaviour at that time
was irrational, racked as he was with personal disasters: his marriage was
not without conflict, he was involved in a bitter legal wrangle with his
father-in-law, Colonel F.H. Custance, and his financial position was
precarious. The last thing he needed was another area of conflict, but as
he saw Ross successful and fêted, dormant jealousies came to life. If
Douglas's behaviour was irrational and illogical then Robbie's subsequent actions were totally out of character. The most obvious and
natural thing would have been for him to advise Ransome to apologise to
Douglas, admit that the offending words could have caused hurt, offer to
make any minor alterations Douglas wished and, above all, insist that no
libel had been intended. Douglas might have been placated and the affair
would have had a happy ending. Regrettably this was not a time for
gentlemen's agreements. The apology was not forthcoming and the writs
were issued.

On learning of the writs, Robbie introduced Ransome to Sir George

Lewis, and between them they set about entering a Plea of Justification. Robbie had obviously learnt nothing from the disasters which followed Wilde's attempt to prosecute the Marquess of Queensberry, and he had certainly not learnt anything from the Freddie Manners-Sutton fiasco. His legal education was going to be costly in financial terms and in terms of his personal contentment. He offered to pay Ransome's legal costs, which Ransome, with a wife and young daughter to support, could ill-afford. The final bill nearly resulted in Robbie's own bankruptcy.

On 31 March he left his job on the *Morning Post*, and the next day, he sat down to write another letter of resignation to Martin Holman, of Parker & Garratt, solicitors to the Wilde Estate. It was fifteen years to the day since Wilde had asked him to be his literary executor; now he felt compelled to relinquish his position:

> I must now ask you to take the necessary steps for relieving me of
> the administration of Oscar Wilde's literary estate at the end of this
> year. I want this done quite irrespective of any issue that may result
> from the libel action now impending against Ransome. It will be
> quite impossible for me in the future to harmonise my own interests
> with my duties as Wilde's executor and the administrator of his
> estate on behalf of his children. For my own protection it might at
> any moment become necessary for me to publish or bring before the
> public in a law court, a correspondence that no one officially, and
> ultimately supposed to protect Wilde's literary reputation, could
> produce without the gravest misinterpretation being put on such a
> proceeding. That any such contingency will arise I hope is very
> improbable. You know however the circumstances as well as any
> one else. During the last three years I have been subject to
> intermittent persecution from Alfred Douglas. I have followed the
> advice which you yourself, the late Sir George Lewis, the present Sir
> George Lewis and all my friends gave me. Meanwhile that
> persecution has not ceased and I shall not feel easy unless I am free
> (when the time comes, if it does come, for my vindication;) to act
> without reference to the interest of living or dead persons.[3]

Robbie did not sign the letter, and it must be a matter of speculation as to whether he sent it to Martin Holman. Probably on reading it through he realised that if he resigned as Wilde's literary executor, Douglas would have won a moral if not a legal victory. It is also doubtful if Vyvyan and Cyril Holland—although they were now both of age—would have accepted Robbie's resignation. When Robbie needed their help they gave it willingly and generously and their support and friendship remained steadfast through all his legal wrangles with Douglas and Crosland.

In May Carlos Blacker invited Robbie down to his home in Torquay, but reluctantly he had to decline the invitation. He was undergoing medical treatment, the strain of the past few months having taken a toll of his very limited physical reserves. As with Edmund Gosse, there was a paradox in Blacker's relationship with Ross; Blacker could not deny he knew the truth of Wilde's sins, nor could he deny that Robbie had been implicated in the scandal. Blacker also knew that Robbie had shared his home for twenty years with More Adey and Freddie Smith, and had never denied his intimacy with Wilde. And yet, although Blacker had two adolescent sons, he did not believe they were in any moral danger from an association with Robbie. Indeed he may even have encouraged a fraternal friendship between them, especially when Pip, his younger son, became acquainted at Eton with Cecil, the only son of Squire Sprigge. In spite of the family connection, Sprigge, a medical man, who would have understood the psychological and physiological needs of the homosexual, would hardly have remained silent if he thought his son and Blacker's were in imminent danger of being seduced by Robbie. The friendship between them survived all the subsequent traumas and ended only when death parted them.

Robbie was not sentimental about the young and, indeed, had firm ideas about the social dangers of introducing the sons of his friends to each other as he admitted to Carlos Blacker:

> I have a decadent little nephew at Eton, called Sprigge. I wonder if
> your sons dislike him very much... My nephew is a clever lazy boy
> who is on the Foundation and is given over, as far as I can make
> out, to Ritualism and socialism.[4]

Robbie may have been too ill to travel to Torquay, but it did not stop him becoming involved in another controversy that was occupying the letters columns of the national press. The dispute concerned the hanging at the National Gallery of a painting (a full-length portrait of Lady Colin Campbell) by Signor Boldini, an artist not yet dead. The controversy attracted the attention of many notable artistic personalities, Sir Charles Holroyd, Director of the National Gallery, admitted that he had been solely responsible for the loan of the portrait from the National Portrait Gallery. Holroyd explained that the Boldini portrait would not have been allowed to hang in the Tate Gallery, which allowed only native British art to be shown; there was though, Sir Charles insisted, no reason why

Boldini or any other contemporary foreign painter should not be exhibited at the National Gallery. Sir Philip Burne-Jones, painter and nephew of Sir Edward, and Marion Spielmann entered into the argument and gave their views on the relative merits of the Boldini portrait. The discussion became broader when claims and counter-claims were made as to whether the Trustees of the National Gallery were tied by a mandatory Charter or by a set of discretionary Rules. Agreement was not to be found, but it was an ungallant comment of Spielmann's that Lady Colin Campbell was 'a clever journalist and certainly made some figure in society' which brought forth Robbie's wrath. He replied in some detail to the major arguments but his most pertinent comments were reserved for the defence of the lady:

> It is not as a clever journalist nor as a clever art critic (Lady Colin Campbell was both) that her portrait was accepted by the Trustees of that institution; but simply because she was acknowledged to be one of the most exquisite and stately types, the appearance of which is always an addition to history.[5]

Frequently in his *Morning Post* articles and in his Letters to Editors, Robbie defended the cult of Beauty. Be it a beautiful woman, a fine piece of porcelain or a picture of exceptional merit, if it was beautiful in design and exquisite in execution, he would defend it. He always admired beauty in women, and his natural chivalrous character would not allow others to make disparaging remarks about them. He was equally eloquent when defending a contemporary artist of exceptional merit against a Royal Academician.

There was also work to be done for the Johannesburg Art Gallery. Lady Phillips was mainly responsible for securing for the Gallery two extremely generous benefactors, Sigismund Neumann and Max Michaelis. She was a person of strong opinions, and she had the determination to carry out her plans without worrying about the consequences of her actions. It was not long before she was giving Robbie very precise instructions, which she expected him to carry out without delay. Michaelis had promised the Gallery £5000, and Lady Phillips was anxious that the money should be spent quickly but expediently. She was inclined to spend the whole sum on sculpture and would even consider casts, but she did not consider them so pleasing. She was adamant that the money should not be spent on the English School of painting, which must have displeased Robbie, who delighted in their work. Michaelis had also been induced to contribute an additional £1000 for the Art Library, and Lady Phillips wanted the money principally spent on books on architecture.

In return for his generosity to the Gallery, Michaelis was not above asking Robbie for a favour:

> I learned that you are a friend of Mr Sargent. I am a great admirer
> of... [his] art and should very much like to possess some works from
> his brush but hear his landscapes are generally disposed of even
> before exhibition. It would also give me great pleasure, were he to
> make a drawing of my wife and little daughter. Do you know
> whether he is likely to be in Paris now, or in England during the
> autumn?[6]

Robbie approached Sargent, but he had not contacted Michaelis before the latter left for Marienbad in June; but as he told Robbie he hoped to be back in England in the autumn and confidently hoped the meeting with Sargent would then take place. As Lady Phillips was acquainted with many members of that select circle of artists and art connoisseurs whom Robbie regarded as his friends his task was somewhat eased. He met Lady Phillips's daughter Edith, and a bond of mutual respect grew between them. Lady Phillips's health was often poor, and much of the communication between her and Robbie was relayed either through Edith or her secretary, Dorothy Keith-Wright. His exact role in the affairs of the Gallery remained ill-defined, but he was constantly sought after by artists, dealers and private collectors who hoped to persuade him to buy their works for the Johannesburg Art Gallery, and his diplomacy as a dealer was often tested.

There were other honours awaiting him, and as if to reward him for his generous praise of their work in the pages of the *Morning Post* and in the correspondence columns in *The Times*, and now that he had a little more free time, the National Art-Collections Fund at their meeting in May 1912 elected Robbie on to the Executive Committee.[7]

The public and official nature of Robbie's appointments was too much for Douglas and Crosland to accept; they were both financially impoverished and virtually unemployed. The trouble was that Robbie's natural discretion made it difficult for them and they had to resort to conspiracy and dirty tricks to try to humiliate him. In these troubled times, as on so many previous occasions, Robbie turned to Edmund Gosse for advice; regrettably, though, he did not heed Gosse's wise counselling to

> adopt a policy entirely passive and neglectful. Your unhappy
> fondness for litigious struggles and fightings, sometimes, if you will

forgive my saying so, causes you to lose a sense of the proportion of
things. You say you are full of anxieties, and I daresay you are, and
I am extremely sorry that you are, but you know that in your heart
you have a love of fighting, and that without some sort of semi-
public quarrel going on with some worthless degenerate or other,
your life would be insipid. I wish you could lift yourself, for once
and all, out of this circle of ideas and people. As to D[ouglas] as a
serious antagonist, or as to his grotesque and insane manoeuvres, I
regard them with contempt: and you should do the same. He is a
criminal, but not a dangerous one, because his mind is loose and
ragged.[8]

Early in July he spent the weekend at Ockham, the Kent home of
Lady Lovelace, where his fellow guests included Henry James and Hugh
Walpole. In August he applied for the position as Valuer of Pictures and
Drawings for the Board of the Inland Revenue. Douglas always main-
tained that Herbert Asquith had made the job for Robbie, and that his
appointment was directly the result of Parliamentary Patronage. This
claim, however, cannot be substantiated: Robbie had to ask his friends
for testimonials. These were forthcoming, including tributes from
Charles Holroyd, Charles Holmes and a glowing tribute from D.S.
MacColl:

> Mr Ross is a learned student of history of painting, and an excellent
> judge. . . . I have had occasion to appreciate the exactness of the
> knowledge thus acquired. A lady known to me applied to Mr Ross,
> as an expert, to value a collection of drawings of Old Masters, many
> of them rather out of the way and difficult to price. His estimate
> almost precisely agreed with the sum ultimately fetched by the sale
> of the collection.
>
> Mr Ross is further a man of the most scrupulous and delicate
> sense of honour, and I know no one who could be more completely
> trusted to give their due weight to all the considerations on which a
> decision should depend.[9]

His appointment was duly confirmed. The post would take Robbie all
over the country as he assessed pictures for death duty valuations. He
would enter many of the great estates of the land and the intimate nature
of his duties would make him more vulnerable to the accusations being
made by Douglas and Crosland. As well as his duties for the Inland
Revenue Lady Phillips was urging him to make greater efforts on behalf
of the Johannesburg Art Gallery. With regard to the finances of the

Gallery she told him: 'I shall put the money in the bank and if you send
me the accounts will pay them and when I leave will let Mr Beit have
them. Is that what you want?'[10]

On 28 September Robbie heard from Dorothy Keith-Wright that the
sum of £1750 had been placed on credit at Coutts Bank for him to spend
on behalf of the Gallery. He did not dwell too long on the question of
spending the money entrusted to him. With the assistance of Henry
Tonks, he acquired a number of notable Pre-Raphaelite paintings,
including *Cromwell on his Farm* by Ford Madox Brown; *The Good
Shepherd* and *The Importunate Friend*, both by Sir John Everett Millais;
and *Regina Cordium* by Rossetti. The Augustus John picture Robbie
acquired was *The Childhood of Pyramus*; an acquisition of which he was
particularly proud. It appreciated enormously in value within the space
of a few years. In collaboration with Henry Tonks, Robbie was also
responsible for the beautiful illustrated catalogue which accompanied the
Neumann Collection when it was finally sent to Johannesburg.

Controversies continued to occupy much of Robbie's time that autumn
of 1912; it had taken Jacob Epstein three years to complete the sculpture
for Wilde's memorial, and the finished work caused many angry protests
and accusations of indecency. The sculpture was of a vast winged figure
in the guise of a swiftly moving messenger. It is difficult to imagine what
sort of obelisk would have pleased all the different factions; a memorial
in the form of a robed angel with a glowing halo would have been
inappropriate, and the figure of a slim-built Greek youth would have
caused a hail of derision from the puritan sections of society. A simple
Celtic cross would have served well, but its essential simplicity would
have been a betrayal of the richness and extravagance of Wilde's life.
There is a grotesque magnificence to the Epstein tomb; rather like
Wilde's own physical stature: it is a vast grey stone mass which has about
it a feeling of permanence.

As Wilde's memorial neared completion the French Authorities considered certain parts of the winged statue were too indelicate and they
ordered the whole edifice to be covered by a tarpaulin until alterations
were made. Epstein refused to make any adjustments and in an attempt
to placate the sensitivities of the Authorities, but without consulting
Epstein, Robbie had a large bronze plaque made to cover the offending
appendages. The fig-leaf might well have saved the blushes of a few
young women, but it was a mistake. The plaque was soon removed by
collectors, and the process would, no doubt, have been repeated *ad
infinitum*, had duplicates been made. Sensitivities appeased, the French
Authorities then confiscated the monument and demanded £120 importa-

tion duties. Epstein was still a relatively poor man, and a fund was begun by Lytton Strachey and his friends. He also organised a petition to persuade the French customs service to repay the duty demanded. Robbie, Bernard Shaw, H.G. Wells and the painter John Lavery were among those who signed the petition, but Robbie must have had other things on his mind, or, he would never have signed a document which proclaimed Wilde as 'an English poet of distinction'.[11] Oscar Wilde had been proud of his Irish ancestry and he would surely have demanded an explanation for the careless lapse from his literary executor.

The affairs of the monument continued to occupy much of Robbie's time. He heard from various sources, in both Paris and London, that the official unveiling of the Epstein sculpture had been postponed, and in a typically irreverent letter to the editor of the *Pall Mall Gazette* Robbie gave the true facts:

> M. Lepine cannot have ordered any postponement of the unveiling of Mr Epstein's beautiful monument to Wilde for the very good reason that no date had been fixed for the ceremony. Even the police cannot postpone an unfixed date. The monument would in ordinary course have remained veiled, at my own instructions, until the ceremony. It is true that the police have taken official possession of this unique work of art, of which I am sure they will take the greatest care.
>
> I regard the arrest of the monument by the French authorities simply as a graceful outcome of the *Entente Cordiale* and a symptom of that determination on the part of our allies to prove themselves worthy of political union with our great nation, which, rightly or wrongly, they think has always put Propriety before everything. I hesitate to say that the rest lies in the lap of the gods, because that is precisely the part of the statue to which exception is taken.[12]

The protests failed to sway the French Authorities, and even with Robbie's bronze plaque shielding the offending features from public gaze, the monument remained shrouded in tarpaulin until May 1914.

His official duties at Somerset House and his work for the Johannesburg Art Gallery were taking up all his time, yet, in October, he could not resist the temptation to become involved in yet another protracted correspondence in *The Times* over the desecration of Philae by the building of the dam at Assuan. And in doing so he took his sphere of interest one step further; however, as with every controversy into which he entered, he had more than sufficient knowledge of the subject to give his views weight and authority. Sir Henry Knollys, the civil engineer responsible for the building of the dam, began the correspondence by trying to defend the decision to destroy the ancient tomb. George Birdwood, an authority on Eastern and Indian art, protested at the destruction by drawing a comparison between the beauties of the Parthenon, Philae and the Taj Mahal, which he described as 'the three most enchanting "beauty spots" on the face of this world',[13] and then asking the readers of *The Times* to decide which they would save if given a free choice. It was a question to which he knew there was no answer; but Knollys had already asked readers to decide which they would save if they were alone in a burning garret with the '*Dresden Madonna*[14] on the walls and a live baby on the floor'.[15]

Robbie took his theme from George Birdwood. He admitted that he was not an Egyptologist, nor had he ever been to Philae, but he did not think that prevented him from having an opinion. He protested that simply because a ruin was of 'a comparatively late period' it was not unworthy of preservation; he was inclined to the view that only their descendants could decide what was and what was not of historical interest. He took issue with Sir Henry Knollys who had suggested it was too fantastic to consider knocking down the Parthenon to feed the Greek nation. Robbie argued that Knollys, as an engineer, was aware that the ruins could be sold to the Americans and removed stone by stone and re-erected in some distant state. Robbie might have been cynical about the destruction of the Parthenon, but he had no such contempt for the possible loss of the *Dresden Madonna*:

> In regard to the pertinent parallel (if it be a true parallel to Philae and the Nile Dam) of the burning garret, the baby and the Dresden Sistine Madonna, let me say at once that I would rescue Raphael's picture first. I might argue that the sale of the rescued picture would build a small Nile Dam, or at least save hundreds of other babies from starvation. But I will not: I will merely ask a question of my own. Had America the right to sacrifice so many human lives in the construction of the Panama Canal in order to save millions of money?[16]

Robbie neither expected nor received an answer to this last question, although the *Globe* newspaper, never a supporter of creative or cultural affairs, took the opportunity to lampoon and ridicule his judgement in advocating the saving of a picture before the life of a child. Miss Adeline L. Newman, in a letter to that newspaper, asked if Robbie would save himself before the picture or the baby. She pointed out that if he saved the baby it could grow up to be another Raphael. Robbie considered her arguments carefully, but he still had no doubt where his duty lay:

> There are many other works of art for which, sitting beside a patent fire-extinguisher, I find it easy to think that I would lay down my life; there are few adults or babies for whom I would make any such sacrifice...I have duly considered the possibility of the child being a second Raphael. But the odds against it are so overwhelming that I do not think it would be worth while risking the *Dresden Madonna* against them, especially after a visit to the Grafton Gallery. Besides, I disapprove of gambling.[17]

Soon the controversies would not be to his liking; he would have little time to defend the destruction of an ancient tomb or the honour of a beautiful woman. He would be too busy defending Wilde's name and his own honour.

In late autumn Crosland went into print with an odious and contemptible parody of *De Profundis*, entitled *The First Stone*. In the Preface, Crosland wrote: 'With the exception of a very occasional row of periods, there is nothing about it to indicate that it is a fragmentary or incomplete work, or that it has been edited into its present form by the simple process of omitting quite half of what the author really wrote.'[18] Crosland maintained that *De Profundis* should never have been published, even in its abridged form, and he hoped it would never be published in its entirety. He declared, 'I have read every word of it and shuddered as I read.'[19]

His confession disturbed Robbie, who did not know how Crosland had gained access to a complete copy of *De Profundis*. Douglas had always argued that he had never seen the complete text of Wilde's prison letter, yet, somehow Crosland had managed to read the entire letter. In his scathing Preface, Crosland said of the letter: 'A blacker, fiercer, falser, craftier, more grovelling or more abominable piece of writing never fell from mortal pen.'[20] In trying to justify his attack on a dead man he declared; 'I admit that in ordinary circumstances common decency would have prevented me. Wilde is dead; let his crowning devilry die with him—yes, Mr Robert Ross, I say, devilry!'[21]

November began badly and ended badly. Douglas intensified his vendetta; between 1 and 5 November he wrote Robbie three offensive and objectionable letters, in which he again accused Robbie of sodomy, anarchy and socialism. Douglas was annoyed that his writs against Arthur Ransome were being contested; he had expected Ransome to capitulate and the affair to be settled out of court and that he would gain

substantial financial recompense from the publishers and *The Times*
Book Club. In the event Douglas was faced with a Plea of Justification
and an army of barristers and legal experts. Not unnaturally he blamed
Robbie for this unpleasant turn of events, and gave vent to his anger in a
series of letters.[22]

The accusation of sodomy frightened Robbie, but Douglas had been
making the same charge for years, and, anyway, it was a crime where the
accuser was, or had been, as guilty as the accused. The charge of
socialism for an old-fashioned Radical was harder to bear; as for anarchy,
that was ludicrous, he believed in firm government, but as a committed
pacifist, he viewed the increasing tension between Great Britain and
Germany with despair. He feared that war, between the nation that had
been his home since he was a child and the nation he respected for their
devotion to Oscar Wilde's works, would cause him to have divided
loyalties.

Douglas fully expected Robbie to sue for libel. Robbie resisted the
temptation but continued to give his full support to Arthur Ransome.

The impending libel against Ransome unfortunately split Robbie's
friends into those who agreed with his support of the young writer and
those who were appalled by his continued disagreements with Douglas.
Max Beerbohm was concerned that Reggie Turner, living so close to
Robbie, would be drawn into the affray, and thought that Turner had
always done all he could to help Robbie. Beerbohm's worry, however,
did not prevent him from writing to wish Robbie success when the case
finally came to court. Beerbohm's attitude was always ambiguous; in
direct communication with Robbie he would be loyal and affectionate;
behind his back and usually to Robbie's most intimate friends he would
be scathing and critical. Robbie was a realist; he never had any illusions
about his friend's complex interpretations of what should have been a
matter of simple fact. Writing to Ada Leverson, Robbie suggested, with
amusement, that she should consult Turner if she wanted to hear the
truth of the problems he was experiencing:

> The really amusing person to give you about six different
> impressions of the situation is Reggie Turner. He prophesies
> according to the *last* person he has seen. After an afternoon with
> Max he thinks "Robbie is very silly!!!" After an afternoon with
> More Adey he thinks "Robbie is in great danger." After an
> afternoon with George Lewis he thinks "Bosie is in great danger and
> also very silly." After an afternoon or evening with *me* he assures me
> that "He is going abroad before Xmas."[23]

On 29 November Robbie attended a party at 34 Queen Anne's Gate, the

London home of Lord and Lady Glenconner. The Prime Minister and Margot Asquith were among the guests; initially Robbie was reluctant to attend; he consulted George Lewis and various friends, who assured him he should attend, as Douglas most certainly would not be there. Robbie had been at the party only a few minutes and was talking to Mrs Belloc Lowndes when Douglas came up to him and said: 'You have got to clear out of this: you are nothing but a bugger and a blackmailer.'[24] Deeply shaken and distressed by the public humiliation but unwilling to retaliate Robbie took his leave of Lord Glenconner. Margot Asquith, angry that Ross had been insulted at the home of her brother, drove him back to Downing Street where he quickly recovered his composure. The next morning Robbie wrote a letter of apology to Glenconner:

> I feel I must write and express to you and Lady Glenconner my deep regret at what occurred last night not merely because of the unpleasantness to myself, but for being the occasion of discord under your hospitable roof. Had I known that Alfred Douglas was likely to be there I would not have availed myself of Lady Glenconner's kind invitation. I do not propose to trouble you with the origin or cause of Douglas's alleged grievances against me but if you wished for an immediate explanation Sir George Lewis would, I am sure, place all the information you may want before you. This will of course be made public in the legal proceedings instituted by Douglas himself, when the pending litigation is heard. I feel sure that any one who may have a curiosity in the matter will be reassured in regard to my reluctant share concerning the incident at your house.[25]

The year of 1912 was coming to a fretful close. As the demands made on Robbie increased so did his disinclination to take any positive action to solve them. He needed to bring an end to the persecution by Douglas and Crosland and he needed to protect Wilde's memory from their evil pens. To add to his burdens Lady Phillips was leaving England for South Africa, and her demands increased as the day of her departure approached. She ordered him to see Sir Hugh Lane and, together with him, persuade Max Michaelis to agree to have his portrait painted for presentation to the Gallery. She wanted William Orpen to be given the commission, unless Robbie had other ideas. Her husband also wanted to present Hugh Lane's portrait to the Johannesburg Art Gallery, but Lane was reluctant to sit, and Lady Phillips urged Robbie to get Lane to change his mind. She was also anxious that Otto Beit should again see the Thomas Baines pictures and she asked Robbie to take him. She thought

Beit could be induced to buy the entire collection, even though Edwards
was proving a reluctant seller. She was sure that with Robbie's intervention the whole matter could be successfully concluded; she had great
faith in his ability to solve all her problems. As the pressures increased he
neglected even more of his duties; Gosse might have thought he entered
into litigation for the pleasure of the fight, but in trying to defend his
honour against Douglas and Crosland, he would pay a terrible price.

Robbie, though, had few illusions about the direction of his life or
about his rightful place in the order of things, as he admitted wryly to
Oscar Browning:

> I am quite happy now; but I would like to have been something
> other than a contributor to *The Times*, and valuer to the Inland
> Revenue and Keeper of Wilde's reputation. I was so ambitious when
> you first gave me your stimulating friendship. Now I am a practical
> hard-headed Scotchman with no ideas except finance and the
> application of literary and graphic art to money. I am the frozen
> executor to four living artists and three living men of letters.
> Fortunately I can laugh at myself.[26]

He would need all his sense of humour as the tranquil years gave way
to two years of bitterness and despair.

III

BITTER YEARS

(1913-14)

O We are wearied of this sense of guilt,
Wearied of pleasure's paramount despair,
Wearied of every temple we have built,
Wearied of every right, unanswered prayer.
For man is weak; God sleeps, and heaven is high;
One fiery-coloured moment: one great love; and lo! we die.

Oscar Wilde, 'Panthea'

Fourteen

The Ransome Case

HE TRIAL of Arthur Ransome on a charge of libelling Lord Alfred Bruce Douglas was due to open on 13 March 1913, but as Douglas was answering a summons before the Court of Bankruptcy, Mr Justice Darling delayed the hearing until 17 April. Arthur Ransome was represented by Mr J.H. Campbell, KC and Mr H.A. McCardie. *The Times* Book Club retained the services of the flamboyant and controversial Member of Parliament, Frederick Edwin [F.E.] Smith, KC, (no relation of Robbie's friend, Freddie Smith) who was assisted by Mr Eustace Hills, and Mr W.G.Howard Gritten. Against these legal heavyweights stood Lord Alfred Douglas's Counsel, Cecil Hayes, who had been a witness at his wedding, Mr H. Benjamin assisting.

By the time the case came to Court, Douglas had withdrawn the writ against Secker and the printers. Secker had sold his interest in the book to Arthur Ransome and formally apologised to Douglas. In spite of all his previous problems with publishers, Ransome, instead of passing the rights of his Wilde book to Methuen, transferred his interests to the maverick publisher Charles Granville. Unfortunately, Ransome fell victim to Granville's charm and plausible lies, even believing, at least for a while, that they were related. Their association was short-lived and Ransome thus learnt another important lesson.

The Times Book Club entered a Plea of Denial, that the words complained of had the meaning that had been alleged in the writs. They further denied negligence in offering the book for sale.

The proceedings were opened by Mr Benjamin, but it was Cecil Hayes who put the case for the plaintiff. He outlined the sequence of events leading to Wilde's imprisonment and his years of exile and early death. Hayes went into considerable detail of how the friendship between Wilde and Douglas developed and he stressed that both men had initially benefited from the association. He said that when the friendship began Douglas was a young and impressionable undergraduate who had been charmed by Wilde's success as a writer and raconteur. Wilde, on the other hand, had been enchanted by Douglas's aristocratic lineage and social connections. Hayes said there had been many friends who had deserted Wilde at the moment of his disgrace:

> But there would always be found a few friends, though very few
> perhaps heroic, perhaps foolish, who would continue the man's
> friends in the after period.... They might continue their friendship
> to the unfortunate man in the belief that his soul might still be
> something to live for and something to hope.[1]

Hayes read the quotations from Ransome's book, which Douglas
thought constituted the alleged libel:

> The letter [*De Profundis*], a manuscript of "80 close written pages on
> 20 folio sheets", was not addressed to Mr Ross, but to a man
> [Douglas], to whom Wilde felt that he owed some, at least, of the
> circumstances of his public disgrace. It was begun as a rebuke to
> this friend [Douglas], whose actions, even subsequent to the trials,
> had been such as to cause Wilde considerable pain.... He had left
> prison with an improved physique, and now that he was able to
> work there was hope that he would not risk the loss of it by leaving
> this life of comparative simplicity. Suddenly, however, he flung
> aside his plans and resolutions, desperately explaining that his folly
> was inevitable. The interacted entreaty of a man whose friendship
> had already cost him more than it was worth, and a newly felt
> loneliness at Berneval destroyed his resolution. He became restless
> and went to Rouen, where it rained, and he was miserable; then
> back to Dieppe; a few days later, with his poem[2] unfinished, he was
> in Naples sharing a momentary magnificence with the friend, whose
> conduct he had condemned, whose influence he had feared.... Soon
> after Wilde left Berneval for Naples those who controlled the
> allowances that enabled him to live with his friend, purposefully
> stopped it. His friend, as soon as there was no money, left him. "It
> was", said Wilde, "a most bitter experience in a bitter life!"[3]

Even on the first day of the trial, Robbie, sitting in the well of the
Court with Arthur Ransome and his Counsel, must have had some
serious misgivings about the conduct of the proceedings. He had feared
that it would not be Douglas's conduct the jury would judge, but the
character and disgrace of Oscar Wilde. Lord Alfred's dominant presence
in the witness-box served only to strengthen his feeling of apprehension.
Although Douglas had aged considerably, his pose and superior bearing
would influence the mainly middle-class jury. There was little in the first
day's hearing to lighten Robbie's sense of gloom, particularly when
Douglas's Counsel referring to Oscar Wilde said that, 'though distinguished in the literary world, [he] was only a Bohemian and literary

adventurer who wanted to get into society'.[4] After Wilde's disgrace it was an often repeated slur, but it had little substance to it. Wilde's wit and genius for conversation had made him popular in society, and he had rarely been dependent on Douglas's introductions. On the contrary, his friendship with Douglas made him unwelcome at many London salons; the boorish behaviour of the Marquess of Queensberry had affected his son's social standing far more than his association with the brilliant, witty Oscar Wilde.

The shallowness of Douglas's case was revealed when he was cross-examined by Mr Campbell.

'Have other books been written making precisely the same charge against you?'

Douglas declared that if there had, he had not read any of them, a deliberate lie, which Campbell quickly refuted. He pointed out that in 1902 Robert Sherard had published a tribute to Oscar Wilde, in which he wrote:

> His [Wilde's] funds had all run out, he had nowhere to go to, and all the while his friend was pleading, fretting, menacing. This young man was in receipt of a considerable allowance from his family, and in his letters he placed his house, a delightful villa at Posilippo, and his purse at Wilde's disposal.
>
> The consequence was the natural one, and a few days later it became known that Oscar Wilde had resumed the friendship which had brought disaster and ruin upon him.[5]

Douglas had, indeed, at the time Sherard's book was published, consulted his solicitor Arthur Newton, but had not proceeded with the action. In the minds of all those who knew the full details of Wilde's last years, there was never any doubt that the 'friend' who had brought Wilde to disaster and ruin was Douglas. And, although, like Ransome, Sherard had not actually named him, the implications of his words were only too obvious; further, in dedicating the book to Robbie, Sherard had only added to the insult. In a moving tribute Sherard accurately assessed the nature of Ross's devotion to Wilde, during the years of his shame:

> In Remembrance/ of His Noble Conduct/ Towards the Unhappy Gentleman/ Who is The Subject of This Memoir, whom/ In Affliction He Comforted, In Prison He visited,/ and in Poverty He Succoured, Thus Showing /an Elevation of Heart and a Loyalty of Character.[6]

It is worth stating that in 1902 Douglas was not then actively engaged

in his campaign against Robbie. Nevertheless, the contrast between the
generous dedication and the blatant accusations made against him in
Sherard's book must have given Douglas a severe shock. Possibly it was
then that the seeds of hatred began to germinate. In 1913 he was ready to
reap a rich harvest.

It was not long before Mr Campbell brought up the subject of *De
Profundis*. Robbie, under subpoena, agreed that Arthur Ransome should
have access to the unpublished parts of the letter in preparing his Plea of
Justification. It was a decision he took with a heavy heart and he had a
foreboding that the repercussions would be distressing. He had not
wanted the general public to know the contents of the letter, nor did he
want it read out in open Court. The libel action was attracting a great
deal of Press attention and they would gleefully quote, probably out of
context, from Wilde's prison letter.

In answer to a question from Campbell, Douglas admitted that Ross
had handed him a copy of the manuscript that purported to have come
from Wilde, but he had destroyed it without reading it. Ransome's
Counsel said he proposed to read the unpublished parts of *De Profundis*
to the jury. Douglas's Counsel objected, but this was overruled by Mr
Justice Darling. McCardie began to read. Some memories faded, but the
picture of Wilde in his prison cell, the words coming fast from his pen,
remained as pertinent as the day they were written. The hurt he had
bottled up against Douglas came pouring forth:

> After long and fruitless waiting I have determined to write to you
> myself, as much for your sake as for mine,...Our ill-fated and most
> lamentable friendship has ended in ruin....Of the appalling results
> of my friendship with you I don't speak at present. I am thinking
> merely of its quality while it lasted. It was intellectually degrading to
> me. You had the rudiments of an artistic temperament in its germ.
> But I met you either too late or too soon. I don't know which.[7]

In the sixteen years since the letter was written it had lost none of its
poignancy, nor its tragedy. During the long reading of the letter, Douglas was ill at ease and interjected to ask if he could leave the witness-box.
Mr Justice Darling inquired if he felt unwell, and on being assured
Douglas was quite well, he was ordered to remain seated. Shortly before
the Court adjourned for the day, Counsel read the paragraph where
Wilde contrasted Douglas's behaviour with that of his other friends:

> I thank God every day that he gave me friends other than you. I owe
> everything to them. The very books in my cell are paid for by

Robbie out of his pocket-money. From the same source are to come
clothes for me, when I am released. I am not ashamed of taking a
thing that is given by love and affection. I am proud of it. But do
you ever think of what my friends such as More Adey, Robbie,
Robert Sherard, Frank Harris, and Arthur Clifton have been to me
in giving me comfort, help, affection, sympathy, and the like?[8]

As the day's proceedings came to an end Mr Justice Darling commented:

'It is plain that Wilde had written this [*De Profundis*] for publication,
because in it he gives himself the *beau* role all the time.'[9]

The case was resumed on the 18th and the reading of *De Profundis*
continued. After some twenty minutes, Mr Justice Darling noticed that
Douglas was not in the witness-box; he was summoned to take his place,
but to the Judge's dismay, and no doubt to many others', he was not to
be found. They waited a further five minutes, and when he still failed to
appear Mr Justice Darling ordered the reading to continue in his
absence. After a further ten minutes Douglas appeared. The Judge was
unhappy at Douglas's cavalier attitude to the Court and accordingly
issued a strong rebuke, not the last that day. Further exchanges between
Douglas and the Judge occurred; Douglas complained that Campbell
was asking the next question before waiting for his answer. He accused
Campbell of not wanting to hear the truth, which brought another
rebuke from Mr Justice Darling:

'Don't be impertinent to learned Counsel.'

'I accept your Lordship's rebuke,' Douglas replied.

'You will not only accept my rebuke, but you will act on it,' Mr
Justice Darling retorted.[10]

The interchange between Douglas and the Judge was a rare moment
of pleasure for Robbie, in what had been a day of unremitting gloom.

'In writing of his [Oscar Wilde's] conviction did you express a wish to
put it on its proper level and call it, "the greatest romantic tragedy of its
age"?' Campbell asked.

'Yes,' replied Douglas.

'That was after he had confessed to you in Holloway that he was guilty
of these practices?' Darling again interjected with an observation.

'Yes,' was Douglas's rather morose reply.[11]

Douglas was re-examined by his own Counsel. Cecil Hayes attempted
to establish his client's reputation as an athlete and sports-loving gentleman. He tried to distance his client from the sins of Oscar Wilde,
although he was prepared to link Douglas with Wilde's literary genius.
The day ended with a dreary catalogue of Wilde's financial problems,

and all that Douglas had personally done to ease them. The bare facts of Wilde's spending habits indicated that he had an irresponsible attitude to money, and an extravagant style of living which far exceeded his wealth. More Adey, in giving evidence, spoke with care and clarity in defence of Oscar Wilde. He was critical of Douglas's attitude to Wilde, both before and after his conviction. He admitted he was aware of the intimacy between Douglas and Wilde, and that it had been the subject of a grave scandal. He also agreed that one of his own personal objects was to prevent Wilde meeting Douglas after his release from prison. He did not dissent when Counsel suggested he had been assisted in this desire by Robert Ross.

Douglas had, indeed, had a bad day. His absence from Darling's Court that morning had been because his presence was required in another Court, that was meant to hear the public examination of his bankruptcy. He had to beg the indulgence of the Recorder for London and Dr Williams, Assistant Official Receiver, to grant a postponement of the hearing. The request was granted and the hearing was suspended until 12 June.

When the Ransome libel case resumed on the 21st, most of the day was taken up by the evidence of Alfred Bute, Director of *The Times* Book Club, who explained in some detail how the Club decided which books to add to their library lists, and which to offer for sale. He denied emphatically that there had been any negligence, on the part of the Club, or by any individual member of the selection committee, in picking the Ransome book. Two further witnesses were then called by Ransome's Counsel: one was M.Didier, the Frenchman who had translated Douglas's article, supporting Wilde's conduct, which he wrote for *Revue Blanche*[12] in 1896. Douglas later tried to blame the editor and the translator for the contents of the article, but there can be little doubt that when first published, the sentiments expressed were very much Douglas's own sentiments. The fact that he had spent the next decade repudiating them did not alter the truth, and when they were introduced they served only to strengthen Ransome's case.

The rest of the day was taken up by Counsel's closing speeches. F.E. Smith, at his eloquent best, put the case not only for *The Times* Book Club, but for Arthur Ransome as well. F.E. was aware that Ransome was in danger of losing his case, and if that happened then *The Times* Book Club would also lose. F.E. hated losing.

> People [F.E. said] as a rule did not read books about Oscar Wilde
> unless they were already familiar with the main features of his
> unhappy story. Could it be suggested that no book about Oscar

Wilde should contain any reference to the tragedy in his life? From
the point of view of history the world was entitled to know what
were the main facts in the history, literary or otherwise, of well-
known men, and how those facts could be stated less offensively
than in Mr Ransome's book, he was at a loss to understand....
Although the plaintiff [Douglas] had denied writing that article,
there was the most amazing correspondence between its language
and that of the plaintiff's letters to Mr Labouchère, they [the jury]
would have carefully to consider the plaintiff's account of the
authorship of that article. His own account was that he had accorded
an interview to a reporter of a *déclassé* paper, and that the reporter
had worked it up into an article. Could they believe that he had read
the article and had taken no proceedings to vindicate his honour? He
was prepared to hear that there were difficulties of procedure in the
way of France. But they had actually found the plaintiff
contributing to further issues of this paper.[13]

It was a powerful speech from the Master Orator; he dominated the
jury and they listened attentively to each argument presented; in conclusion he said:

With regard to Oscar Wilde, that unhappy child of genius, years had
passed since his fall, and men were beginning to be glad to think of
the artist rather than of the man's life. And now this legacy of
infamy had been resurrected, unnecessarily resurrected, again.[14]

Summing up on behalf of Arthur Ransome, Campbell stressed that
nowhere in *Oscar Wilde: A Critical Study* had the author named Lord
Alfred Douglas, and only those intimately connected with the Wilde
tragedy would know to whom the references applied. As F.E. had done,
Campbell also challenged Douglas's loss of memory about his articles
and correspondence with Labouchère. Campbell said it seemed that the
plaintiff's lapses of memory were extremely selective, and appeared only
to occur when it suited his purpose, and only when he was confronted
with the evidence of his own letters did his memory improve. Dealing
with the production of *De Profundis*, Campbell said the plaintiff's change
of feelings had followed the publication of the document. He had been
told by Ross that he would never publish the entire letter in the lifetime
of either of them. He went on:

There were still left from the wreck of Wilde's sordid tragedy men
who had stood loyally by him, such as Mr Robert Ross, who desired

> to collect such material of Wilde's work in the hope that the stigma
> of his private character might be palliated by the better
> demonstration of his literary greatness.[15]

In putting the counter-arguments, Cecil Hayes began by pointing out that Robert Ross had been in Court throughout the hearing, yet he had not been called to give evidence. He wanted to know how *De Profundis* came into the possession of Ross, and under what conditions he had given it to the British Museum, when it was so clearly the property of his client. Hayes was still speaking when the case was adjourned for the day. The next, and last, day of the hearing began with Cecil Hayes resuming his closing statement to the jury. During the morning, there was a spirited exchange between him and Darling, when Hayes again asked why Ross had not been called to give evidence.

'You may call him now if you wish,' Mr Justice Darling offered.

'But the onus of proving their justification lies on the defendants,' Hayes replied.

'Mr Ross is not a party to this action, and the decision of the question as to whether he should be called or not did not rest with him. It is my duty to protect him,' Mr Justice Darling remarked.

'He ought to have been called by the defendants. I could not cross-examine him as my witness, and should be bound by his answers,' Hayes protested, with little effect.

'I have listened in vain for any reason why he should have been called. He was only Wilde's literary executor,' Mr Justice Darling reminded the unfortunate Counsel.[16]

Hayes, however, was not to be denied the last word on the subject, and snapped angrily: 'I believe Mr Ross is well equipped to prove all my client's charges to be true.'

The exchange between Judge and Counsel continued for a little longer, but Robbie was not called to give evidence. In fact, the decision not to call him had been carefully orchestrated by Campbell, and supported by F.E. Smith. If Robbie had gone into the witness-box to support Ransome he would have been cross-examined by Cecil Hayes, and there was no knowing what harm would have ensued. Under oath, Robbie might inadvertently have condemned himself and earned the contempt of the Court and the hostility of the jury.

Cecil Hayes made some reference to the money his client had spent on Wilde after his release from prison; Douglas had come into Court only to clear his character and had never been motivated by the desire to obtain a large sum of money in settlement of damages. But, Cecil Hayes continued, his client should nevertheless be awarded something to show that his character was cleared and then he would not again have to defend his honour in a Court of Law.

Summing up, Mr Justice Darling said:

> Mr Ransome's book related to a very bad man of genius. Was nobody to write about him because his moral character was bad, or read his plays or see them?...Mr Ransome's book was published because Wilde was a great literary artist and manager of words. Whether they liked his work or not, whether they considered his paradoxes too laboured or not, he was nevertheless a great artist in written words and he wrote plays which were being performed at the present day...*De Profundis* was a most remarkable and interesting document. It must be read as a study of what a bad man, but a man of genius, went through in prison, and what the effect of prison was upon him, as written from day-to-day. It would be a great mistake to take all that he said as Gospel truth. The document was an excuse and an apology.[17]

Darling left the jury in no doubt that he regarded Ross as a man of honour, who had suppressed Wilde's condemnations of Douglas, until Douglas had issued the writs for libel against Ransome. Indeed, said Darling, 'It [*De Profundis*] might never have seen the light at all unless the plaintiff had brought his action. When he had attacked the defendants and Mr Ross he could not complain that they should bring the whole of the document so that the jury should have Wilde's own word as to what were the relations between Wilde and the plaintiff towards the end of the former's life.'[18]

The jury were out for only an hour and fifty-five minutes, and when they returned, it was to announce, that while they found the words complained of by the plaintiff did constitute a libel, they were, however, true in substance, and therefore they found for Arthur Ransome. *The Times* Book Club were cleared of negligence in circulating the book.

The findings were entered for the defendants and they were awarded the costs of the action. Robbie was delighted with the outcome of the case, believing that all his efforts on Wilde's behalf had been vindicated. Wilde's crimes had been forgotten, if not forgiven, and from then on only his literary genius would be important. Robbie was soon disillusioned. Methuen was quick to appreciate the commercial advantages to be gained from the favourable verdict. He told Robbie[19] that when the new edition was produced Ransome could remove the contentious passage, thereby calming Douglas's wrath.

Arthur Ransome behaved impeccably after his victory. He deleted the offending paragraph when the book reappeared under the Methuen imprint. He also made one or two other significant alterations to the text, and there can be little doubt that these were on the insistence of Robbie.[20]

To celebrate his victory Robbie dined on 25 April with Edmund Gosse, but his euphoria quickly faded. Douglas thought he had been robbed of the verdict by the intervention of Ross, and with Crosland's connivance, he set about getting even with the man responsible for his public humiliation. The fury the verdict caused in the hearts of Douglas and Crosland was out of all proportion to the importance of the action. It would have been much better if Douglas had recalled the words of Alexander Pope: 'To err is human, to forgive, divine.' Crosland could not understand why he, such a prolific writer, suffered from financial starvation, while the followers of the cult of Wilde grew rich and fat on the proceeds of their loathsome works. It was particularly irksome to Crosland to see London theatres again staging Wilde's plays and to see Methuen reprinting Wilde's works in cheap, mass-produced editions. It was the final indignity.

Fifteen

Interlude

FTER THE successful conclusion of the Ransome libel action, Robbie received so many letters of congratulation, that he was forced to dictate his replies for Millard to type. In spite of his pleasure at winning such a small victory, he was still bitter at the way Douglas's family were rallying round him, and in a letter to William Rothenstein, he gave free rein to his anger:

> Douglas has lodged an appeal which will be heard in July; and though I have no anxiety as to the result yet I feel as if the wretched thing would never be buried. Douglas obtains unlimited financial and moral support from his aristocratic relations, the Wyndhams, who appear to me by their action to be very much more dangerous members of the community than Alfred Douglas himself. Loyalty to a relative is one thing: but to supply a bankrupt relative with the means of blackmailing and persecuting other people is a singular comment on English social life.[1]

There is a lovely handwritten postscript to this letter which reveals that even at the height of a crisis, Robbie's sense of humour was never far from the surface, but could bubble over whenever an opportunity presented itself: 'My love to Alice if I may send it.'

The thought that Douglas would appeal against the verdict continued to concern Robbie; George Lewis warned him that if such an eventuality did occur, the expense of fighting the appeal would be substantial. He was, though, fortunate: both Alex and Edmund Gosse assured him that, if Douglas did go ahead with the appeal, they would help with the financial burden. Indeed such was the support Robbie received from his family and friends that it led Lewis to say; 'I don't think you [Robbie] deserve quite such splendid friends as that.'[2]

As early as December 1912 Robbie had been aware he was being watched and followed by strange and somewhat frightening men. In January, driven to the point of despair, he approached one of his followers, and was told he was a private detective employed by Douglas. He admitted he had been watching Robbie, on and off, since June/July 1912,

189

and that he had been instructed to give Douglas details of all Robbie's and Freddie Smith's movements. Smith was an obvious choice for anyone wishing to blackmail Robbie. The detective complained that Douglas had been dissatisfied with the contents of the reports and had refused to pay certain of the expenses. He further indicated that Douglas had obtained the services of a struck-off solicitor to draw up an anonymous statement, charging Ross with committing 'unnatural offences' with Freddie Smith. This statement, the detective said, had been sent to Scotland Yard early in December. His extraordinary revelations were soon confirmed by others. More Adey and John Lane said that Douglas had been bragging that he had heard on good authority that Robbie was about to be arrested.

On the evening of Thursday 5 June 1913, Robbie and Alex attended a party at the home of Edmund Gosse. Among the other thirty-three guests was Siegfried Sassoon,[3] the twenty-six-year-old nephew of Gosse's friend Hamo Thornycroft. Sassoon was a tall, shy, good-looking man with the dark eyes of his Jewish ancestors, who spent his time indulging in country pursuits—hunting, point-to-point racing—and cricket though he dreamed of a different existence as a poet. Robbie was instinctively drawn to the idealistic poet, who so obviously fulfilled all the spiritual and cultural elements he desired in a friend. But with Douglas's persecution threatening to engulf him, Robbie could not risk involving another young man in his problems, and it was eighteen months before he felt able to offer Sassoon the hand of friendship.

As events conspired to shatter his peace of mind, and as he was often physically and mentally exhausted after his day's work at the Board of Inland Revenue, he continued to neglect his duties for the Johannesburg Art Gallery. Such was his preoccupation that when he accepted the gift of Walter Sickert's picture *The Pork Pie Hat* from an anonymous donor he forgot to acknowledge receipt of the picture, and Sickert had to write direct to the Gallery because he had not been paid. Lady Phillips's incessant demands convinced Robbie that he would have to relinquish his position. He wrote to her giving an explanation, if not an excuse, for his sloth:

> I was not surprised to hear from [Hugh] Lane that you were
> becoming impatient with me. Please do not think that it is on that
> account that I am writing as I do. I am more than sensible of your
> kindness and patience. After very grave consideration I have decided
> that I must give up my Directorship of the Johannesburg Gallery.

Some of the reasons I gave to Mr Solomon before he sailed, which
reasons unhappily are still paramount. He will possibly have told
them to you and I therefore need not go into the question.[4]

In his letter to Solomon, Robbie had written: 'Douglas is bringing out
a book of *Memoirs*;[5] and while I hope sincerely that it may not be
necessary for me to take any action in the way of an injunction or libel, it
is very likely that I may be compelled to do so. There are other material
reasons quite apart from this; and I fear that anything which you or Lady
Phillips or the Johannesburg Committee could do would not obviate
them.'[6]

No doubt these thoughts were in Robbie's mind as he continued his
letter to Lady Phillips, but he was unsure how to communicate the
indelicate detail of his problems:

My name being associated with what seems likely to become a
perpetually recurring scandal would eventually do the Gallery harm.
So far, I am glad to think, no harm has been done, except that the
stress and anxiety of eight months made it physically impossible for
me to give that attention to the affairs of the Gallery which was
required.[7]

He admitted frankly that the remuneration he received from Johannesburg was insufficient for him to risk neglecting his other duties in
preference to the business of the Gallery. It was with no sense of his own
importance that he added somewhat modestly, 'leaving out of the question what my undivided attention to the interests of the Gallery is
worth'.[8] He urged Lady Phillips to delay announcing his resignation
until a successor had been appointed. He hoped that when Hugh Lane—
who was about to leave England for South Africa—arrived, Lady Phillips would have the opportunity of discussing with him a suitable
successor. He said he did not think he had earned his £150 salary and that
he proposed to repay all but £50 which he intended to keep for petty
expenses. In spite of his resignation, he would retain an interest in the
Gallery and would work on an informal basis when freed from his
litigation battles.

Solomon expressed his profound regrets at Robbie's resignation,
adding that the South African papers had carried a long interview with
Douglas, in which he discussed the forthcoming publication of his
Memoirs. He hoped that Robbie would not be drawn into another legal
wrangle. In a fair assessment of Robbie's complex character Solomon
said that Robbie frequently, because he was so close to a problem,

allowed a 'molehill to become a mountain'. Solomon then suggested: 'Why not come out for a trip with Lane when he visits us and so see things in their right proportions from out here?'[9]

It was an invitation Robbie should have taken up. If he had gone on an extended visit to South Africa, it is just possible he would have escaped unscathed from the persecution of Crosland and Douglas. Solomon concluded his letter with even more good advice: 'Patience has always been to me the most dramatic of remedies. With all good wishes and the hope that your hobby of litigation, as *Who's Who* has it, may soon be at an end.'[10]

Lady Phillips was equally sad to receive his resignation and she readily agreed not to make his split with the Gallery public until he was ready. She was adamant that she would not accept the return of his salary, insisting he had already earned it:

> I am extremely sorry that you should be feeling hurt about anything,
> but no doubt you have had more than your share of worry (of which
> I only heard quite lately from Mr Solomon) and later on when we
> can meet, I hope that you will get your mind disabused of any idea
> that you are suffering from any grievance, as far as I am concerned.
> You always were so perfectly charming and kind to me when I was
> in London, that I have (and always shall) only the very warmest and
> kindest feelings for *you*.[11]

Solomon somewhat underestimated the situation. The molehill did not become a mountain but a vicious, uncontrollable volcano; Robbie must have wondered if he would ever again be free from the constraints of litigation. On 16 August he knew he was right to end his connection with the Johannesburg Art Gallery. Norman Farr, a former St Paul's schoolboy and now a medical student, came to see him and had an alarming story to impart. Robbie had met Farr ten years earlier at the home of Lady Alfred Douglas, but had seen him only occasionally since. Farr said he had been approached by a barrister, working for Douglas, who offered him a large sum of money if he would come forward and say he had had immoral relations with Robbie. He had categorically denied the allegation and declared he was deeply offended at being asked to commit perjury in return for a bribe. He had told the barrister he had met Robbie only once socially, and once when he had asked for an opinion on the value of a picture. Farr said he had been so alarmed by the impropriety of the barrister's suggestions, that he felt it was his duty to tell Robbie exactly what had taken place.

Deeply conscious that there were those, among his friends and relatives, who thought he was suffering from a persecution mania, Robbie, nevertheless, informed Sir George Lewis of Farr's visit. Farr was encouraged to make a written statement detailing what had taken place between him and the barrister, but he was unwilling to become too involved in a *cause célèbre* as it would irretrievably damage his position as a medical student.

Sir Charles Mathews, the Public Prosecutor, however, was sufficiently convinced of the truth of Douglas's allegations that he personally instituted enquiries. He interviewed Digby La Motte, a master at St Paul's School, and showed him a letter written by Douglas in which he accused Robbie of seducing St Paul's schoolboys over a period of twenty years. La Motte emphatically declared there was not a shred of truth in the allegations, but his eccentric and intemperate opinions only strengthened Mathews's feeling that he was lying to shield Ross. Mathews then interviewed Adolf Birkenruth at Little Grosvenor Gardens and Birkenruth's evasive answers further convinced Mathews that Douglas's allegations were based on solid fact. Unfortunately, he had insufficient proof to be able to issue an immediate warrant for Robbie's arrest, but he was sure Douglas would be able to find corroborative evidence and then the Law could issue a warrant.

Robbie had always tried to shield Douglas's family from the accusation that Douglas had been mainly responsible for Wilde's downfall, but if he expected gratitude from Douglas and his family, then he was to be sadly disillusioned. If asked by inquisitors whether Douglas had ever had sexual intercourse with Wilde, Robbie always maintained an air of ignorance of such matters. He had published nothing against Douglas, and he would have faithfully kept his promise, if Douglas had not intensified the hate campaign. He could have endured the slurs on his own good name, but when Douglas began to defile the memory of Wilde, that was more than Robbie could stomach. Douglas compounded his crime when he sought to publish the first of his autobiographies, *Oscar Wilde and Myself*. The book, said to have been written largely by Crosland, was riddled with half-truths, innuendoes and flagrant breaches of copyright. Robbie had no alternative but to issue an injunction to stop the publication of the most damning parts.

Douglas did not proceed with his appeal against the verdict in the Ransome case, and in August 1913 he lost another round in the legal battle, when Charles Mathews informed George Lewis that no warrants would be issued as a result of Douglas's allegations.

During September Robbie was away from London; he had been invited by M. Lykiardopulos, of the Moscow Art Theatre, to attend the first production in Russia of *Salome*. Robbie arrived in Paris on Friday the 5th, but could not get a sleeper train to Moscow until the 15th. The prospect of ten days in Paris did not displease him and he settled happily into his old quarters at the Hôtel Regina in the place Rivoli. He had left Millard to handle his private and business correspondence, and alone in Paris he had time to reflect on his year of despair, and in particular his deteriorating friendship with Freddie Smith:

> I have at last reduced Freddie by tenacity to conforming in some way to my wishes. Every other appeal was made in vain. He attempted every kind of subterfuge and elaborately ignoring the causes of my indignation with him and pretending that I had some other motive. I need not tell you that my only motive was to insist that the person who is living with me or supposed to be living with me, should not shut up the two rooms he does not occupy. His head, of course, is quite turned and I shall never be able to resume the real terms of affection. Freddie is the one friend besides Oscar and Douglas for whom I have made sacrifices, and he is the one friend who showed neither affection nor regard nor sensitivity nor appreciation of my appalling position. The clerks in George Lewis's office have been kinder to me.[12]

He spent time wandering round the Louvre, enjoying as always the splendours of the great gallery. He met and dined with many old friends, but one old friend he did not meet was Reggie Turner. Millard had written to say that there was a rumour circulating round London that Turner had left Paris before Robbie arrived rather than risk meeting him. In refuting the rumour, Robbie gave vent to his anger:

> Reggie Turner could not have left Paris on my account for he never knew I was coming here and indeed I did not know myself. He wrote to More suggesting I should meet him at Dieppe or come over for one day, an invitation I rejected. However I suppose from what you say, that he has been making the usual disagreeable and critical observations about me which I often notice about him and hearing that I am annoyed by his stupid remark to Birkenruth, *invented* the flight from Paris. However it is much better that we should not meet.[13]

The increase in tension between Robbie and his friends was undoubtedly caused by a fear which they all faced, that Douglas's very public allegations against Robbie would rebound on them. If Douglas provoked the Authorities sufficiently, they could well initiate a campaign to hound and prosecute all known homosexuals. Millard, the least discreet member of the côterie, as Robbie's secretary and friend, was subjected to intense police surveillance. In trying to shield Millard, Robbie laid himself open to further abuse and, whereas he was discreet and did not seek to justify his proclivities, Millard was prepared to stand up and proclaim to all. Although both were converts to the Roman Catholic Faith, they found it possible to live with their Christian beliefs and their sins—unlike Douglas, who believed his conversion gave him a religious duty to impose sexual and social constraints on all sinners except himself.

On the morning of 18 September, just as Robbie arrived in Moscow, Charles Nehemiah Garratt was arrested as he left Millard's flat. When he appeared before the Magistrate, Millard was imprudent enough to speak up for him, but he earned himself a sharp rebuke from the Bench. The incident was reported in the Press and shortly afterwards Millard was visited by a Private Inquiry Agent named Carew, who said he was working for Douglas and Crosland. Carew offered Millard money if he would steal some of Robbie's letters. To his credit, Millard would not be bribed, and on Robbie's return from Russia, he informed him what had happened and together they told George Lewis of Carew's offer.

If there was a tangible benefit from the legal battles with Douglas, then Robbie would have been the first to agree that it brought him closer to and more dependent on his brother, Alex. It had not been easy for Alex to tolerate or understand his brother's vices, but when Robbie most needed his help and advice, Alex had not let him down. After leaving Cambridge, Alex had for a while devoted his time to literature, but by 1913 he had become a partner in a successful firm of City stockbrokers and enjoyed the benefits of a substantial fortune. He was a perfectionist and although his needs were modest he demanded the best that money could buy. He was generous to those less fortunate than himself, though his acts of generosity were made with the same wish for secrecy that governed most of his life. Alex's character was the opposite to Robbie's. He preferred to stay in the background, never giving his opinions unless especially asked to do so, and then he did not expect his advice to be acted on. Robbie was fully aware of Alex's generous and tolerant character, as he told Jack back in 1904: 'But I venture to urge you to be adamant on one or two points; George,[14] as you must know, is a great deal more stern in *theory* than in practice. When it comes to a point he is fearfully apt to make things easy for people out of pity and a charming disposition.'[15] Alex, like Robbie, was a confirmed bachelor, and although he moved in much the same literary and artistic circles as his brother, the whiff of scandal did not cling to him. If he sinned, then his sins were those usually associated with a man about town and he paid for the maintenance and care of his mistress and her offspring. And the world was left in ignorance, unlike Robbie, whose sins were paraded for all to see.

Robbie's journey from Paris to Moscow was not without incident. On the train to Berlin a fellow traveller recognised him as Wilde's literary executor. He was inclined to deny his identity but, mindful that St Peter had denied a friendship, he admitted the truth. But when the Jew urged Robbie to break his journey in Berlin in order to meet his wife, Robbie was sure he should have followed St Peter's example and denied all knowledge of Wilde. He refused the offer of German hospitality and hurried on to Warsaw. He was not impressed by the scenery between Warsaw and Moscow. He found it monotonous and it reminded him of Canada. At the frontier between Poland and Russia he was saved customs examination much to the annoyance of other British people on the train.[16]

Lykiardopulos and a deputation from the Moscow Art Theatre were at the station to greet him when he arrived in Moscow. Robbie was embarrassed by the warmth of their welcome and after an agreeable supper they took him to a music-hall. He was a little concerned that he did not speak Russian and although he had been told before leaving London that English and German were both spoken at the hotel, he found he could make himself understood only by gesticulations; although his Canadian-French was of limited benefit.

While in Moscow he wrote frequently to Alex.[17] He could not admit to his brother that he was lonely, but to Millard he was willing to say exactly what he was missing. Even with the pressures crowding in on him, he could not resist the temptation of telling Millard that homosexuality as such did not appear to exist in Russia:

> You will be surprised (as indeed I am) but among the multitude of people I have met here I have not seen any purple people or any who avowed they were or looked in the least like it. Nor does one see them in the streets. It is rather depressing.[18]

Robbie was planning to go on to St Petersburg, but as his expenses in Moscow were greater than he anticipated, despite the generosity of his hosts, he decided he would have to forgo the trip. He was disconcerted to find that the museums in Moscow were closed for cleaning, and he was embarrassed by the kindness of curators and others who opened them especially for him. His inability to understand the Russian language was a terrible disadvantage at all social occasions, and without the presence of the attentive Lykiardopulos his visit would have been less happy. He was overwhelmed by the hospitality of his Russian hosts and the affection in which they held Wilde: 'They admire his work not, as is so often the case, merely for his unimpressioniste [sic] tastes. Grave and white-haired professors are trundled up to me and make long speeches. Their names are all unpronounceable, and their French is only a trifle more intelligible than mine.'[19]

A childhood passion for religious ritual still remained part of him, and in Russia he was able to indulge himself, with 'positive *orgies* of ceremonies'. The elaborate services of the Greek and Russian Orthodox Churches appealed to his love of ecclesiastical ritual, and he told Alex that the singing was the best he had ever heard, but he thought their religion degraded the Russian people. Robbie was not to know, nor could he have predicted, that before the decade was over, the Tsar and his family would be dead, and for decades to come the Russian Orthodox Church would be outlawed.

His visit to Moscow had been but a brief interlude of pleasure in the midst of his litigation battles. He would now have to begin in earnest his struggle with Douglas and Crosland. The world he loved was coming to an end, and as he informed Millard of his plans for his return journey, he knew that the final break between him and Freddie Smith would have to be made although he would always mourn the ending of that bitter/sweet relationship:

> I leave here next Friday going straight to London via Ostend. I
> arrive sometime on Sunday following and should like you if possible
> to come and meet me. Don't tell Freddie. I have especially arranged
> to arrive on Sunday when he will be away in the natural course of
> events. His presence would moreover upset me and his artificial
> enthusiasm would annoy me.[20]

Robbie arrived back in London on 5 October. Exhausted as he was by his long journey, he had barely time to recover before he became acutely aware of the scale of the problems which were about to engulf him. Thanks, though, were due first to Millard for his secretarial work, although such was his tiredness that he misdated his letter by one day:[21]

> I must thank you for the complete and perfect manner in which you
> have attended to all my correspondence and affairs. It took me the
> whole afternoon to examine the letters! Though they were all in
> order and exactly as you described them. I could never have gone

away without knowing that you would look after everything for me
and that you would do so with perfect care and discretion.[22]

Robbie had little time to rest. The magazine *Outlook* proposed, in their
October issue, to print some of Wilde's letters without the courtesy of
asking Robbie's permission. He had no option but to instruct Lewis &
Lewis to obtain an injunction against the publishers and their agents. He
had no doubt that when the case was finally heard, in the Chancery
Division of the High Court, he would be successful in obtaining a
perpetual injunction.[23] He was, however, not as optimistic about the
interim injunction that he had taken out last August against Douglas and
his wretched book *Oscar Wilde and Myself.* He could apply to make the
injunction perpetual, but although the British copyright of *De Profundis*
and Wilde's other works were secured, there was nothing to stop Douglas publishing his book in the United States, unless he could also protect
the American copyright. Robbie moved swiftly and resolutely; he still
had a typed draft of the *De Profundis* manuscript in his possession, and
he quickly arranged for it to be sent to a New York publishing friend,
Paul R. Reynolds. Millard warily informed Walter Ledger of the situation:

> Ross has decided to get it set up in America for copyright purposes
> to avoid eventualities that may occur, and, I suppose, to prevent
> anyone from printing even those parts published in the London
> papers last April. Only 25 are to be done[24] (by Reynolds the man
> who did *The Duchess of Padua*).
>   Robbie Ross is sure to send you a copy so I need say no more
> about it. And, of course, keep it private.[25]

The book was hurriedly printed, and as Robbie was unable to check
the page proofs, it contained many errors. For the purposes of American
registration, two copies were given to the Library of Congress, and to
comply with the copyright legislation, one copy was offered for sale by
Reynolds. Robbie was not keen for the book to be sold, and with
Reynolds's connivance, the book was offered for sale at an exorbitant
price, and much to the dismay of Robbie and his publisher, a man
walked into the shop and bought the book. The remaining copies were
sent to Robbie, who distributed some of them among his friends, extrac-
ting from each a vow of secrecy as to the contents of the book. The
recipients all had some connection with Wilde: Vyvyan Holland, Viscount Haldane, Sir Edmund Gosse, A.L. Humphreys, John Lane,
Algernon Methuen, Sir George Lewis, Christopher Millard and Martin

Holman. It is to be regretted that he did not send a copy to Lord Alfred Douglas; if he had, Douglas might have seen it as a gesture of reconciliation, and might have been able to accept the contents of the book, and consequently draw back from his attempts to shame and ruin Robbie.

The publication of *Oscar Wilde and Myself* was finally announced for November. Robbie told Edmund Gosse: 'Of course [it] will be libellous as John Long the publisher makes a speciality of sailing near the wind. I expect however both publisher and author have been careful to avoid the reprisals of prosecution for obscene literature and they are fortified by knowing that I will not prosecute for libel on my own account: I can only hope that the press will not discuss it too much.'[26] Robbie expressed his opinion of the book in no uncertain terms to Robert Sherard: 'I have just been allowed to see privately a copy of Douglas's book. You and I are attacked vigorously. I dare say you will be able to get damages, if it is libellous, out of John Long, but of course I don't know.'[27] In the end, neither Robbie nor Sherard took any action against Douglas and his publisher.

It was inevitable, with the injunction against him made perpetual and the American copyright protected, that Douglas would be forced to retaliate. The arrest of Charles Garratt and Millard's attempt to help the boy were reported by the *Reynolds* newspaper. Douglas sent the cutting and an extremely offensive letter to Sir George Lewis; once again he repeated his allegations of sodomy, anarchy and socialism against Robbie. In desperation Robbie turned to Edmund Gosse for help; Gosse arranged for him to see Haldane, who, as Lord Chancellor, was in a position to recommend a course of action which would finally stop Douglas repeating his allegations. Gosse coached Robbie on what to say and how to conduct himself for he was worried that Robbie's 'ill-timed candour'[28] would create more problems than it would solve. Gosse need not have worried, Haldane soon put Robbie at ease, and after the meeting Robbie was happy to tell Gosse what Haldane had suggested:

> I am to write down a complete account of the persecutions which I
> have endured for the last four years, the causes which are supposed
> to have provoked it and the various manifestations thereof, and I am
> to supply a set of copies of all letters written to me by Douglas and if
> possible copies of letters written to others, containing abusive
> references to myself or other people.[29] Lord Haldane suggested, I
> am glad to say, that I should tell Lewis of my interview and obtain
> his assistance in the preparation of the report. Lord Haldane made it
> quite clear that while he could not promise that any protective
> measures would be taken officially on my behalf and could not give

an opinion as to whether it might be possible for the Crown to
interfere until he had weighed the matter carefully and examined the
case from every possible point of view. But he promised to do all he
could for me in his personal capacity and expressed a real hope that
he might find himself empowered to do something in his official
capacity.[30]

Sir George Lewis was not the least of those who were impressed by the
willingness of Robbie's friends to come to his assistance. Margot Asquith
was dismayed at the way the police and Scotland Yard were treating
Robbie, and she was determined 'to have it out'[31] with Charles Mathews,
the Director of Public Prosecutions. If it had not been for the support of
his friends, the stress imposed by Douglas would have been too great for
Robbie to bear. As it was, although he suffered a good deal, he was still
able to lead a fairly normal life. He spent the weekend of 25/26 October
at The Wharf, Sutton Courtenay, with the Asquiths; among his fellow
guests were Guy Charteris and his wife Frances, Jaspar and Nathalie
Ridley and Tommy Lascelles, who, recalling the weekend in his journal,
expressed his own view of Robbie's persecutor: 'Douglas seems always to
have been an absolutely amoral man, and is now mad into the bargain.
Lady Glenconner subsidises him from time to time v. misguided
charity.'[32]

As if his own personal affairs were not complicated enough, Robbie was
also concerned over the continuing problems of Wilde's Memorial at
Père Lachaise. There had still been no official unveiling and the Epstein
sculpture was attracting a good deal of adverse publicity. Robbie told
Edmund Gosse: 'I received an official document today from the Prefect
of the Seine at Paris notifying me that the Wilde monument has been
mutilated by unknown persons.' Such was Robbie's state of mind that,
mindful of his persecution by Douglas, he added a final heartfelt comment, which summed up so accurately his attitude to life at that point in
time: 'But I don't think Douglas has anything to do with that.'[33]

A couple of weeks later a group of British artists and poets, led by
Aleister Crowley, decided to take the matter of unveiling into their own
hands, and organised an unofficial ceremony. Jacob Epstein was far from
amused by the incident. Robbie was not unduly concerned: he had no
great wish to see Wilde's tomb perpetually shrouded by tarpaulin.

Lord Haldane may have prevented Robbie from being arrested on the
charges laid by Douglas, but he could not protect him from the worst
aspects of Douglas's harassment. The affair simmered on through

November and December. On 15 December Robbie moved again, this time to a service apartment at Georgian House in Bury Street, close to the Carfax Gallery. On 23 December, as a most unwelcome Christmas present, Robbie received from Mrs Garratt, issued on behalf of her son, a writ charging him with improper conduct and asking for damages. Robbie immediately handed the writ to Lewis & Lewis, and it was thus that he spent Christmas with the shadow of the affair hanging over him.

On 28 December Robbie travelled to Scotland for three days' holiday, and when he returned to London it was to find Douglas had taken rooms in Georgian House! He immediately complained to the hall porter; only to be told that Douglas had been making enquiries about him, and had tried to bribe a waiter to steal any papers he could from Robbie's apartment. Robbie gained a tactical advantage by ordering the hall porter to answer all Douglas's questions candidly and honestly. Robbie then sent for the proprietor and told him the whole sordid story. The proprietor agreed that Douglas's actions were reprehensible but did not feel able to evict Douglas that evening, though he promised that Douglas would be asked to leave the next morning. With Douglas under the same roof Robbie could not remain in his rooms; at the Reform Club he found the peace and tranquillity he needed to tell Gosse what had occurred over the past few days. He drew a fearful picture of the events which were leading him into the quagmire of litigation, something which he neither sought nor welcomed. The final paragraph of Robbie's letter to Gosse revealed the extent of his desperation:

> This is AD 1914 and you will not think me either melodramatic or
> mock heroic when I tell you that I return to my rooms tonight with
> firearms. Have you seen the newspaper tonight? Douglas had
> another triumph in the police courts! A fitting place for his
> triumphs.[34]

It was no wonder that Robbie felt beaten and demoralised. Even Millard could not comprehend the lengths to which a man would go to discredit a friend. To Walter Ledger he wrote of his dismay: 'A.D. has taken the most amazing step against R.R. and myself; of which I will tell you something when we meet. It seems almost incredible. But the end thereof no man can foretell!'[35]

Odd moments of pleasure did present themselves. On Saturday 7 January Robbie was best man at the wedding of Wilde's younger son, Vyvyan, to Violet Mary, younger daughter of Edmund Warren Craigie. Robbie was worried that Douglas might cause some kind of scene at the wedding, as he told Gosse:

> Tomorrow I go to the wedding of Wilde's son and by Lewis's advice
> I have not attended any of the arrangements. Detectives disguised as
> guests and members of the theatrical profession are to be both at the
> Church and the House in case Douglas has organised a
> demonstration. If I had followed my own inclination I should have
> absented myself, but I see the point of not showing the *white feather*
> even though I carry it in my pocket.[36]

It crossed Robbie's mind that history had a cruel way of repeating itself: Wilde had been scared that the Marquess of Queensberry would disrupt the first performance of *The Importance of Being Earnest* when it was staged at St James's Theatre on 14 February 1895. Queensberry had been arranging to present Wilde with a bouquet of rotting vegetables and it was possible that Douglas would try to emulate his father. Vyvyan Holland did not share Robbie's concern; he thought that despite all Douglas's eccentricities he was far too well bred to make a scene at a wedding.

The moments of happiness were soon extinguished. On the Monday after the wedding, Robbie heard from Crosland that the conspiracy being waged against him was well founded. Crosland was a moralist who believed passionately that his allotted task was to rid the world of all evil. Paradoxically, he was an intemperate drinker and in consequence his health suffered, and he spent many long periods in hospital. He had a passion for gambling and spent money he could ill afford on trips to Monte Carlo. And despite being a married man, with three sons, he had a mistress with whom he lived. The irony of Crosland's beliefs was that all the time that Wilde's works were available only in vellum-bound editions, printed on hand-made paper, he took no action, believing that the wealthy and educated could take care of their own moral decline. But when the common man was able to buy cheap editions of Wilde's books, Crosland was outraged. In his letter Crosland repeated all the allegations he had previously made against the writings and the life of Oscar Wilde, before he gave Robbie an ultimatum with regard to his future conduct. He ordered him to resign as Wilde's literary executor and to make a public statement that he had been wrong to restore Wilde's literary and moral reputation.

If Crosland thought that on receipt of the letter Robbie would immediately resign and renounce Wilde, then he was mistaken. However, events moved swiftly. At the end of January Lewis & Lewis wrote to Cecil Holt, Mrs Garratt's solicitors, informing them that if the statements of claim were not delivered they should withdraw the writs for damages against Ross and Millard. The statements of claim were not delivered, and on 4 February the writ against Millard was dismissed. A week later the writ against Robbie was similarly dismissed. Lewis & Lewis wrote again to Cecil Holt, asking for payment of costs. Eventually Holt informed Lewis that there were no funds available. Robbie added another grievance to the long list he had against Douglas and Crosland.

On 14 February Charles Garratt was again arrested and charged with importuning. A week later, at the Marlborough Police Court, he was sentenced to six months' hard labour. It had been only two months since his release from Pentonville Prison for the previous offence.

Crosland and Douglas were both convinced that they had right on their side. They thought their use of *facts*, as they called them, was all the evidence they needed to condemn Wilde and Ross. Irrefutable evidence that would convince a Court of Law was another matter. Neither of them believed they would have to substantiate their allegations with incontrovertible proof. They expected Robbie to retire and slip quietly into obscurity, a disgraced and ruined man. Robbie, however, was prepared to fight and let the Law give its judgement on his guilt or innocence. Unlike Wilde, he had no reason to fear there would be a gang of young rascals willing to come forward to give perjured evidence against him.

Crosland sent Robbie yet another abusive letter. He was annoyed that Robbie had not taken action against Douglas. He said he had heard that Ross had refrained from taking action against Douglas because of his social standing. He hoped that Ross would have no such scruples about proceeding against him, a common man and undischarged bankrupt. Crosland then repeated his previous disgusting libels and challenged Ross to issue a writ for libel, which he would be delighted to defend in a Court of Law.

It is doubtful if Robbie's refusal to prosecute Douglas had anything to do with his finer feelings for Douglas's rank and position. What is more likely is that he was concerned that a protracted Court action would cause great suffering to the Dowager Marchioness of Queensberry. Robbie decided, however, that Crosland's letters were the final straw. The time had come to take his revenge against Bosie Douglas and Thomas Crosland. He had been very patient but now all the strands of the drama had come together.

Fate, possibly with a little help from Sir George Lewis, played into Robbie's hands. Colonel Custance, Douglas's father-in-law, decided to continue the action for libel he had brought against Douglas in the previous year. Douglas had on many occasions broken the conditions of his own recognisances and Colonel Custance sought to have his son-in-law arrested and sent to prison. Douglas fled to France. Robbie then played his trump card skilfully, and the gamble very nearly paid a just dividend. On 24 March he filed for criminal libel against Douglas and at the same time issued writs against Douglas and Crosland for criminal conspiracy and perjury. Crosland was also in France, gambling and consorting with Douglas. Robbie rather hoped that neither of them would return to face the charges. Unfortunately his wish was not granted, although in the end, it was only Crosland who stood in the dock.

With the arrogance and showmanship that only he could display, Crosland returned from France to face his accusers on the evening of Easter Sunday, 12 April 1914.

Sixteen

Conspiracy and Perjury

HE ARREST of Thomas Crosland excited yet depressed Robbie Ross. It was now inevitable there would be a preliminary hearing before a Magistrate and later a full trial at the Central Criminal Court. Once begun, the Law had a way of perpetuating itself. The action could not be reversed and the day would arrive when a jury would finally decide the guilt or innocence of Crosland.

That Crosland was guilty there could be no doubt, but it was often easier for the Defence to prove innocence than for the Prosecution to prove guilt. The Prosecution had few ways of proving the charges against Crosland, and in the witness-box Crosland would be able to say what he liked. In the end it would be Robbie's word against Crosland's. The principal witness for the Prosecution would be Charles Garratt, an unreliable person, who, on his own admission, was an inveterate liar, and judged alongside the moral, upstanding Crosland, fighting evil wherever he found it, Garratt would be a liability. The trial could not possibly be a fair one with only Crosland in the dock. The jury would have to banish from their minds the fact that Alfred Douglas should also be there, as he should have been when Wilde stood trial. It would be difficult for them to convict one guilty man while the other man went unpunished. It was also inevitable that the jury would never be able to forget the crimes and disgrace of Oscar Wilde.

Crosland spent Easter Sunday night in police custody, and came up before the Magistrate, Paul Taylor, on 13 April 1914. Detective-Inspector John McPherson, in giving details of Crosland's detention and charge, said that in reply to the charge Crosland had asked:

'Why don't you arrest Robert Baldwin Ross? We gave you all the information about what these fellows did to the boy Garratt. We have been to great expense and trouble to do all that the police ought to have done.'[1]

Cecil Holt, the solicitor that Douglas used in his attempts to extort money for the Garratts, did not act for Crosland, who was represented by Bell, of Carter & Bell, another of Douglas's solicitors. In his opening statement to the Bench, Bell made much of the fact that his client had not attempted to evade arrest but had deliberately returned to England in

205

order that the trial could proceed. In reply Lewis & Lewis's senior clerk, Lister, asked for a remand for a week and at the same time vigorously, but unsuccessfully, opposed bail. Sholto Johnstone Douglas, a cousin of Alfred's, was accepted as surety for £500, reaffirming the clan tradition that members or their close friends should stand together. They even came forward when Oscar Wilde needed surety.

Crosland's remand was the first of many. On his second appearance eight days later, Sir George Lewis asked for a further remand, explaining that Ernest Wild, KC, who was to appear for Ross, was engaged in another Court, and that the Prosecution also wished to give Lord Alfred Douglas every opportunity to attend the Court and take his rightful place beside Crosland in the dock. He said it was the desire of the Prosecution that Douglas should have full notice that a warrant was out against him. Douglas had been in Boulogne for the past six weeks and it would be a simple matter for him to attend the Court, if he desired to do so. Crosland objected vehemently, asserting that the remand was merely a device by the Prosecution to keep him waiting, thereby trying to wear him out. Sir George assured him he would have no further reason for complaint, as the Prosecution were anxious to expedite the proceedings. Crosland's excited outburst provoked a sharp reply from the Magistrate, but a further remand was granted. Crosland's solicitors then asked to be allowed to see the information on which the warrants were issued. After careful consideration, Taylor said he was of the opinion that to provide such information would not be in the interests of justice, and it should not be made available until it was disclosed in open Court.

Crosland was ordered to appear again on the following Monday at 2.30. The adjournment was not without incident. Crosland and Douglas were in contact by letter, and it was inevitable that Douglas should try to influence the impartiality of the inferior Court by writing to Paul Taylor. In his letter Douglas offered to return to England to give evidence, if he could be granted immunity from the warrants issued by his father-in-law, Colonel Custance. Unfortunately for Douglas, the letter was published in the Press prior to its delivery, much to the embarrassment of the Defence.

Crosland stood charged with fourteen counts of conspiring with Douglas to accuse Ross, falsely and unjustly, of committing acts of gross indecency with Charles Garratt.

The Prosecution contended that the beginning of all the evil design stemmed from the Ransome case, when, in forming his Plea of Justification, Ransome produced documents supplied by Ross. Douglas lost that action, and from that moment he began to make serious allegations against Ross, including an accusation of blackmail. They then sought an accomplice. When they had read of Garratt's arrest and Christopher Millard's involvement, the whole elaborate plot was born.

While Garratt served the first of his sentences for importuning, he was visited by Fairhall, an employee of Cecil Holt & Co. He showed Garratt a photograph of Ross, and said that if Garratt would say he knew him, they (the people he represented) would help him when he was released. Crosland, in the meantime, went to Countesthorpe to see Garratt's mother. He told her that it was not her son who should be in prison but Ross and Millard. Crosland is alleged to have said that if she would help him and the man behind him, he would see Ross and Millard were punished. In return he said they would help her son when he came out of prison. There matters stayed until Garratt was released, when he was, as expected, met and taken to the offices of Cecil Holt. Douglas and Crosland were waiting for him and they again tried to make him sign a statement accusing Ross of having immoral relations with him. Garratt refused to sign the statement saying it was a lie.

Fearing they would lose their only creditable witness, Crosland again turned to Mrs Garratt and, on Douglas's instructions, offered her ten shillings a week if she would have her son back home. On 20 December 1913, she had received two writs in the post which required her signature. She thought they were for a criminal charge against Ross and Millard, but on reading them she found that they were for damages against Ross. In due course both writs were issued, but were later withdrawn for the want of action by the claimant.

In the witness-box Mrs Garratt told a sorry tale of the harassment and coercion she had endured from Crosland. It was obvious, from her attitude that she was a woman of little education. She had been dragged into the affairs of her son, and had neither the intelligence nor the wit to know she was being used by unscrupulous men for their own ends.

The hearing was adjourned for the weekend, and Robbie went to Paris, to supervise the final unveiling of Wilde's memorial. As Millard reported to Walter Ledger: 'The monument at Père Lachaise is now uncovered. I have a photograph of it *in situ*...'[2] Robbie had difficulty in finding a suitable hotel room. At the Hôtel Regina they proposed to charge him sixteen francs for a room 'which looked out into an *oubliette*';[3] Robbie was much annoyed and refused to accept the offer, but he had to try eight further hotels, before at last he found an attic room in his old haunt at the Hôtel Louvis on the Left Bank.

Maurice Gilbert met Robbie at Gare du Nord and, when they dined together, Gilbert showed him a letter he had received from Reggie Turner, in which he had written: 'I always thought that Ross provoked

Douglas and I did not think Ross ought to have used documents in the Ransome case which he had received when they were friendly. However I wish him well. I know that Douglas has attacked me but I don't think he should be treated like ordinary people.'[4] Turner was not alone in believing Douglas should not be treated like other people, and that was why Douglas was so dangerous. He thought he could do and say exactly what he liked, and that no one had a right to object or argue with him. Sir Charles Mathews, Adolphus Birkenruth, the Recorder of London, Paul Taylor, the Home Secretary, and Ernest Wild, Robbie's own Counsel, all believed that Douglas's behaviour was irrational and illogical and should be pitied rather than prosecuted.

It must have been particularly galling for Robbie to read of Turner's attitude while in Paris. He and Turner had shared many encounters, but the relationship could not be sustained if Turner supported Douglas. All the time Robbie remained silent and ignored Douglas's taunts his friends stood by him, but when he fought back he found just how fickle some of those friendships had become. Millard had warned him that human nature being what it was he could expect nothing more. Robbie had been unwilling to accept his judgement, but from Paris he wrote, 'Is there no one who can be trusted? You [Millard] said not. I thought it was cynical. But you were quite right.'[5]

On his return from Paris, Robbie, still hurt by the contents of Turner's letter to Maurice Gilbert, formally broke the friendship which had lasted twenty years. In a rare show of pique he exposed the deep hurt he felt at the lack of understanding of his old friend:

> I am sure you will agree with me that the friends [who] are precious
> are those with whom one has *not* been too intimate. Circumstances
> made us too intimate in the past.... It will I am sure be a still
> greater relief to you if I say now that I regard our friendship as
> having definitely ceased.[6]

Robbie could not, however, sustain his anger against Reggie Turner and before a year had past they had regained their former intimacy. In trying to stop the activities of Douglas and Crosland, Ross received much abuse from friends and enemies and from those who would rather have had the affair hushed up. There had been too many scandals, but in defending his own honour he was in danger of again dragging Wilde's name through the mire.

When the hearing resumed, Mrs Flude, Garratt's sister, was called to corroborate her mother's evidence. She said that in December her mother had brought Crosland to her husband's cottage, and he told her that two people named Millard and Ross had made Charlie drunk and that her brother remembered no more until he awoke the next morning dressed in women's clothes and smelling of perfume. Later, she had accompanied her mother to London, and Crosland had told them that if the case against Ross and Millard went through, her mother would receive £1000. But at the solicitor's office, Charlie had refused to make the statement and had run away. Mr Holt had told her that he would like to take the boy by the scruff of the neck and see what he could do with him. He also told her that Crosland and Lord Alfred Douglas would not let the matter drop if they could help it.

Charlie Garratt followed his sister into the witness-box; Robbie was called forward, and Garratt swore on oath that he had never seen him before. Under some searching questions from Crosland's Counsel, he admitted he may have met Ross, but he could not really be sure. If he had, it had been at the Avenue Hotel. He had not heard the gentleman's name when the introduction was made, and the meeting had been brief.

Garratt went into considerable detail about the visits he had received, while in prison, from the solicitors Cecil Holt. Fairhall, Holt's senior clerk, had wanted him to make a statement saying he had had sexual relations with Ross but he had refused because it was a lie. Fairhall had told him that if he changed his mind the prison authorities would give him Holt's address. He admitted that on the day of his release from prison, he had gone straight to Millard's flat and told him what had happened while he was in Pentonville. Millard had taken him straight round to see George Lewis and he had made a statement. He refuted his sister's evidence, denying that he had been drugged or dressed as a woman, or that it had anything to do with Ross. When he left the offices of Lewis & Lewis, he had gone to Holt's where he met Douglas, who asked him if he knew Ross. Garratt said he did not. Even so, Douglas gave him half a sovereign and took him in a taxi to get his luggage, and then on to a restaurant near Victoria station for lunch. During the meal Douglas left and when he returned he had Crosland with him. In Garratt's hearing he said to Crosland. 'Look here, this boy knows Millard, Ross's secretary, it would be quite easy for him to say he knew Ross.'[7]

Garratt agreed that Douglas's sole purpose was to get Ross into trouble, declaring that Ross had caused him great injury. Douglas and Crosland had begun to write a statement, and when it was finished they said that he should take it to Scotland Yard. Douglas had told him that if he made the statement against Ross, he [Ross] would lose his important position and would have to leave the country to escape the consequences of his shameful conduct.

Garratt recounted how they had all gone to Scotland Yard, where he made a statement. He did not like the police and the police did not like him, although they had treated him politely. The first weekend he was free, he had seen a great deal of Douglas and a man called Carew. He had dined with them on Saturday. They had changed taxis three times in going to Euston, because Douglas was afraid Millard was trying to follow them. On Sunday they had gone to Kensington where they wanted him to swear before a Commissioner of Oaths that the statement he had made against Ross and Millard was true, but he had become frightened and refused to do as they ordered. Douglas had flown into a temper and used filthy language. Carew had advised him to swear the statement, but he had still refused.

Garratt denied that Ross or Millard had ever given him money to keep him out of the way. In comic detail Garratt explained how he had stayed in Carew's house at Earl's Court, and how, when he had wanted to leave, he had found the door of his room locked and his boots missing. It was not until he had been taken to Holt's office that he had been able to make good his escape.

The weekend break in the case provided a pleasant interlude for Robbie; on 8 May, he received a note from Margot Asquith which raised his flagging spirits. She had heard that on the 14th he was taking her step-daughter Violet to the revival, by George Alexander, of Wilde's *An Ideal Husband*. Margot said she was not going to the play although she would have enjoyed an evening in Robbie's company and she suggested he should dine at Downing Street on the 13th and take her daughter Elizabeth to a better play. In a mood of self-congratulation she told him 9 May was her twentieth wedding anniversary.

Margot Asquith's invitation was well received. It would have been easy for him to have shied away from social contact yet he continued to lead a full social life, including taking the Prime Minister's daughter to a play by Wilde and dining at Downing Street with the smartest set in the land. It says much for his genuine feelings of respect for Margot Asquith, that such an apparently minor thing as selecting a present for a woman on her twentieth wedding anniversary was no trivial matter. But Robbie was a generous, caring man, who chose gifts with consideration, always mindful of the tastes of the recipient. His efforts were appreciated by Margot Asquith: 'How sweet you are to remember my great day today.'[8]

On 13 May Robbie entered the witness-box. He spoke well, for he was a gifted public speaker, but he did not enjoy giving evidence and had to work hard to control his nervousness. He outlined briefly the position he held at the Board of Inland Revenue, gave details of his family background and listed the political appointments held by his father and grandfather. He spoke sincerely about his friendship with Oscar Wilde, making a point of saying that since Wilde's death he had published many of his works, but had received no payment for his efforts. The royalties, which had been substantial, had been paid into the accounts of Wilde's sons.

In recalling the Ransome case, he said he had been subpoenaed to produce the whole of the manuscript of *De Profundis*. After the verdict had been delivered, Douglas had shown great enmity towards him and had expressed his feelings in a letter dated 1 November 1912. To a hushed Court Robbie read Douglas's damning words:

> No doubt to your dirty blackmailer's mind this is a fine *coup* and
> you and your filthy associates, who are the scum of the earth,
> imagine that I shall be very much perturbed. As a matter of fact, as
> I was always aware that you had in your possession the original of
> the letter with all its plain lies and obvious absurdities concocted by
> the filthy swine Wilde in prison for the express purpose of giving
> him a hold over me and my family and as I was equally aware that
> you were keeping this for the express purpose of blackmail, I was
> neither surprised nor disturbed by its production. I *knew* that you
> were at the back of this filthy scoundrel Ransome and his
> scoundrelly solicitor.... I am going straight ahead with my action
> and my only hope is that you will go into the witness-box and give
> me a chance of having you cross-examined. I shall smash you all
> inevitably and finally because I have right on my side and because I
> am a decent straight man fighting a lot of filthy rats.[9]

Douglas condemned himself but he was safe in France and it was Crosland, a lonely and broken man, who had to endure the reproaches from the public gallery.

'Have you ever seen Charles Garratt in your life until you saw him in Court the other day?' Ernest Wild asked.

'Never,' Robbie replied clearly and decisively. 'I heard of his existence first on my return from Russia, when an obscene letter about him was sent to Sir George Lewis.'[10]

Robbie went on to describe his meeting with Carew, who called on him, saying he was writing an article about Oscar Wilde for an American encyclopedia. He had not known that Carew was employed by Douglas, but he had mistrusted Carew's motives, and had asked his secretary Millard to deal with him. He recalled how on 14 November the previous year, Millard had come to see him and had showed him a letter he had received from a man called Murray. They consulted Lewis & Lewis, and it was agreed that Millard should keep an appointment with Murray, but he should be accompanied by a detective. Millard had gone to the Café Royal, where he found Douglas and a man he now knew to be Carew, a private inquiry agent.

On 28 January 1914 Robbie said that he had received a telephone call from a man who identified himself as Hughes; he agreed to see him and he came the next day. Hughes told him that if he would give him £100 he would see the whole Court business was dropped. Robbie refused to have anything to do with the man and had communicated the details of the meeting to George Lewis, who wrote a letter of complaint to Holt's. But before the letter could be sent, Hughes telephoned again and told him that, 'they [Douglas and Crosland] were not going on with the civil action, but were going to proceed with a criminal charge.'[11]

On the Wednesday evening Robbie dined pleasantly at Downing Street with the Asquiths; it was a world of peace, tranquillity and gaiety, in sharp contrast with the drab and dreary proceedings in Court. For Douglas, far away in Boulogne, the events of the day were somewhat different. Hampstead Police Court issued a summons against him for the non-payment of rates on his Church Row property. This, added to all his other problems with his father-in-law, made it difficult for him to return to England, at least until his mother had once again paid his debts. Crosland fared little better; the previous day another petition for bankruptcy had been made against him.

On the Thursday morning Christopher Millard entered the witness-box. Millard was a tall, impressive-looking, middle-aged man . He spoke with all the arrogance and confidence of his class. He did not normally take much interest in his appearance, but that morning, in comparison with the unkempt Crosland, he looked well groomed, prosperous even, and showed little signs of nervousness or indecision.

He confirmed he had first met Garratt on 19 August. On 17 September together with four other friends he had dined at a restaurant in Soho. After dinner they had gone back to his flat. Garratt left about 11.30 p.m., and the next morning he heard the boy had been arrested. He had attended the Court on the boy's behalf, but his actions had been misunderstood by the Magistrate, and misreported in the newspapers.

Millard explained that after Ross had returned from Russia, they discussed the matter and Ross had dismissed him. He had been very upset by the loss of his paid employment and had written to Douglas complaining that his intervention had caused him a great deal of hardship. He had tried to counter Douglas's accusations, by stating that Douglas, as a fellow Catholic, should be more forgiving in his attitude. He said Douglas had, after all, been previously guilty of compromising behaviour. Douglas had replied but had pointed out that as a fellow Catholic he could not possibly condone evil committed by other Catholics. He had written that anything he did which 'has the effect of cutting you off from a man like Ross, who is probably the foulest and most filthy beast drawing the breath of life, can only be an ultimate gain to you: and if there were anything I could do to help you to get out of the quagmire of corruption in which you are floundering, I should be most pleased to do it.'[12]

Millard went on to describe the interview he had had at the Café Royal with Douglas and Carew, who had told him of the statement Garratt had made against Ross. Douglas had told him they would use the statement when Garratt came out of prison.

'Did Lord Alfred Douglas tell you what the statement said?' Prosecution Counsel asked.

'He said, it was enough to get Mr Ross arrested, if not convicted,' Millard replied.[13]

Douglas, Millard said, suggested that they should leave a card at Ross's house with an offensive message on it, exactly as his father, the Marquess of Queensberry, had done at Oscar Wilde's club. Douglas told him if he could obtain information against Ross, he would give him money. Three days later he had another meeting with Douglas at Church Row where again Douglas had suggested that if he could get hold of any letters of a compromising nature, which Ross had written, he would buy them.

Douglas said he would take them to Sir George Lewis and exchange them for the compromising documents Ross had given them. One of the conditions of the exchange was that the suppressed part of *De Profundis* should never be published, but should be burnt.

The hearing was adjourned for the weekend and did not begin again until the following Tuesday. In spite of Margot Asquith's suggestion that he should take Elizabeth to a better play, on 14 May Robbie was in the audience for the revival of Wilde's *An Ideal Husband*. He must have remembered the first production of the play in January 1895, when he had attended the glittering first night, in the company of Wilde, Douglas and a circle of admiring friends.

When the hearing resumed Robbie was recalled. In reply to a question from Paul Taylor, he said at one time he had been a great friend of Douglas, but that they had not spoken for nearly six years. He said that he had not wanted to break the friendship, but once Douglas began writing abusive letters, he felt he had no alternative. Asked about Douglas's friendship with Oscar Wilde, Robbie said that at the beginning of the association—he was loath to use the word friendship, because Douglas had dishonoured that word by his later actions—Wilde had been thirty-six or thirty-seven and Lord Alfred twenty or twenty-one.

'Wilde was a mature man and Douglas practically a boy?'[14]

Robbie agreed but when Taylor suggested that the criminal proceedings against Wilde had showed that the boy had been corrupted by the mature man, Robbie vehemently objected, declaring that that was not his reading of the case. He said Douglas's grievance against him stemmed from his allegation that he had coached Ransome, but he repudiated this accusation. He had merely answered questions, as indeed he had answered similar questions put to him by other biographers of Wilde.

'Although you possess the copyright of the unpublished letters from Wilde to Lord Alfred Douglas, you would not object to their being published, if they were published *bona fide* by Lord Alfred, for the purpose of exculpating himself from what he might look upon as the improperly informed judgement of the Public?'

'No, sir, so long as I was allowed to see them. My object is to protect the children of Oscar Wilde,' Robbie replied.[15]

Paul Taylor commented that he could not help feeling that Lord Alfred had been a young man in the hands of a genius with depraved habits, and that the young man was the victim of the older man. Robbie did not answer, against such prejudice there was nothing he could say.

'Why did not this man [Ross] save himself?' Crosland shouted from the dock.[16]

There was no reply except from Taylor, who told him to contain his outburst. Anyway the question was unanswerable, Robbie could no more have explained to Crosland than he could have answered the prejudices of the Magistrate.

On 25 May, freed from attendance at Court, Robbie, from his office at Somerset House, wrote a letter of thanks for the support he had received from his old and valued friend, Robert Sherard:

> I am so deeply touched by your letter which is only a further
> justification of Oscar's famous description of you in *D.P.*[17] The
> fearful delays of the case are what prostrate me. Crosland is trying to

> get the Old Bailey trial postponed until the autumn. Garratt comes
> out of prison on July 15th and then Douglas will be able to get *at*
> *him* and having spirited him away pretend that I have done so.[18]

Robbie was not paranoid. He had some justification for being concerned. Crosland, while giving evidence, had implied that Ross and Millard had tried to buy Garratt's silence by offering him employment in Tunbridge Wells. If Crosland had managed to prolong the trial until Garratt was free, he and Douglas would, without doubt, have attempted to buy Garratt's silence. Robbie's postscript to Sherard was particularly poignant: 'This is a fatal day as you remember [nineteen years since Wilde was imprisoned] and also my natal day. I am 45!'[19]

If Robbie was utterly dejected by the events in the Magistrates' Court, he had some luck on his birthday. In the Reform Club Derby sweepstake he drew Dunbar II; he was, though, philosophical about drawing an outsider. Two days later the French-trained colt, appropriate for a French-born man, came in a winner at odds of 20/1 beating Hapsburg and Peter the Hermit by a length and a half. If Robbie had been a gambler, which he was not, he could have put £100 on the horse and he would have collected sufficient winnings to pay his legal expenses. It would have been like using Douglas's own money; Douglas, a singularly unlucky gambler, had lost most of his inheritance on the race tracks of France.

There was a lengthy postponement in the proceedings when Crosland was taken ill, but when it resumed on 28 May, Crosland was called to give evidence. Paul Taylor cautioned him and read the eight charges that had been placed against him. Crosland made no reply and the hearing was adjourned until the next morning. He looked much older than his forty-eight years. His features were drawn and his grey complexion showed the serious nature of his cardiac illness. The bags under his eyes emphasised his dark staring expression. He had a receding hairline and his sparse grey hair was pushed untidily to the side. His clothes were formal yet he looked unkempt.

He spoke well in his own defence, but there was a rough edge to his voice. He vehemently denied there was any foundation for the charges laid against him and he emphatically rejected the suggestion he had tried to blackmail anyone. He said he thought Ross and Millard ought to be in prison and he could not imagine why the authorities did not act against them. He had seen Garratt the day after the interview at Scotland Yard, and the boy had told him that Ross and Millard wanted him to go to Tunbridge Wells, where they promised to find him lodgings. He warned

Garratt that he would be ruined if he went, and would, in all probability, spend a great deal of time in prison. Crosland insisted that he did all he could to persuade the boy to go back to Leicestershire and lead a tidy life, but he refused all his offers of help. Douglas had become angry with the boy's reluctance to do as he was told, and had refused to pay his expenses while he was in London. Crosland said that he had gone to Leicestershire himself to try and enlist the help of Mrs Garratt in getting the boy to go back to the safety and security of his home.

Following an overnight adjournment Crosland continued to give evidence. He denied he had ever said Garratt was dressed as a woman, or that he had been drugged. He agreed he might have said that the whisky the boy had consumed had put him off his guard. He further denied he had said Ross was present on the first occasion when Millard met the boy; neither had he said Ross and Millard shared a flat. What he had said was that Ross visited Millard's flat. Asked by Paul Taylor, if the statement Garratt had made at Scotland Yard had ever been before the Public Prosecutor, he replied that he did not know. He said the police had told him that the Public Prosecutor did not proceed with these matters unless forced to do so. This, he said, was a scandal, and in his opinion Scotland Yard had hanged men on less evidence than they had against Ross.

Comyns Carr, Defence Counsel, painstakingly took Crosland through the detailed evidence of the Garratts, Ross and Millard, and in answer to each question he reiterated that he and he alone was telling the truth. Crosland, sensing victory looming on the horizon, thumped the rim of the witness-box, and declared. 'I've been ten years trying to bring this thing about, and I am here now, very happy and comfortable.'[20]

The last day of the Magistrate's hearing began on 2 June with the cross-examination of Crosland by Ernest Wild. In reply to a question from Wild, Crosland said he believed Ross had received payment for the work he had done for the Wilde Estate. He added that he had always understood that Ross considered *De Profundis* to be his property. Wild reminded him that Ross had sworn that he had never received a farthing from the Estate.

Wild pointed out that through Ross's efforts the Wilde Estate was out of bankruptcy, and Wilde's sons were now assured of an annual income. Crosland agreed that in his own parody, *The First Stone*, published in 1912, he had suggested Ross had done improper things to Wilde's manuscript of *De Profundis*.

Crosland flew into a rage when Wild suggested that Crosland had dined with Garratt, whom Paul Taylor described as 'a dirty boy'. Wild continued to taunt Crosland, and there was a spirited exchange between the two men, with Crosland becoming increasingly angry. In the end

Wild said he would not ask any more questions and it could go down in the deposition, that the defendant had refused to answer.

'After being insulted by Counsel,' Comyns Carr interjected.[21]

In committing Crosland for trial, Paul Taylor said that he saw no evidence whatever that either Crosland or Lord Alfred Douglas had been actuated by a desire to obtain money, nor was there a shred of evidence which would justify their allegations against Ross of committing any criminal offence.

The newspapers, the next day, incorrectly reported that bail had been refused. In fact it was granted with Sholto Johnstone Douglas again standing as surety. It was an unhappy end to what had been an extremely hard seven weeks, and they would have to go through the whole sordid business again at the Central Criminal Court. Crosland's presence in the witness-box would impress any jury. He was a lone voice of reason in the wilderness of depravity and vice. His defence of honesty, decency and moral standards would make a powerful impact on any jury. In counter-argument the Prosecution had only the pathetic testimony of Charlie Garratt; Millard's testimony was tainted. He would hold his own in the witness-box, but it would be insufficient to discredit Crosland or Lord Alfred Douglas.

Seventeen

At the Old Bailey

HERE WAS little that Robbie could do to settle his mind between the end of the Magistrate's hearing and the beginning of the trial at the Old Bailey. He did, however, experience a sense of righteousness when, in the recess, Cecil Holt was arrested for 'the fraudulent conversion of clients' accounts'. On 18 June he appeared before Paul Taylor, the same Magistrate who had sent Crosland for trial. Holt said he was not now practising and within the last month had been made bankrupt. As his catalogue of crimes became known, Millard did not hesitate to broadcast the news to his friends: 'Cecil Holt, the rascally solicitor who acted for Douglas and Crosland, was arrested yesterday for embezzling the money of his clients (those clients obviously not being A.D. and T.W.H.C!). His clerk Fairhall has turned King's Evidence.'[1]

For almost a year since his resignation as London Director of the Johannesburg Art Gallery, there had been no contact between Robbie and Lady Phillips, but shortly before the trial at the High Court he wrote to her:

> My unpleasant *case* is expected to come on this week; and therefore, before you suggest an appointment for me to see you or your representative, I will ask your further indulgence to postpone it until my case is over.
>
> I fear that in the strain of worry which has overwhelmed me the Aronson matter escaped my attention. So far as I can recall, the busts have not been delivered. Do you wish me to send the cheque for £100 to you or to the Solicitors at once? You will remember that you gave me a cheque on November 18th 1912 to cover the amount.
>
> Since you wrote to me in August last acknowledging my letter of resignation I have been expecting your return; and I have, not from any slackness but from dire necessity, been obliged to adopt an attitude of *masterly inactivity* with regard to the Johannesburg Art Gallery. But, of course, I realised that you were delayed by the dreadful attack on Sir Lionel Phillips. And I myself have been occupied entirely with my own sordid affairs, I am afraid.[2]

His admission of *masterly inactivity* was far from the truth. Robbie had been much occupied on behalf of the Gallery. As usual his attention to detail was precise, and everything was in its allotted place, although he admitted he felt like 'the steward in scripture who buried the talent and restored it to his master.'[3] He had arranged for the Tate Gallery to store all the paintings and sculptures that had been bought on behalf of the Gallery. He was aware that certain people had expressed concern that a picture he had purchased from Augustus John[4] was disliked, but he assured Lady Phillips it could be sold for a substantial profit, if she so chose. The gift of the Walter Sickert picture particularly pleased him, and although Sylvia Gosse thought he might dislike the paintings of Harold Gilman and Spencer F. Gore, he was quite happy to accept her gift of Gilman's *The Reapers*, Spencer's *The Promenade* and Walter Bayes's *Le Petit Casino*.[5] On Robbie's advice Lady Michaelis later presented the Gallery with one of Sylvia's own pictures, *Market Place, Trequier*.

The trial of Crosland opened on 27 June at the Central Criminal Court, before Mr Justice Avory. The Prosecution was led by the flamboyant Frederick Edwin [F.E.] Smith, a tall, slim, athletic, attractive man in his middle forties. His sleek black hair was hidden behind the rakish angle of his wig, and his black Court gown was worn as if it were already trimmed with ermine and gold. He knew the full extent of his abilities and there was a hint of arrogance in his dark eyes which few could fail to notice. He had a wit which could ridicule and satirise in a single sentence. He could demolish a defence argument with his brilliant intellect. The judiciary, often on the receiving end of his insolent, invective tongue, viewed his presence in their Court with unconcealed glee, and if the chance came to put the elegant, eloquent Counsel in his place, the moment did not go unchallenged.

Against a downtrodden, moral crusader such as Crosland, it was perhaps a mistake for Robbie to retain the services of such a controversial leading barrister. The all-male jury were likely to be prejudiced against F.E. and certainly his reputation for high living and extravagances would not help him to gain the sympathy of the Court. F.E. was assisted by Ernest Wild and Eustace Fulton. Cecil Hayes appeared again for the Defence. It was in some ways reminiscent of the line-up of Counsel in the Ransome case. The only disturbing aspect was the presence of Mr Horace Avory, who had been a junior member of the Crown's Prosecution team when Oscar Wilde had been tried twice for the same crime. There was no reason why Mr Justice Avory should allow his personal disapproval of the Wilde cult to influence his judgement of the present case, yet in the minds of the Prosecution there must have remained a nagging doubt.

The proceedings began with F.E.'s opening statement. He told the jury that the inquiry on which they were about to enter would be of an unusual, disagreeable and somewhat protracted nature. The defendant, in trying to bring the charges against Ross, knew they were unwarranted and baseless. F.E. went into considerable detail into the background to the friendship between Ross and Douglas, and the late Oscar and Constance Wilde. He said that when Wilde had been released from prison Ross had done his best to prevent the unfortunate man from rejoining Lord Alfred Douglas and that this intervention had been much resented by Douglas. Crosland, F.E. said, had deliberately and persistently set out to annoy Ross whenever the opportunity presented itself. For a period of nearly ten years Crosland and Lord Alfred Douglas had been confederates in business. Cecil Hayes interposed, to object to the word 'confederates'. F.E. ignored the interruption and repeated the word in his very next sentence. He stressed that the hatred of Crosland and Douglas had not softened with the passage of time nor by adversity, nor was it subdued by the repeated failure of their efforts to bring Ross into a Court to answer their false charges. In outlining the details of the Ransome case, F.E. said that Ross felt he owed it to the memory of Oscar Wilde to produce the documents known as *De Profundis*. The jury had found for Arthur Ransome, and his Plea of Justification had been accepted. Hayes again interrupted to dispute F.E.'s interpretation of the jury's verdict.

The proceedings at the Central Criminal Court followed closely those held at the Marylebone Police Court, with the witnesses repeating their earlier evidence. But when Cecil Hayes, during the cross-examination of Christopher Millard, produced a copy of *The Picture of Dorian Gray*, a murmur of expectancy echoed round the Court. The introduction of Oscar Wilde's most notorious book was deliberately intended to revive in the minds of the Judge and the jury, all the sordid details of Wilde's trials. Reading from the Preface, Cecil Hayes quoted:

' "There is no such thing as a moral book or an immoral book. Books are well written, or badly written. That is all". Do you consider *Dorian Gray* is an immoral book?' The voice belonged to Cecil Hayes, but the words were those uttered by Sir Edward Carson during the trial of Queensberry.

Millard did not try to repeat Wilde's eloquent defence of the literary merits of *The Picture of Dorian Gray*, he simply replied. 'No, I do not.'

'Do you approve of the book as a moral book?' Mr Justice Avory enquired.

'I see nothing immoral in it.' Millard lacked Wilde's sparkling wit, yet, there was about his answers an intellectual sureness which could not be easily ignored. 'I don't see how printed words can be immoral. They might be indecent.'

'Do you mean that no printed words could have an immoral tendency?' Mr Justice Avory asked.

'That', Millard said, 'is a hypothetical question. I don't consider that they have any immoral effect upon me. I fail to see how they could have an immoral effect on anybody.'[6]

Robbie followed Christopher Millard into the witness-box. He had none of Millard's arrogance, but he was self-assured without being over-confident, and there were odd moments when his sparkling wit matched Wilde's as he countered Counsel's questions. He spoke sincerely of his efforts to restore Wilde's financial and literary fortunes, and he reiterated that he had never received any remuneration from the Wilde Estate. He gave the simple facts concerning his argument with Douglas which resulted in the ending of their friendship. He again repeated on oath that until the proceedings had begun he had not met Charles Garratt.

Cross-examined by Cecil Hayes about the dinner he had with Millard after Garratt had been imprisoned, Robbie said it had been a business meeting to discuss various aspects of the present case.

'Did you think it might give people a false impression?' Hayes asked.

'No, because everybody knows what my character is. I can afford to dine with anybody.'

'Are you above suspicion?'

'Absolutely.'[7]

He was questioned closely on his relationship with Douglas before Wilde's imprisonment. Robbie objected strongly when Cecil Hayes tried to introduce into evidence a letter he had written to Douglas more than twenty years before; and when asked by Mr Justice Avory, if he considered *The Picture of Dorian Gray* to be a perfectly moral book, Robbie assured him it most certainly was. At the end of a long day in the witness-box, asked if in his opinion there was such a thing as an immoral book, Robbie could not resist the temptation to provide a little light relief.

'Yes, I know heaps of them. Lord Alfred Douglas's poems, for instance.'[8]

Perhaps it was wrong to score bonus points against the absent Douglas, since it only brought forth an excited incoherent protest from Crosland. It did, however, bring the day's proceedings to an end on a triumphant note. Avory indicated that he was well aware of Robbie's attitude towards Douglas. It was obvious he viewed Robbie's cool and controlled pose with as much displeasure as he did the presence of F.E. and he became increasingly antagonistic towards the Prosecution.

Cecil Hayes opened the case for the Defence, by apologising for being a humble member of the Bar, whose inability and incapacity were the only reasons why the Judge did not instruct the jury to throw out the case, once the Prosecution's evidence was completed. If the Defence had been put by the learned Counsel for the Prosecution, he firmly believed that the case would have now ended and his client would be a free man cleared of all the ridiculous charges against him. Hayes argued it was one of the most ingeniously devised schemes that had ever emanated from one of the most brilliant firms of solicitors in London. George Lewis and all the brilliant specialists of the Bar, he said, had been employed in a desperate attempt to whitewash and establish forever the reputation of Robert Ross. The whole movement to whitewash Oscar Wilde and to propagate his works by his disciples was repulsive to Crosland. Crosland's friendship with Douglas was purely literary and he sympathised strongly with Douglas's endeavour to live down his past associations with Wilde and his efforts to prevent the foisting on the world of all the books on Wilde with their odious references to himself.

In his evidence, Crosland, explaining his attitude to Wilde's writings, said he 'considered them—and I do not say this out of bitterness but as a critic of literature —dangerous works because, although clever and brilliant, they deal only with half-truths.'[9]

He went on to admit that at the time he wrote his first denunciation of Wilde's writings, he had not read *The Picture of Dorian Gray*.

'If I had read it,' Crosland continued to defend the indefensible, 'I should have been furious. I did not read the book until after the Ransome case.'

'What were your feelings then?' Hayes enquired.

'I should not like to express it in the witness-box,' Crosland replied, bringing a burst of laughter from the public gallery. 'I was disgusted with the whole thing. Wilde's expression, "there is no such thing as an immoral book", is the stand-by for all people who write dirty books.'[10]

F.E. rose to begin his cross-examination. He and Crosland had crossed swords on a previous occasion. Crosland was a born performer and the witness-box an excellent stage, and in Crosland's mind he was the leading player and F.E. the incompetent and inexperienced supporter. The cut and thrust of the argument ranged back and forth, with F.E. attacking and Crosland parrying. In trying to counter-argue that Douglas held the view that a man's vices ought to be allowed to die when he had written a great book, Crosland stated that he thought it was not possible to improve a good story by putting a moral in it.

History was again replayed when F.E. began to quote from Douglas's poem 'Two Loves', which ends with the provocative line, 'I am the Love that dare not speak its name.'[11] Mr Justice Avory would have recalled that those damning verses had been read during the trial of Oscar Wilde. Mr Gill, in cross-examining Wilde, had quoted from the same poem with unexpected results. Wilde's moving defence of the 'Love that dare not speak its name'[12] had brought a spontaneous burst of applause from the public gallery. There would be no eulogy this time since Crosland did not have Wilde's ability or sensitivity.

F.E. did not pursue the subject of homosexuality but turned to other matters, particularly Crosland's personal affairs, and in reply to a question about his marital relations Crosland said he had been married for nearly twenty years and he lived on terms of affection with his wife, although for legal reasons it had been necessary for them to live apart. He did not explain what the legal reasons were, nor did F.E. press him for an explanation.

'Who is Mrs Powell?'[13] F.E.'s question sounded naive, but it was heavily laced with disdain.

Crosland replied somewhat coyly that she was the tenant of the flat where he resided.

'In a case like this,' F.E. retorted, 'a man need not be ashamed to say that he has a mistress.'[14]

It was such a singularly innocent insult, yet behind it was all the Machiavellian finesse of a great legal mind. Crosland had condemned Ross for dining with a male friend and colleague, but he hesitated to call the woman he lived with his mistress, and by doing so he stepped neatly into the trap laid by the Prosecution Counsel.

Questioned on his attitude to what F.E. called the *De Profundis* affair, Crosland said he thought Ross's action in handing the manuscript to the British Museum was 'damned treacherous'.

'I will not allow those words to be used here. I don't know where they are going to stop. You must restrain your language,' Mr Justice Avory rebuked him for his intemperate remarks.[15]

Crosland's response brought forth a renewed burst of laughter from the gallery when he declared that he wanted the jury to look after him. 'I am here to fight with one of the best intellects [F.E.] in England, and I am going to fight. Two thousand quids worth of counsel against a poor man.'[16]

A little later Crosland said he would take no pleasure in seeing Ross or any of his associates suffer. There was no way F.E. could let such a lie pass unchallenged, and he scoffed. 'Your one object throughout the whole proceedings was to make Mr Ross suffer.'

'My point was that the public interest was greater than the suffering of anybody,' Crosland replied virtuously, and then went on to say that it was a good thing, 'To bring this out about Ross, as it would interfere with the Wilde Movement. Mr Ross and Millard had made Wilde from an insignificant author, into one whose works they boasted had the largest sale of any. It was his view that Wilde's works were most dangerous.'[17] He then repeated what F.E. had said earlier, 'about a man's works should be remembered and his sins forgotten'. Crosland said he could not share that opinion.

The closing speeches began on 6 July, thirteen weeks after Crosland's arrest. Cecil Hayes, in an impassioned speech, defended his client's puritan beliefs and ideals. He stressed that the jury could not punish his client because he had a ferocious dislike of vice. Nor did he feel they should suspend the well-known maxim that 'birds of a feather flock together'.

The moment arrived for F.E. to make his final effort. The Court was his theatre and like all great actors he knew the measure of his audience. An orator *par excellence*, it was his habit to dominate the centre stage with his vibrant personality. He went straight on to the offensive, pointing out first that some observations which the Judge had let fall during the case appeared to express views which he [F.E.] had not put before them. The case, he said, was surrounded with an atmosphere of prejudice and mutual hostility, which it was necessary for the jury to eliminate from their minds before they could come to a proper decision. He concluded his speech by inviting the jury to say that it was incredible that Crosland could ever have believed the story told to him by Charles Garratt. If that were so, then the jury had no alternative but to find the defendant Guilty.

Avory began his summing up at 3.10 p.m.. In great detail he took the jury through each point of Law. He stressed to the jury that 'the fact that Lord Alfred Douglas had not surrendered himself to the charge and the fact that he had remained abroad, not subject to the jurisdiction of this Court, must not prejudice the defendant in the jury's eyes.'[18] He said it would be difficult for the jury to understand that although Douglas and Crosland had been close friends, there could, in the eyes of the Law, still be evidence of conspiracy against one man but not against the other.

He drew the attention of the jury to F.E.'s initial remarks. It was unnecessary he said, for them to be reminded not to be influenced by any view that he [F.E.] might take of the facts. They should not be influenced by the views of the Prosecution Counsel. The jury, he said 'were not there for the purpose of admiring the advocacy of Mr Ross's learned counsel, and certainly they were not there to convict anybody merely because Mr Ross had the good fortune to secure the services of one of the most eminent and most eloquent of the counsel at the English Bar.'[19] He also warned the jury that if they acquitted Crosland it would not imply that Ross was guilty of any offence, but he said, 'if a man allowed himself to be associated with such a person as Oscar Wilde... if he chose to run that risk, could he complain if a person who was not carried away by admiration for the literary genius of Oscar Wilde said a man was known by his companions? If he persisted in associating on friendly terms with such a person right up to the time of his death, Mr Crosland said he, at all events, was entitled to take that into consideration.'[20]

The Judge's summing-up was such that the jury needed only half an hour's deliberation before they found Crosland NOT GUILTY.

True to their nature, Crosland and Douglas were soon squabbling over who should pay the costs of the action. In the end neither of them paid; any bills that were eventually paid were settled by the generosity of the Dowager Lady Queensberry and other members of the Queensberry family. Douglas could not refrain from composing and offering for sale, on the receipt of nine penny stamps, an odious satire against F.E.[21] If, as Douglas prophesied, 'O, Smith you've taken Ross's "thou", You'll take the Chiltern Hundreds now?'[22] he was to be bitterly disappointed. F.E. did not sink into oblivion; before a year had passed he became Attorney-General, and was better placed to keep a close legal eye on the activities of Douglas and Crosland.

There was only humiliation and sadness for Robbie. He had lost a fight he should have won. Crosland was at best a hypocrite, at worst a liar and a cheat. His opposition to the moral behaviour of others did not stop him leading a life of debauchery. It would, perhaps, have been possible to feel sympathy for him if he had confined his actions to the written word; at least he could have said it was his honest opinion. With the power of his pen he could have conducted a moral crusade against Wilde's works with impunity, but to use perjury and blackmail to discredit and ruin another man merits the strongest condemnation. In appointing himself judge and jury of another man's sins, he assumed a role for which he was not qualified. On his own admission Crosland was an alcoholic. He made no secret that he had a mistress, although he declared he still had a loving and devoted wife and family whom he continued to maintain. He borrowed money from a moneylender in order to go to Monte Carlo with his mistress. At the same time he accepted a gift from the Royal Literary Society to ease the poverty of his wife and family. He despised Ross for his personal wealth and for his rich and powerful friends, yet he did nothing to improve his own financial standing. He wrote profusely, and then objected when his work did not attract the same financial rewards as the writings of Oscar Wilde.

Robbie could not face life in London after the iniquitous verdict and he retreated to Jesmond Hill,[23] the home of his sister, Mary. And from the security and comfort of her Pangbourne home he slowly began to recover his spirits and resolve to rebuild his shattered life. In spite of being the innocent prosecutor he had no alternative but to resign from his position as Assessor of Picture Valuation. The job brought him into contact with many of the leading families in the land, and he was required to enter their homes to perform his duties on behalf of the Crown. He could not risk his employers or his clients being embarrassed by his presence. Sir Matthew Natham and his staff had warmly supported Ross all through the Crosland case, but they could do no more than accept his resignation. It was a further triumph for Douglas and one that Robbie resented as bitterly as he resented Crosland's acquittal.

As in all previous moments of crisis he turned to Edmund Gosse for support. In writing to Gosse he gave full vent to his anger. He blamed the Home Secretary, Reginald McKenna, and the Director of Public Prosecutions, Charles Mathews, who was an intimate friend of Mr Justice Avory, for failing to protect him against Douglas's allegations. He did, though, appreciate

> that poor Millard was the difficulty for the authorities. But looking at the whole situation calmly I think it is obvious that both Mathews and the Home Secretary were *not* merely *not* protecting me but using Crosland and Douglas and propose to do so in the future by allowing Douglas to return to England. I know this sounds fantastic but it is the generally held opinion of many barristers. If the blameless Colonel Custance is not allowed protection from Douglas or the benefit of his verdict, how much less shall I be allowed protection after the Avory attitude and verdict of last Monday![24]

Robbie told Gosse that he had no firm plans for the future. He said he was loath to continue with his libel action against Douglas, even if he should be foolish enough to return from France. Aware that the Law would not protect him, Robbie told Gosse that perhaps his best course of action would be to get certain of his parliamentary friends to raise the whole matter in the House or get his friends to organise a press campaign on his behalf. He thought either action would be more successful than further litigation, but he had no illusions about the value of such an action. 'The object being not to rehabilitate me, that is impossible, but at least to rid this country of Douglas and Crosland and break the influence of the Wyndhams. I know the world must be as sick of the subject as I am. But Douglas has become a real danger to the community.'[25]

Gosse was not prepared to remain silent after the grossly unfair verdict. He was one of the first of Robbie's friends to suggest they should organise a petition and fund to pay his legal expenses. He was, though, of the opinion that nothing should be done until after the libel action against Douglas had been heard or withdrawn. Dugald MacColl was not so reticent. On 27 July he wrote to Maurice Bonham Carter, Asquith's Private Secretary, suggesting, now that Robbie was free of all his other duties, that the Government, with the approval of the Trustees of the National Gallery, should appoint Ross Administrator. MacColl said of Robbie, 'He would strengthen the administration just when it is at present weak, namely in knowledge of the market value of pictures and of the ways and wiles of the picture dealing kind.'[26] Bonham Carter, as MacColl suggested, did put the matter to Asquith, but it was felt that in the circumstances it would be better if they proceeded with caution, but he said that the Prime Minister would consult the Trustees of the National Gallery.[27]

The support and encouragement of his friends was deeply appreciated, and Robbie was only too aware of the debt he owed them, but his main obligation was to Gosse. 'It is largely due to you, dear Gosse, that I have kept up my health let alone my failing courage during the last year.'[28] Of the many letters of support Robbie received, the one from John Maynard Keynes pleased him most; he hastened to reply:[29]

> I was really more touched than I dare to say by your kind letter of sympathy. While I appreciate deeply the loyalty and confidence of the many friends who have endeavoured in every possible way to break the fall for me, expressions of sympathy from such as yourself mean even more to me. Crosland has started proceedings against me for *malicious prosecution* so I have a further ordeal to go through in the winter when the case will be heard in the King's Bench. I am going abroad for a couple of months, but I hope I may one day have the pleasure of thanking you personally. I sometimes go to Cambridge to stay with my nephew-in-law Donald Robertson.[30,31]

In reality, in the Crosland trial, it was Wilde—not Crosland—who was the prisoner in the dock. Every time Douglas used the Law to settle his quarrels, it was Oscar Wilde the jury were trying. Until the day dawned when Oscar Wilde was allowed to rest in peace, and only his literary genius allowed to influence a Judge or jury, there could be no justice for any of them. Justice was not served when twelve good men and true found Thomas Crosland not guilty, thus allowing him to continue his puritanical crusade.

Eighteen

Plea of Justification

HERE SHOULD have been nothing but sympathy for Robbie when Crosland was acquitted of the conspiracy charge. It was as if the judiciary had given every scoundrel and blackmailer in London a licence to harass Robbie and demand money in return for their silence.[1] The acquittal of Crosland was also the spur Douglas needed to intensify his own campaign of hate, and he took full advantage of Robbie's disinclination to retaliate.

Homosexual acts other than sodomy had not been a criminal offence until Section 11 of the Criminal Law Amendment Act 1885 had been placed on the Statute Book. The crime of homosexuality was given undue prominence by Mr Justice Wills when he sentenced Wilde to two years' hard labour, for what was, even then, only a misdemeanour. In the years since the Amendment was passed there had, in relationship to the numbers involved in homosexual activities, been very few prosecutions. The charge most often used was importuning, which even today is still on the Statute Book.

If Mr Justice Wills thought the misdemeanour which Wilde had committed was so bad that he could not find the right language to describe it,[2] then he obviously did not know what was taking place in the last decades of the nineteenth century. He was, however, not alone in his narrow denunciation of homosexuality; Crosland's obsession with the vice bordered on madness. He was prepared to condemn all those who had an association with a known homosexual, no matter how trivial.

There was, and indeed still is, a marked difference in Society's attitude to a man who commits adultery and to one who commits buggery. This difference of attitude was put into perspective by the social reformer W.T. Stead, who wrote at the time of Oscar Wilde's disgrace:

> The male is sacrosanct: the female is fair game. To have burdened
> society with a dozen bastards, to have destroyed a happy home by
> his lawless lust of these things the criminal law takes no account.
> But let him act indecently to a young rascal who is very well able to
> take care of himself, and who can by no possibility bring a child into
> the world as the result of his corruption, then judges can hardly

229

contain themselves from indignation when inflicting the maximum
sentence the law allows.[3]

Had Robbie seduced a young woman, and had she borne his child, he
would have been regarded by Society as a 'proper fellow'. Had he stolen
another man's wife, Society would have been shocked but the scandal
would have soon been forgotten; indeed, there would have been those
who would have shaken his hand and congratulated him on his 'manli-
ness'. But he did not seduce young girls, nor did he commit adultery. He
did, unfortunately, enjoy the company of young men—not always for
sexual gratification—and for this he was hounded, abused and held up to
public ridicule. He sought the protection of the Courts but found only
prejudice and intolerance. The Law did not understand that a man could
be different sexually from other men and yet still have a high standard of
morality. Having seen what the Law, in its infinite wisdom, did to
Wilde, Robbie should have been more careful in his affairs, and he
should at least have heeded the warning signs.

In his visits to Wilde in prison he had observed the intolerable
conditions of prison life and should not have gambled so recklessly with
his own freedom. He had seen Wilde made bankrupt and he had known
the agony of paying off the debts before the bankruptcy could be
annulled. Knowing all the penalties, it is inconceivable that Robbie
would have corrupted and debauched hundreds of innocent young boys
and continued to do so as Douglas claimed. Robbie was not a monster,
nor was he a sexual beast who needed to satisfy an insatiable appetite. He
did occasionally need the love of another man. Certainly, he would have
been judged a lesser man if he had sought this comfort from a woman of
the streets or from an innocent young virgin.

The trial of Crosland was a clash between the activities of Ross the
homosexual and the heterosexual Crosland with a wife and mistress. The
jury should not have been asked to make a comparison since all com-
parisons were subjective. If the jury had been able to decide which of the
two men was more compassionate and caring in his treatment of those
less fortunate than himself, then Robbie would have walked out of court
with his reputation untarnished. F.E. had told the jury that after extensive investigations by officers at Scotland Yard, they had found no
evidence with which to convict Ross of practising homosexual acts. The
presumption of Ross's guilt came primarily from Lord Alfred Douglas.
And few men have been more guilty of perpetrating a lie. Robbie was not
a saint, but he should have been judged on his own style of living and on
the evidence he gave in his own defence, not on the perjured testimony of
others.

In trying to seek the reasons behind Douglas's continuing vendetta, it is not necessary to look further than his own autobiography, published in 1929.[4] He gave a clear and unequivocal declaration of his intention to destroy Ross, as his father had destroyed Oscar Wilde. The pity of it is that he nearly succeeded, although he admitted it took him two years because Ross failed to respond to his libels. He boasted that he did it without friends or money and with only the support of his mother. He said that as he had finally driven Ross to retaliate, it was nothing short of a miracle.

Douglas was always inclined to exaggerate. There was nothing miraculous about his actions; they were simply the vicious, petulant actions of a spoilt, arrogant, social snob. Ross, despite what Douglas and Crosland thought, was tough and for a long time took all their insults without comment. Finally, though, he was driven by sheer exhaustion to seek the redress of the Law; even then, he did not act as Douglas and Crosland had expected.

In the early summer of 1914, Robbie took rooms at 40 Half Moon Street, Mayfair, where he was under the watchful and compassionate eyes of the admirable and dependable Nellie Burton, his mother's former maid. The redoubtable Miss Burton was just the foil Robbie needed to see him through the dark years of the Great War. She was a lady of large stature with a round beaming face; dressed elaborately in silk and velvets and ostrich feathers, but her sense of panache did not hide her loyal, shrewd and caring personality. Nellie Burton was the perfect landlady. With her native Hampshire dialect she could scold in the plainest and heartiest terms, but 'the scoldings were directed at the erring and wayward, since Miss Burton held firmly that it is in the nature of gentlemen to err and behave strangely'.[5]

Half Moon Street was Robbie's first settled home since he had left Vicarage Gardens and he was able to bring together all the treasures he had collected over the years:

> The tones of the room were mellow and subdued, half Italian and
> half Oriental, yet essentially imbued by London homeliness. There
> was a richly-looming Roman landscape by Richard Wilson. A few
> small Chinese prints and pieces of faience, refined and delicate in
> colour, harmonized with the Persian carpet and the curtain at the
> tall windows which opened onto a balcony.... In the large old glass-
> doored bookcase... an assortment of... "poetry and *belles*
> *lettres*"... Along the middle of the room, parallel with the bookcase,
> was the table on which he did his writings.[6]

The table was littered with papers and copies of recently published books which required Robbie's attention, but the table would always be set ready to tempt his guests, with brandy and glasses, tins of biscuits and boxes of Turkish delight, fresh figs, and boxes of his favourite Egyptian cigarettes. Above the mantelpiece was the Giovanni di Paolo devotional panel of *St Fabian and St Sebastian*,[7] which made a magnificent backdrop to the room.

With the declaration of war on 4 August, Douglas decided it would, after all, be better to leave France and return home. Since Crosland's acquittal, he believed that all he had to worry about was the bench warrant issued after his libel on his father-in-law, Colonel Custance. He reckoned without George Lewis's cunning and shrewd manipulation of the outstanding warrants, and a severe shock awaited him when he arrived ashore at Folkestone on 4 September. As well as the outstanding warrant by his father-in-law, he was also arrested on the warrant dated 24 March 1914, for unlawfully and maliciously writing and publishing a false and malicious libel concerning Robert Ross. Christopher Millard admirably expressed the views of many, when he said in a letter to Walter Ledger: 'Douglas is in Brixton till tomorrow (I would much prefer for him to be in Boulogne, where at least there would be a chance of the Germans shooting him as undesirable).'[8]

Douglas's arrest added to Robbie's overwhelming sense of impending disaster. He felt vulnerable and lonely; Alex was away on a short muchneeded holiday and he was loath to disturb him; George Lewis was also out of town, and, as in other moments of extreme crisis, Robbie turned to Edmund Gosse. It was unfortunate that just when he most needed a compassionate and understanding friend, Gosse failed him. It can be a matter only of speculation as to what caused the argument between them, but it is likely to have been caused by Douglas's arrival in England. Perhaps, feeling as depressed as he was, Robbie wished to withdraw from yet another bruising legal fight, perhaps Gosse warned him that, if he did, he would lose the last shred of credibility he possessed. Perhaps it was the exact opposite, Gosse imploring him to withdraw and Robbie determined to continue. Whatever the cause, the row only added to his misery and he wrote to Nellie Gosse, trying to lift some of the blame from his own shoulders. He was confident that she, at least, would

> understand something of what I suffered today *when* Gosse tore me
> to shreds and Gosse will understand why I am not more elated when
> he reminds me as others remind me of all the highly placed friends

> who "sympathise" with me so much. I *asked* for protection both
> from the law and from highly placed friends. I realised that neither
> could have done more for me than sympathise; the law did not even
> do that. Gosse was the *one* person who really tried to *act* for me, by
> practical steps. That he could do nothing only makes my obligation
> to him greater. I am where I was five years ago at the mercy of two
> vindictive families, minus everything except my devotion to Gosse
> and his family.[9]

Douglas made his first appearance at Marylebone Police Court on
Saturday morning, and was remanded. He spent the first five days in
Brixton Prison, before coming up before the Recorder of London at the
Central Criminal Court, on the bench warrant for libelling Colonel
Custance. As he was more interested in his forthcoming battle with
Robbie, Douglas offered his regrets and made a full apology to the Court
and his father-in-law. He was ordered to enter into his own recognisances
of £500 together with two further sureties each of £250; he was warned
that failure to keep his word not to repeat the libels on Colonel Custance
would mean he would be brought back to the Court and sentenced to six
months' hard labour. It was easy for him to give such an undertaking; he
had no conscience about not keeping his word.

In forming his Plea of Justification Douglas was to encounter more
problems than he expected. He believed that as his father had had no
difficulty in finding evidence against Wilde, he would also find a group of
young scoundrels who would be delighted, for a monetary consideration,
to give evidence against Ross. In the end Douglas was able to cite only
four incidents of Ross's homosexual activities. The first citation was
twenty years old and involved the boy at Biscoe Wortham's school in
Bruges. Carter & Bell, Douglas's solicitors, wrote to Wortham on 4 June
1914.[10] Unfortunately, the letter does not now exist, but it is possible to
make a number of assumptions about it; if the letter was sent to Biscoe
Wortham, why wasn't it addressed to the Reverend Biscoe Wortham?
Was it, in fact, addressed to his son Philip? Wortham replied to Carter &
Bell, and again its contents can be only a matter of speculation. But
Wortham did not appear as a witness for Douglas, nor was he subpoenaed. Did Philip, after an interval of twenty years, regret his youthful
confession that he had been seduced by Robbie? As a precocious adolescent he may have thought nothing of 'lying' to his father, but as a
successful mature man, to lie under oath, was quite a different matter.
He might also have been concerned that if he agreed to be a witness for
Douglas, he could under cross-examination, confess that Douglas had
also seduced 'the boy involved in the Bruges incident'. It is also worth

noting that Douglas did not subpoena Alfred Lambart, who at the time was languishing in prison, and as such would not have presented a respectable front to the jury. Nor did he call Danney or Dansay as a witness.

The second citation inevitably involved Charles Garratt although it had already been established that there was no legal foundation for such an accusation. Freddie Smith was named in the third citation, but Douglas was more concerned with Smith's improved social and financial status than his homosexual activities. It was a source of continued annoyance to Douglas that Smith, under Robbie's careful tutoring, had become a cultured and refined young man, and financially secure now that he had inherited a considerable sum of money from the Estate of a distant relative. The fourth citation was even more ludicrous than the previous three, based on the evidence of a Mr Edwards of Campden Hill,[11] who stated that his son had been seduced by Robbie.

In recounting how he came upon Mr Edwards, Douglas wrote in his autobiography[12] that it was only at the last moment he heard of Edwards but on going to the address in Campden Hill, he had found to his dismay that the occupants had never heard of Edwards. He prayed to Anthony of Padua, his favourite Saint, and lo and behold, when he turned round, a beautiful young boy offered his assistance. He took his hand and escorted him to the far end of the road and showed him where Edwards could be found. Douglas hurried to the front door, but, on turning round to thank the child, found he had disappeared.

If Douglas had not been so blinded by his own morality he would have seen there was something highly suggestive in a beautiful young boy becoming his soul-mate. He had spent years declaring, to all who would listen, that he was not, nor ever had been, a homosexual, yet, when he needed help, it was 'a beautiful young boy' who came forward to give him assistance. With such formidable opponents ranged against him, Robbie had no more chance of walking away unscathed from the legal fray, than Wilde had done two decades earlier. He was already worn out by his fight to clear Wilde's name and literary reputation, and now he had to defend himself against Douglas, the Saints and a choir of angels!

It did not occur to Douglas that his difficulty in getting evidence against Ross was because the evidence was not there to get. Eventually Douglas produced fourteen witnesses, but they lacked credibility.

Douglas appeared for trial at the Central Criminal Court on 19 November 1914 before Mr Justice Coleridge. Douglas's Counsel was Comyns Carr, assisted by E.J. Purchase. Robbie was represented by Ernest Wild, KC, and Eustace Fulton, under instructions from Lewis & Lewis. The presence of F.E. Smith as Prosecution Counsel was sadly missing as he was serving in France with the Indian Brigade. Although an able deputy, Ernest Wild's performance lacked F.E.'s incisive thrusts. The trial was scheduled to last six days.

Douglas pleaded not guilty and entered a Plea of Justification. The Defence said that they would prove the truth of the allegations made and therefore they could not be libellous. The Prosecution said that they proposed to produce letters written by Douglas over the previous five years.

Robbie did not make a very good impression on the jury. He lacked his usual sparkle, the strain of the past years showing clearly on his face. He offered very little defence against the tainted evidence submitted by Douglas, and was defeated as much by his own apathy as he was by the brilliance of the Defence's advocacy. On the second day of the trial, Robbie spoke of his friendship with Wilde during and after his imprisonment, and of his appointment as Wilde's literary executor. The strain of the proceedings was clearly self-evident when he declared. 'After Wilde's conviction in 1895 I visited him constantly in prison, and was very friendly with his *father*.'[13]

It was indeed a Freudian slip. Sir William Wilde had died on 15 April 1876, ten years before Robbie met Oscar Wilde.

In contrast to Robbie, Douglas, when he entered the witness-box, made a very favourable impression on the Judge and jury. He stressed that he was a repentant and reformed man and that he was trying hard to live down the reputation he had earned from his friendship with Oscar Wilde. During the cross-examination by Ernest Wild, Douglas asked if it was fair to draw any inference from the letters he had written twenty years earlier. Douglas admitted that in 1895 he had been a young scoundrel but he had not deserted Wilde in his hour of need. He argued that his behaviour at that time had been 'the result of the teachings of Wilde and Ross, and the pernicious books they gave him to read in their efforts to corrupt him.'[14] In a plea to the jury Douglas said he could not understand why he should not be given back the letters he had written twenty years before. He wanted to know how much longer they were going to be used against him by 'this gang of people'—his description of Ross's supporters.

Albert Edwards, giving evidence for the Defence, said that his son William had come home in 1908 with the name Ross on his collar and shirtband. In 1912 he had read in the newspaper of a Mr Ross at the unveiling of the statue to Oscar Wilde, and he realised the name on his son's collar was that of Robert Ross.[15] Crosland and his solicitor Bell were also called to give evidence. Crosland made his usual lively attack against the Wilde movement, again stressing that his one desire was to protect the ordinary man and woman from moral corruption.[16] Emma Rooker, a fellow member with Freddie Smith in an amateur dramatic society, in evidence, recalled a time when she and other members of the company had rehearsed in Ross's home. She was extremely bitter about Smith's position as Robbie's secretary and the social benefits he enjoyed and resented the fact that he had risen above his station. In reply to a question from Purchase she said she had seen Ross put his arm round Smith's shoulders and had heard him call Freddie 'my darling'. The Reverend Andrew Bowring said that, in his opinion, Freddie Smith was not competent to be a secretary to a man of literature, and similarly objected to Smith's enhanced financial standing. He added that he had seen Smith with paint and powder on his face, and in consequence he had stopped him serving at Mass as an acolyte.

The Prosecution, in rebuttal, called four witnesses, including Alex, who under a merciless cross-examination by Comyns Carr had to admit that Robbie had twice had a nervous breakdown and had been forced to spend a period of convalescence in Davos.

Alex was given little opportunity of stressing the essential goodness of his brother's nature.

H.G. Wells said he had known Ross for twelve or thirteen years. Ross had been a visitor to his home and was on very friendly terms with himself and his wife. He said that he had met Freddie Smith occasionally in Ross's home but he had never seen powder or paint on Smith's face.

In cross-examination of Wells, Comyns Carr dealt with Wells's own moral and literary reputation, although it is hard to understand what relevance either had to do with proving or disproving the accusation of libel against Douglas.

'Have you come here as a supporter of conventional morality?'

'I have come here to give evidence for Mr Ross as to his moral character,' Wells replied.

'Do you remember when Lord Alfred was editing the *Academy*, there were attacks upon your writings and it was suggested that you had written an improper book called *Ann Veronica*?'

'Yes, there was an ill-mannered article of that kind.'

'Was it an accurate description of that book to say that it was a glorification of people living together as man and wife without being married?'

'No, it is a stupid rendering of the case,' Wells replied.[17]

As Oscar Wilde had been cross-examined as to the morality or immorality of *The Picture of Dorian Gray* and on his letters to Douglas, so H.G. Wells found himself subjected to a scathing attack on his written work.

'Have you not constantly written advocating the view that the ordinary ideas of marriage are nonsensical?' Carr asked.

'I have done nothing of the sort,' Wells replied.[18]

Wells was followed into the witness-box by Edmund Gosse. He said that he had first met Ross in 1890 and since that date Ross had been a dear and loyal friend to both him and his wife. He stressed that he had never seen anything in Ross's life or conduct which led him to believe he was an immoral man. He was, though, a man of flighty disposition, and his judgement of men could be faulty. Gosse said that, in his opinion, Ross was a totally honest and unselfish man, who had done splendid work for the Wilde family and had worked incessantly for the benefaction of the poor and unfortunate.

The most impressive witness for the Prosecution was Vyvyan Holland, Wilde's younger son. He said he was a member of the Bar and an officer in the Army, as was his brother, who was at that moment in the trenches in France. Ross, he declared, had been a second father to him and had never received any money for the work he had done for his late father's Estate.

There can be no argument that in writing letters, as Douglas was prone to do all his life, he committed many gross acts of criminal libel. It is, however, extremely difficult for a man to prove the libels perpetrated on him are false, and for a man with a past it is almost impossible for him to get justice, as Oscar Wilde found to his great discomfort. Robbie, in spite of his denials and the glowing references by his eminent friends to his character, never stood a chance of proving his innocence against Douglas's allegations. He had endured the sordid harassment for five years, but in trying to bring an end to Douglas's vendetta, Robbie was fortunate that he did not suffer a term of imprisonment as Wilde had done when he tried to bring an action for libel against Queensberry.

If Mr Justice Wills, in his summing-up, had been prejudiced against Wilde, then Robbie suffered from the same judicial prejudice. In his submission, Mr Justice Coleridge laid much stress on the fact Ross had not, in any written or verbal statement made over the previous twenty years, condemned the practice of homosexuality. 'Indeed,' said Mr Justice Coleridge, 'I don't recollect that there is any copy or extract which has been produced indicating that he [Ross] disapproved or that he viewed this kind of vice with disgust.'[19]

Mr Justice Coleridge should not have required Robbie to condemn the practice of homosexuality. It was asking him to admit there was some truth in Douglas's allegations. Robbie could not deny the practice of homosexuality, nor could he publicly condemn the practice which Wilde, Douglas and he had once shared. He could not dismiss the past.

To associate himself with such a fraudulent action would be the final snub to Oscar Wilde, and this he could not do, even to clear his own name.

As the jury in Wilde's trial failed to agree, so did the jury who stood in judgement on Douglas. Douglas was ordered to come up for re-trial at the December sessions and bail was granted on the same sureties. After the inconclusive verdict Douglas maintained that one of the jurymen had been planted by George Lewis, and it was this man who had been solely responsible for the jury not acquitting him. The accusations were typical of Douglas. Having lost, he had to blame someone for fixing the result to his detriment. If there had been a shred of truth in Douglas's allegations, then any member of the jury could have brought the matter to the notice of the Judge or the Police; the trial would then have been stopped, and a new jury sworn in. In attempting to lay the blame for the verdict on the shoulders of George Lewis, a successful and influential member of the Jewish faith, Douglas was guilty of anti-semitism.

Two weeks later, on 11 December, the case was due to be resumed, but George Lewis applied to the Attorney-General for a *nolle prosequi*. It was said by Douglas's supporters that the Prosecution withdrew from the case for lack of evidence. What is more likely is that Robbie and his legal advisers knew they would be unable to counter-argue the tainted evidence Douglas produced in his Plea of Justification. There is, after all, no legal defence to prevail against sheer stupidity and blind bigotry. There was little Robbie could do to defeat Douglas, and to proceed, and fail again, would absolve Douglas of all blame.

It must be asked, however, if Robbie knew before or after he entered the *nolle prosequi* that Mr Justice Avory would preside over the second trial. If Robbie knew before, it could have influenced his decision to withdraw. He had already experienced the 'impartiality' of Avory's decisions and he would not have relished the prospects of another encounter. Avory would have vigorously denied that he was unable to divorce the previous trials from the present case; but this was a judgement Robbie could not risk. He withdrew wounded and only the passing of time would hide the scars.

The papers of the case were sent to the Director of Public Prosecutions, who decided in his wisdom, there was no case for Robbie to answer. It is also apparent that neither the D.P.P. nor the Law Society accepted the truth of Douglas's allegation that George Lewis bribed a member of the jury. No impeachment of the solicitor followed, nor was he debarred from practising.

Robbie's behaviour was understandable. He was not, in spite of all the so-called evidence produced in Court, a man who frequented public places for the sole purpose of importuning male prostitutes. A youthful wild escapade hung over him, and Douglas used it as a lethal weapon in his campaign of hate. Douglas was never able to produce new evidence or persuade Robbie's many influential friends to testify against him. It is also significant that the Defence could not prove that Robbie had ever approved of Wilde's style of life. It was a part of Robbie's complex character that he refused to admit the truth, yet he also denied the lie. It was in his nature to play the clown and like all good clowns his humour disguised a deep and sincere spirit. In acts of generosity he was a peer without equal, but he was unable to accept the thanks of the multitude who never had a chance to know the private man.

Douglas's harassment was based on malice and greed. It was only when he realised that Robbie was successful, popular and accepted by the highest in the land, that he deliberately set out to destroy him. Justice did, eventually, have sweet revenge on Lord Alfred, though regrettably it came too late for Robbie to enjoy. In January 1923 Mr Justice Avory sentenced Douglas to six months' imprisonment for libelling Winston Churchill. Perhaps, after all, justice was not prejudiced but simply a little slow at coming to the right decision.

IV

YEARS OF DESPAIR

(1915-18)

We may forget those transient things
That made your charm and our delight:
But loyal love has deathless wings
That rise and triumph out of night.

Siegfried Sassoon, 'Elegy'

Nineteen

Testimonial and Scholarship

HE YEAR 1914 had been a bad one both in world and personal terms. The legal battles between Robbie, Douglas and Crosland had been very bitter, and little of any lasting significance had been achieved. All three of the litigants were now out of work; Robbie had hoped that he might be re-employed by the Board of the Inland Revenue. He had received a telephone approach from Green, an important official at Somerset House, who enquired, 'Was there any other reason for your resignation other than the one you gave because if not, would you be prepared to write a letter to the Board asking whether your resignation had yet been accepted, as if you did I think the matter would be reconsidered?'[1] But as Robbie told Nellie Gosse, his hopes were soon dashed. 'I followed the instructions to the letter. A week later I received a formal reply informing me that the incident was closed and that my resignation *had* been accepted!!! *After* such a ghastly snub, after walking into such a trap, more humiliating than...anything I have suffered during the last five years.'[2] Robbie was bitter, believing that losing his position at the Inland Revenue gave Douglas a moral victory and he resented that victory as much as he resented his failure to beat Douglas in a Court of Law.

After some discussion between their respective legal advisers, it was decided that Ross and Douglas should exchange written declarations not to harm each other in the future. In the declaration Douglas still maintained that the charges he had made were true, but he agreed not to repeat them, providing Robbie did not allow anyone to use Wilde's letters. They both, however, reserved the right to break their undertakings during the action Crosland was bringing for malicious prosecution. Robbie also stipulated that if he was forced to take action against Frank Harris and his forthcoming biography of Wilde, he would use every scrap of information at his disposal to stop Harris perpetrating further lies against Wilde. Robbie further promised not to oppose Douglas's wish to gain possession, from the British Museum, of the manuscript of *De Profundis*. In spite of his efforts Douglas never gained stewardship of Wilde's prison letter and on Robbie's death copyright passed to Vyvyan

243

Holland, and he, not Douglas, enjoyed the financial fruits of Wilde's greatest literary work.

If Robbie cherished the thought that the war in Europe would curb Douglas's actions, then he was soon disillusioned. The ink on the declarations was hardly dry before Douglas restarted his own war of attrition. He wrote to the Prime Minister repeating his wild and inaccurate statements about Robbie's conduct. He gave precise details about the conduct of his libel trial, asserting that it was only after Ross's solicitors had offered to pay his legal expenses of £600, that he agreed to the *nolle prosequi* being entered. Douglas ordered Asquith to end his friendship with Ross and to refrain from entertaining him again at either The Wharf or Downing Street. Douglas threatened that if Asquith did not act on his instructions, he would, through the good offices of sympathetic newspaper editors, make his allegation public, to the embarrassment of the Liberal Government. His letter was not well received by Asquith and neither he nor his Private Secretary Sir Maurice Bonham Carter bothered to acknowledge it, but passed it on to Charles Mathews. Mathews, who was, at least in Robbie's opinion, an ally of Douglas, passed the letter on to the Home Secretary, Sir John Simon, hoping that if there was some substance to Douglas's allegations, he could begin criminal proceedings against Robbie. Simon quickly disappointed him, telling Mathews that Douglas's letter was full of errors. He explained that the *nolle prosequi* was granted only after an application by Counsel for both prosecutor and defendant, and not, as Douglas claimed, only by the prosecutor's Counsel. Simon said he would not have been able to grant such an application if it had been made by only the prosecutor's Counsel. As to Douglas's allegation that he agreed to the *nolle prosequi* only because the prosecutor had agreed to pay his legal costs, Simon declared that that was the first he had heard of such an arrangement, and if such an action had occurred he would not have granted the *nolle prosequi*.[3]

Frustrated that neither Asquith nor his Cabinet colleagues took his complaints seriously, Douglas spread his campaign far and wide, including the Committee of the Reform Club, where Robbie had been a longstanding and well-respected member. Douglas wrote an infantile verse damning Ross and, suggesting the Committee could not let the result of the case go unnoticed, insisted that Ross should be asked to resign. There were very few members of the Reform who had any sympathy with Douglas's outbursts. On the Committee were Herbert Asquith and Squire Sprigge and they had no intention of allowing Douglas to dictate to them.

Not deterred by their silence, Douglas persisted and he always believed the Committee met and requested Ross's resignation, but withdrew their demand after they received his poem. The truth is somewhat different. The Committee Minutes of the Reform Club show they did not even discuss Robbie's membership, and certainly they were not influenced by Douglas's poem. It is probable Robbie was asked by the Chairman of the Committee to explain his appearances in Court and he was able to reassure them. In April 1911 Robbie had also been elected a full member of the Royal Automobile Club, and in spite of Douglas's worst efforts, there is no record in the Committee Minutes that they asked for his resignation, nor was Robbie's future membership ever discussed.

In the second week of January 1915 Robbie paid a long-delayed visit to Carlos Blacker at Vane Towers, Torquay. It is significant that Blacker was so unconcerned by the allegations made against Robbie that he thought his sons were in no moral danger from Robbie's sexual activities. Indeed, as with the Gosse family, Robbie was a favourite with Carrie Blacker and her children. He had particularly fond memories of the children as he told Carlos: 'I have the most lively memory of the precocity of one of them.'[4] But Blacker's sons were not at Torquay. With Cecil Sprigge and Wilde's sons they were on active service in France. At a time when they should have been enjoying the freedom and delight of university and the company of pretty young women, their young lives were being torn apart by war. The war, however, would increase Robbie's circle of young friends, his rooms at Half Moon Street becoming a safe haven for the literary and intellectual young warriors.

On his return from Vane Towers Robbie contracted bronchitis and, as Nellie Gosse was also ill, he told her, 'I hope to be up tomorrow and out on Monday [15th] if it is nice. Shall I be allowed to come and see you soon? I am rather good with convalescents. I *trust* you are in that group (though I am quite useless with the sick in the serious stages, at least sick friends always tell me so).'[5] The war would give Robbie endless opportunities of using his skill with convalescents as more and more of his young friends were injured in mind and body. In particular he would become a source of comfort and support to Siegfried Sassoon, the idealistic poet, who would suffer wounds to mind and body. Robbie was passionate in his condemnation of the war. He never visited the battlefields of Europe but he sensed the agonies of the front-line soldier, and did not flinch from voicing his fears. He had little sympathy with the shortcomings of the military authorities. He thought they were guilty of grossly undervaluing the suffering caused by trench warfare. War was ugly; but the newspapers reported only the victories and failed to tell the true story of the battlefield horrors. Sassoon said of Robbie's hatred of war:

> My verses appealed to his flair for anything lively and enterprising in
> the arts, and were aimed at the type of person he most disliked,
> among whom were what he used to call "the screaming scarlet
> Majors". There was an element in his nature which delighted in
> provoking opposition; he hated the war, and was unable to be
> tolerant about it and those who accepted it with civilian bellicosity,
> and self-defensive evasion of its realities.[6]

With the end of Douglas's libel action, Edmund Gosse and Dugald MacColl completed their plans to raise a subscription and testimonial to Robbie. Gosse became Chairman of the Committee, Lord Plymouth agreed to act as honorary treasurer and MacColl and Robert Witt were appointed honorary secretaries. After some discussion Gosse refused to write the Address, and the task was left to MacColl, although Witt and Gosse edited his rough draft. A printed letter was sent to possible subscribers in the hope they would respond to the 'opportunity of testifying publicly to their admiration and regard for one who has been unfailingly at the disposal of any who claimed either his sympathy or his help. The calls that have thus been met with rare loyalty and courage will never be fully known, but in our time there has been no friendlier influence in the world of Art and Letters.'[7]

The response was overwhelming, nearly three hundred people signed the testimonial, including the Prime Minister and Mrs Asquith, Sir James Barrie, Thomas Hardy, H.G.Wells, J.T.Agg Gardner MP and Sir Herbert Beerbohm Tree. George Prothero and Nathaniel Wedd signed as a token of friendships which had begun in 1888 at King's College, and which had survived all the tribulations of the intervening years. Ellen Beardsley signed, in spite of the fact that she had publicly expressed reservations about her son's friendship with Robbie, after the publication of his book on Beardsley. The signatories were a very conservative section of the literary, political and social élite of the day. Bernard Shaw, at the time, was pleased to add his name to the list, though he later changed his mind and, writing to Douglas, said: 'Ross did not get his testimonial for nothing. Only a great deal of good nature on his part could have won over that distinguished and very normal list of names to give public support to a man who began with so very obvious a mark of the beast on him.'[8]

Two old friends, Reggie Turner and Max Beerbohm, however, had belated misgivings about signing the declaration. Turner believed that

Robbie had been wrong to sue Douglas for libel, and Beerbohm, with typical duplicity, signed and then told Turner he wished he had not done so. Sidney Colvin was more blunt in his refusal to sign, and even when MacColl wrote personally to ask him to reconsider his decision, he would not be swayed

> and in spite of your appeal must decline now, to take any step which
> would associate me with approval or condemnation of Oscar Wilde-
> ism, the most pestilent and hateful disease of our time, with the
> taint of which Ross, by association at least, is unhappily so deeply
> tarred. (Why on earth must he, the moment he hears of a
> professional bugger let out of jail, go and engage him as private
> secretary?)[9]

Robbie was not a rich man but Alex had borne most of the burdens of his legal expenses and, not wishing to benefit unduly, he asked that the money raised by the Testimonial Committee should be used for a worthy cause. The Committee readily agreed, but insisted that £50 should be set aside for the purchase of a personal gift as a gesture of their regard. More Adey told MacColl that Robbie would like a repeater watch purchased from Frodshams, 'the model RR wants is the more modern one totally without any artistic value, because it is in better order and the one with the pretensions to "art" has an incurable wheeze in the striking, which I agree with him would be peculiarly intolerable to a man liable to asthma.'[10] Robbie also expressed the wish that the names of the subscribers should be engraved on to the watch, and although Frodshams assured More Adey that they could engrave the names of all the subscribers, Adey was sceptical and thought only a selection should be inscribed.

Robbie decided the money should be offered to the Senate of University College for the foundation of a scholarship at the Slade School. At a meeting on 24 March 1915, chaired by Sir Alfred Gould, the Vice-Chancellor, the gift was accepted. The terms of the scholarship were precise. Robbie, in helping to draft the final regulations, insisted that the award was for *male* students only. What Sylvia Gosse and Robbie's ardent feminist nieces thought of such a blatant act of sex discrimination can only be guessed, but it is highly probable that he was subjected to a lecture on the subject when they next met. Robbie probably had his tongue in his cheek when he outlined the conditions of the scholarship, and he would have immensely enjoyed the wary comments made later by Wilde's biographers. He always enjoyed the hypocrisy of others.

A prize of £25 was to be made annually to a student who had

completed nine consecutive terms and who, in the opinion of the Examiners, was likely to achieve most in his future career in drawing, painting, sculpture and architecture, or other branches of the creative arts, (which now include stage and television design). The war and the lack of well-qualified students prevented the first award from being made until after Robbie's death. In 1920 J. White was the first recipient of the prize and it has been made every year since, with the exception of 1940 and 1943, when war again depleted the number of qualified students.

The testimonial and the public declaration of support did not halt Douglas's campaign of harassment—if anything, it galvanised him into further actions. He had threatened Asquith that he would use the Press to further his campaign of attrition and Charles Palmer, editor of the *Globe*, became his willing accomplice when he printed on 30 March a letter from Douglas repeating that he had agreed to the *nolle prosequi* only because Ross had agreed to pay his legal costs and reimburse his personal expenses. George Lewis had no option but to answer the impropriety and flagrant untruths contained in Douglas's letter and on 3 April Lewis & Lewis were granted the right of reply. They repeated yet again, that the Attorney-General could not have entered the *nolle prosequi* plea until he had received a written request from both Ross's and Douglas's Counsel. They also pointed out that it had been agreed between the parties that Ross was in no way personally responsible for paying Douglas's costs.

Four days later, perhaps with the misguided idea that Robbie would be embarrassed, the *Globe* published the declarations which he and Douglas had signed on 8 December 1914. Lewis & Lewis tried to counter the further damage to Robbie's reputation, but in the end, it was Asquith and his Government who had a moment of sweet revenge. In November 1915, for a period of two weeks, they seized and suppressed distribution of the *Globe* for reporting prematurely that Lord Kitchener had resigned. On 20 November, when the *Globe* appeared again, Charles Palmer had been replaced.

That one man could inspire such love, such devotion and such compassion was a reflection of his urbane character. That the same man could also attract such hatred, such viciousness and such anger is hard to understand. If Douglas was a Jekyll and Hyde character then it must be said so was Ross. And there perhaps is the cause of their quarrels. They were both so alike, spoilt, arrogant, charming, generous, witty and utterly unforgiving of each other's faults. They both wanted to be Wilde's saviour, but it was Douglas who was Wilde's *âme damnée*[11] and he resented Ross's domination of Wilde's life and art.

Robbie's trial for bringing a malicious prosecution against Crosland began on 13 April 1915, in the King's Bench Division, Old Bailey, before Mr Justice Bray and a Special Jury (jurors selected from those within a higher property qualification group). Crosland, as ever, was aided and abetted by Douglas, and the two conspirators sank to new depths of obduracy as they sought yet again to destroy Robbie's reputation. The war had begun to take a gruesome toll of young lives. Almost every family in the land from Downing Street to the most isolated croft of the Western Isles was affected by the slaughter, yet the war did not touch the pair. Douglas offered his services to the Crown but as he was regarded as *persona non grata* his request was politely refused. Crosland was too old and too ill for military or active service and he was not offered a post as a war correspondent.

Robbie was represented by Mr Schiller, KC, and Mr McCardie, who had assisted Mr Campbell when Arthur Ransome had justified his libel on Douglas. The Defence Counsel were certainly well versed in the sordid history of the action. Crosland was again represented by the ever-faithful Cecil Hayes, instructed by Mr W. Ewart Craigon, but on the second day of the trial Crosland asked leave of the Court to change his solicitor, and Carter & Bell were again appointed.

The trial lasted four days and it soon became obvious to all those in Court that it would not be a re-run of the previous hearings. Mr Justice Bray was free from the taint of prejudice which had hung over Mr Justice Avory, nor did his Court resemble a vaudeville as had the proceedings of Mr Justice Darling. In a long opening statement Cecil Hayes detailed the prosecution of Crosland the previous summer; an action, he emphasised, which had resulted in Crosland being acquitted. Ross, declared Cecil Hayes, had devoted the last fifteen years of his life to editing and publishing the writings of Oscar Wilde, a man who had been imprisoned for his advocacy of unnatural practices. Schiller objected to the implication in the jibe, Bray also intervened to inquire if he was going to bring evidence to prove his charge. Hayes assured him he would prove the truth of the allegation.

Twice in his opening statement Hayes said that Wilde had been sent to prison, not for committing acts of gross indecency, but for advocating the practice of unnatural acts. Did he really expect the jury to believe that it was for spreading the doctrine of homosexuality, and not for taking part in homosexual practices, that Wilde spent two years in prison? If this were so, then the sentence was grossly unfair and Wilde should have received only a caution from the Bench. It also means that the words on Queensberry's card, 'posing [as a] somdomite'[*sic*], were, after all, correct. Wilde was *posing*, not practising, the crime for which he was arrested, charged and sentenced—such an assertion was nonsense.

Much of that first day was taken up by Hayes, repeating the detailed evidence of the previous action. He was particularly scathing in his condemnation that Robbie had not gone to Scotland Yard to see the statement made by Charles Garratt. He complained that: 'Mr Ross [had] refused to charge Mr Crosland with criminal libel, so that the question of his [Ross's] relations with Garratt could not be tried. By prosecuting Mr Crosland and Lord Alfred Douglas for conspiracy, Mr Ross fogged the issue.'[12]

In not playing the game according to the rules laid down by Douglas, Robbie was accused of muddying the waters. Even allowing for a degree of legal licence it was still a shameful presumption by Crosland's Counsel.

When Hayes complained: 'Mr Ross knew when he launched the prosecution against Mr Crosland and Lord Alfred Douglas that they were both abroad.' Mr Justice Bray then reminded him: 'You had been goading him to take action, so I do not see that you can complain when he did take action.'[13]

The proceedings did not go well for Crosland and Douglas. They were very good at saying they knew the facts of Robbie's crimes, but when asked to supply proof that would bear the scrutiny of the Law, they could produce only letters written twenty years earlier, when Robbie was a young man—and what young man has a completely sin-free youth!

On 15 April Schiller began the cross-examination of Crosland, and he soon proved an able replacement for the flamboyant and brilliant F.E. Smith; and if Mr Justice Bray had any prejudice against Oscar Wilde, he was prepared to let it remain hidden. There was a spirited exchange between Bray and Crosland, when Crosland, in answer to a question put by Schiller, declared his objection, 'to the spreading of Wilde's doctrines among the cheap public, shilling public. The thinking public could take care of themselves.'

'What public?' Mr Justice Bray enquired.

'The "cheap" public, the street public, office boys and others. I thought that the publication of Wilde's works in this cheap form was a damage to public morals.'

'And you thought that justified you calling Mr Ross opprobrious names?'

'I didn't use opprobrious epithets, I only used words which were justified, as I knew the facts about Mr Ross. Mr Ross had an ulterior interest in booming Wilde's works, not a literary interest.'[14]

Schiller took Crosland through his evidence, but Crosland had very little new to say. He admitted he had never written a word of praise about Wilde's work, although he did consider him a genius. He repeated that he thought *The Picture of Dorian Gray* was a very foul work, but admired *The Ballad of Reading Gaol*. Schiller suggested that Crosland was very fastidious. Crosland retorted that he did not know the meaning of the word, but if it meant that the writings of a man like Wilde should always be treated with suspicion, then he was prepared to say he was fastidious.

Cross-examined about his involvement with the libel action Douglas had brought against Arthur Ransome, Crosland said that he did not know Ransome could justify his action. He did not know there was such a thing as a Plea of Justification in a civil action. Schiller treated that statement with derision, and reminded him that he had justified his action, when in March 1911 Horatio Bottomley had sued him for libel. Crosland boasted that he had received damages from Bottomley but Schiller had been well briefed and Crosland had to admit that his damages had been only three farthings, a farthing against each defendant. Schiller said that in that action he [Crosland] had been charged with being a blackmailer. Crosland vehemently denied the charge and said he would give £500 if anyone could prove it. Schiller reminded him that he hadn't even got five hundred pence. Crosland was intensively questioned about his relationship with Douglas. He said that Lord Alfred had denied, on his honour, that there was any truth in the allegation that he had gloried in the practices for which Wilde had been convicted.

At the start of the hearing on 16 April, Mr Justice Bray withdrew the case from the jury, saying the case was one for him and him alone to decide. Hayes handed Bray five questions which he submitted should be left to the jury: (1) Did Ross take reasonable care to inform himself of the true facts of the case? (2) Did Ross honestly believe the facts which he laid before the Magistrate? (3) Did Ross honestly believe the facts which he laid before the Central Criminal Court? (4) Did Ross honestly believe Crosland to be guilty? (5) Did Ross take reasonable care to inform himself whether Crosland was guilty?[15] Bray wanted to know what evidence there was that Ross did not take reasonable care when instructing his solicitors to issue the warrants against Crosland and Douglas. Hayes again repeated that Ross should have gone to Scotland Yard and seen Garratt's statement, although he knew there was no chance of Ross being allowed to see the document. Bray interjected to say that the case hinged on whether Garratt's evidence had been corroborated and that raised the question of whether there had been reasonable and probable cause for a charge to be made. After further argument Bray said he would withdraw questions one and five from the jury, and he would hear from Schiller on the question of reasonable and probable cause.

In his summation Schiller said: 'In all cases of conspiracy the evidence on which one had to rely was tainted, but it was not necessary before instituting proceedings, for a man to have obtained anything more than *prima facie* evidence.'[16] He reminded the jury that Crosland and Douglas could not have believed Garratt's original allegation of impropriety against Ross, because at the time of the alleged incident they knew Ross had been in Russia.

Schiller made an impressive speech, and it was well received by Mr Justice Bray: 'I think I appreciate your argument. What do you say, Mr Hayes?'[17] It must have seemed to Robbie that he was being given an early birthday present; it was the first time in his long association with the judiciary that he had ever heard a remark that was in his favour.

Hayes, seeing his arguments dissipate before him, made one last attempt to put his client's case in a favourable light. He did not deny there was hostility between Douglas and Ross, but he said he could use that argument to show that Ross was actuated by malice and spite in proceeding against his client: 'It was difficult for him to look upon the defendant as a reasonable and discreet man, but the question was: Would a reasonable and discreet man have believed what the boy Garratt said, when he knew, as Mr Ross knew, that Garratt had been twice convicted, and that he was, on his own showing, a liar?'[18]

It had been twenty years since Mr Justice Wills had summed up in the trial of Oscar Wilde, and in the intervening years Robbie had listened to many other judgements and he must have wondered if he would ever hear a member of the judiciary sum up in an impartial manner. The whole conduct of the trial before Mr Justice Bray gave him a glimmer of hope that, at last, he had met a man of high principles and incorruptibility. Dealing with the five questions put by Cecil Hayes, Bray said that he had already decided that questions one and five should not be put to the jury, and that of the remaining three he had to decide if the defendant [Ross] showed an absence of reasonable and probable cause when he had brought the charge against Crosland. Bray said that there had never been any evidence to suggest that Ross was guilty of the charges laid against him and therefore he must assume Ross was Not Guilty. In dealing with Garratt's evidence, he said that there were indeed many points on which the boy's story was corroborated. Bray recalled that over the last few years Douglas had written several letters to the defendant 'threatening to expose him and calling him opprobrious names' and, said Bray, Ross could not ignore the threats nor could he ignore that one of them [Crosland or Douglas] 'would not be above trumping up a false charge. In my judgement, therefore, a reasonable man might have believed that the boy's story was true. There is no other question that is material. If the plaintiff fails on this point he fails altogether, however malicious the defendant may have been. There is therefore no question to go to the jury, and I must give judgement for the defendant, with costs.'[19]

The victory was very sweet indeed. Millard was certain that at long last justice had been done, as he told Walter Ledger:

> I have just come back from the Law Courts where I have been for the last four days. You will see that Crosland has lost his case, which is virtually (though not legally) a reversal of the monstrously unjust verdict given before *Justice* Avory in July. It was good to hear the whole story of the vile conspiracy exposed before a just Judge who made no bones about saying that C. and D. were both trying to blackmail Robbie. He emphasised many of the points which Avory swept aside because they were in favour of Robbie. I now hope that R. will be left in peace... at long length some sort of justice has been awarded to him.[20]

Millard's faith in justice was premature. Immediately after the rejection of their claim for damages, Crosland and Douglas instituted proceedings for an appeal against the findings. On Saturday, the day after the judgement, McCardie, on behalf of Robbie, applied to the Master of the Rolls and Lord Justice Pickford for an order for security of the costs of the appeal to be entered by Crosland. McCardie intimated that if the case went to appeal, it would be extremely expensive as there was a great deal of documentary evidence to be assessed and he therefore asked for a substantial security. Their Lordships made an order that Crosland should make £75 available within ten days if the appeal was to proceed. McCardie said that Crosland had been served with the notice of application but he had not appeared to resist the order. Lewis & Lewis had telephoned Crosland and told him the application was due to be heard that day but to no avail. Crosland's Court costs were taxed at more than £600 but nothing was paid.

Crosland never found a way of discrediting Ross or diminishing his loyalty and devotion to Wilde's memory. He had used all the resources of the Law, but, in the end the Law protected Ross more than it protected him.

Twenty

Lost Generation

EATH IS the inevitable consequence of war, and Robbie suffered the loss of many good and dear friends. On 9 May 1915 Cyril Holland, Wilde's elder son, fell victim to a sniper's bullet at the battle of Neuve-Chapelle. A life which had begun just three decades before with such joy and promise ended prematurely in the mud of France. As a nine-year-old child, at the time of Wilde's arrest, Cyril's world had been shattered beyond repair and he was never able to rebuild it or even trust his own instincts. He became a professional soldier to quieten any suggestion that he was his father's son. Indeed, he once wrote to Robbie, 'I am fitting myself for the world. . . . They shall not say "a talker, the son of a talker". I will hold my own with the best of them, I too have something to inscribe on the pages of that little history book.'[1]

In the last years of his short life Cyril gained no respite from the gnawing pains that ate into his soul. He found little comfort in his father's writings, he could not bear the bitterness in *De Profundis*. Nevertheless, he did appreciate the support he received from Robbie and from that small group of people who still held Wilde in high esteem. He understood the debt he owed to his father's loyal friends for all their acts of selfless devotion to Oscar and Constance. 'Love without loyalty' [he wrote to Robbie], 'that's a contradiction in terms, though may express the facts of life. You and those others were loyal indeed. The more I experience of life in all its sordid vulgarity and mediocrity, in all its cowardice and egotism, the more I realise the nobility of your conducts.'[2]

Vyvyan Holland was in France at the time of his brother's death and Robbie was unable to share his grief with the young man. Vyvyan had grown into a sensitive, reserved man but with a wry sense of humour. If Cyril had found a place in the world as a professional soldier, Vyvyan had not been so lucky. He had been called to the Bar, but found the practice as a barrister not to his liking or sufficiently financially rewarding. His wife's extravagances did little to help him settle to a routine of domesticity. Robbie tried to guide him along the right path. He introduced Vyvyan to writers and men of letters, and he found their company much more to his liking. Vyvyan wanted to write, but he lacked his father's creative genius. He was an affable man who would not survive in the jungle of hack journalism, and the war brought a welcome relief to his search for meaningful employment. After the war, Scott-Moncrieff introduced him to the art of translation and Vyvyan was able to use his creative talents to the full.

Robbie was worried by Vyvyan's restless, extravagant behaviour. Perhaps he saw in Wilde's younger son too many of his father's characteristics and not enough of Constance's essential goodness. In a letter to Carlos Blacker, Robbie admitted: 'Vyvyan Holland is behaving very badly just now. A short while ago I would have [been] very distressed. But I have become frozen to all emotions about the Wildes. As Oscar would have said I shall die of an embattled heart.'[3]

In Cyril Holland's will, he bequeathed to Robbie one-half share of Wilde's Literary Estate, the other half going to Vyvyan, who a few years earlier had sold his share to his brother. The gift was greatly appreciated, but, as it happened, Robbie gained very little reward. The events which destroyed one life made it virtually impossible for him to gain financially from the production of Wilde's works. There would be very few royalties during the remainder of his life, but after Robbie's death, Wilde's works would gross many thousands of pounds before the copyright ceased.

In an atmosphere of national hysteria and pseudo-patriotism it was essential that Robbie experienced some pleasure. More Adey was the most constant of his old friends, and most evenings would find him occupying his favourite armchair at Robbie's Half Moon Street chambers. He contributed little to the conversation, preferring to let Robbie dominate the centre stage. Pip Blacker gave the best insight into More Adey's relationship with Robbie when he wrote to Cecil Sprigge: 'I regard [More] as one of the sweetest, gentlest and kindest souls I know. He always speaks, if one asks his opinion about anyone, of "we", i.e. he and Robbie as if they held all their opinions inseparably.'[4]

Alex was another frequent evening visitor. He would drop in on his way back to his own apartment, after an evening at the theatre or dining with friends. But it was the companionship of young soldiers, on leave from the trenches, that became Robbie's salvation. Siegfried Sassoon, commissioned into the Royal Welch Fusiliers, was not least among the artistic intelligentsia who found Robbie's home an oasis of peace. Robbie was often fatigued at the end of the day, yet he would not retire until the last of his guests had reluctantly drifted away. Sassoon left what is perhaps the most accurate description of Robbie as he was in those dark days of war:

his face tired and old before its time masking the sadness of
wounding experience with a mood of witty reminiscence and word-
play, while he bestowed on others the influence of his resolve to
evoke gaiety and good sense in despite of the pervasive dullness and
hostility of human affairs. There he would stand, in his loose grey
alpaca jacket, wearing a black silk skull-cap and smoking his
perpetual cigarette in its jade-green holder, emphasizing his lively
pronouncements with controlled gestures of the left hand, on the
third finger of which was a fair-sized scarab ring.[5]

Robbie's friendship with the soldier-writers was often altruistic as he
frankly admitted: 'You must forgive me for being such an incorrigible
chaperon... but making other people a success is my only real vocation.'[6]
He was very successful in his own right, but was never able to appreciate
his own gifts; much of his talent and genius was used only in the service
of others. He had an extraordinary capacity for knowing the 'right
people', he could introduce young writers to publishers or young artists
to wealthy patrons. He bullied, cajoled and persuaded. His judgement in
literary matters was not, however, always sought. When Cecil Sprigge[2]
and Topsy Jones considered publishing an anthology of their poems
Squire Sprigge warned his son:

It is, I think, no good asking Robbie anything about it. His
judgements on the published book may be all right, his opinions on
unpublished work are entirely a matter of mood. To the book he
returns, reconsiders and becomes just; to a manuscript he is
momentarily sweet and momentarily sour, as his mood may be, and
the criticism is worth nothing.[7]

But in helping others, Robbie became a noble and 'impresario' parent
fulfilling a role for which he was eminently fitted, an adoring, forgiving
and compassionate friend. There should be no misunderstanding of his
role. It was that special relationship which exists between a father and a
son or between an older and a younger man, a relationship which Wilde
so eloquently described from the witness-box at the Old Bailey:

"The Love that dare not speak its name" in this century is such a
great affection of an elder for a younger man as there was between
David and Jonathan, such as Plato made the very basis of his
philosophy, and such as you find in the sonnets of Michelangelo and
Shakespeare. It is that deep, spiritual affection that is as pure as it is
perfect. It dictates and pervades great works of art like those of

Shakespeare and Michelangelo, and those two letters of mine, such
as they are. It is in this century misunderstood, so much
misunderstood that it may be described as the "Love that dare not
speak its name", and on account of it I am placed where I am now.
It is beautiful, it is fine, it is the noblest form of affection. There is
nothing unnatural about it. It is intellectual, and it repeatedly exists
between an elder and a younger man, when the elder man has
intellect, and the younger man has all the joy, hope and glamour of
life before him. That it should be so the world does not understand.
The world mocks at it and sometimes puts one in the pillory for it.[8]

In May the Keepership of the National Gallery of Ireland became vacant.
Roderick Meiklejohn, a senior Treasury Civil Servant, told MacColl that
Bailey of the National Gallery in Dublin approved of Ross being
approached. Robert Witt was also approached, but he told MacColl,
'When I heard I had been asked to consider the Dublin Gallery I did not
know and I have only just this moment heard that Robbie Ross was a
possible candidate. I have written to Lady Gregory to tell her that in no
possible circumstances would I entertain it against him.'[9] Robbie considered the matter but in the end he told MacColl, 'that I do not care to run
for Dublin. I am particularly well now without any gout or grievance but
my nerve and courage, such as it was, have entirely gone. My energy has
also dissipated but I hope that is only temporary... Politics enter so
much into everything at Dublin and I am too much of a partisan not to be
dragged into the vortex.'[10]

In July Robbie went to Jesmond Hill to stay with Mary. The peace and
quiet of her beautiful home did much to restore his physical and mental
well-being. His health was causing concern because his fragile strength
had been stretched to the limit by his litigation battles. Crosland did not
proceed with his appeal against the Not Guilty verdict in the malicious
prosecution case. He had been unable to raise the money required by the
Court as security of costs.

Death broke into Robbie's life again when, in October, Robin Carlos
Blacker was killed in action. Robbie hurried to Vane Towers to give what
support he could to Carlos and Carrie Blacker, the young man's grieving
parents. It was a duty he would perform again and again as the war
dragged to its bitter conclusion. There were, however, happier things
with which Robbie could occupy himself. He produced two highly
amusing books in the form of a parlour game where the participant was
asked to give his or her opinion on various aspects of art and literature.
In *The Connaught Square Catechism or Confessions to Mrs Robert Witt*,

Robbie was unabashed with his own answers and named his old friend Charles Ricketts as among the four best living experts. He acknowledged Augustus John as the greatest living draughtsman, although he prefaced his confession with 'as evinced in his paintings'; in answer to the question, 'Who is the worst deceased painter in [the] European school of any considerable reputation or held in any esteem?' he wrote Van Dyck, and then added, Van Dyck is 'the first snob in art according to Sargent. He retarded the English School for a hundred years by representing a fictitious autocracy which was in reality as brutal, vulgar and vicious as its present descendants in the 20th Century.'[11] Modesty prevented him from naming himself as the best living critic or expert, but he did not feel inhibited from naming Sidney Colvin as the worst critic.

He continued the question-and-answer theme in *Really and Truly: A Book of Literary Confessions: Designed by a late Victorian* published by Arthur Humphreys in December 1915. Aware that he needed to offer Max Beerbohm an olive branch after the cooling of their relationship, and always an admirer of Beerbohm's work, Robbie asked him to do the jacket cover. Beerbohm was reticent and not so easily persuaded: 'I have been wondering whether I could design a cover at all worthy of the idea of your Confession Album. My first impression was that I couldn't, and alas, this impression has gradually hardened into certainty.'[12] Beerbohm admitted he had designed covers only twice, and one of them, which he regarded as very successful, W.H. Smith had refused to sell and it had to be recalled and recovered before they would consider restocking it. Beerbohm suggested that Henry Tonks should be asked. He said that Tonks was better equipped to produce the required work. Robbie thought over Max's suggestion, and the cover-design for *Really and Truly* was eventually done, but regrettably the name of the artist has been lost.

The confessions game could be played on cold winter evenings instead of games of cards which Robbie hated because they disturbed the art of conversation. Additional difficulties could be introduced by excluding Shakespeare and the Bible from 'favourite writers and books'. The parlour games provided a little light relief but there were other things which more fully occupied his time. The war in Europe went on unabated, decimating a generation of young men. On New Year's Day 1916 Robbie was at Comarques in Essex with Arnold Bennett. Charles Masterman was another guest, and the conduct of the war was among their topics of conversation. Bennett was more realistic about the war than Robbie: 'I was startled to find Ross believing in the legend that the Germans had been cooking all their mortality figures since 1870. Whenever Ross talks about the war his whole face changes.'[13]

Throughout the winter Robbie continued to be a welcome and honoured visitor at the homes of his friends, but his peace was again disturbed by Christopher Millard's reckless and indiscreet behaviour. On 31 March, the Magistrate Paul Taylor issued a warrant charging Millard with gross indecency. Millard fled to the safety of friends at Kirk Newton in Northumberland and such was his hasty departure that he had to appeal to Robbie to send on his luggage. In spite of his wish not to get involved in yet another sordid scandal, Robbie continued to befriend Millard and, to ease his poverty, paid him a monthly allowance.

Cecil Sprigge also ran foul of the Military Authorities. He was court-martialled and cashiered for unspecified crimes, although at the time, it was thought he had indulged in acts associated with 'the love that dare not speak its name'. The truth of his crime, if crime there was, was more likely to have involved a *femme fatale* or even more probably an embarrassing inability to pay his mess bills. There is no evidence that Douglas was responsible for laying a charge against Cecil Sprigge, yet it must have crossed Robbie's mind that it was the sort of thing that Douglas could have done. Cecil Sprigge immediately enlisted as an ordinary seaman in the Royal Navy and served with honour for the rest of the war.

In May Robbie spent another weekend at The Wharf with the Asquiths. On Sunday afternoon, the 21st, together with the Prime Minister, his daughter Elizabeth and Mrs George Keppel, the late King Edward VII's mistress, he motored over to Garsington. Lady Ottoline Morrell was away from the house on a picnic with Clive Bell, Lytton Strachey, Dora Carrington and Dorothy Brett when the party from The Wharf arrived. As the day was hot and sunny, Lady Ottoline had given permission for her maids and Lucy, a young land-girl, to bathe in the Garsington pond. Lucy had told her employer that she was a competent swimmer and had indeed won medals and had life-saving diplomas.

At the approach of the Asquith party, Lucy suddenly cried out that she was drowning. Robbie, ever gallant, sprang instantly into action, but not before removing his precious testimonial watch did he plunge into the water to rescue the pretty fair-haired girl.

The rescue was an anti-climax since the pond was only four feet deep. Lucy had been indulging in a little play-acting and had not been in danger of drowning. Robbie was less than amused by her stunt. He did not enjoy being made to look foolish in front of his eminent host and he had also soaked his best suit. He had to borrow some of Philip Morrell's clothes before returning to The Wharf. Asquith, however, enjoyed the whole performance, and thereafter always greeted Lady Ottoline with 'How is Lucy?' Lady Ottoline's comment on the whole incident and

Robbie's 'heroic' gallantry summed up his impulsive nature: 'He's always jumping into the water to pull people out, isn't he?'[14]

On Monday, dry and with his humour restored, Robbie considered the incident so unimportant that in writing to tell Christopher Millard of his weekend he did not even mention the rescue. He could not, however, hide his feelings of pleasure at spending yet another weekend at the home of the Prime Minister with Mrs Keppel, Edwin Montague and his wife Venetia Stanley and Count Benckendorff, although he had to admit that he liked Mrs Keppel the most as she had 'no airs and graces and tells amusing stories'. Asquith had been greatly concerned with the political problems of Ireland, following the Easter Rising in Dublin, but as Robbie told Millard he betrayed no confidences:

> I cannot resist writing to you from an address of such repute. . . . The
> P.M. is of course very interesting about his wide experience and also
> his visit to the Pope when he went to Italy. Apparently there is not
> going to be any Lord Lieutenant again which is a very good thing
> and one gathers that there is to be a sort of transportation scare in
> Ireland, but that can be gathered from the Press. I observe that
> nothing of any consequence is ever revealed at the Prime Ministerial
> Board. There are only revelations about the past never the present.
> However, I am told (what you will see in tomorrow's papers) that
> Skeffington's murderer[15] really is going to be tried for his life and
> not promoted as I expected. . . . Yesterday morning I motored into
> Oxford with the P.M. alone to visit Anthony at his school there.
> Unfortunately the effect of this was somewhat lost as nobody in the
> school knew who I was! except Anthony and that was not of much
> consequence.
>
> However today I motor up to London with the great man! But
> alas I fear it will not be noted by the press. Enough of this drivel.[16]

If spending weekends at The Wharf gave him enormous pleasure, then so did his friendship with the Morrells. He was at Garsington again on 24 June and no doubt he had to endure further expression of their gratitude for his rescue of the pretty young Lucy. He spent part of the summer at Jesmond Hill with Mary, but it was in the company of Siegfried Sassoon, Robert Graves and Osbert Sitwell that he gained the most pleasure. Naturally, literature was the main topic of conversation and the war only intruded when absolutely necessary though none of them was isolated from its horror. On 20 July, during the battle of the Somme, Robert Graves received injuries and was reported 'killed in action'. Fortunately he was rescued by an alert dressing station orderly, who, while clearing away the dead, noticed one of the corpses was still breathing.[17] After a spell in hospital in France and England, Graves recovered sufficiently to spend a few days with Robbie. His convalescence continued at Sassoon's home at Weirleigh in Kent, from where he wrote to Robbie, 'Those were two very jolly days and apart from a sudden access of strength that has come from the mental and moral stimulation of Half Moon Street I am deeply indebted to you.'[18]

Robert Graves was not the only casualty that summer. In June Sassoon was awarded the Military Cross, but in August he caught trench fever and was sent home to convalesce at Somerville College. On the 10th Robbie visited the invalid, a visit that Sassoon remembered with obvious enjoyment when he came to recall it in later years:

> Although seventeen years my senior, his intuitively sympathetic understanding of youth made him seem a benevolent and impulsive bachelor uncle with whom one could feel on easy terms of equality, while consenting to be guided by his astute and experienced advice.
>
> Anyhow there he was, coming across the college lawn where I had been awaiting him under a tree, a small man in a light grey suit, wearing his soft black hat at a jaunty angle and carrying the ebony stick which somehow suggested his profession of art critic. My heart went out to his careworn face, lit up by pleasure at seeing me home from the war in an undamaged condition. My heart went out to him, as it always did, and as it does now; for he was one whose memory lives on through his gaiety and courage and the friendship which never failed those who benefited by it.[19]

Finding Sassoon more or less fully recovered, Robbie suggested that rather than just relaxing in the grounds of the College, they should spend the afternoon in a more amusing fashion. When Sassoon asked: 'Who is Lady Ottoline Morrell?' Robbie proposed a visit to Garsington. Sassoon found the eccentric and colourful Lady Ottoline a perfect companion for an afternoon's visit; although, like Robbie, he never became a full member of the Garsington set.

At least while he was at Oxford, Sassoon was safe from enemy shells and bullets but the list of those killed at the front and known personally to Robbie grew daily. On 7 September tragedy struck very close when Edward Jones, the eldest son of his sister Mary, was killed. And since it was to Jesmond Hill that Robbie retired when he needed to recover his own physical and mental equilibrium, he could give her wise and sympathetic counsel. He could help Mary to come to terms with her loss, although he had never forgiven Edward for his hostility and dislike of

Freddie Smith when the young man first shared his home. Robbie rarely held a grudge for long, but he did not expect to be told, either by his family or by his many friends, how to live his life or with whom he should share his home. He was arrogant and thought he was above criticism for he believed he alone should be the arbiter of his own behaviour.

It was not just the young who were being sent to the front to serve their King and Country. Forty-four-year-old Christopher Millard, in an attempt to escape the writ that was still out against him, joined the ranks of the Royal Sussex Regiment and was soon in France.

Neither the outbreak of the war nor the destruction of a generation of young men, nor Robbie's protracted appearances at the Central Criminal Court were allowed by Lady Phillips to disrupt her determination to have the Johannesburg Art Gallery finished and fully equipped at the earliest opportunity. Robbie, in spite of his resignation as Director of the Gallery, continued to deal with Max Michaelis, and a 'curious and harmonious relationship'[20] developed between them; poor Michaelis suffered much anguish by having a German name, and Robbie with his pro-German sympathies was an ideal companion, although he strongly disapproved of the war and the atrocities being committed.

In September Robbie arranged for all the pictures, bronzes, sculptures and books, which had been stored at the Tate, to be packed and shipped to Johannesburg for the official opening of the Gallery in April 1917. Later in the month Robbie was in communication with Sigismund Neumann as to whether Neumann had promised the sum of £4500 to the Gallery. In a letter to Robbie, Neumann denied he had ever made such a promise, Robbie was equally adamant that it had been made and therefore he expected the promise to be honoured. He could not, though, have known that less than a week later Neumann would be dead; wryly he told Dorothy Keith-Wright: 'My application to Sir Sigismund Neumann about the gallery seems to have killed the poor man.'[21] It would be a year before Neumann's executors finally agreed to honour the debt. Robbie's heart remained firmly with the Johannesburg Art Gallery, and he always felt its success—or failure—was largely his responsibility. He was quite happy to work for the Gallery without payment and when Lady Phillips offered to compensate him for his efforts he politely refused.

The affairs of the Johannesburg Gallery were not the only artistic distractions Robbie encountered that autumn. When the *Lusitania* was sunk by enemy action, Sir Hugh Lane was among the passengers who perished. In a codicil to his will, Sir Hugh bequeathed to the National

Gallery of Ireland thirty-nine French Impressionist pictures, but since
the codicil was not witnessed, the National Gallery in London refused to
part with them.[22] Outraged at such behaviour, Lane's aunt, Lady Gregory, a prominent Irish playwright and an ardent Nationalist, appealed
among others to Robbie to help obtain the pictures for Ireland. Robbie,
as always when a request was made to him, responded. He consulted a
good many people, read for himself the constitution of the National
Gallery, and even consulted two barristers, which must have been a
refreshing change after all his previous consultations with members of
the Bar. But reluctantly he had to report to Lady Gregory his efforts had
largely been in vain:

> I trust you will not think I am a depressing friend but I do not
> believe it is possible, *except by an Act of Parliament* for the Trustees
> to repudiate the bequest, except on the ground that the pictures
> were forgeries or quite worthless.... Supposing for the sake of
> argument that the Trustees and the Treasury were moved by your
> appeal and illegally handed over the pictures to Ireland: it would be
> open to any tax payers to bring an action against the Trustees for
> breach of trust. But I don't believe for a single moment that the
> Trustees will entertain the idea for a moment however sympathetic
> they may feel towards yourself. They have been subjected to severe
> criticism both in Parliament and in the Press and they would hardly
> subject themselves to such a risk of further (from the English point
> of view) justifiable attack of mere sentiment.
>
> I will try and come on Thursday next as you so kindly suggest.
> Unless my visit is postponed I am due to stay with the Asquiths next
> Saturday and I will speak to the P.M. on the subject if he is there,
> but I know he will express no opinion without consulting the
> permanent officials and Lord Curzon.[23]

His visit to the Asquiths was not postponed and from The Wharf he
apologised for being unable to see Lady Gregory the previous Thursday,
and admitted his attempts to get Asquith's personal help had not been
successful, although the Prime Minister was

> entirely sympathetic to your views. He asked me various small
> details of the subject which I was able to answer. He confessed
> however what I have already written to you that the whole matter
> would require legislation to enable the Trustees to act. However
> benevolent to your pleas they might be separately or collectively
> they could do nothing. The P.M. also admitted that he had nothing

whatever to do with their powers as Trustees. Still you may be
congratulated in having his "moral support" which will weigh very
much.

If I may suggest it to you I strongly urge you for diplomatic
reasons (quite apart from what Mr Birrell will of course tell you in
due course) *not* to tell people or to quote what the P.M. thinks. The
Trustees will hear that you have done so and might become hostile
out of mere "cussedness" to the whole scheme.[24]

While a guest at The Wharf Robbie's mind was not wholly occupied
that weekend with Hugh Lane's unresolved codicil. On 28 October
Freddie Smith left England to become a temporary secretary at the
British Legation in Stockholm.[25] He would always miss the company of
the young man who had helped fill the void left by Wilde's untimely
death, but he could rejoice in Freddie's good fortune in being spared the
horrors of trench warfare. The parting was made slightly easier by his
weekend with the Asquiths, but, as he admitted in a letter to John Lane,
his pleasure was marred by the insistence of his hosts on playing cards:

> The party here is a very delightful one, but I feel very much out of it
> by not playing bridge. The Asquiths are so kind that they never
> mind anything, though one feels, as you may suppose, rather a drag.
> To my old-fashioned Victorian taste, when there is so much to
> discuss, hear and learn, from life, art and literature, it is murdering
> time to play cards. Just when the Prime Minister is telling us
> something of astounding interest, or commenting on some European
> event in his own "inimitable" way, there is a general move to the
> bridge table. If I were a Bishop or puritan minister of some
> denomination I should preach against what I regard as a social
> disease.[26]

Robbie's genial and compassionate personality made him a pleasant
house-guest as Asquith himself recognised in a letter to Venetia Stanley:
'Ross proved to be a very agreeable companion and what John Burns
calls a "good raconteur".'[27] A fortnight later Robbie was a guest at
Corpus Christi College, Oxford, with Edward Warren, an old and valued
friend from the days when the Carfax Gallery was the centre of his
existence. If he lacked a 'paid' profession he was nevertheless still
extremely busy in solving the artistic and literary problems of his friends.

Twenty-One

Honour and Duty

S THE third autumn of the war dragged on, there was still no sign that peace would come quickly or that the battle was being won by either side. Robbie was concerned by the loss of talented and gifted young men and he did all in his power to prevent them being sent back simply as 'trench fodder'. In November, when it looked as if another artist would be sacrificed, he wrote to Charles Ricketts to offer what advice he could to avert another tragedy:

> I am so deeply distressed about [Ernest Alfred] Cole. But I burden you with this letter only in the endeavour to persuade you that something really *can* be done if the right "stops" are sounded and the right wires pulled. I admit that Kitchener being dead makes the matter more difficult. ... I am convinced if the seriousness of Cole's case is rightly presented to the right people he may be saved. The person to get at is Lord Curzon. ... Curzon, if convinced of what Cole is capable of, would be flattered, I believe, at being asked. Drawings—the *more obvious* drawings—should be shown to him. One might even be given to him "accidently on purpose": or perhaps afterwards. If you could get some Frenchman to back the opinion it would be valuable. It might shame the authorities into giving way. On no account should any demand for exemption be made: merely substituted non-combatant work; R.A.M.C. or something of that sort. No conscientious objector or peace people, I need hardly say must espouse his cause. [1]

Robbie was never afraid of using his influential connections to help others, but he rarely used them for his own benefit. He could, when helping others, be devious and cunning, but was totally incapable of using such traits to defend his own honour. He had no such scruples, however, when it came to protecting Oscar Wilde's memory. Early in 1916 Frank Harris, in self-imposed exile in America and short of money, was anxious to complete his book on the life of Oscar Wilde.[2] Robbie viewed the project with deep misgivings; Harris would not hesitate to denigrate Wilde's reputation, although Robbie was sure the book would

be more about Frank Harris and his many acts of generosity and kindness towards Wilde during his last tortured years. The prospect appalled
Robbie, but as Wilde's literary executor, he was duty bound to give what
assistance he could to prevent the worst excesses of Harris's literary
exuberance. The book would be an unreliable account of Wilde's life,
but it would place the blame for his disgrace squarely on the shoulders of
Douglas.

Predictably, Douglas would complain bitterly to Harris, and modifications to the text would be made. Harris could not find a publisher in
Britain who was willing to face the inevitable writ from Douglas, and
even in the United States he had to publish it himself. Bernard Shaw
never doubted that Harris's book should be published in Britain and
thought it would be after the war; he declared, 'the book says what needs
saying better than any of the others.'[3]

While the book was in preparation Harris wrote often seeking Robbie's advice. Robbie was less diligent in answering, but on 1 February
1917 he settled down to reply in detail to Harris's five previous letters. He
told Harris that Bernard Shaw had given him a copy of the letter he had
sent to Harris.[4] Robbie said that he had also spoken to both Shaw and to
George Moore, but, he had to admit, he did not agree with either of these
eminent writers' comments on Wilde. He thought Wilde appealed differently to different people and that was his strength and his weakness,
for each man perceived him in a different light. He was reluctant to
disclose his own opinion of Wilde, and indeed, throughout his long
stewardship as Wilde's literary executor he had rarely written anything
that could be taken as a personal assessment of Wilde's character or style
of living. He had, he said, been quite proud when Douglas

> objected to what he called my "detached and patronising attitude"
> about Wilde's writing. But I will confess to a certain craft in
> exercising a reticence which I do not propose to break. In the first
> place, my views of Wilde as a writer would not be regarded as of any
> importance; and my views of Wilde as a man would be regarded as
> too biased. . . . Douglas and Crosland sought vainly to discover some
> word of approval of Wilde or his life among my sparse contributions
> to the literature on the subject. That they failed to do so was one of
> the most gratifying tributes I have ever received.[5]

Robbie's reluctance to give an assessment of Wilde did not stop Harris
paying him a rather elaborate tribute, which must have further annoyed
Douglas. 'It became the purpose of his [Ross's] life to pay his friend's
debts, annul his bankruptcy and publish his books in a suitable manner,

in time to clear Oscar's affairs from reproach while leaving to his lovable spirit the shining raiment of immortality.'6

With the resignation in December of Asquith and the appointment of David Lloyd George as Prime Minister, there was the usual hand-out of honours to those who had loyally served the previous Prime Minister. Robbie, who liked honours as much as most men, was nevertheless disgusted when Charles Mathews was included in the New Year's Honours list. He did not blame Asquith or the Monarch for awarding the undeserved honour. In a very intemperate letter to Millard, he showed he had no doubt where the blame should be placed:

> The baronetcy conferred on Sir Charles Mathews seems to me most appropriate. He has protected so many of the aristocracy (including Douglas) from the consequences of their crimes, that it would have been ungenerous of the King not to have rewarded him for his combination of snobbishness and servility and corruption of the public office he occupies. Though I am sure the poor King had nothing to do with it. The Wyndham family probably arranged it.7

The political changes, however, made it possible for the Art Establishment to contribute further to Robbie's rehabilitation. All the time Asquith was Prime Minister, Douglas would have seen any position Robbie was given as political patronage and he would have created a great deal of adverse publicity, to the embarrassment of Robbie and the Government.

In January 1917 Baldwin Spencer, of the National Gallery of Victoria in Melbourne, Australia, while on a visit to London, sought to appoint an adviser for the purchase of works of art for the Gallery and for the Felton Bequest. Spencer asked Charles Holmes, Sir Cecil Smith, Sir Hercules Read and Dugald MacColl for their opinions and assessment of Robbie being appointed.8 The letters of recommendation were forthcoming and on return to Australia Spencer laid them before the Trustees of the Gallery, and Robbie was formally offered the position as adviser. Robbie accepted the honour and immediately began to make plans for a visit to Melbourne but ill-health and the vagaries of war delayed the start of the trip. It was his first paid occupation since resigning from the Board of the Inland Revenue in 1914, and he was soon extremely busy. He purchased a number of important pictures, including *The Garden of Pan* by Sir Edward Burne-Jones and *The Forum in Rome* by Canaletto. He also bought a number of works by William Blake which included thirty-six watercolours from the series of illustrations to Dante's *Divine Comedy*; two watercolours, illustrations to Milton's *Paradise Lost*; three coloured engravings of Blake's own poems; and twenty-one engraved illustrations to the *Book of Job*.[9]

His rehabilitation continued a few weeks later, when he received a letter from the Prime Minister's office offering him a position as a Trustee of the Tate Gallery.[10] This was the post he most cherished. It was an overt indication by the Establishment that he had been forgiven for the embarrassment he had caused by his litigation with Douglas and Crosland, and his steadfast support of Oscar Wilde. The appointment was duly confirmed by a Treasury Minute on 24 March. The Board, when it was constituted, included the Earl of Plymouth, Lord D'Abernon, Robert Witt, Lord Henry Cavendish-Bentinck, John Singer Sargent (though he resigned his position soon after), D.S.MacColl, and J.R.Holliday,[11] and two *ex-officio* members, Charles Holroyd, Director of the National Gallery, and Charles Aitken, Keeper and Director of the National Gallery of British Art (Tate).

At the first meeting of the new Board on 3 April, a subcommittee, composed of MacColl, Witt, Aitken and Ross, was asked to draw up a list of painters who ought to be represented in, and pictures which ought to be acquired by, the Gallery, and to consider the means of representing in the new Gallery works of British art after Hogarth.

His days were not so fully occupied that Robbie could not continue to enjoy an active social life. He lunched at the Reform Club frequently, often in the company of Arnold Bennett, H.G. Wells, Roderick Meiklejohn and Henry William Massingham (editor of the *Nation*). Dining with Robbie and Massingham was like being 'the meat in a sandwich of two pacifists', Arnold Bennett observed.

On 13 May, Robbie gave a celebration lunch at the Royal Automobile Club for Edmund and Nellie Gosse, and among the guests were Elizabeth Asquith, Mrs Sybil Colefax, Arnold Bennett and Dr Tancred Borenius. In early June, together with Roger Fry, Robert Graves, T.S. Eliot and Kathleen Mansfield, he was a guest at a dinner given by St John and Mary Hutchinson at River House, Hammersmith.

He still found it hard to pick up his pen again for serious articles on art or literature. Indeed, in the whole of 1917 he wrote only four contributions for publication, the Art Review for the *Annual Register*, a Monthly Chronicle for the *Burlington Magazine* on the sale of Whistler's lithographs; a letter to *The Times* on Victorian Relics in Berlin, which lacked his usual controversial edge; and an obituary on Sir Herbert Beerbohm Tree (who died 2 July 1917), published in the *Revue Bleue*. Naturally he was pleased to write an appreciation of the great actor-manager, though he probably prayed that the article would not cause the same controversy as had Douglas's *Revue Bleue* article on Wilde. If he could not find the will to write, he was, nevertheless, increasingly active in his role of 'gamekeeper turned poacher' as he told Lady Phillips: 'Owing to these hard times, I have to revert to my old profession of picture valuer. But instead of acting for Somerset House, I now assist the bereaved to resist the exactions of Inland Revenue for Death Duties.'[12]

The war went on relentlessly. Air-raids on London, particularly the East End, provided occasional horrific drama, and the sighting of a Zeppelin or a Gotha bomber overhead became more of a topic for conversation than the merits of the latest play at the St James's.[13] The nobility and aristocracy still entertained, although not as lavishly as in pre-war times. They privately mourned their dead sons, husbands and lovers. Their beautiful daughters were seen during the day in VAD uniforms, but at night they changed again into débutantes.

As much as he would have wished Robbie could not isolate himself from the ravages of the conflict. Millard served 228 days of exemplary service with the Royal Sussex Regiment, but the awful conditions of trench warfare and atrocious winter weather brought on a near fatal heart-attack. He was repatriated and in July was discharged with a pension. After a short period of convalescence he took up an appointment at the War Office as a civilian decipherer and for the moment no one bothered him and the warrant issued in March 1916 was not served. Robbie was relieved that at least one of his friends was spared further suffering. He, himself, was a fundamental pacifist. He detested all forms of killing but he did not believe that in bringing about the end of the war anyone should commit acts of treason or sedition. His loyalty and pride in King and Country never wavered although he found it hard to accept the bellicosity of the military who thought it the duty of the young to die for their country. Indeed such was his disgust at the conduct of the war that Squire Sprigge informed his son, 'Robbie has been lunching with the ruling classes somewhere, and his language had caused one lady seriously to say that she should report his conversation to the Provost Marshal.'[14]

Robbie was not a lone voice of protest that summer of 1917. Sassoon, sickened by the ceaseless slaughter, decided he would have to take action to bring his concern to the notice of the appropriate authorities. He was apprehensive, however, that his action would be seen as a sign of cowardice, as he had been offered a post as instructor to a Cadet Battalion and was unlikely to be sent to France again. If he was worried about the attitude of his 'enemies' to his anti-war statement, Sassoon was also unsure of Robbie's reaction, and in consequence, as he admitted, he had

> been avoiding Robbie lately; but on my way to Charing Cross I
> called at the Reform Club on the chance of seeing him there. As it
> was the middle of the afternoon I found the Club almost deserted.
> The door-porter having told me that he was probably in the library,
> I went up the stairs to the gallery which overlooks the noble
> columnar entrance hall. There I discovered him, with his coat off, at
> the top of a step-ladder, cleaning one of the embrowned and more
> than life-sized portraits of Victorian Liberal statesmen which are let
> into the walls. He was wearing his black silk skull-cap and looked
> small and somehow touching as his tired face brightened to greet
> me.[15]

Sassoon could not bring himself, that afternoon, to tell Robbie about his proposed action, but as he said his 'duplicity towards Robbie made me feel rather wretched, and he must have noticed that something was wrong; for when I was saying good-bye on the steps of the Club he suddenly asked whether I had anything on my mind, as I didn't look at all well. I muttered something about sleeping badly and London not agreeing with me, and changed the subject.'[16] Sassoon had rightly judged Robbie's attitude. It was typically ambivalent. He could applaud Sassoon's sensitivity but he was horrified that in making his anti-war statement Sassoon would be committing an offence for which he could be court-martialled, and if found Guilty he would serve a long period of imprisonment or he could even be shot for cowardice.

In his statement Sassoon argued eloquently that there should be a political solution to ending the war. He believed that the reasons for which he and the front-line soldier had first entered into the conflict had, over the years, been changed by the military and political establishments.[17]

Robbie was at the Hotel Albion, Brighton, with Alex and Ethel Sprigge, who was unwell, when Sassoon's statement reached him on 8 July. Immediately he wrote expressing his fear at the likely outcome of his friend's compassionate but impulsive action:

> I am quite appalled at what you have done. I can only hope that the
> C.O. at Litherland will absolutely ignore your letter. I am terrified
> lest you should be put under arrest. Let me know at once if
> anything happens.[18]

Sassoon was not, as Robbie gloomily prophesied, arrested and court-martialled, and although his friends disagreed with his actions, they came to his aid. On 19 July when Robbie returned from Brighton he was able to tell Gosse the latest events:

> [Robert] Graves wrote an excellent letter to the C.O. at Liverpool and received a most kind sympathetic letter in reply, saying that Siegfried would be ordered a Medical Board and the best would be done to treat the whole thing as a medical case. Siegfried consented to go to Liverpool and passed through London last Thursday, slept at my rooms and *said* he was going to Liverpool. I was away at the time. He is hurt with me because I am unsympathetic and to be precise that I did not give my blessing to his insane action. I came on Tuesday and met Graves by appointment but he had no news. He (Graves) went to Liverpool on Wednesday (yesterday) and is to let me know how things are going....I fear lest Siegfried is under arrest, but in a way that is the best that could happen. I have promise of powerful help if necessary at the War Office. At present it is premature to do anything. When I have news you shall have it.[19]

Sassoon's statement was discussed in the House of Commons on 30 July. Although some were sympathetic to his views, there was predictably some hypocrisy from those who had never experienced life in the trenches and could not understand the ordeal of being perpetually cold, wet, hungry and terrified of the enemy's merciless attacks. The statement was printed as a leaflet by Francis Meynell at the Pelican Press and copies were circulated around London from the Henderson Bookshop, a pacifist meeting place in Charing Cross Road, known somewhat inappropriately as the 'Bomb Shop'. The Pacifist Group, led by Bertrand Russell, whom Sassoon had met at Garsington, tried to use the statement as propaganda for their cause, but Sassoon never approved of their stand and was certainly not ready to become a pacifist martyr. He appeared before a Medical Board at Litherland, diagnosed as suffering from battlefield neurasthenia, and was sent for treatment to Craiglockhart War Hospital at Slateford near Edinburgh. Three days after his admission, having obviously recovered a sense of proportion and a little of his fine sense of humour, he addressed a letter to Robbie as coming from 'Dottyville'.

Robbie may well have repeated those immortal lines from one of Sassoon's most poignant war poems: 'My friends are dying young; while I remain, /Doomed to outlive these tragedies of pain'.[20] At least for the moment Sassoon was safe, and Robbie was grateful for that; a period of rest and relaxation would be good for both of them. At Craiglockhart Sassoon met another young soldier-poet, Wilfred Owen, and when at the end of October he left Edinburgh, Sassoon gave him an introductory letter to Robbie. True to his generous nature, Robbie, on 9 November, lunched the young soldier at the Reform Club, and introduced him to Arnold Bennett and H.G. Wells. The next evening Ross again dined with Owen at the Reform Club. They may have returned to Half Moon Street later in the evening, where in all probability Owen met More Adey, who rarely missed an evening seated in his favourite armchair. Such was the pleasure Owen experienced with Ross and his circle of literary friends, that when, in May 1918, Owen was again on leave, he rented a flat above Robbie's rooms in Half Moon Street.

Robbie was out of London a good deal that summer, which gave Nellie Burton time to redecorate his rooms; as Squire Sprigge told his son, '[Robbie] is having his rooms decorated entirely in gold as a protest against the morbid wave of economy, as he would consider one's social behaviour today. Your mother and I called on Sunday to borrow a bottle of whiskey from Burton... and found Burton in a mauve dressing-gown, smoking a cigarette and superintending the hauling of Robbie's furniture. Burton looked exactly like a bad character in a Hogarth print... the background of gilt paper, splendid books and pictures, bits of bronze, bits of sacking and workmen's tools recalled some such moral picture as *The Debauchee's Downfall* rather than *Autumn Cleaning in a Gentleman's Home*.'[21]

The redecorating was completed by the time Sassoon left Craiglockhart on 26 November. He spent some time in London and on 5 December he and Robbie went to see a performance of *Dear Brutus*. In spite of having to endure a series of noisy air-raids he was very happy to stay with Robbie at Half Moon Street and as usual Robbie proved a delightful host and the admirable Burton pampered and petted two of her favourite 'gentlemen'. Robbie entertained his war-weary guest with delightful tales of the 'heroism' of the civilian population, including his own small act of gallantry. One night returning along Piccadilly during an air-raid, he had encountered a frightened, bewildered 'old lady standing on the pavement opposite the Ritz. Unable to think of any other method of reassuring her, he put up his umbrella, offered her his arm, and gravely escorted her across to the shelter of the Ritz arches. There had seemed nothing ridiculous... in his holding the umbrella over her, and it evidently gave her a sense of security.'[22]

At the Coltart sale Robbie was able to secure for the Tate Gallery two

Madox Brown pictures, and at a meeting of Trustees on 27 November, he was given a grateful vote of thanks. Mrs Sybil Colefax arranged a late afternoon poetry reading for charity on 12 December. Robbie was coerced into overseeing the event and Gosse agreed to act as Master of Ceremonies, but as he told Robbie, the arrangements were fraught with difficulties, as he had another social occasion later that evening.

The poets taking part in the reading included Aldous Huxley, Osbert and Edith Sitwell, Robert Nichols, T.S. Eliot and Irene Rutherford. The Countess of Wemyss and her daughter Lady Cynthia Asquith were in the distinguished audience, Robbie was accompanied by Tancred Borenius; Arnold Bennett refused Edmund Gosse's invitation to attend, and Sassoon, although expected to read one of his own poems, was not all that keen on attending. He told Robert Graves he thought it would be a bit of a bore. As it turned out, the evening was a great success; even Gosse was delighted with the performances—including his own:

> I am pining to know what you thought of Wednesday. You must
> acknowledge I did my best?
> Scott-Moncrieff has written me a most beautiful and enthusiastic
> letter. His coldness at your lunch must have really come from *excess*
> of feeling. What perfect dears the Sitwells are, and R[obert]
> N[ichols] is a portent of tragic splendour.... Viola Tree was very
> charming.[23]

Robbie's interest in the affairs of the Johannesburg Art Gallery never wavered; he was always willing to publicise its achievements whenever an opportunity presented itself. In late 1917, when General Smuts accepted an anonymous gift for the Gallery in Pretoria, the *Morning Post*, in acknowledging the generosity of the donor, implied that the Pretoria Gallery was the only one of significance in South Africa. Robbie could not let such a mistake go unchallenged and in a letter to the *Morning Post* dated 16 December, he gave the history of the Johannesburg Art Gallery. He paid a well-deserved compliment to Lady Phillips for her foresight in establishing the Gallery. He also stressed that without the tireless efforts of the late Sir Hugh Lane the Gallery would have remained only a good idea. While he could not deny that the gift to Pretoria was a generous one, the Johannesburg Art Gallery, he said, had many generous benefactors, including Otto Beit, Sir Sigismund Neumann and Max Michaelis. He was, though, unable to recognise fully his own contribution to the Gallery. Modesty is an admirable trait but with Robbie it was a positive obsession. Lady Phillips summed up his complex character when she said, 'He was a victim of his own integrity and devotion'.[24]

As the third year of the Great War drew to a close, Robbie found the days growing more wearisome. The time he spent in the company of his friends were moments to savour, and in the diversity of his friends Robbie was a wealthy man. He still enjoyed the company of old friends, but he had shared with them too many bitter memories, and it was with the young war-poets, writers and artists that he found much of his relaxation and peace of mind. The young men who came to his Half Moon Street rooms in the sombre days of 1917 were not all pederasts but neither were they the 'Johnny-come-lately' extroverts who saw the war as an excuse for mindless violence and patriotic blustering. With the young men who shared his precious free time Robbie found a union of aesthetic and artistic tastes.

Robbie was never a rich man in the monetary sense, nevertheless, he bought his friends presents with a generosity which bordered on the extravagant, a precedent he inherited from his mentor, Oscar Wilde. Robbie's pleasure in giving was always greater than his joy of receiving. Only to hear of a friend's desire for a book, a drawing or a picture would provide him with the *raison d'être* to purchase the desired object. He once told Sassoon, 'Telling one's friends to buy a book is a waste of time.... One has to produce it from one's pocket and press it into their hands. The least one can hope for is that they'll leave it lying about in their drawing-rooms and talk as though they'd read it!'[25] There should be no suggestion that he bought friendships—that would be a complete misinterpretation of his generous nature; to a gregarious man the act of giving is its own reward. Robert Graves, for one, spoke kindly of Robbie's generous spirit: 'When he heard of my grand passion for him [John Skelton, 1460-1525, court poet to Henry VII] Robbie embarrassed me rather by buying me the only complete edition of J.S., 1843, very rare and beautifully bound.'[26]

The war took the life of many of Robbie's friends but he still needed to plan for the time when the enemy would be conquered, peace restored and life was normal again. He could once more hold up his head with pride; he was again accepted by the art establishment. He would travel to Melbourne as soon as restrictions had been lifted and his professional reputation would be further enhanced. It was a time to make plans and think of the future. They all had their dreams, not least Robert Graves, who, writing to Scott-Moncrieff, was clear what his idea of paradise was:

> It's a bad idea to make plans for after the war especially during the great Hun offensive, but I do think a farm on the Downs would be great fun. You could manage the office, SS [Sassoon] the horses. I and Nancy the ploughing, sowing and spuds. Bob Nichols the sheep

with an oaten pipe. Robbie Ross would hang the pictures and act as mess president.[27]

In the margin of his letter, Graves added a poignant postscript: 'I hope poor Robbie is all right. He hasn't answered letters for a long time. Please go and see.'

Twenty-Two

Final Injustice

HE YEAR 1918 started badly. On 9 January Christopher Millard was arrested for committing acts of gross indecency. Not that it was a surprise. He had avoided the day of reckoning for nearly two years. The Authorities had probably hoped that he would die a hero's death on a French battlefield as so many other brave men had, but Fate did not play her cards according to their wishes, and Millard had to stand trial for a second time in twelve years. He appeared at the Central Criminal Court on 2 March before the Recorder of London, Sir Archibald Bodkin. Since there was never any doubt he would be found Guilty, the only issue to be decided was the nature of his punishment. In sentencing him to twelve months' imprisonment, Bodkin tempered his judgement with a little mercy by insisting that, in deference to his war service, loss of pension rights and his poor state of health, the sentence should not include hard labour.

It was inevitable that in reporting the verdict, the Press would remind its readers that Millard had been a witness for Robbie Ross in the trials of Crosland. Douglas used the further disgrace of Millard as the signal for a new round of persecution against Robbie. Exhausted and depressed by continued harassment from the police, from moral crusaders and from vindictive old friends, Robbie was almost at the end of his tether, as he admitted to Walter Ledger:

> So many thanks for your kind letter of 17 March, too long
> unanswered. Like yourself I am seeking oblivion in strenuous work
> at the War Museum and the Propaganda. I wonder if you have seen
> Douglas's latest attacks on me. He has sent it round very freely. I
> wish I did not mind so much. Of course the disaster to Millard was
> for him a very good opportunity.[1]

Millard's imprisonment was a double blow. Sassoon had returned to active duty in France on 11 February, and Robbie had gone to Waterloo with Sassoon's mother to wish the departing warrior 'God's speed'. Even with pressures and depression that daily surrounded him Robbie still had the courage to face an active social life. On 3 March he was at Gosse's reception and among the guests were Lord Haldane and the Sitwells. Max Beerbohm's mother died on 13 March. Robbie had been very fond of the old lady, as she of him, and on the following Friday he attended her funeral at the Church of the Annunciation in Bryanston Street.

There can be little doubt that Douglas was behind the attacks orchestrated by Noël Pemberton Billing, Independent Member of Parliament for Mid-Hertfordshire. On 26 January, in a magazine he owned and edited called the *Imperialist*, Billing published a blatant attack on the Government's conduct of the war. He declared that there were men in positions of authority who were more interested in profit than in achieving a victory against the enemy. He claimed that a *Black Book*, compiled by the German Secret Service, contained the names of 47,000 prominent English citizens, who were engaged in 'the propagation of evils which all decent men thought had perished in Sodom and Lesbos'.[2]

Billing continued the attack on 16 February in the *Vigilante*, the renamed *Imperialist*, under a heading of sexually explicit language, the like of which had never before been printed in a British journal. There appeared a paragraph which effectively linked the corruption in Government and the conduct of the war with the crimes of Oscar Wilde and his circle: 'To be a member of Maud Allan's private performances in Oscar Wilde's *Salome* one has to apply to Miss Valetta, of 9 Duke Street, Adelphi. If Scotland Yard were to seize the list of these members I have no doubt they would secure the names of several thousand of the First 47, 000.'[3]

In this offensive manner, Billing and the author of the article, Captain Harold Spencer, established a link between Maud Allan the dancer; Jack Grein, the drama critic and impresario producer of the Independent Theatre; Oscar Wilde; Robbie; and the *Black Book*. Billing received many letters of support, including one from Marie Corelli, who claimed, 'It would be well to secure a list of subscribers of this new upholding of the Wilde cult among the 47,000.'[4] Marie Corelli had a fetish for defending the moral character of the nation. She had also many times been the butt of Robbie's incautious humour. Indeed, on a cold winter afternoon in Davos in 1894, in his lecture to the Literary Society, he had been extremely rude about her and now she would seek her revenge. There can be little doubt that the motive of Billing, Douglas and their associates was to discredit yet again Wilde, the Asquiths and their German-Jewish friends and Ross.

There were those in the Government who thought Billing should be arrested and charged; F.E., now Sir Frederick Smith, Attorney-General, had long held a personal grudge, and would dearly have loved to have brought a legal action against the odious Billing. But even F.E. had to admit reluctantly there was not a crime on the statute book which fitted the case. F.E. argued that a Government prosecution would give undue prominence to Billing's offensive allegations, and thus provide him with the opportunity of reaching a much wider audience. He rather hoped that if the Government ignored the accusations in Billing's publications, they would deprive him of the publicity he sought. No doubt at the back of F.E.'s mind there was the hope that if Billing continued to make his allegations, some upright citizen would eventually seek the redress of the civil law. In the end this is what happened. Maud Allan and Jack Grein issued writs for libel.

Jack Thomas Grein, a naturalised British subject of Dutch origin, had approached Robbie for permission to stage *Salome* at his Independent Theatre. He offered the part of Salome to Maud Allan, who wanted to broaden her experience in the theatre with a dramatic speaking role. Robbie saw no reason to refuse Grein's request since Wilde's books and plays were enjoying a popular revival but it was an act of extreme carelessness on Robbie's part.

Billing was arrested and charged at Bow Street Magistrates' Court on 6 April. Initial evidence of the libel against Maud Allan and Jack Grein was heard and the case adjourned for a week, when Sir John Dickinson committed Billing for trial at the Central Criminal Court.

The trial was fixed for 29 May. In the meantime, Robbie had to cope with continued harassment and visits from the police. But, as he told Charles Ricketts he was no longer surprised or upset by their visits:

> I don't know if it is a *post hoc* or a *propter hoc*, but yesterday morning [6 March 1918] as I was opening my letters, including one from yourself, detectives arrived from Scotland Yard. I concluded of course that it was the usual thing. (I have long become accustomed to the Douglas cum Scotland Yard conspiracy, for it is really nothing else, to drive me either to murder or madness.) However I found that it was a cheerful change. Information has been laid against me that...[I was] an art critic! a pacifist, a consorter of the company of conscientious-objectors, a sympathiser with and visitor of German prisoners: a former professed Roman Catholic and now a professed and militant atheist. They were rather flabbergasted when I said it was all perfectly true, and that I could produce documentary evidence to prove it.
>
> It is so grotesque that I am not in the least alarmed, and would not have recorded the matter to you at all, except as an explanation

> of why I cannot, as I intended, do anything further about the person
> of whom you wrote, at all events for the present.
>   By a brilliant instinct, when the detectives arrived, and assuming
> a search of my rooms, I hurled your letter into the fire. I mention
> this lest you should anticipate similar enquiries, of which, of course,
> there is no fear. But everyone must be careful.[5]

If the police thought their visits would bring a reduction in Robbie's activities they were soon disillusioned. He continued to support all those persecuted people who needed his support. Not for the first time in his life, the views and actions of the private man were in opposition to the views and actions of the public man. In his official capacity he was extremely busy with the newly formed British War Memorials Committee, and the fact that he worked in close co-operation with Arnold Bennett delighted him. He had always admired Bennett's hard-headed common sense and lack of pretension. Charles Masterson, Lord Beaverbrook and Lord Rothermere formed an executive quorum; Alfred Yockney was Secretary to the Committee; and Muirhead Bone was another of the art advisers. It was Robbie who suggested to the Committee that they should have an 'art memorial'. In outlining his proposals he stressed that to be effective the Memorial Collection should be designed to have an unmistakable unity and identity. He was never hesitant to disagree with his fellow advisers especially if their views offended his aesthetic tastes.[6]

The Great War would be commemorated with memorials in every city, town and village. The great Cenotaph in Whitehall and the cemetery memorials were designed by Sir Edwin Lutyens, one of the architects of the Johannesburg Art Gallery. Robbie would have been horrified to find that the British War Memorials Committee's art memorial would not occupy one room attached to an existing gallery, as he expected, but would become a separate museum devoted wholly to the remembrance of war.

The Billing trial began at the Central Criminal Court on 29 May 1918, and it was, perhaps, doubly unfortunate that the Judge was Mr Justice Darling, a senior member of the judiciary who had a reputation for unorthodoxy and whose comments, from the Bench, were frequently not in the interests of impartial justice. The prosecutors were officially Maud Allan and Jack Grein, but again it was Oscar Wilde who was really on trial. Billing conducted his own case.

The case was scheduled to last six days, and as the three indictments were to be heard separately, only the libel against Miss Allan was heard.

The trial was an admirable example, nauseating in the extreme, of the inability of the Law to protect the innocent. After nearly four years of war, public hysteria and anti-German resentment were running at fever-pitch, and an outburst of cheering from the public galleries was a particular feature of the proceedings whenever Billing made a robust patriotic statement. The Defence called an array of expert witnesses, but they were distinguished only by their ineptitude and sheer silliness. Captain Harold Spencer, the author of the article, who spoke of being shown the infamous *Black Book* by Prince Wilhelm of Weld, admitted he had not read all 47,000 names, but had recognised the name of Asquith.

Billing's witnesses, without exception, viciously attacked Wilde's life and work and tried to ridicule Ross's love and devotion. Ross's friendship with the Asquiths was abused and degraded but he was given no chance to rebut the allegations. His hatred of the war and the pseudo-patriotism of the professional warmongers were given as an excuse for the libels. Billing's witnesses mouthed platitudes to justify the slaughter. They declared the war was a crusade for the honour and dignity of the British nation against the infiltration of the German menace.

Predictably, Billing's star witness was the 'reformed' Lord Alfred Douglas, now a paragon of virtue and Christian morality, who used the privilege of the witness-box to make a vitriolic attack on Wilde. Asked by Billing if he regarded Wilde as sexually evil, Douglas replied, 'No, he was the agent of the devil in every possible way. It was his whole object in life to attack and sneer at virtue and to undermine it by every means.'[7]

The *Black Book* was never produced, but its influence successfully distorted the Prosecution's evidence; Billing made full use of the public sympathy for his war on sexual perverts. In the minds of the jury, the battle for public morality and the battle being fought against the German nation were one and the same thing. The defeat of one would automatically bring about the defeat of the other. The fact that, at least according to Billing, there were 47,000 people in high places addicted to 'unnatural practices' was cited as the reason why politicians were not fighting the war with full vigour. The jury might have been persuaded differently if the Defence had called one serving soldier to give his view on the war. They might have decided it was not the German influence on the Government which was at fault but the ineptitude of the military machine.

Billing continued to play on the sympathies of the jury, using the cheers of the gallery to press home his attack. It is to Darling's credit that he did try to keep hold of the proceedings, but against Noël Pemberton Billing, declaring that he knew nothing of the rules of evidence and that all he wanted was to get at the truth, the trial became a farce.

In spite of a masterly summing up by Darling in Maud Allan's favour, the outcome of the trial was a foregone conclusion. The jury were clearly prejudiced in favour of Billing and there were scenes of unprecedented rejoicing when they returned a Not Guilty verdict. It took the ushers and the police some time to clear the public gallery and the demonstrators at the back of the Court. Only a few officers in uniform were allowed to stay to hear the closing stages of the trial.

A postscript on the three main defence witnesses proves that the verdict was a serious miscarriage of justice. Mrs Villiers-Stuart, it was revealed, was Billing's mistress and later that year was sent to prison for nine months for bigamy. Captain Harold Spencer was invalided out of the Army, certified as insane and unfit for further military training. He was later imprisoned for publishing a defamatory libel and was further fined for committing an act of indecent behaviour. And Douglas, inevitably, libelled one man too many, and served a six-month sentence.

Robbie never doubted that Billing would be found Not Guilty. Charles Ricketts wrote expressing his distress and indignation at the grossly unfair verdict; and in his reply Robbie revealed his perverse sense of humour, even at the blackest times:

> Your letter both touched and soothed me. You are perfectly right about the English dislike of tragedy, though I never thought of your admirable explanation of the reason: the favourite scene in *Hamlet* is that of the jesting gravediggers, and that is a confirmation of your theory. I foresaw the result of the Billing case, and warned Grein not to bring the action. When the trial began, everyone thought I was mad because I said Billing would be acquitted.... The English, intoxicated into failure, enjoyed tearing poor Maud Allan to pieces, simply because she had given them pleasure, and kicking Oscar's corpse to make up for the failure of the 5th Army...
>
> However, I have not lost all sense of proportion, and these things are small compared to the fate of Paris, which will be lost and destroyed owing to the vanity and incompetence of the English generals. On that point I fear I am with the majority. Every soldier from the Front, wounded or unwounded, tells the same story.[8]

The touching naïvety in Robbie's letter is notable; despite all his trials and tribulations of the past eighteen years, he still regarded them as small compared to the imminent destruction of his beloved Paris. For once his pessimism was ill founded. Paris remained virtually intact, practically unscarred. In a sparkling summary of the Billing case, he wrote to Cecil Squire Sprigge who was on active service in India:

I have been used as a piece of mud...or rather to make a more
suitable image; once a lion in the zoo of Alfred Douglas, I am now a
minnow in the Pemberton Billing Aquarium! For a few days
London forgot all about the war, in its excitement over the case.
The populace were entirely on the side of Billing and, as he
succeeded in the trial, are quite convinced that all he says must be
true. Kicking the corpse of Wilde has also been a pleasure to the
English people even if they disapprove of Billing's methods.[9]

In a reply to his father, Cecil, in commenting on the Billing case,
summed up eloquently what must have been the opinion of many right-
minded people: 'Out of this absurd case I have derived one pleasure,
namely that of seeing all the elements of society I despise in league
against all the people I most honour: Asquith, Haldane, Grey....How
excellent to hear that H.H.A. treated the whole thing with the contempt
it deserved.'[10]

It was too much to hope that Robbie would be allowed to carry on
with his official duties without fresh insinuations and accusations being
made against him. Lord Beaverbrook, although a fellow Canadian, was
alarmed by Robbie's pacifism and pro-German sympathies, and, following the revelations in the Billing case, Beaverbrook tried to have Robbie
removed from all the Committees connected with the War Museum.
Arnold Bennett, disgusted at Beaverbrook's narrow attitude, wrote a
spirited defence of Robbie's moral and sexual character:

There can be only one reason for getting rid of Ross....his friendly
relations with Oscar Wilde are well known; and Alfred Douglas is
his declared enemy. Ross is an entirely honest man. He stuck to
Oscar when Oscar was ruined, and without reward of any kind he
has put Oscar's family on its feet. He is not a sodomist, never was,
and never defends sodomist doctrines. He merely has a weakness for
looking after people in adversity....It is inconceivable to me that
such a man should be got rid of merely because Alfred Douglas has
hooked himself on to Billing and there is a fear of Ross being
attacked in the House or elsewhere. To get rid of him would be a
very dangerous thing. It would be equivalent to stopping Billing in
the Strand, putting up one's hands, and crying "Kamerad"....Any
newspaper proprietor who cared to spend £5000 on the job could
with the aid of documents in the possession of George Lewis burst
up the present scare in a month....My opinion is that if any
question is asked in the House about Ross a straightforward answer
would dispose of it at once. It would assuredly arouse such a protest

in the press as would surprise the questioner. Ross's friends, and he
has many powerful friends, would see to that. I should certainly see
to it.[11]

One element in Bennett's letter needs explanation. Ross was always
disinclined to use all the resources he had at his disposal, and he never
defended himself as vigorously as the situation demanded. He was,
therefore, never able to beat Douglas. He did, however, make one
exception and in a show of uncharacteristic pique he wrote to Sir Charles
Mathews, Director of Public Prosecutions. The pent-up emotions of the
previous ten years boiled over:

> I write to congratulate you on the complete rehabilitation of your
> protégé, Lord Alfred Douglas. Your connivance at his campaign
> against myself and subsequently against others of much greater
> importance in the world than I can pretend to be, has been crowned
> with a success which must have been unforeseen even by yourself.
>
> Unless my memory fails me your collusion with him began with
> your visit to Mr Digby La Motte, and the High Master of Little
> Grosvenor Street. You were well aware at the time of the character
> of the man who was making the charges against me, but you were
> ready to investigate them; and since, you have shown your
> unreadiness and unwillingness to investigate or interrupt his
> campaign of calumny, which has now been brought to such a
> triumphant issue. For some time I was a little puzzled, but now I
> understand what Shakespeare intended in presenting so vividly the
> venom and snobbery of a bastard, particularly the bastard of a
> mummer.[12]

In trying to understand the attitude of Robbie's friends to his single-
minded determination to rescue Wilde's tarnished reputation, it is essential to realise that they viewed his loyalty and dedication as nothing short
of miraculous. Charles Ricketts wrote perhaps the best testimonial to
Robbie's devotion to Wilde and the terrible price he paid for that
devotion:

> It [the Wilde trial] has been a constant burden to R. Ross, the heroic
> self-constituted literary executor of Wilde, the man in fact who has
> helped to negative the iniquitous consequences of the verdict. To
> this day he is subject to persecution from ignoble quarters, a little
> uncertain in mental and bodily health, as a consequence an old man
> before his time.[13]

As the restrictions on travel began to ease, Robbie completed his
arrangements for his long-promised visit to the United States and to the
National Gallery of Victoria in Melbourne. Preparations occupied much
of August and September and he viewed the coming adventure with a
mixture of trepidation and apprehension. Not having been abroad since
the outbreak of war, he was nervous and excited, almost as if he were an
inexperienced traveller about to embark on his first overseas expedition.
He had last made his will on 3 October 1914, but there were alterations he
wished to make before embarking on his protracted visit. With the death
of Cyril Holland it was now necessary to leave his share of Wilde's
Literary Estate solely to Vyvyan. He had long been concerned that,
should he die, a number of his closest friends would be impoverished,
and he planned to set up a trust fund. More Adey would be the main
beneficiary, Nellie Burton would have an annuity of £100, and Christopher Millard, Cecil Sprigge and Alfred Lambart would each receive an
annuity of £50.[14] The papers were drawn up. Alex and William Jones, as
his executors, would be responsible for seeing that Robbie's last wish was
carried out, even though he did not sign the new will before he died.

As the day of his departure approached Robbie was busy saying
farewell to his many friends. Sassoon arrived in London on 30 September; in July he had been shot in the head by one of his own sergeants,
who mistook him for the enemy. They lunched at the Reform Club the
next day with Arnold Bennett and Maurice Baring and in the evening
they went to a performance of the Russian Ballet's *Papillons*. On 2
October they lunched at the Royal Automobile Club with Massingham,
Edith Sitwell and Clive Bell. Lady Ottoline Morrell and E.L.[Billy]
Greaves joined them for tea at Half Moon Street. On Thursday Sassoon
spent the evening at Half Moon Street in Robbie's company:

> He had told me that he would be spending the evening alone, as his
> preparations for departure had worried and over-tired him. I found
> him sitting at his table reading a little red-bound Bible. He
> explained that he wasn't getting ready to meet his Maker; he had a
> fondness for the Old Testament because there were such a lot of
> good stories in it.[15]

Sassoon's wish to spend a quiet evening alone with Robbie was
dispelled when Charles Scott-Moncrieff and the young Noël Coward
arrived to disturb the tranquillity. Confessing he had a splitting head-
ache, Sassoon took his early leave of Robbie:

> I said good-bye to Robbie with tormented abruptness, and when I
> was downstairs and about to let myself out of the front door he came
> quickly down and stood beside me. He said nothing, but took my
> hand and looked up at me for a long moment. His worn face, grey
> with exhaustion and ill-health, was beatified by sympathy and
> affection. The memory of it will always remain with me. How
> should I forget that look, with what afterwards seemed to have been
> its presentiment of final farewell?[16]

Robbie spent part of the evening writing letters. Even with his departure so close he still wanted to see Lady Phillips and settle a few
problems concerning the Johannesburg Art Gallery. He wrote to Squire
Sprigge and told him that, finally, he had seen Arnold Bennett and had
been able to pass on Sprigge's letter. Bennett had promised him an early
reply. In a postscript he expressed his delight at the rehabilitation of
Sprigge's son: 'He [Cecil] seemed in great spirits and permitted himself
certain very healthy criticisms of certain old idols. It cheered me very
much that his dreadful experiences, poor darling, have really been of
intellectual use to him.'[17]

On Saturday afternoon, 5 October 1918, Robbie returned home at
about four o'clock from lunching with friends. He told Nellie Burton he
was suffering from indigestion pains and asked if she had any of 'Arnold
Bennett's tablets'. She was unable to supply the magic pills, but she
assisted him to his bedroom to rest until the pain subsided. When she
went to wake him to dress for dinner he was dead. Sassoon put into
perspective the awful tragedy of that unexpected event:

> While resting before dinner, he died of heart failure. It seems
> reasonable to claim that this was the only occasion on which his
> heart failed him, either in personal courage or in generosity towards
> his friends. For them his death made a difference which could only
> be estimated in sorrowful conjectures. It deprived us of an ever-
> ready helpfulness that might have changed many human discords to
> harmony.[18]

As with all sudden inexplicable deaths there was a postmortem carried
out by Dr J.C. Jewesbury, pathologist at Charing Cross Hospital. The
subsequent Inquest was held at the Westminster Coroner's Court on 9
October. Alex Ross told the Coroner that his brother had been comforta-
bly off, and, as far as he was aware, had had no trouble of any kind. He
said that, somewhat to his own amusement, his brother had fussed a
good deal about his forthcoming visit to Australia, although he was

looking forward very much to the trip. Nellie Burton, in evidence, said that Robbie had been distressed about the state of his health since September, when he had not been graded by a Medical Board. The Coroner, Mr Inglebury Oddie, said that death had been entirely natural and gave the cause as 'syncope caused by chronic bronchitis and gastritis'. He stressed there were no suspicious circumstances, and there was no question that the death was anything other than the result of the deceased's chronic ill-health, which he had endured since childhood.

There were many glowing tributes from family and friends, Squire Sprigge wrote to his son:

> It is enormously pleasant to think that his life, in the last two years or more, has been so peaceful, and has brought him many new friends young and old, and has confirmed him in the love of his old friends. He was looking forward with whimsical trepidation but with real interest to his journey to Australia. . . . I have known him utterly intimately since he was little more than a child and I was little older than you are now. We differed bitterly more than once, but we never even squabbled once: from the beginning to the end in our family friendship we were perfectly frank in our divergency of opinion and mutual regard notwithstanding. He leaves a gap in my life. . . he will leave a gap in your life and it is the tragedy of the days we live in that our young people are being asked to endure the blows which belong to the generation senior to them.[19]

Robbie's obituary notices in *The Times, Daily Telegraph* and the *Manchester Guardian* expressed the feelings of many. *The Times*, in particular, said: 'It was his foible to pretend to be a trifler in all things and to gibe at the greatest reputation; but he knew more and did more than many solemn people and, in acts of kindness, he was always in earnest.'[20]

Vyvyan Holland was in France on active service, when he read of Robbie's death and the news devastated him. The war had already cost him dearly with the death of his only brother, and before he had time to come to terms with Robbie's death his wife would die in tragic circumstances. Vyvyan Holland wrote to Alex, 'I am writing to offer you all my sympathy in what I know must be a terrible bereavement. You know without my telling you what it means to me. Robbie has always been my dearest friend, and I have always looked to him when I wanted sincerity and advice. . . . I can only add my sorrow to yours at the untimely death of the dearest man I have known.'[21]

The death of Robbie Ross saddened many people, but for More Adey it brought an end to a friendship which had endured for three decades. In writing to Cecil Sprigge five days after Robbie's death More Adey poured out his distress and his loneliness:

> I am ten years older than dear Robbie and his vitality of mind and of resistance—especially—had in 30 years' close and devoted friendship communicated itself to me, and had prevented me from enclosing myself within a wall of impenetrable reserve. I see that effect of Robbie in everyone who knew him, as well as the strong feelings of affection which he inspired in all sorts and kinds of minds, even when he was opposed to them as with great acumen over business matters!... it struck me when I saw him about one and half hours after death that he could not have suffered in articulo mortis, there was no sign of any struggle. That is some comfort. I never have been able to make out why, but suffering by Robbie has always seemed to me more poignant to see than in anyone else. It is also a blessing that he had not started for Australia; I always hated the idea of his going....No one can ever be to you what Robbie has been, no one can ever be to me what he has been, but I should like to make up to you, dear Cecil, whatever little I can of the loss, and you can always count on me as long as I live.[22]

There was deep family concern that with Jack dying without a son, and Alex and Robbie never marrying, there was no male heir to continue the name of Ross. Robbie, who valued the continuity of the family name, would have been delighted by the gesture made shortly after his death, by William, Mary's second son, who by Deed Poll changed his surname to Ross and so secured the name for at least two more generations. The name of Jones was secured, because although Edward had been killed, he had two sons to carry on the lineage.

Robbie's new will remained unsigned and for Probate purposes Alex had to use the will dated 3 October 1914, almost exactly four years to the day of Robbie's death, and written before he knew the outcome of his libel action against Bosie Douglas. In both the old and new will Robbie left instructions that would have had Oscar Wilde laughing in heaven. It was his final gesture of defiance to a society which had hounded him mercilessly all his life:

> I direct that my remains shall be cremated at Golders Green Crematorium with the ordinary burial offices of the Catholic and Roman Church. And I direct that my ashes shall be placed in a

suitable urn and taken to Paris and buried in the tomb of the said
Oscar Fingal O'Flahertie Wills Wilde. If however it should prove
impossible to obtain the licence of the necessary authorities for this I
direct that my ashes shall be scattered in Père Lachaise.[23]

Thirty-two years were to elapse before his wish was granted. To have
removed Robbie's ashes to Père Lachaise, before the death of Lord
Alfred Douglas in 1945, would have brought the wrath of that unforgiving man down on the heads of Robbie's relatives. The Second World
War delayed matters further, but on 30 November 1950, the fiftieth
anniversary of Oscar Wilde's death, Margery Ross, William's wife, took
Robbie's ashes to France and laid them to rest in the special chamber
which Robbie, thoughtfully, had asked Jacob Epstein to design. Their
spirits finally united, in that noble, majestic memorial, the two friends
are together for eternity, forever freed from the struggles of an earthly
existence.

> So, in the days to come, your name
> Shall be as music that ascends
> When honour turns a heart from shame...
> O heart of hearts!...O friend of friends![24]

Notes on Sources

Abbreviations for location of MSS & Letters.

Austin:	Harry Ransom Humanities Research Center, University of Texas at Austin.
BL:	British Library.
BM:	British Museum.
Berg:	Berg Collection, New York Public Library.
Bodley:	Bodleian Library, Oxford.
Bogle:	Edra Bogle, Life and Literary and Artistic Activities of Robert Baldwin Ross 1869-1918. PhD Thesis. University of Southern California.
BRT:	Brotherton Library, University of Leeds.
Clark:	William Andrews Clark Memorial Library, University of California, Los Angeles.
CRO:	Central Record Office, Chancery Lane, London.
CUL:	The Syndics of Cambridge University Library.
Friends:	*Robert Ross: Friend of Friends*, (ed.) Margery Ross.
GU:	University of Glasgow, Special Collections.
HGT:	Houghton Library, Harvard University.
Holland:	Merlin Holland.
IWM:	Imperial War Museum, London.
JAG:	Johannesburg Art Gallery.
KCC:	King's College, Cambridge.
Letters:	*Letters of Oscar Wilde*, (ed.) Rupert Hart-Davis.
MacGuire:	J. Robert MacGuire.
MPost:	*Morning Post*, articles by Robert Ross.
NLS:	National Library of Scotland, Edinburgh.
OAT:	Ontario Archives, Toronto.
RUL:	Reading University Library.
Ross:	J.-P.B. Ross.
Slade:	Slade School of Fine Art, University College, London.
Sprigge:	Prof. and Mrs T. Squire Sprigge.
TLS:	*Times Literary Supplement*.
TML:	Toronto Metropolitan Library.

Notes

I MORAL DILEMMA (1869-1900)

1 Early Influences

1 Hon John Ross (1818-71). Lawyer, politican and businessman. Married Margaret Crawford early in 1847; she died in childbirth later that year, the child died shortly after. Married Augusta Elizabeth Baldwin February 1851. Solicitor-General for West Canada 1851; Attorney-General 1853; Receiver-General 1858. Appointed to Senate 1867. Director Northern Railway Co. of Canada.
2 Hon Robert Baldwin (1804-58). Canadian statesman, Member of Executive Council 1836. Solicitor-General 1840; Attorney-General 1842 & 1848-51. Premier of Upper Canada 1842-3. Married Augusta Elizabeth Sullivan, his first cousin, who died after a Caesarean-section.
3 I spoke at length to the late Prof. Giles Robertson and to J-P.B. Ross during 1985-6 on the relationship between Ross and his family, and all statements made are as a result of those conversations. I have also had access to private correspondence between members of the Ross family, and to the unpublished *Memoir of Mary Jones*.
4 Bogle, p.22.
5 *Bystander*, "The Literary Log", 23 Nov. 1910.
6 Lord Alfred (Bosie) Bruce Douglas (1870-1945). Poet, journalist and litigant.
7 Hart-Davis, Ross to Humphreys, 16 Dec. 1900.
8 *Letters*, p.225.
9 *Granta*, 1 Mar. 1889.
10 Ibid.
11 KCC, Browning to Prothero, 9 Mar. 1889.
12 KCC, Prothero to Browning, 13 Mar. 1889.
13 Mrs Ross's telegrams to Browning did not specify the nature of the attacks. There can be no certainty that Ross was suffering from a nervous breakdown or pneumonia. Alex Ross admitted once that his brother had

291

had two nervous breakdowns, but he did not say when these had occurred.

14 KCC, Statement by J.E.Nixon.

15 Ibid.

16 KCC, Nixon to Browning, 6 May 1889.

17 KCC, A.G. Ross-Browning, 30 June 1889.

2 Friendship and Journalism

1 KCC, Ross to Browning, Sept. 1889.

2 Ibid.

3 KCC, Mrs Ross to Browning, Feb. 1890.

4 Samuel Squire Sprigge (1860-1937). Caius College, Cambridge, 1878, MRCS. St George's Hospital, 1886. Married Ada Beatrice Moss, 18 Sept. 1895; two children, Cecil and Elizabeth Miriam. Second marriage to Ethel Jones, 24 June 1905; one daughter: Annabel. Editor of *Lancet* from 1909. Knighted 1921.

5 Clark, Ross to Wilde, [c1890].

6 *Letters*, p.271.

7 *Friends*, p.23.

8 Robert Ross, *Masques and Phases*, Arthur L Humphreys 1909, p.48.

9 Clark, Ross Deposition, ?1913.

10 Rupert Hart-Davis (ed.), *Diaries of Siegfried Sassoon: 1923-1925*, p.25.

11 William More Adey (1858-1942). Keble College, Oxford. Editor, *Burlington Magazine*, 1914-19. Lived at Under-the- Hill, Wotton-under-Edge, Glos. After Robbie's death, he became more eccentric and spent his declining years confined to a psychiatric hospital.

12 BRT, 16 Mar. 1892.

13 The full text of Wilde's letter to Ada Leverson where he mentioned his reasons for taking the name Melmoth is in *Letters*, p.566.

14 Robert Ross, *Aubrey Beardsley*, John Lane 1909, p.15.

15 *Friends*, p.27.

16 *Aubrey Beardsley*, op. cit., p.46.

17 There is some disagreement among biographers of Wilde/Douglas about the identity of the boy involved in the Bruges incident. It is my contention that it was Alfred, son of Brig.-Gen. Edgar Allan Lambart, (1857-1930). My reasons are threefold: Ross supported Alfred Lambart throughout his life and after his death through his Trust Fund, and when he sued Douglas for libel in 1914, Douglas tried to involve Wortham in connection with the Bruges incident, and not Danney as identified by the late Prof. Ellmann or Dansey as identified by Anstruther. Douglas could not involve Alfred Lambart, as he was serving a three- year prison

sentence for "false pretences" and it would have created quite the wrong impression to have as his chief witness a man with a criminal record. In 1930 Sassoon wrote to Lambart sending him a copy of his anthology of poems. In the letter he said, "It will remind you of him [Ross] a dear and generous friend." The book was given to its present owner by J.H.L. Lambart, the youngest son of Brig.-Gen. Lambart. See Note 18/10 p.233.

18 KCC, Wortham to Browning, 15 Oct. 1893.
19 KCC, Ross to Browning, 16 Oct. 1893.
20 Sir George Henry Lewis (1833-1911). Solicitor in English Criminal Law. Succeeded by his son George.
21 The cruel schoolmaster in *Nicholas Nickleby* by Charles Dickens.
22 *Daily Telegraph*, 24 Nov. 1914.
23 Hart-Davis, Beerbohm to Ross, Nov. 1893.
24 Ibid.
25 Reginald Turner (1869-1938). Writer and journalist.
26 W.G.Gorman (ed.) *Converts to Rome*, Sands & Co. 1910 p.237.
27 The lady was not identified either by Ross or by the editor of the *Davos Courier*.
28 *Friends*, p.30.

3 A Life Destroyed

1 *St James's Gazette*, 18 Jan. 1895.
2 Arthur Bellamy Clifton (1862-1932). Solicitor and writer. Wrote under the pseudonym of Arthur Marvel.
3 Holland, Constance Wilde to Ross, 26 Dec. 1894.
4 Holland, Constance Wilde to Ross, 1 Feb. 1895.
5 The late Prof. Richard Ellmann, with the assistance of R.E.Alton, in his biography of *Oscar Wilde*, Hamish Hamilton, 1987, interpreted the words on Queensberry's card as "To Oscar Wilde posing somdomite", although later in court the words were given as "posing as a somdomite".
6 *Letters*, p.384.
7 Alfred W. S. Taylor (c 1862). Well educated and financially independent. He was charged along with Oscar Wilde, refused to turn Queen's Evidence and was sentenced with Wilde. After his release he lived in North America. As Wilde's friendship with Taylor ensured he would be found guilty of homosexuality thus so it was with Ross's friendship with Millard.
8 *Letters*, p.386.
9 H.Montgomery Hyde (ed.), *Trials of Oscar Wilde*.
10 Henry Labouchere (1831-1912). Liberal M.P. (1866-1906). Moved the Amendment to the Bill which was originally designed to protect women

and girls from prostitution. This had the effect of making all homosexual
acts a criminal offence. The Amendment became law on 1 Jan. 1886, and
was responsible for the prosecution of Oscar Wilde.

11 Evan Charteris, *Life and Letters of Sir Edmund Gosse*, p.248.

12 CUL, The Book of Gosse. (Visitor's Book.) (Copy in BRT).

4 Love for the Imprisoned

1 Oscar Wilde, *De Profundis*: a letter written to Lord Alfred Douglas
during the last months of his imprisonment. It was first published by
Ross in 1905 and in 1908 he brought out a longer version. In 1948, Vyvyan
Holland published what was thought at the time to be the whole letter,
but in 1960 when the manuscript became available to historians and
writers, Sir Rupert Hart-Davis was, for the first time, able to compare the
versions and subsequently restored many of Robbie's "corrections". In
1962, Wilde's original letter was published in its entirety in *Letters*.

2 *Letters*, pp.459-60.

3 £2000 is equivalent to £60,000 at today's values.

4 KCC, Ross to Browning, 21 Oct. 1895.

5 Ibid.

6 Ibid.

7 *Friends*, pp.39–43.

8 Wilfred Scawen Blunt, *My Diaries: Part Two (1900-1914)*, Knopf, 1923,
p.121.

9 The full letter appears in *Letters*, p.326.

10 Sir Frederick Treves (1853-1923). Founder of the British Red Cross
Society. Was responsible for many improvements in surgical techniques
and was best known as the surgeon to Joseph Merrick, the "Elephant
Man".

11 *Letters*, p.407n.

12 *Letters*, pp.512-15.

13 The title of *De Profundis* is said to have been suggested by E.V.Lucas,
but Ross said the title was his own suggestion, see Ch.7 p.94

14 *Letters*, p.550.

15 Holland, Constance Wilde to Ross, 27 July 1896.

16 *Letters*, p.557n.

17 More Adey (ed.), *After Berneval: Letters of Oscar Wilde to Robert Ross*,
(London 1922).

18 *Letters*, pp. 564-5

19 Ibid.

20 It has been impossible to discover exactly what were Ross's views on
freemasonry, but the Roman Catholic Church still forbids its members to

be freemasons (in France in particular, freemasonry and anti-Romanism are strongly identifed).

21 *Letters*, pp.564-5.
22 *Letters*, the full letter is on pp. 568-9.
23 *Letters*, p.581.
24 *Letters*, p.577.
25 Ada Leverson, *Letters to a Sphinx*, Duckworth, 1930, p.48 (Limited Edn.).
26 *Letters*, p.624.
27 Clark, *Two Approaches of Oscar Wilde*, John Espey, 1976, p.42.
28 *Letters*, p.644.
29 *Letters*, p.675n.
30 *Letters*, p.649.
31 Stetson Catalogue, p.397: 25 Nov 1897: Ross to Leonard Smithers. (Copy in Bodley).
32 *Letters*, p.691.

5 Death of a Decadent

1 Mrs Ross lived at 11 Upper Phillimore Gardens, London until Nov. 1899.
2 *Letters*, pp.577-8n.
3 *Letters*, p.679.
4 *Letters*, p.735n.
5 *Aubrey Beardsley*, op.cit., pp.53 and 55.
6 *Letters*, p.729-30n.
7 Holland, Constance Wilde to Ross, 21 June 1896.
8 Bogle, p.143.
9 William Rothenstein (1872-1945). Artist and portrait painter, studied Slade School and Paris. Principal, Royal College of Art, 1920-35.
10 John Rowland Fothergill (1876-1957). Studied Slade School and London School of Architecture. In later life became a restaurateur and earned for himself the dubious reputation of being the rudest host of an inn, but such was the excellence of his *haute cuisine* that his patrons endured his insults in silence and delighted in their feast.
11 HGT, Ross to Rothenstein, 11 Sept. 1899.
12 Bernard Berenson (1865-1959). American art critic, expert on Italian Renaissance and prolific writer on Italian Art.
13 HGT, Ross to Rothenstein, 27 Nov. 1899.
14 Ibid.
15 HGT, Ross to Rothenstein, 6 Feb. 1900.
16 *Letters*, p.819.
17 *Letters*, p.821.

18 Reprinted in *Masques and Phases*.
19 *Letters*, p.833.
20 Sophie Lily Wilde (née Lees). Second wife of William Wilde, Oscar's
   brother. After his death, in 1900 she married Alexander Louis Teixeira
   de Mattos (1865-1921).
21 William Wilcox Baldwin (1830-1893). Larchmere, Whitechurch and
   Toronto. Director of Law Stamps.
22 Dalau & Co., Catalogue 161, item No 51.
23 Ellmann in his book *Oscar Wilde* identified the doctor as Paul Cleiss,
   p.547n, but Ross spelt the name Kleiss, and I have used that spelling.
24 Adrian Charles Francis Hope (1858-1904). Connected by marriage to
   Constance Wilde. Guardian of Cyril and Vyvyan Holland after Wilde's
   imprisonment and Constance's death. Secretary of the Hospital for Sick
   Children, Great Ormond Street, from 1888.
25 After Wilde's imprisonment Constance changed her name and that of her
   sons to Holland.
26 Vyvyan Holland, *Son of Oscar Wilde*, p.153.
27 HGT, Ross to Rothenstein, 11 Dec. 1900.
28 *Letters*, pp.858-63.
29 Hart-Davis, Ross to Humphreys, 16 Dec. 1900.
30 Humphreys may have written a memoir, but he did not, as far as I can
   ascertain, ever write a definitive biography.

II   TRANQUIL YEARS (1900-13)

6 The Carfax

1 HGT, Ross to Rothenstein, 25 Aug. 1901.
2 Ibid.
3 Ibid.
4 *Friends*, p.73
5 *The Times*, 10 Dec. 1901, "Art Exhibitions".
6 Hart-Davis, Beerbohm to Ross, Oct./Nov.1901.
7 Lord David Cecil, *Max*, p.220.
8 Olive Custance (1874-1944). Married Lord Alfred Douglas, 4 Mar. 1902.
9 *Friends*, p.75.
10 *Friends*, p.74.
11 Walter Edwin Ledger (1862-1931?) Qualified as an Architect. A member
   of the RNVR, the Royal Yacht Club and Royal Horticultural Society,
   Kew. After his death, on the advice of Donald C.L.Cree, his extensive
   Wilde library and letters from Ross and Millard were presented to Uni-

versity College, Oxford, and are now on deposit at the Bodleian Library as the "Robert Ross Memorial Collection".

12 Ross and More Adey shared rooms at 24 Hornton Street for over ten years.

13 HGT, Rothenstein to Ross, 8 Dec. 1902.

14 Ibid.

15 HGT, Ross to Rothenstein, 11 Dec. 1902.

16 KCC, Ross to Fry, 30 Apr. [1903].

17 Berg, Ross to Marsh, 29 Mar. 1904.

18 Christopher Hassall, *Edward Marsh*, p.112.

19 *Friends*, p.137.

20 Berg, Ross to Marsh, 1 Mar. 1904.

21 Ibid.

22 *The Times*, 21 June 1904, "Art Exhibitions".

7 Poisoned Chalice

1 *Letters*, full text is on p.512.

2 Wilde, *De Profundis*: Prefatory Dedication to *De Profundis*, Methuen, 1908.

3 Ibid.

4 Ibid.

5 Bodley, Ross to Ledger, 10 Feb. 1905.

6 Wilde, *De Profundis*, Methuen, 1905.

7 Ibid.

8 *De Profundis*, op.cit., 1908.

9 Ada Leverson, op. cit.

10 Ross, Robbie to Jack Ross, 2 Feb. 1904.

11 Hart-Davis, Beerbohm to Ross, 16 Mar. 1905.

12 Prefatory Dedication, op.cit.

13 Lord Alfred Douglas, *Motorist & Traveller*, 1 Mar. 1905.

14 *TLS*, 24 Feb. 1905.

15 Ibid.

16 *Friends*, p.95.

17 Dan H. Laurence (ed.), *Collected Letters of G.Bernard Shaw, 1898-1910*, p.521.

18 Bodley, Ross to Ledger, 19 Dec.1905.

19 Christopher Sclater Millard alias Stuart Mason (1872-1927). Son of Canon J.E. Millard, a former Master of Magdalen College School; educated at Keble College, Oxford, and a convert to the Roman Catholic Faith. In 1905 he published a translation of André Gide's personal memoir of Oscar Wilde.

20 *Academy*, 16 Dec. 1905, p.1316.
21 *Academy*, 23 Dec. 1905, p.1340.
22 *Academy*, 30 Dec. 1905, p.1364.
23 *Academy*, 6 Jan. 1906, p.21.

8 Bibliography Men

1 Clark, Ross to Millard, 30 Mar. 1906.
2 Bodley, Millard to Ledger, 12 Apr. 1906.
3 Clark, Ross to Millard, 3 Apr. 1906.
4 Bodley, Ross to Ledger, 29 Apr. 1906.
5 Ibid, 6 May 1906.
6 Edward Jones (1876-1916). Married Margery Garrett and had two sons: Charles Garrett and Ronald Garrett Jones.
7 *Friends*, p129.
8 *Academy*, 27 Jan. 1906, p.95.
9 Ibid.
10 Butts Collection—50 small tempera paintings by William Blake, 1799-1805. Sold by Blake to his patron Thomas Butts.
11 *Academy*, 23 June 1906, p.600.
12 *Academy*, 10 Feb. 1906, p.140.
13 *Academy*, "En Revenant de la Revue", 17 Mar. 1906, p.262.
14 *Academy*, "Mr Arthur Symons' Morality", 21 Apr. 1906, p.383.
15 Ibid.
16 *Academy*, "Impatience", 13 Apr. 1907, p.364.
17 Oscar Wilde, *Salome, La Sainte Courtisane, A Florentine Tragedy*: Preface to *Salome*, Methuen, 1921, 7th edn.
18 Ibid.
19 Ibid.
20 Clark, Ross to Millard, 26 Sept. 1906.
21 *Academy*, "The Eleventh Muse", 7 July 1906, p.12.
22 *Academy*, "The Jew in Art", 24 Nov. 1906, p.527.

9 Art of Friendship

1 CUL, Speech by Ross to Poetry Club, 17 May 1911.
2 *Friends*, p.147.
3 *Friends*, p.138.
4 *Academy*, "Mr Benson's Pater", 31 July 1908.
5 *Friends*, pp.132-6.
6 *Academy*, "Blunderbore", 6 Apr. 1907, p.340.

7 Clark, Ross to Millard, 27 May 1907.
8 Clark, Ross to Millard, 5 May 1907.
9 *Academy*, "Mr Ricketts and Mr Shannon at the Carfax", 6 July 1907.
10 *TLS*, letter to the editor, 28 June 1907.
11 Ibid.
12 Vyvyan Holland, *Son of Oscar Wilde*, p.185.
13 Ibid, p.165.
14 *TLS*, 3 Oct. 1907.
15 American publisher was A.R. Keller & Co.
16 *TLS*, 3 Oct. 1907.
17 *TLS*, 10 Oct. 1907.
18 *Academy*, 5 Oct. 1907.
19 Thomas William Hodgson Crosland (1865-1924). Writer, poet and hack journalist. Moral crusader who misused the Laws of Libel to justify his caustic attacks.

10 Fulfilment of a Promise

1 Bodley, Ross to Ledger, 23 Jan. 1908.
2 Oscar Wilde, *The Picture of Dorian Gray: An Editorial Note*, Charles Carrington, Paris, 1908.
3 Clark, Ross to Millard, 23 Jan. 1908.
4 *Masques and Phases*, pp.277-8.
5 Bodley, Ross to Ledger, 1 Apr. 1908.
6 Bodley, Ross to Ledger, 29 May 1908.
7 *TLS*, "The Works of Oscar Wilde", 18 June 1908.
8 *Daily Telegraph*, "Dramatic Censorship Once More", 19 Aug. 1908.
9 Oscar Wilde, *Reviews*: (Preface), Methuen, 1908.
10 Ibid.
11 *TLS*, *Reviews* by Oscar Wilde, 5 Nov. 1908.
12 Clark, Ross Deposition, pp.16-17.
13 *Friends*, pp.156-7.
14 See pp. 227 and 257.
15 *Friends*, pp.156-7.
16 *The Times*, "The Trial of Pembleton Billing", 3 June 1918.
17 Film, *The Trials of Oscar Wilde*: starring Peter Finch, produced by Ken Adam, directed by Ken Hughes.

11 Confederates in a Vendetta

1 *Aubrey Beardsley*, op.cit., pp.27-28.
2 Compton Mackenzie, *My Life and Times*: *Octave 3*, pp.271-2.
3 Violent Wyndham, *The Sphinx and her Circle*, André Deutsch, 1963.
4 *Letters, De Profundis*, p.445.
5 Clark, Ross Deposition, pp.15-17.
6 *Academy*, 6 Mar. 1909, pp.843-4.
7 There is some dispute about the actual date the removal of Wilde's remains took place. I have taken the day given by Vyvyan Holland, who was, after all, there as confirmed in his *Time Remembered After Père Lachaise*, p.14.
8 Frank Harris, *The Life and Confessions of Oscar Wilde*, Constable, 1938, p.16.
9 Vyvyan Holland, *Son of Oscar Wilde*, pp.196-7.
10 *Friends*, p.164.
11 *Masques & Phases*, pp.X-X11.
12 *TLS*, review of *Masques & Phases*, 28 Oct. 1909.
13 *Friends*, p.166.
14 Hart-Davis, Ross to Beerbohm Sept. 1909.
15 BM, Ross to Sir Frederick Kenyon, 1 Nov. 1909.
16 Slade, Ross to Lang, 23 Nov. 1909.

12 Tranquil Years

1 Hon. Henry Frederick Manners-Sutton: Heir to Viscount Canterbury. Manners-Sutton proposed marriage to Olive Custance; after she married Bosie Douglas they all remained friends, and he became godfather to their son. In 1908 when the *Academy* was in financial difficulties, Douglas sent Crosland to ask Manners-Sutton for the loan of £500. Manners-Sutton refused and, within days, the *Academy* published a flagrant and offensive article concerning Manners-Sutton, Greenings & Co and the publisher John Long. Manners-Sutton sued for libel, but he was a "man with a past" and Crosland was found Not Guilty. It is also worth noting that in 1914 when Douglas wanted a publisher for *Oscar Wilde and Myself* he used John Long, although in the *Academy* he had admitted that Long published books only of "an unsavoury kind".
2 André Gide, *Si Le Grain Ne Meurt*, 1910, p.288n. (*If It Die*, trans. by Dorothy Bussy.)
3 *New Age*, 27 Jan. 1910.
4 *New Age*, 3 Feb. 1910.
5 Bodley, Ross to Ledger, Mar. 1910.

6 Robert Ross, "Present & Future Prospects for English Art", pp.19-21.

7 *MPost*, "Post-Impressionists at the Grafton", 7 Nov. 1910.

8 *Bystander*, 16 Nov. 1910.

9 *MPost*, "History of *Salome*", 8 Dec. 1910.

10 CUL, Add.7035, Simpson to Bax.

11 Ibid.

12 CUL, Speech by Ross to Poetry Club, 17 May 1911.

13 Ibid.

14 Ibid.

15 Wilfred Scawen Blunt, *My Diaries: Part Two (1900-1914)*, pp.146-7.

16 *Friends*, p.327.

17 BRT, Ross to Ransome, 8 June 1911.

18 BRT, Ross to Ransome, 19 Aug. 1911.

19 BRT, Ross to Ransome, 29 Aug. 1911.

20 BRT, Ross to Ransome, 10 Oct. 1911.

21 Arthur Ransome, *Autobiography*, pp.142-3.

22 National Art-Collections Fund founded in 1903 (*see* Ch 13, note 7).

23 *Friends*, p.221.

24 *MPost*, "National Gallery Administration", 4 Jan. 1912.

25 *MPost*, "Old Masters at Burlington House", 30 Dec. 1911.

26 *MPost*, "Mr Abbey's Drawings", 11 Jan. 1912.

27 BRT, Ross to Gosse, 15 Feb. 1912.

28 *Friends*, p.225.

13 Ups and Downs

1 *Friends*, p.225.

2 MacGuire, Ross to Blacker, 7 May 1912.

3 Clark, Ross to Holman, 1 Apr. 1912.

4 MacGuire, Ross to Blacker, 12 May 1912.

5 *The Times*, 9 May 1912.

6 JAG, Dr Thelma Gutsche's notes, p.5.

7 National Art-Collections Fund AGM, 1912.

8 Bogle, p.292.

9 *Friends*, p.231.

10 JAG, Lady Phillips to Ross, 31 Aug. 1912.

11 Michael Holroyd, *Lytton Strachey*, Heinemann, 1967, p.53.

12 *Pall Mall Gazette*, letter to the editor, 30 Sept. 1912.

13 *The Times*, 1 Oct. 1912.

14 The Sistine Madonna by Raphael. Painted in 1512. Dresden Art Gallery.

15 *The Times*, 1 Oct. 1912.

16 Ibid.

17 *Globe*, 5 Oct. 1912, p.4.
18 W. Sorley Brown, *Life & Genius of T.W.H. Crosland*, pp.284-5.
19 Ibid.
20 Ibid.
21 Ibid.
22 Clark, Ross included the full text of Douglas's letters in his Deposition, pp.35-6.
23 Clark, Ross to Ada Leverson, 18 Nov. 1912.
24 Clark, Ross Deposition, p.38.
25 Clark, Ross Deposition, p.39.
26 KCC, Ross to Browning, 30 Sept. 1912.

III   BITTER YEARS

14 The Ransome Case

1 *The Times*, "Libel Action by Lord Alfred Douglas", 18 April 1913.
2 Wilde, *The Ballad of Reading Gaol*, Leonard Smithers, 1898.
3 *The Times*, op. cit.
4 Ibid.
5 Robert Sherard, *Oscar Wilde: The Story of an Unhappy Friendship*, 1905.
6 Ibid.
7 *Letters*, pp.423-7.
8 *Letters*, p.495.
9 *The Times*, op. cit.
10 *The Times*, 19 Apr.1913.
11 Ibid.
12 Douglas wrote an article for *Revue Blanche*, published on 1 June 1896, in which he said "that in France he was regarded as 'the young friend of Oscar Wilde, or to be more explicit, the child that Oscar Wilde loved', and as such he was pitied by some and detested by others." Douglas also wrote a series of letters and petitioned the Queen for Oscar Wilde's release, and in doing so earned the wrath of Labouchere and other leading reformers. Ross's Counsel made use of the letters and articles, much to Douglas's discomfort.
13 *The Times*, 22 Apr. 1913.
14 Ibid.
15 Ibid.
16 *The Times*, 23 Apr. 1913.
17 Ibid.
18 Ibid.

19 BRT, Methuen to Ross, 22 Apr. 1913.

20 *Spectator*, "What Killed Oscar Wilde?", 24/31 Dec. 1988.

15 Interlude

1 HGT, Ross to Rothenstein, 9 May 1913.

2 BRT, Ross to Gosse, 7 May 1913.

3 CUL, Book of Gosse.

4 JAG, Ross to Lady Phillips, 18 July 1913.

5 Lord Alfred Douglas, *Oscar Wilde and Myself*, John Long, 1914. Douglas later repudiated much of the book explaining that it had been written mainly by Crosland.

6 JAG, Ross to Solomon, 18 July 1913.

7 JAG, Ross to Lady Phillips, 18 July 1913.

8 Ibid.

9 JAG, Solomon to Ross, 31 Aug. 1913.

10 Ibid.

11 JAG, Lady Phillips to Ross, 11 Aug. 1913.

12 Clark, Ross to Millard, 6 Sept. 1913.

13 Clark, Ross to Millard, 12 Sept. 1913.

14 Alex was always known within the family circle as "George".

15 Ross, Robbie to Jack Ross, 2 Feb. 1904.

16 It is possible that Robbie still held a Canadian passport and this would explain why he was treated differently from other British visitors at the frontier.

17 Full text of letters in *Friends*, pp.251-5.

18 Clark, Ross to Millard, 13 Sept. 1913.

19 *Friends*, p.253.

20 Clark, Ross to Millard, 13 Sept. 1913.

21 The letter was dated Monday the 7th but Monday was actually the 6th.

22 Clark, Ross to Millard, 7 Oct. 1913.

23 The case was heard on 19 Nov. 1913 before Mr Justice Joyce; the defendants agreed to a perpetual injunction restraining them from publishing any of Oscar Wilde's letters, and the costs of the action were awarded to Ross.

24 There is some dispute about the number of copies printed, some people say it was only fifteen.

25 Bodley, Millard to Ledger, 3 Sept. 1913.

26 BRT, Ross to Gosse, 17 Oct. 1913.

27 RUL, Ross to Sherard, 25 May 1914.

28 BRT, Ross to Gosse, 17 Oct. 1913.

29 Ross composed a deposition which ran to sixty-two pages; it was a comprehensive account of the five years of harassment he had suffered.

30 BRT, Ross to Gosse, 17 Oct. 1913.

31 Ibid.

32 Duff Hart-Davis (ed.), *End of An Era: Letters and Journals of Sir Alan Lascelles 1887-1920*, p.150.

33 BRT, Ross to Gosse, 17 Oct. 1913.

34 BRT, Ross to Gosse, 2 Jan. 1914.

35 Bodley, Millard to Ledger, 26 Dec. 1913.

36 BRT, Ross to Gosse, 6 Jan. 1914.

16 Conspiracy and Perjury

All the details of the law actions used in this and the succeeding chapters have been taken from the Central Record Office files, *The Times*, *Daily Telegraph* and *Morning Post* Court reports. Where actual quotes are used the item is identified.

1 *The Times*, "Arrest of Mr Crosland", 14 Apr. 1914.

2 Bodley, Millard to Ledger, 28 May 1914.

3 Clark, Ross to Millard, 3 May 1914.

4 Ibid.

5 Ibid.

6 Clark, Ross to Turner, May 1914.

7 *The Times*, "The Charge against Mr Crosland", 6 May 1914.

8 *Friends*, pp.260-1.

9 Clark, Ross Deposition.

10 *The Times*, "The Charge against Mr Crosland", 14 May 1914.

11 Ibid.

12 *The Times*, 15 May 1914.

13 Ibid.

14 *The Times*, 20 May 1914.

15 Ibid.

16 Ibid.

17 *Letters*, "Robert Sherard, that bravest and most chivalrous of all brilliant beings," p.453.

18 RUL, Ross to Sherard, 25 May 1914.

19 Ibid.

20 *The Times*, "Mr Crosland Committed", 3 June 1914.

21 Ibid.

17 At the Old Bailey

1 Bodley, Millard to Ledger, 16 June 1914.
2 JAG, Ross to Lady Phillips, 21 June 1914.
3 Ibid.
4 Augustus John, *The Childhood of Pyramus*.
5 JAG, List of works acquired by Ross.
6 *The Times*, "The Crosland Trial", 2 July 1914.
7 Ibid.
8 Ibid.
9 *The Times* "The Crosland Trial", 3 July 1914.
10 *The Times*, "The Crosland Trial", 4 July 1914.
11 Lord Alfred Douglas, "Two Loves" and "In Praise of Shame"; these two poems were quoted *ad nauseam* to prove that Douglas was once addicted to the same sins as Wilde and Ross.
12 Wilde's speech from the witness-box is quoted in full on pp. 256-7.
13 In the reporting of the trial of Crosland, his mistress is referred to as "Mrs Parnall"; her correct name was Winnie Powell.
14 *The Times*, "The Crosland Trial", 4 July 1914.
15 Ibid.
16 Ibid.
17 Ibid.
18 *The Times*, "The Crosland Trial", 7 July 1914.
19 Ibid.
20 Ibid.
21 Lord Alfred Douglas "The Rhyme of F. Double E".
22 Ibid.
23 Jesmond Hill, Pangbourne, Berkshire, the home of Mrs Mary Jones. Named after Jesmond Dene in Newcastle, where the late Major Charles Jones was a gunnery expert for Vickers after his retirement from the army.
24 BRT, Ross to Gosse, 13 July 1914.
25 Ibid.
26 GU, MacColl papers, B455.
27 GU, MacColl papers, B456.
28 BRT, Ross to Gosse, 13 July 1914.
29 KCC, Ross to J. Maynard Keynes, 21 July 1914.
30 The Malicious Prosecution case was heard in April 1915: see Ch. 19.
31 Donald Struan Robertson (1885-1961). Professor of Greek at Cambridge. Married Petica Jones (1883-1941).

18 Plea of Justification

1 From a conversation with the late Prof.Giles Robertson and Mr J.-P.B. Ross.
2 Hyde, *The Trials of Oscar Wilde*, p.339.
3 *Review of Reviews*, "The Progress of the World", July 1895.
4 Lord Alfred Douglas, *Autobiography*, Martin Secker, 1929, p.42.
5 *Manchester Guardian*, "Miss Burton of Half Moon Street", 11 Oct. 1935.
6 Sassoon, *Siegfried's Journey*, p.31.
7 *St Fabian and St Sebastian* by Giovanni di Paolo (National Gallery Catalogue, 242) was bought by the Carfax Gallery on 26 May 1911 presumably on behalf of Robbie Ross. Ross lent it to the Burlington Fine Arts Club in 1915/16. After his death it was presented in his memory by the National Art-Collections Fund to the National Gallery in 1919.
8 Bodley, Millard to Ledger, 6 Sept. 1914.
9 CUL, Add 7035/15.
10 CRO, CRIM/1 - 005704. List of Exhibits, Nos 75 and 76. See Ch. 2 Note 17.
11 Douglas must have known that Ross lived in Campden Hill between 1901-2.
12 Douglas, op. cit., pp.286-7.
13 *Daily Telegraph*, "Trial of Lord Alfred Douglas", 21 Nov. 1914.
14 *The Times*, "Lord Alfred Douglas—Letter Writer", 26 Nov. 1914.
15 Mr Edwards's statement should have been challenged. The Epstein monument was never officially unveiled. As an example of the type of witness Douglas produced, Edwards was about par for the course. It is surprising his evidence was not struck from the trial records.
16 Douglas always insisted Crosland refused to give evidence for him, but the Court papers show this was not so, although Crosland did not say much that was new or relevant to either Prosecution or Defence. If Crosland was a witness for Douglas, then it must be said, Douglas did not return the compliment when Crosland was finally brought to book.
17 *The Times*, "Mr Crosland's Evidence", 27 Nov. 1914.
18 Ibid.
19 Robert Le Diable "The story of Frederick Stanley Smith: The Past, The Present and the Future", *Winning Post*, 16 Nov. 1918.
   The Devil was assumed to be Douglas. In a long article Le Diable, commenting on Ross's recent death, raked over old ground and said that in doing so he had access to the short-hand notes taken during Douglas's trial for libel, which proved beyond doubt that Ross and Smith had been engaged in homosexual practices for years. He also managed to imply that

Smith's inheritance had been obtained by blackmail and that Ross was also implicated in the crime.

IV YEARS OF DESPAIR (1915-1918)

19 Testimonial and Scholarship

1 GU, MacColl, W173.
2 CUL, Add 7035/15.
3 Bodley, Asquith Papers MS.26.
4 McGuire, Ross to Blacker, 7 May 1912.
5 CUL, Add 7035/17.
6 Sassoon, *Siegfried's Journey*, p.29.
7 GU, MacColl, R158.
8 Douglas, *Autobiography*, p.12.
9 GU, MacColl, C265.
10 CU, MacColl, A18.
11 Susan Lowndes (ed.), *Diaries & Letters of Marie Belloc Lowndes: 1911-1947*, Chatto & Windus, 1971, p.37.
12 *The Times*, "Mr Crosland's action against Mr Ross", 14 Apr. 1915.
13 Ibid.
14 *The Times*, "Mr Crosland's Action against Mr Ross," 17 Apr. 1915.
15 Ibid.
16 Ibid.
17 Ibid.
18 Ibid.
19 Ibid.
20 Bodley, Millard to Ledger, 16 Apr. 1915.

20 Lost Generation

1 *Friends*, p.248.
2 Ibid, p.244.
3 MacGuire, Ross to Blacker, 1 June [19..?].
4 Sprigge, Pip Blacker to Cecil Sprigge, 18 Dec. 1918.
5 Sassoon, *Siegfried's Journey*, p.32.
6 Ibid, p.31.
7 Sprigge, Squire Sprigge to Cecil Sprigge, 7 May 1918.
8 Merlin Holland, Oscar Wilde's speech from the witness-box at the Old Bailey, 30 Apr.1895.
9 GU, MacColl, W182.

10 Ibid, R160.
11 Bodley, Robert Ross, *The Connaught Square Catechism or Confession.*
12 Hart-Davis, Beerbohm to Ross, 21 Sept. 1915.
13 Newman Flower (ed.), *Journals of Arnold Bennett: 1911-1921*, Cassells, 1932, p.200.
14 Sassoon, *Siegfried's Journey*, p.11.
15 Francis Sheehy Skeffington. An Irish writer, advocate of minorities— socialism, pacifism, vegetarianism, women's suffrage; pro-German, arrested and shot in April 1916, on the orders of a British army officer.
16 Clark, Ross to Millard, 22 May 1916.
17 Paul O'Prey (ed.), *In Broken Images: Selected letters of Robert Graves 1914-1946*, p.55.
18 *Friends*, p.290.
19 Sassoon, *Siegfried's Journey*, p.6.
20 Thelma Gutsche, *A Woman of Importance*, Howard Timmins, Cape Town, 1966, p.346.
21 JAG, Ross to Miss Keith-Wright, 24 Sept. 1916.
22 The problems concerning Sir Hugh Lane's codicil were not resolved until 1959 when a compromise was found and the Collection was split and it now spends five years at the National Gallery in London and five years at the Dublin Municipal Art Gallery.
23 Berg, Ross to Lady Gregory, 24 Oct. 1916.
24 Berg, Ross to Lady Gregory, 29 Oct.1916.
25 Freddie Smith was appointed Honorary Attaché to HM Legation in Dec. 1917. He resigned in 1922. In 1918 Douglas wrote an article "O.H.M.S. Frederick Stanley Smith" and was convinced that his article was the cause of Smith's resignation, but as there were four years between the appearance of the article and Smith's departure this would seem not to be so.
26 NLS, Ref 9925 Folio 19, Ross to John Lane, 29 Oct. 1916.
27 Michael and Elenor Brocke (eds.), *H.H.Asquith Letters to Venetia Stanley*, letter 15.

21 Honour and Duty

1 BL, Ross to Ricketts, Add MSS 58090-58091.
2 Frank Harris, *The Life and Confessions of Oscar Wilde*, The Author, New York 1916, 2 vols.
3 Shaw, *Collected Letters*, p.414.
4 Harris included Shaw's letter entitled "Memories of Oscar Wilde" when he reprinted, *The Life and Confessions of Oscar Wilde*, in 1918.
5 Austin, Ross to Harris, 1 Feb. 1917.

6 Frank Harris, op cit., p.373.
7 Clark, Ross to Millard, [c.1917].
8 GU, MacColl, W272.
9 *Friends*, p.299.
10 Ibid, p.300.
11 Tate Gallery, Treasury Minute, 24 Mar.1917.
12 JAG, Dr Gutsche's notes, p.48.
13 On 13 June 1917 Gotha biplane bombers dropped a 110lb bomb on the infants' class of Upper North Street School, Poplar. 15 children were killed outright; 3 fatally injured, and 27 others maimed for life.
14 Sprigge, Squire Sprigge to Cecil Sprigge, 4 June 1917.
15 Sassoon, *Siegfried's Journey*, p.54-5.
16 Ibid.
17 Full statement on pp. 173-4 of *Sassoon's Diaries*.
18 Ibid, p.179.
19 Ibid, p.181.
20 Ibid, p.185.
21 Sprigge, Squire Sprigge to Cecil Sprigge, 17 Sept. 1917.
22 Sassoon, *Siegfried's Journey*, p.84.
23 *Friends*, p.321.
24 Gutsche, *A Woman of Importance*, p.307.
25 Sassoon, *Siegfried's Journey*, pp.54-5.
26 O'Prey (ed.), *In Broken Images*, p.69.
27 NLS, Graves to Scott-Moncrieff. Ref ACC 7243.

22 Final Injustice

1 Bodley, Ross to Ledger, 4 Apr. 1918.
2 *The Times*, "Mr Billing's Trial", 30 May 1918.
3 Ibid.
4 *The Times*, "Mr Billing's Trial," 31 May 1918.
5 BL, Ross to Ricketts, Add MSS 58090-58091.
6 IWM, Minute 460a/10, 8 Apr.1918.
7 *The Times*, "Mr Billing's Trial", 3 July 1918.
8 *Friends*, pp.333-4.
9 Ibid, p.335.
10 Sprigge, Cecil Sprigge to Squire Sprigge, 21 Aug. 1918.
11 House of Lords, AB 0117, 12 June 1918.
12 Hart-Davis, Ross to Sir Charles Mathews, 6 June 1918.
13 *Friends*, p.334.
14 Conversation with the late Prof. Giles Robertson Nov. 1986, who held the Trust Papers.

15 Sassoon, *Siegfried's Journey*, p.82.
16 Ibid, p.84.
17 Sprigge, Ross to Squire Sprigge, 3 Oct. 1918.
18 Sassoon, *Siegfried's Journey*, p.84.
19 Sprigge, Squire Sprigge to Cecil Sprigge, 10 Oct. 1918.
20 *The Times*, 7 Oct. 1918.
21 *Friends*, p.344.
22 Sprigge, More Adey to Cecil Sprigge, 10 Oct. 1918.
23 Will of Robert Baldwin Ross. Probate Registry, Somerset House, London.
24 Sassoon, *Selected Poems*, Faber & Faber, 1968.

Selected Bibliography

Ackroyd, Peter, *The Last Testament of Oscar Wilde*, Hamish Hamilton, 1983.

Amor, Anne Clark, *A Woman of Some Importance*, Sidgwick & Jackson 1983.

Anstruther, Ian, *Oscar Browning*, John Murray, 1983.

Behrman, S.N., *Portrait of Max*, Random House, 1960.

Bell, John (ed.), *Wilfred Owen: Selected Letters*, Oxford University Press, 1985.

Benson, E.F., *As We Were: A Victorian Peep Show*, Longmans, 1930.

Bentley Joyce, *The Importance of Being Constance*, Hale, 1983.

Birkenhead, 2nd Earl of, *The First Phase* and *The Last Phase*, Thornton Butterworth Keystone, 1933,1935.

Brocke, M. & E. (ed.), *H.H.Asquith: Letters to Venetia Stanley*, Oxford University Press, 1982.

Brown, W. Sorley, *The Life & Genius of T.W.H. Crosland*, Cecil Palmer, 1928.

Campbell, John, *F.E. Smith: First Earl of Birkenhead*, Cape, 1984.

Cecil, David, *Max*, Constable, 1964.

Charteris, Evan, *Life and Letters of Sir Edmund Gosse*, Heinemann, 1931.

Croft-Cooke, Rupert, *The Unrecorded Life of Oscar Wilde, Bosie, Feasting with Panthers*, W. H.Allen, 1972, 1963, 1967.

Drabble, Margaret, *Arnold Bennett*, Penguin Books, 1985.

Edel, Leon, *Henry James: The Master, 1901-1916*, Hart-Davis, 1972.

Ellmann, Richard, *Oscar Wilde*, Hamish Hamilton, 1987.

Ervine, St John, *Oscar Wilde: A Present Time Appraisal*, Allen & Unwin, 1951.

Harrison, Fraser, *The Yellow Book*, Boydell Press, 1982.

Hart-Davis, Duff (ed.), *End of An Era, Letters & Journals of Sir Alan Lascelles, 1887-1920*, Hamish Hamiltom, 1986.

Hart-Davis, Rupert (ed.), *Letters of Oscar Wilde*, Hart-Davis, 1962. *Max Beerbohm, Letters to Reggie Turner*, Hart-Davis 1964. *Siegfried Sassoon Diaries 1915-18, 1920-22, 1923-25*, Faber & Faber, 1983, 1981, 1985.

Hardy, Gathorne R. (ed.), *The Early Memoirs of Lady Ottoline Morrell* and *Ottoline at Garsington*, Faber & Faber, 1963,1974.

Hassall, Christopher, *Edward Marsh*, Longmans, 1959.

Hepburn, James (ed.), *Letters of Arnold Bennett Vols 2 & 3*, Oxford University Press, 1968 & 1970.

Holland, Vyvyan, *Son of Oscar Wilde*, Hart-Davis, 1954. *Time Remembered After Père Lachaise*, Gollancz, 1966.

Hyde, H. Montgomery, *Oscar Wilde, The Aftermath*, Methuen, 1963. *Oscar Wilde*, Methuen, 1976; (ed.), *Trials of Oscar Wilde*, Hodge, 1948. *Lord Alfred Douglas*, Methuen, 1984.

Jenkins, Roy, *Asquith*, Collins, 1964.

Jullian, Phillipe, *Oscar Wilde*, Granada Publishing, 1971.

Laurence, Dan H. (ed.), *Collected Letters of Bernard Shaw 1898-1910, 1911-25*, Max Reinhardt, 1972 ,1985.

Mackenzie, Compton, *My Life and Times Octaves 2,3,4,5*, Chatto & Windus, 1963, 1964, 1965, 1966.

O'Prey, Paul (ed.), *In Broken Images: Selected Letters of Robert Graves*, Hutchinson, 1982.

Pearson, Hesketh, *Life of Oscar Wilde*, Methuen, 1946.

Pearson, John, *Façades: Edith, Osbert & Sacheverell Sitwell*, Macmillan, 1978.

Pullar, Phillipa, *Frank Harris*, Hamish Hamilton, 1975.

Queensberry, Marquess of, and Coulson, Percy, *Oscar Wilde and Black Douglas*, Hutchinson, 1949.

Ransome, Arthur, *The Autobiography*, Cape, 1976. *Oscar Wilde: A Critical Study*, Methuen, 1913.

Reade, Brian, *Sexual Heretics*, Routledge & Kegan Paul, 1970.

Roberts, Brian, *The Mad Bad Line*, Hamish Hamilton, 1981.

Ross, Margery (ed.), *Robert Ross: Friend of Friends*, Cape 1952.

Rothenstein, William, *Men and Memories*, Faber & Faber, 1932.

Sassoon, Siegfried, *Siegfried's Journey*, Faber & Faber, 1945.

Seymour-Smith, Martin, *Robert Graves: His Life and Works*, Hutchinson, 1982.

Sitwell, Osbert, *Left Hand, Right Hand* and *Noble Essences*, Macmillian, 1946, 1950.

Stallworthy, Jon, *Wilfred Owen: A Biography*, Oxford University Press, 1974.

Sutton, Denys (ed.), *Letters of Roger Fry, Vols 1 & 2*, Chatto & Windus, 1972.

Thwaite, Ann, *Edmund Gosse: A Literary Landscape*, Oxford Univeristy Press, 1984.

Wilde, Oscar, *Collected Works*, Methuen, 1908.

Index